Hoodwinking Churchill

TITO'S GREAT CONFIDENCE TRICK

Hoodwinking Churchill

TITO'S GREAT CONFIDENCE TRICK

Peter Batty

SHEPHEARD-WALWYN (PUBLISHERS) LTD

First published in 2011 by
Shepheard-Walwyn (Publishers) Ltd
107 Parkway House, Sheen Lane,
London SW14 8LS
www.shepheard-walwyn.co.uk

British Library Cataloguing in Publication Data
A catalogue record of this book
is available from the British Library

ISBN: 978-0-85683-282-6

Typeset by Alacrity,
Sandford, Somerset
Printed and bound through
s|s|media limited, Wallington, Surrey

Contents

To Anne

Introduction

MUCH NEW INFORMATION has come to light since Tito's death in 1980. What this reveals is a deception so successful that it surprised Stalin and is still largely accepted today. It led the staunchly anti-communist Winston Churchill in December 1943 to back the communist Tito wholeheartedly and to cease aiding completely the anti-communist resistance forces in the former Yugoslavia. The ruse is all the more shocking because of the evidence of British skulduggery – some of it in high places.

But for that decision, Tito would not have overcome his political opponents within Yugoslavia and emerged as its undisputed ruler. That Churchill was conned into so deciding cannot now be doubted. Tito misinformed him and played on the weaknesses and wanton ambitions of many of those British officers he came into contact with. He wilfully broke, too, the promises made regarding "free and unfettered elections" and the participation of non-communists in his government's affairs.

It was a decision our American allies had not favoured, nor everyone in the British Foreign Office – a decision that condemned the Yugoslavs to more than forty years of communist rule and encouraged Stalin in his aspirations to seek political and physical sway over the Balkans and Eastern Europe. Tito's success in securing power in Belgrade came within a hair's breadth of prompting a communist takeover in Greece. Had Greece gone communist, Italy's survival would have been that much more precarious – and had Italy succumbed to communism the momentum might well have affected the delicate political balance in France. Thus Britain's connivance in the imposition of communist rule in Yugoslavia very nearly led to its spread throughout much of continental Europe.

However it was a decision taken when Churchill was clearly under considerable stress – something his closest colleagues had begun to notice and to have grown alarmed at. Just two days later he was stricken with pneumonia and forced to convalesce for several weeks.

The conventional image of Tito is of the daring partisan leader – plucked from obscurity by Winston Churchill – who had fought the Germans continuously throughout the war and liberated his country virtually unaided, unlike the rest of occupied Europe. That he used most of the munitions received from the British and Americans not to kill Germans, as he had promised Churchill, but to eliminate his political rivals, has been glossed over by Tito's supporters in the West. More Yugoslavs were murdered by each other than were killed by Germans – a stunning fact! The Partisans' pestering of the Germans was at best merely peripheral and only occasional. Hitler's ability to utilise to the full the local abundance in oil and minerals so vital to his war machine was never truly hindered. His decision finally to withdraw from the Balkans was dictated not by the activities of Tito's Partisans but by events elsewhere. The German retreat was largely unharassed by the Partisans, to Churchill's intense chagrin. It was the Red Army which really freed Yugoslavia.

While Tito was accusing his political opponents of accepting weapons from the Italians, he was himself proposing joint action to the Germans to resist an Allied landing in the Balkans. This would undoubtedly have led to British and American casualties. He nearly went to war with the Western Allies in May 1945 over his ambition to annex Italian Trieste. In the months following the War's end he massacred in cold blood countless thousands of anti-communist Yugoslavs handed over to him by the British in good faith. By then Churchill bitterly regretted his decision of two years earlier. Tito, though, boasted to his cronies about how he had "outsmarted and deceived that old fox Churchill". Within weeks of his much-vaunted "difference of opinion" with Stalin in June 1948 Tito was keenly trying to rejoin the Soviet camp. He was less than helpful to the rebellious Hungarians in 1956 and to the dissident Czechs in 1968. Yugoslavia had its own gulags on barren islands in the Adriatic, where thousands of Tito's political foes were incarcerated and humiliated.

That it has taken so long for the full story to emerge suggests a concerted cover-up, connected maybe with a glittering generation having had a vested interest in sustaining the myths surrounding Tito that they had helped to beget – a generation which has only now passed away. In questioning Tito's rise to power it is not enough to look simply to the left-wing influences, to the communist moles within the secret services who clearly cooked the books. As one insider graphically put it to me, "It's not so much the reds under the bed that were the more influential, as the blues *in* the bed." Many of

Tito's most loyal and loquacious supporters were pillars of the British Establishment!

When Yugoslavia began breaking apart during the 1990s, some in the West rued Tito's passing. They recalled longingly how he had unified his unruly compatriots. Yet it was only his utter ruthlessness – aided by a brutal secret police abetted by a countrywide army of paid informers – which had kept the lid on Yugoslavia's competing minorities. This, however, merely delayed a more permanent solution of its ethnic problems.

Recent access to Soviet and Yugoslav files has thrown a clearer light on the 1948 contretemps between Tito and Stalin. It has also clarified the mystery of what Tito's communists were doing in the period between the August 1939 Hitler-Stalin pact and the Nazi invasion of Russia in June 1941 – most especially during the two months prior to that invasion when Yugoslavia was already occupied. That they were denigrating the British as warmongering imperialists was perhaps only to be expected from such hardline Stalinists. Less anticipated was that they had been eagerly denouncing to the Germans all those resisting the occupiers, in particular Serbs loyal to the Yugoslav government-in-exile in London, backed then of course by Churchill.

In making his fateful December 1943 decision in the heat of war, Churchill relied heavily on advice from close associates who depended largely on information passed their way by Tito. That they were duped by the Partisan leadership is now clear. How far they knew this, and allowed themselves to be so, is, to put it charitably, less obvious. That many of them promoted the Partisan myths for their own ends after the War – and benefited from the creation of a "Victor's History" – is less forgivable. Intriguingly, there are indications of a carefully orchestrated plot by well-placed Soviet sympathisers within the Cairo headquarters of the Special Operations Executive handling Yugoslav affairs, who played on the gullibility of some of those associates. Documents were doctored. Briefs from liaison officers in the field critical of Tito's Partisans did not find their way to Churchill and the other decision-makers. The BBC played a substantial and controversial role in the disinformation campaign – a role so far not fully revealed.

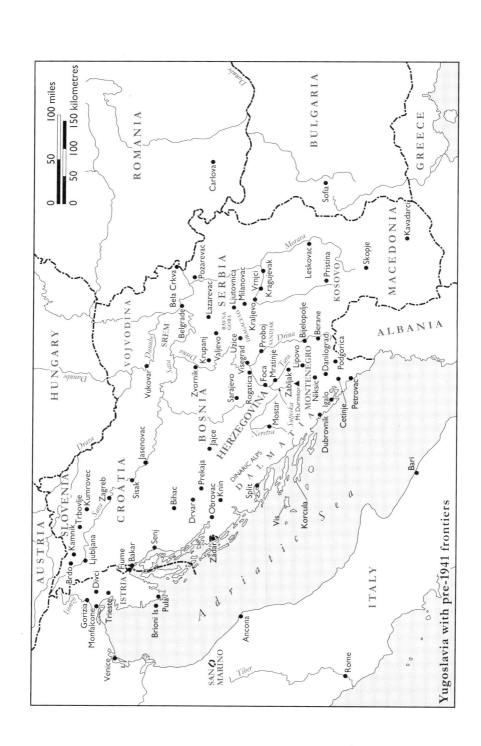

Yugoslavia with pre-1941 frontiers

CHAPTER ONE
Josip Broz, alias Tito

TITO'S FUNERAL in May 1980 was the pinnacle of his fame, witnessed as it was by hundreds of world leaders, more than had attended the obsequies of Winston Churchill or John F. Kennedy. The newspapers of the day listed the kings, princes, presidents and other VIPs from 122 different countries. Millions more watched it on TV beamed live to over fifty networks worldwide. It had been a stunning ascent for the grandson of a serf.

Little is known for certain of Tito's early life, save that he was born Josip Broz on 7 May 1892. Thereafter much depends on seeing through the more obvious exaggerations and omissions of his politically biased chroniclers. He himself was not averse to romanticising his past; he was forever loath to correct the myths that grew up about him. However we do know his place of birth was Kumrovec, a village in the area of Croatia known as Zagorje, close to the border with Slovenia, thirty miles or so north-west of Zagreb. It was in what was then Austria-Hungary. Although picturesque, with wooded hills and fast-flowing trout streams, the land itself was not particularly fertile.

He was the seventh child born to Franjo and Marija Broz. Franjo was a Croat and Marija a Slovene. They had fifteen children in all but only seven survived infancy; four had already died before Josip arrived. Of the seven just four were to reach adulthood. They were Catholics. Josip was confirmed and served for a time as an acolyte – until, it's said, the priest hit him for being slow in helping him change his vestments after a mass. He never again set foot in the local church. The name Broz was a shortened form of Ambroz or Ambrose. The family claimed the Brozes had migrated from the border region between Bosnia and Dalmatia. Before that they may have come from Montenegro.

Croatia had been part of the Roman Empire. The Croats were thought to be one of the tribes, like the Serbs, Slovenes, Bosnians and Montenegrins, that had come out of western Asia centuries earlier. Because the Romans had converted to Christianity, Croatia remained Roman Catholic after the Empire fell, and even when the Eastern Orthodox Church based in Constantinople separated from the Pope's Church in Rome. The Serbs were to opt for the Eastern Orthodox Church and they were a dominant force over much of the Balkans until defeated by the Ottoman Turks in the fourteenth century. Thereafter they endured Ottoman suzerainty for almost five hundred years. Unlike the Bosnians and Albanians, who were pressured into becoming Moslems, the Serbs remained Orthodox Christian.

Croatia was conquered by Hungary in the early twelfth century, while Slovenia succumbed to a succession of German ducal families. Eventually it passed into the hands of the Habsburgs who held it for six centuries. When they became Archdukes of Austria, Slovenia became an Austrian province. Croatia, too, was to fall under Habsburg sway when they secured much of Hungary from the Ottoman Turks in the sixteenth and seventeenth centuries. Croatians formed a substantial part of the victorious army at Blenheim in 1704 when Winston Churchill's great ancestor, the first Duke of Marlborough, was allied with the Habsburgs. Croatian soldiers then had a terrible reputation for pillage and rape. For their part in helping defeat Napoleon in 1815, the Habsburgs were rewarded with the Venetian Adriatic province of Dalmatia. Fifty-two years later their Empire became the Dual Monarchy of Austria-Hungary. In 1878 it acquired Bosnia-Herzegovina from the Turks through the Congress of Berlin, called to carve up the weakening Ottoman Empire. Serbia was allowed to become independent.

Josip's father owned fifteen acres of land. His house, inherited from his father, was one of the biggest in the village, with four rooms plus a kitchen and hall. It was shared with a cousin's family. Josip's paternal grandfather had been born a serf, though serfdom was to be abolished during his lifetime. Josip's father also ran a small cartage concern. But he was not business-minded and fell heavily into debt, taking to drink as a result. Nevertheless, he lived into his eighties. It was Josip's mother who brought up the family. She was the eldest of fourteen children of more prosperous peasants from across the border in Slovenia. To ease the family finances, Josip went to live with his maternal grandparents at an early age, returning to Kumrovec when he was eight years old to work on his father's farm and attend the recently opened school. Elementary education in Croatia had become compulsory.

Croatia's farmers then were finding it difficult to compete with imports of cheaper grain, mostly from America. There had been, too, a succession of poor harvests. Many were migrating to America or moving into the towns in search of work. Croatia had begun industrialising. Josip's elder brother Martin had already gone to Vienna as a railwayman. At the age of fifteen, through a cousin, Josip got a job as a skivvy in a regimental canteen in the garrison town of Sisak, sixty miles away, south-east of Zagreb.

Menial work was not to his liking. He wanted a skill. Within a short time he managed to become apprenticed to a local locksmith. This entailed attending evening classes at a technical school twice a week. He got on well with his teachers, and with his boss. Later he was to claim that the three years spent in Sisak were among the best of his life. Apparently it was where he got his taste for showy uniforms! In 1910, now eighteen, having qualified as a locksmith's assistant and general mechanic, Josip left for Zagreb. He found work in a small engineering factory and registered with the Metal Workers' Union. Zagreb, Croatia's capital, with more than 75,000 inhabitants, had doubled its population in twenty years. It was to double it again in far fewer years. As elsewhere then, trade unionists were interested mostly in securing higher wages and better working conditions but demands were also increasing for a wider suffrage. In Kumrovec, for instance, there were only three voters among nearly two hundred families.

Croatia then was administered from Budapest as part of Hungary. Those speaking Hungarian rather than Serbo-Croat tended to get the best jobs. Dissatisfaction with this brought Serbs and Croats together; not only Serbs living in Croatia but also those of independent Serbia. It was the beginning of the so-called South – in Serbo-Croat *Yugo* – Slav movement pressing for a single state of Serbs, Croats and Slovenes. As the Serbs were the most politically active, the Austro-Hungarian authorities were always suspicious of them. At the turn of the twentieth century Serbs were a quarter of Croatia's population. The Habsburgs played Croats off against Serbs, exploiting their cultural disparities and religious differences – Roman Catholicism and Orthodox Christianity.

Josip went home to help his mother towards the end of 1910 but soon left to seek jobs, without success, in Slovenia's capital Ljubljana and in the Austrian port of Trieste. In March 1911 he returned to Zagreb, where he found work repairing bicycles, motor cars and small machines. There he experienced his first strike – for a shorter working day and higher pay – which was partly successful. Within months he was off again to Ljubljana, and then to nearby Kamnik in Slovenia, where he got a job at a metal-goods factory employing 150 workers. He was there barely a year before it went bankrupt. Declared redundant, he and his fellow workers were given a month's wages in advance and sent to a larger factory in southern Bohemia. When faced with violence from frustrated strikers, they realised they had been recruited as blackleg labour. Luckily Josip found temporary employment nearby, at the Skoda arms works in Pilsen. He was soon on the move to Germany, taking jobs here and there, even as far afield as the Ruhr. While working in Mannheim he seriously considered migrating to America. Instead he joined his elder brother Martin, the railwayman who was living near Vienna, and procured a job at Daimler in Wiener-Neustadt thirty miles away.

Having reached his twenty-first birthday, Josip had to return to Croatia in the autumn of 1913 to undertake two years' compulsory military service. Sent to an infantry regiment based in Zagreb, he was quickly promoted to corporal, and then to sergeant – on account, he said later, of his skill at skiing and fencing. When Austria-Hungary attacked Serbia in July 1914, following the assassination at Sarajevo of the Habsburg Archduke Franz Ferdinand, allegedly on Serbian orders, he was sent to fight the Serbs. Communist historians later tried to conceal this. His party colleague Milovan Djilas admits it was "hushed up because the Serbs were sensitive on the subject."[1]* At the beginning of 1915, he was transferred to Galicia in the Carpathian Mountains to face the Russians, who had joined in the war against Austria-Hungary and Germany.

Later he would claim to have disliked the war, participating only to end the rule of the hated Habsburgs, but eventually he admitted to Djilas that he had enjoyed army life and had not been politically minded at that time. Clearly he must have been more of a conformist then than a rebel or his military bosses would not have promoted him so speedily.

When the Russians struck in the spring of 1915, Josip was part of a reconnaissance group operating behind enemy lines. His apologists were to claim that he had been unwilling to spy on the Russians, and had readily surrendered to them, but researchers after his death discovered that he had frequently been praised by his superiors for

* Sources for references can be found in Notes on pages 349-58.

bravery and resourcefulness while reconnoitering. He had taken so many Russian prisoners that he had been recommended for a gallantry award. In March 1915 he was seriously wounded and captured when Russian cavalry surprised his unit near the little town of Okno. It took him more than a year to recover from his injuries. Much of the time was spent in a military hospital, deep inside Russia, where he learned Russian and soon became fluent. Thereafter his native Serbo-Croat was so peppered with Russian nuances and phrases that he was often thought a Russian who had learnt Serbo-Croat rather than the reverse!

Unlike many of his fellow Croat prisoners-of-war, Josip did not switch sides and join the Russian army. Instead he chose to work as a mechanic in a mill near the prison camp, before, in the autumn of 1916, being transferred further east, to Kungur in the foothills of the Urals. Here he helped maintain the railway lines and rolling stock. Surveillance was evidently lax after the February 1917 Revolution, so he was able to escape that June and make his way to St Petersburg, already called Petrograd – not to join the Bolsheviks, but to find better work. He later told Milovan Djilas he had not expected the Revolution to succeed! He tried to cross into Finland but was caught and sent back to prison in Petrograd. Returned to Kungur, he was soon on his way to Omsk in western Siberia, once more working on the railways.

When the Tsarist White Guards drove the Bolsheviks out of Omsk in July 1918, Josip sought sanctuary in a Kirghiz village twenty-five miles away, where he worked in a flour mill. He claimed to have joined the Communist Party at this time. His party card says he registered with the Omsk section on 19 January 1919 yet the Reds did not recapture Omsk until the autumn. Most Serb historians maintain he did not join the Party until October 1920 at the earliest. But by 1919 the Great War was over. Austria-Hungary was no more. The Kingdom of the Serbs, Croats and Slovenes had already been proclaimed – Yugoslavia for short, meaning "land of the southern Slavs", though it was not officially called this until 1929. Serbia's Belgrade was its capital and Serbia's King Peter its monarch.

Serbia had been on the winning side; Croatia and Slovenia had not. Serb losses had been appalling. More than a million were thought to have died, almost a quarter of Serbia's pre-war population. Also the country had been wrecked by the retreating German and Austrian troops. The Serbs' heroism in resisting the Austrians and Germans had won the admiration of the British and French.

When the victorious Allies came to carve up the Habsburg Empire it was clear they would favour Serbia.

The Serbians had dropped a strong hint in September 1914 that when the war was won they would expect the Allies to "create out of Serbia a powerful south-western Slavic State; all the Serbs, all the Croats and all the Slovenes would enter its composition". Yugoslavia, which came into existence on 1 December 1918, was created out of the Austro-Hungarian provinces of Croatia, Slovenia, Bosnia-Herzegovina, Dalmatia and Vojvodina, together with the independent states of Serbia and Montenegro. The Montenegrin king, fleeing to Italy, had surrendered his country to the Austrians in late 1915, leaving his subjects in the lurch. They had deposed him on 26 November 1918 and proclaimed union with the Serbian dynasty. The United States recognised Yugoslavia fairly speedily, in February 1919, as did the other Allied powers. Italy was the last of the victors to do so, in November 1920, following a dispute over its borders.

It was perhaps inevitable that the Serbs would dominate Yugoslavia. Between the wars, two out of three cabinet ministers were Serbs, as were two out of three top civil servants. Only Serbia had had an army at the end of the First World War. The victorious Allies had disbanded the Croat and Slovene militias. Although officers and men from those were later allowed to join the Yugoslav army, few did. Officers from the former Imperial Russian army, who had taken sanctuary in Serbia, were encouraged to join. Many did. On the eve of the Second World War just 10 per cent of the Yugoslav Army's officer corps was Croat while 70 per cent was Serb. There were 21 Croat and 10 Slovene generals compared with 199 Serb generals.

Consequently the army was associated with Serbian hegemony. It became an instrument for widening the gulf between the various national groups rather than uniting the country. Nor had the Allied leaders imposed on the rulers of the new kingdom any constitutional safeguards for minorities, as they had elsewhere. That this might be storing up trouble for the future – as the Croats in particular would not willingly accept Serb domination – was something the Allied leaders had plainly not contemplated – or, more likely, had chosen to ignore. Most Croats did not identify with Yugoslavia. The Serbs, being the most numerous of the southern slavs, saw Yugoslav identity as simply an extension of their own. For many of them Yugoslavia was *Serbo*slavia. Therein lay the rub in their relations with their fellow Croats, Slovenes, Bosnians, Macedonians and Montenegrins.

Those Croats absconding to the Allied side before the war's denouement had evidently been led to believe the proposed south slav kingdom would be a federation of national groups, each with a certain amount of autonomy and all considered equal, not a centralised, unitary state dominated by Serbians. The attention of those same Croats had been diverted into trying to prevent the equally victorious Italians from taking over the Croatian provinces of Istria and Dalmatia. The Italians claimed, with some justification, that they had been promised them as a reward for joining the Allies. The city of Trieste and much of Istria was eventually given to Italy, as were Zadar on the Dalmatian coast and a few small islands.

The Serbians thought the Croats ungrateful for being liberated from the harsh Habsburgs. The Croats viewed the Serb kings as equally loathsome, and with a less illustrious pedigree. The Serbian dynasty owed its accession to a bloody coup as recently as 1903. Hence Serbs and Croats were suspicious of each other from the outset. Thus was set in train the tussle between Serbian centralism and Croat regionalism that was to dominate Yugoslav politics between the wars.

The Croats, with their greater mixture of Western influences and traditions, considered themselves culturally a cut above the Serbs. They wrote in Roman script like most Europeans; the Serbs used Cyrillic, thought less civilised. In many ways the difference between the two was epitomised by their capitals. Whereas Zagreb resembled a European city, Belgrade remained an eastern stronghold.

The Italians, aggrieved at being denied all their promised spoils, continued to cast envious eyes towards Yugoslavia. This set them at loggerheads with the government there. When the Italian dictator Mussolini came to power during the 1920s, he encouraged militant anti-Serb organisations, such as the Ustasha of Croatia. He financed them and granted them sanctuary when they were banned in their own country. Hungary and Bulgaria had also conceded territory to Yugoslavia, and both looked for opportunities to regain it. A disagreement between Yugoslavia and Albania over borders came to blows. It was not until the summer of 1926 that Yugoslav troops withdrew from the disputed area.

The new Yugoslavia was slightly bigger than the United Kingdom. But almost 90 per cent of it was mountainous or forested. Of its twelve million inhabitants, 40 per cent were Serb, 23 per cent Croat,

9 per cent Slovene and 6 per cent Bosnian Muslim. The rest included about half a million each of Germans, Hungarians, and Albanians, as well as 150,000 Turks, 64,000 Jews and 20,000 Russian émigrés. Quite a mixture! Fourteen languages were recognised. Whereas Serbs, Macedonians and Montenegrins were Orthodox Christian, Croats and Slovenes were Roman Catholic, and Bosnians mainly Muslim.

As the political parties ran largely on lines of nationality, the discontent of minorities was destined to be exploited by the more extreme politicians. The Croat problem, and to an extent the Macedonian wish for some form of autonomy, dominated Yugoslav politics between the wars, in the same way as the Irish question had dominated British politics before 1914. There was the same fanaticism, violence and religious rivalry.

Although Croatia brought a coastline, and hence ports from which to trade, as well as some industry, four out of five citizens of the new Yugoslavia earned their living from the land. By and large a country of peasants, it was desperately poor. Crop yields were low and animal husbandry primitive. Illiteracy was high and the country's financial institutions antiquated.

Sadly, once they had established Yugoslavia, the victorious Allies seemed to lose interest in it. Apart from the French, who had assisted Serbia during the war. A French general had commanded the largely Serbian force that eventually liberated the country. To the British there appeared little to be gained from a close association with Yugoslavia. For them it was just another of those far away countries likely to prove problematic. It had the misfortune to be in a part of the world most British people considered beyond the pale. The Balkans were associated with assassinations, blood feuds, boundary disputes, *coups d'état*, religious wars and other unspeakable horrors. The region was seemingly in perpetual turmoil; violence and intrigue were part of everyday life. The age-old cry of "trouble in the Balkans" still sent shivers down British spines. To diplomats of the British Foreign Office, "typically Balkan" meant something peculiarly shady and devious. In their book the Balkans were best avoided like the plague!

Josip married during the summer of 1919, in an Orthodox church in Omsk, a Russian girl, Pelagija Belousova, twelve years his junior. The daughter of a local peasant, she was said to have been uncommonly beautiful. Not tempted to stay and be part of the first Communist

Revolution, he immediately began the long trek home, taking her back with him to Kumrovec. They arrived in October 1920.

He had been away six years and was now twenty-eight. His mother had died two years earlier and his father had moved to another village. They spent some time with him before going on to Zagreb, because Josip urgently needed paid employment. He did not see his father again. Pelagija gave birth to a child who died within days. At least three more were to follow. Only a son, Zarko, born in 1924, would survive through infancy. Josip had a number of temporary jobs in Zagreb, then a city of 120,000 souls. In early 1921 he found a more permanent position, helping to run a flour mill in a prosperous village, Veliko Trojstvo, about sixty miles east of Zagreb. Here they stayed four years.

Like many of his contemporaries, participating in the War had been the making of Josip Broz. His harsh experiences were to have a lasting effect on him. Importantly, it had brought him into contact with dedicated communists, which was to change his life decisively. His die had effectively been cast. Clearly he was a survivor, as his disease-ridden childhood had shown. Equally clearly, he was now under suspicion from the authorities of his new country, indicated by the opening of a police file on him. But the file does not reveal that he had sought contact with those of his countrymen who had already become communist, as he was later to claim. Nor does it show any overt militancy on his part, although these were violent times in Yugoslavia. He rejoined his trade union, no doubt more as a means of obtaining employment as a metal worker than for deeper political reasons.

The Bolsheviks had expected communism to sweep the world after their success in Russia. When it did not, they established, in early 1919, the Communist International – or Comintern, as it came to be known. It was meant to maintain the revolutionary momentum outside the Soviet Union through agitation and propaganda (agitprop). Later that year, when British and French troops intervened in the civil strife following the Russian Revolution, the Comintern called upon workers throughout Europe to strike in protest. Winston Churchill had enthusiastically advocated intervention against the Bolsheviks.

A Yugoslav Communist Party of sorts had been formed in Russia in the spring of 1918 by a group of Croat and Slovene former prisoners-of-war. They returned home soon after the November 1918 Armistice. Together with the more radical, militant wing of the pre-war Serbian Social-Democratic Party, they established in Belgrade, in April 1919, the "Socialist Workers Party of Yugoslavia (Communists)". The call for a general strike in Yugoslavia three months later, at the Comintern's behest, met with scant success. Many of the strikers were imprisoned and foreign citizens suspected of subversive activities expelled from the country. The Yugoslav authorities had been more perturbed over a mutiny close to the Hungarian border by two Serb units of the newly formed Yugoslav Army that had coincided with the general strike. Eight soldiers had been killed. Led by some of the newly returned prisoners-of-war from Russia, the mutiny had occurred during the Bolshevik takeover of Budapest. Although brief, it had alarmed Belgrade.

The abortive general strike was followed in April 1920 by an initially much more successful transport strike, again organised by the communists. It was broken by the authorities conscripting the strikers into the army after thirteen of them had been killed by soldiers summoned to tackle the expected disorder. Furious with their leaders for meekly obeying the conscription call, rank-and-file communists convoked a congress for June 1920. The leadership was changed. So was also the Party's name, to the simpler "Communist Party of Yugoslavia".

Able to exploit the economic discontent, and with the Russian Revolution still fresh in working people's minds, the Party did well in the municipal elections that summer. Emerging as the strongest political grouping in both Zagreb and Belgrade, they went on to win 12 per cent of the votes in the first nationwide elections held in November 1920. This made them the third largest party in the Assembly that was to draw up a constitution.

But power through the ballot box was never going to be achievable. The control they sought must come through revolution as in Russia (though this was something the new Yugoslavia was not yet ready for) or as a result of existing institutions being destroyed (which the authorities were not prepared to countenance). When more strikes called by the communists the following month threatened to disrupt coal supplies, the authorities took tough measures to thwart them. Troops were sent to intimidate the miners in Bosnia and Slovenia. The Party's offices and newspapers were shut down. A young Serb communist tried to assassinate the Prince Regent in June 1921. A few weeks later a Bosnian communist killed the minister responsible for repressing the Party. All communist propaganda was forbidden on pain of death. Communist deputies were expelled from parliament. The Party's leaders were arrested and imprisoned, thus effectively banning it.

Support and sympathy for the Party faded away. Its numbers soon dwindled to a mere handful. Many activists went into exile, mostly in Moscow. Those remaining became a prey to police informers. The regime sought to neutralise left-wing influence among the village folk by distributing land formerly owned by the Austrian, Hungarian and Ottoman aristocracies. By the end of the decade almost 90 per cent of peasant households owned some land.

With the Yugoslav Party in such disarray, the Comintern stepped in. A former Croat officer prisoner-of-war, Stevo Sabic, was sent to reorganise it. He had joined the Bolsheviks during his captivity and had participated in the Russian Revolution, even serving in the Red Army. From this time onwards Moscow was always in control, dictating the Party's policies and appointing its leaders.

Yugoslavia was seen as part of the *cordon sanitaire* the Versailles victors had established to shield the western world from what they considered the Bolshevik bacillus. The Fifth Congress of the Comintern in 1924 advocated Yugoslavia's breakup into its separate ethnic communities, believing this would facilitate their becoming Bolshevik republics. Croat and Macedonian dissidents were encouraged to greater militancy. Seeking secession from the Yugoslav state of all non-Serbs was official communist policy for the next decade.

During 1923 Sabic persuaded Josip to distribute leaflets among his workers and other trade unionists encouraging militancy. No doubt Josip was paid for this. Having a young family, he needed money from whatever source. Bettering himself was clearly a driving force in his life. For someone of his background, with little formal education, communism presented a way forward. Although the Party was banned, the trade unions, many of which the communists had infiltrated, remained legal.

Economic conditions were bad. Some employers sought to reduce wages. Josip's political activities had obviously been noticed. When his employer died in 1925, the new owner of the mill demanded he give them up and, when he refused, fired him. In future his choice of jobs was to be influenced more by political than personal economic needs, as he came to rely on Sabic's subsidies. He worked first in the Kraljevica shipyards near Bakar on the north Adriatic coast, becoming a shop steward. Sacked for organising a strike, he managed in October 1926 to obtain a job in the railway-carriage works at Smederevska Palanka, near Belgrade. Fired in March 1927 for criticising conditions there in a trade union journal, he moved back to Zagreb where he found employment in a large engineering factory. Drawn increasingly into Party affairs, he became a full-time functionary. His cover was his appointment as secretary of the Metal Workers' Union of Croatia, one of the country's biggest trade unions. His wife was now working for the Party too.

But the Party was still in the doldrums. From about fifty thousand in 1920, its membership had dropped to a few hundred by 1927. It had little influence on national politics within Yugoslavia. Still proscribed, it had to operate in secret. Its headquarters had been moved from Belgrade to Zagreb because it had more members there. Zagreb was Yugoslavia's most industrialised area, with more than four thousand metal workers alone. Nearly a third of them were unemployed, due to the recession.

The move suited Josip and helped him succeed within the Party hierarchy. Because of the paucity of members he probably had little competition. He was gaining a reputation for loyalty to his party superiors and proving a diligent organiser. The Party at that time was split. Some wanted a revolution within Yugoslavia on the lines of the Russian one but had no clear idea of how to achieve this, other than with the help of Moscow, which had enough problems of its own at the time. Others, mainly Croats, were more interested in local autonomy. Josip spoke out against these disputes and appealed for unity. To that end he wrote to the Comintern, which brought him to Moscow's notice.

In early 1928, as a result of Comintern pressure, he became secretary of the Party committee for Zagreb. Arrested for distributing illegal literature, he was sentenced to seven months' imprisonment, reduced to five on appeal. Meanwhile he had gone into hiding. When caught, he was tried on the more serious charges of plotting sedition and of being a member of a banned organisation, namely the Communist Party. His sentence was increased to five years.

That same year the leader of the Croatian Peasant Party and two of his colleagues were assassinated in parliament by a Serb deputy. For many Croatian nationalists this was the last straw. Most were reluctant to resort to terrorism personally, but they became increasingly willing to condone others subverting the hated Serbian-dominated state. The more fanatical of them fled to Hungary and Italy to form the Ustasha ('Uprising') terrorist movement under a lawyer and former member of the Yugoslav parliament, Ante Pavelic.

The Ustashi were prepared to use terror and violence, however extreme, to achieve Croatian independence. They spoke as much of racial and religious identity as of Croat nationalism. They were willing to accept the Italian dictator Mussolini's money to those ends. Pavelic modelled his Ustashi on the Italian Fascists, with their blood oaths and pseudo-military organisation. Mussolini had his eyes on Yugoslav territory. Anything undermining the Yugoslav state was grist to his mill. Hungarians, keen to recover land lost to Yugoslavia in 1918, also had a reason to stir up trouble for their neighbour. An Ustasha training camp founded near the Slovenian border was soon attracting hundreds of recruits, particularly unemployed Croat workers. Other camps were located in Italy.

Sharing the wish to break up their country, the Yugoslav communists maintained close links with the Ustashi. Milovan Djilas confirms this in his *Memoir of a Revolutionary*: "We instinctively felt that the Ustashi action could only help further our own aim: the destruction of Yugoslavia." *Proleter*, the official organ of the Party's Central Committee, declared in December 1932 that it was "the duty of all Communist organisations and of every Communist to help" the Ustasha movement. Pavelic had often defended communists in the courts. Communists and Ustashi on occasion found themselves in the same prisons. Friendships resulted.

Josip was incarcerated at Lepoglava, in his native Zagorje, where many other communists were held. Unlike ordinary convicts, they were allowed to socialise with each other and to receive and exchange political literature. They even created Party cells and studied Marxism openly. The rules were probably relaxed because the guards were Croats, not Serbs. Less sympathetic commentators claim the guards were bribed with Moscow money. Josip would later liken Lepoglava to a university, saying it was "where I learned most". In 1931, after trying to escape, he was transferred to the stricter Maribor prison in Slovenia and then, in late 1933, to Ogulin, before being freed in March 1934.

His time in prison coincided with the autocratic regime of King Alexander, who had succeeded to the Yugoslav throne on the death of his father in August 1921. A military man with little enthusiasm for politics – but with an obsession for Packard cars of which he owned twenty-three – he decided, on 6 January 1929, after four general elections and twenty governments, that he had had enough of democracy. He was prompted by the assassination of the Croat leaders, and student riots in Zagreb the previous month that had resulted in a dozen deaths. Dispensing with parliament, he suspended the constitution and thereafter governed by decree. It was a royal dictatorship. All parties were dissolved and political publications, including those Communist-related, were banned. Press censorship was imposed, as were restrictions on the right of assembly and to demonstrate.

Most ordinary people appeared to be sickening of politics too. There was little opposition to the King's coup. Working folk were concerned more with the dire economic climate. Yugoslavia was to be hit hard by the world slump following the Wall Street Crash of October 1929. The prices of her exports – mainly agricultural produce and raw materials – fell faster than those of the manufactured goods she imported. This reduced the purchasing power of the population as a whole. Unemployment soared. What little revolt the communists attempted was firmly suppressed. Many were killed or arrested. The Party became almost extinct as its leaders fled abroad. The authorities were unrelenting in their repression of anything communist. It was the Croats and the other "troublesome minorities" who were their biggest bugbear during the 1930s.

To the disgust of the Croatian nationalists, Alexander now chose officially to name his realm Yugoslavia. The formation of a national, albeit largely Serbian, identity was aided by a new flag which replaced the old Serbian, Croatian and Slovenian ones flown hitherto in the separate "tribal" areas. Now only the Yugoslav flag was permitted for public display. He forbade, too, the use of the old regional names such as Serbia and Bosnia. The country was divided into nine provinces named after the rivers running through them – save for Dalmatia, which was renamed Littoral. He tried, unsuccessfully, to abolish the Cyrillic script. It was all meant to make a break with the past – a way, perhaps, of curbing nationalism, especially of the Croat sort. The opportunity was taken to crack down on non-Serb dissidents, whether politicians or intellectuals.

Pressed by the French, who were dangling the offer of a substantial loan, Alexander restored a modicum of constitutional rule in 1931. It made little difference and he became a bitterly hated figure. It was no surprise when, at the start of a state visit to France on 9 October 1934, Alexander was assassinated in Marseilles. A Macedonian agent of the Croatian Ustasha movement, based then in Italy, was the culprit. Alexander's son became King Peter II. Only eleven years old, he required a regent until his "majority" was reached in

September 1941. Alexander in his will had named his cousin Prince Paul as regent.

Ironically, Alexander's visit to France had been to shore up Yugoslavia's alliance with Czechoslovakia and Romania. France had promoted this so-called "Little Entente" as part of the *cordon sanitaire* to protect Western Europe from the Bolshevik pestilence, and then as a possible containment of Germany. Its members had more immediate worries. Hungary hungered to restore the Habsburgs and to recover lost territory. Alexander had been hoping for a military alliance with France. His host on that visit, the French Foreign Minister Louis Barthou, also died in the assassination. Barthou, like Winston Churchill, had recognised Hitler's aggressive ambitions early on. He was determined France should withstand them, possibly by allying with the Soviets as well as with the British. Thereafter France was cursed with weak, appeasing foreign ministers. Barthou's immediate successor was the infamous collaborationist Vichy wartime leader, Pierre Laval. Yugoslavia's attempts to seek redress for the assassination from Italy, through the League of Nations, were blocked by France and Britain, anxious not to embarrass Mussolini. Surprisingly to us today, Mussolini was looked upon then as a potential counterweight to the rising power of Hitler.

On his release, Josip was required to live in his native Kumrovec and to report daily to the police. But he again went into hiding in Zagreb, resuming his place in the Party hierarchy, living under assumed names and adopting disguises. He grew a moustache and dyed his hair red. It was now that he became Tito, the most lasting of his many aliases. Some have suggested that it was an acronym of "Third International Terrorist Organisation" (which has the same initials in Serbo-Croat). Others that Ti-to was Serbo-Croat for "do this – do that". His own explanation was more mundane: it was a common nickname in his native area, from the Latin Titus. He now became a full-time paid official of the Comintern. In late July 1934 he was sent to Vienna, where the Yugoslav Party had located its headquarters. Two years earlier the Comintern had put a Czech, Milan Gorkic, in charge of the Party. Under him it was beginning to recover. Gorkic had been given large funds for the task.

Tito's family life had ended with his imprisonment. His wife Pelagija had spent some time in custody herself during 1928. She had then been sent by the Party, with Zarko their son, to Moscow. There she worked for the Comintern before being posted to Kazakhstan as a teacher. Zarko was left behind in a children's home in the Soviet capital. She divorced Tito in 1936, remarried and had a daughter by her second husband. Caught up in the purges, she was exiled to Siberia in 1938. Rehabilitated in 1957, she returned to Moscow in 1966 and died there two years later. Zarko, after a peripatetic childhood, joined the Red Army and lost an arm early in the war.

The continuing economic depression of the 1930s led to much dissatisfaction among urban and agricultural workers. This helped the communists in their agitation and brought new audiences for their propaganda, especially among the young. They were aided, too, by the easing of restrictions on political activity by the more liberal regime that followed Alexander's assassination. The Yugoslav Party was thought to have sufficiently recovered to consider holding regional conferences inside the country, concluding with a national gathering. All of this Tito helped arrange. He already had a reputation in communist circles for hard work and obedience. His trial and imprisonment had now given him a suitable revolutionary pedigree.

The secret national gathering held in Ljubljana in late December 1934 elected a new leadership. Tito was included for the first time. In line with Moscow's wishes, it agreed to work towards weakening Yugoslavia's ruling classes by setting them against each other. Croatian and Macedonian separatism were to be encouraged. The troublesome minorities were to blame their miseries on the Serb monarchy. To these ends separate communist parties were established in Croatia, Slovenia and Macedonia. The Party leadership strengthened its links with the Ustashi, seeing them as natural allies in the revolutionary struggle. Leaflets were distributed praising them as "national revolutionaries" and "Croat patriots", and promising them "solidarity in their struggle".

Moscow sought to exploit the rebellious potential of the resentful non-Serbs. This was why Croats, Slovenes and Montenegrins came to dominate the Party, which suited Tito. It was why there was an anti-Serb element in the Party's policies. Apart from a few intellectuals in Belgrade, the Party had little support in Serbia and was non-existent in the countryside. Ivan Avakumovic, in his *History of the Communist Party in Yugoslavia,* maintains that in 1939 Belgrade University had fewer Communist Party members than Cambridge, despite having many more students than the English university!

Gorkic sent Tito to Moscow in early 1935 to be the Party's representative in the Comintern's Balkan Secretariat. His arrival coincided with the start of Stalin's ruthless purges and the notorious

"Treason Trials" that were to see the wholesale extermination of Stalin's former colleagues. Tito lodged at the infamous Hotel Lux, where all Comintern's foreign visitors stayed. It was a hotbed of informers and Soviet secret police. He attended the Comintern's Seventh World Congress that summer as a Yugoslav delegate, seeing Stalin for the first time. The personality cult of the Soviet leader was reaching its peak. Obeisance to him was obligatory in the most obsequious terms. Tito was to recall that every time Stalin's name was mentioned it was greeted with thunderous and prolonged applause.

Fearing the consequences for international communism of German rearmament and Italy's growing strength, the Congress called for alliances with other political parties opposing fascism throughout the world – so-called "Popular Fronts". The Soviets had made military pacts with France and Czechoslovakia the previous year, as well as joining the League of Nations.

The line on Yugoslavia changed too. Moscow now considered the West's *cordon sanitaire* a useful protection against the eastward ambitions of Hitler and Mussolini! The Party was to cease agitating for Yugoslavia's ruin – a *volte-face* it did not find easy to perform and which did not appeal to its Croat and Macedonian members. No agreements were reached with any other Yugoslav party and it relapsed into internal squabbling. It was further weakened by a fearsome crackdown by the authorities that included the arrest of many party activists. While in Moscow, Tito met an Austrian communist, Lucia Bauer, whom he married in October 1936, a few days before his return to the Yugoslav Party's headquarters in Vienna. He was to go through four marriages in his time.

The Comintern made him Gorkic's deputy. He was given the additional task of recruiting volunteers to fight alongside the Republican Army against Franco in the Spanish Civil War. All the communist parties around the world were being asked to provide such volunteers for what came to be known as the "International Brigades". The Yugoslav Party moved its headquarters to Paris to escape the attention of the Austrian secret police, now strongly anticommunist. Many Yugoslav communists living in Vienna had already been arrested.

Paris was Tito's first taste of the West. It was also the first time he had handled big money. The Comintern had given him lavish funds to recruit volunteers. He was responsible for finding more than a thousand. Several hundred were to make their way from Yugoslavia where a French merchant ship was charted for the journey. The authorities got wind of this and most of the recruits were seized before embarking. Tito managed to escape blame for the fiasco which, in Moscow's eyes, fell on Gorkic. Of the seventeen hundred or so Yugoslav communists who eventually made it to Spain, more than half were to die there, not always in battle. Of those who survived, twenty-four became generals in Tito's Partisans during the Second World War.

Tito did little later to settle the mystery of whether or not he had gone to Spain himself, preferring to be deliberately vague. Most Serb historians are now convinced he must have gone. Also that the Comintern had given him the task of supervising the liquidation there of dissident communists, especially so-called Trotskyists, in line with the long reach of Stalin's paranoiac purges. Some have specifically accused him of managing a prison ship in Barcelona harbour used by Stalin's secret police for their nefarious purposes.

I found buried away in the British Foreign Office files a letter from an Edith Wedderburn dated 20 May 1944 to the then Secretary of State, Anthony Eden, in which she wrote:

> I should like to remind you that there are in this country, émigrés who fought for the Republican cause in the Civil War in Spain, and who were tried by the Military Courts set up by Tito, who was a member of the Yugoslav Comintern in Spain, to try "Trotskyists" and other rebels who refused to submit to the GPU [Stalin's secret police] Dictatorship set up in Spain in 1936-37. One man who was brought to this country, through the good offices of a professor in Cambridge University, was imprisoned for many months, with many other members of the International Brigade, in a GPU prison ship anchored off Barcelona. It was "Marshal" Tito, and the GPU agent Hans Kahle, now in this country, who were responsible for these methods of terrorisation in the Civil War in Spain.

The Foreign Office official deputed to answer the letter minuted: "As far as I know Tito did take part in the Spanish Civil War but I have not so far heard that he committed atrocities."[2]

The British historian Hugh Thomas, in his seminal *The Spanish Civil War,* says:

> Tito denies having ever been in Spain but, in view of the surprising number of people who claimed to have seen him there, it seems possible that he at least visited the [International] Brigades' headquarters for one reason or another.

The Oxford historian Richard Crampton, commenting in his *Eastern Europe in the Twentieth Century – and After* on how Tito was able to escape the Stalin purges of the 1930s, considers it "primarily because he spent much of the time in Spain".

Tito had by now learned how to survive in the communist world – doing what he was told and keeping his mouth shut when required. Outwardly charming, he was clearly ambitious, single-minded, determined, and, when necessary, a ruthless opportunist. He needed nerves of steel to have eluded so far the traps and tripwires of the Comintern. No intellectual and no bourgeois, he shunned philosophical squabbles, unlike many of his peers who relished political debate. Their eagerness for it often led to their downfall. Tito left ideology to others.

Milovan Djilas was to complain later that Tito was "lacking in original ideas".[3] Maybe this was his salvation, as was a strong instinct for self-preservation! From the start he had been prepared to toe the party line, unthinkingly and unquestioningly: the perfect *apparatchik*; no theoretician, but a simple, reliable Stalinist field-worker. Once he had decided to become a communist he knew he needed to be seen to be intensely loyal to Moscow, in particular to the Comintern where power over his life and death lay. He appreciated, too, very early, that he must be prepared to report on his comrades in detail and, if necessary, to denounce them. How much he knew of the gulags and of the millions of innocent deaths from forced collectivisation he never disclosed. Perhaps to him they were, as Stalin insisted, simply rumours put about by wicked imperialists!

Gorkic was ordered to Moscow in July 1937, where he promptly disappeared, a casualty of Stalin's continuing reign of terror. Hundreds of Yugoslav communists living in Moscow had been arrested and charged with deviation, fractionalism and treason. Few were ever released. Djilas says Tito put it about that Gorkic had been a British spy, but this was thought to be a Stalinist fabrication.

Tito was asked temporarily to take over the Yugoslav Party. Not all the members approved. For a while there was a rival leadership located in Paris, but by the middle of 1938 he had moved the Party headquarters back to Yugoslavia. It was a time of great anxiety for Yugoslavs. Hitler's takeover of Austria earlier that year had brought the Nazis to Yugoslavia's northern borders. The fascist Italians were already at its western borders. Within the year they would also be at its southern borders when Mussolini occupied Albania.

Researchers at the British Foreign Office, when asked by Churchill in May 1945 "for the fullest possible dossier on Tito", revealed that he had in 1937 worked at Adriatic Shipyards Limited at Split, owned then by the British firm Yarrows. They also discovered that, at this time,

> he quickly organised strong Communist cells in the industrial centres of Dalmatia, Croatia and Slovenia; that widespread strikes followed, that he seemed to make a special target of British and American concerns, that he seemed to be financed from a centre in Vienna.

He had started a big strike in the Shell refinery at Caprag during August 1937 and other strikes in partly British owned spinning and weaving mills in Slovenia.[4]

In the summer of 1938 Tito put together his first politburo, though it was not called such until two years later. It included the Slovenian Edvard Kardelj, a schoolmaster, who became his chief ideologue. The Montenegrin Milovan Djilas, a perpetual student, looked after propaganda, and the Serbian Aleksandar Rankovic, a journeyman tailor, was charged with party discipline. He would later head Tito's secret police. The three were to remain his closest lieutenants until the mid-1950s. Djilas had first met Tito in 1937. The Comintern chiefs were not yet convinced Tito was up to the job, although he had sought their approval for his every move. They worried about the frictions within the Party and evidently considered disbanding it, as they had recently done with the Polish party.

He was summoned to Moscow in August 1938 to discover his wife Lucia Bauer had been arrested on suspicion of being anti-Stalinist. He managed to secure her release, but little mention is made of her thereafter. He never took her to Yugoslavia. Staying inevitably at the Lux, he again spent much time compiling copious reports on his colleagues and being questioned on their contents. He also helped produce a Serbo-Croat translation of Stalin's *Short History of the Bolshevik Party*. It was only after he undertook to liquidate the remaining "alien and vacillating elements" within the Yugoslav Party without delay that his leadership of it was finally confirmed in January 1939. He returned to Yugoslavia almost immediately. His official biographer, Vladimir Dedijer, maintains that about eight hundred Yugoslav Communists were purged at this time, including at least twenty former members of the Party's Central Committee. Tito never spoke about it. Ironically, he was more successful than the Yugoslav authorities at killing communists!

Djilas maintains Tito could not have been appointed leader unless

> his loyalty to the Soviet leadership [had been] tested, or, rather, his
> disloyalty to the factionalists within his own party [been] confirmed.
> Many other Communists had been checked out in that same fashion
> and they had not survived. Later, Tito said of that time: "I made no
> friends among the factionalists, I minded my business, and I was
> careful about what I said, particularly in rooms with telephones."

In pondering whether Tito betrayed or slandered his comrades,
Djilas reminds his readers that for Communists, especially pre-
Second World War ones, collaboration with Soviet intelligence was
"regarded as an honour worthy of recognition". Tito, he says, was
certainly loyal to Stalin. Otherwise "how could he have survived".
Hence he "energetically purged his own party".[5] It was as a result of
the purging that Djilas himself – nineteen years younger than Tito –
rose to power within the Party having, presumably, successfully
shown *his* loyalty to Tito.

Evidently Tito was to report back to the Comintern in person in
the summer of 1939. He appeared to be in no hurry to do so, taking
a roundabout route to Moscow via Genoa and Paris (where inevitably
a woman had caught his eye), then by sea from Le Havre to
Leningrad, bypassing Germany. By the time he arrived in early
September the infamous Hitler-Stalin non-aggression pact had been
signed and Britain and France were at war with Nazi Germany,
following the latter's attack on Poland. Although applauded in the
Moscow press as a great victory for peace, and a defeat for those
French and British imperialists anxious to embroil the Soviet Union
in a war with Germany, the Pact shocked many communists in the
West. Droves left the Party.

Not so Tito and his comrades. They praised the Pact enthusiastically and accepted unquestioningly Stalin's explanation that it was a
war between bourgeois powers which the Soviet Union would do well
to stay out of. They issued a manifesto in September 1939 claiming:

> the Soviet Union, led by the Bolshevik Party and Comrade Stalin,
> the leader of genius of all progressive humanity, have unmasked the
> imperialist warmongers' foul trap. German fascism has been com-
> pelled to capitulate before the strength of victorious socialism, the
> USSR, and to conclude a non-aggression pact with it.

The manifesto ended: "Through the Non-Aggression Pact with
Germany, the Soviet Union has won a great victory and limited the

range of the present war."[6] By contrast, the French and British communist parties immediately pledged loyalty to their respective countries and denounced the Germans as aggressors.

When, in line with the unpublished clauses of the Hitler-Stalin Pact, the Red Army occupied its agreed share of defeated Poland, Tito's comrades loyally welcomed it. Djilas says they "were thrilled by the partition of Poland". In their opinion, "the Soviet Union had taken the field and was broadening the territory of socialism".[7] The 30 November 1939 edition of the German newspaper *Die Welt* quoted Tito as declaring:

> The Pact for Mutual Aid between the Soviet Union and Germany, and the entry of Soviet troops into western White Russia [Tito's euphemism for what had been eastern Poland!], have aroused great enthusiasm amongst the broad masses of the Yugoslav population.

An aide of Tito's, Lola Ribar, wrote in the Communist youth monthly *Mladost*: "Thanks to this pact the peoples of Yugoslavia will be spared a new slaughter, a slaughter in which they have nothing to gain, and in which they would only fight for foreign interests."[8]

Nor did Tito complain when the Soviets attacked Finland that same month, although innocent lives were lost in the bombing of Helsinki. He hailed the Russian successes as nailing "once and for all the foul lie about the weakness of the Red Army... The bourgeois dogs must now acknowledge the power and might of the Red Army and the Soviet Union and its peace-loving policy."[9] One of his lieutenants dismissed Finnish resistance to the Soviets as an "instructive example of how not to defend the independence and sovereignty of a small nation". It was blamed on more powerful states behind the scenes urging, in "their own interests", the Finns to fight.[10] Another maintained:

> the Finnish war was provoked by English imperialist agents with the aim of bringing the Soviet Union into the war and using Finland as a base for operations against Russia, as they did twenty years ago.

Earlier, in September 1939, Tito's communists had provoked a Croat infantry regiment to mutiny by spreading rumours that it was being sent to France to man the Maginot Line! Tito's colleagues agitated against any military preparedness by Yugoslavia. Call-up was opposed and recruitment discouraged. Soldiers were urged to disobey orders. Djilas admits they "stood against mobilisation" because "mobilisation had an anti-German character".[11] Strikes were organised in ordnance plants and aircraft factories. One, the longest then in Yugoslav history, lasted almost three months. The strike organisers were in cahoots with the German-speaking community. A Party leaflet distributed that autumn declared: "Hitler at the moment presents no danger whatsoever to the independence of Yugoslavia." It protested against the "decrees of mobilisation and evacuation of the civil population, etc., which are clearly designed preliminaries to dragging the country into the war."[12]

Tito's official biographer, Vladimir Dedijer, mentions in his *War Diaries* that they organised an anti-war demonstration in Belgrade on 14 December 1939. Banners and slogans attacked the British and French premiers, but none berated Hitler. Similar rallies were held in Zagreb and elsewhere, in which Croat Ustashi and other extreme nationalists participated. In May 1940 Tito's politburo branded the Anglo-French war against Germany "unjust" and "imperialistic". Similarly, when Hitler attacked Scandinavia and the Low Countries, the misfortunes of people there were blamed on "the imperialists of London and Paris". Tito and his comrades claimed that:

> The crude violation of the Scandinavian countries by England and France forced Germany to move troops into Denmark and to occupy strategic positions in Norway... Thanks to the obstinate efforts of the English and French imperialists to drag small nations into the war on their side, four independent states, Denmark, Norway, Holland and Belgium, have been occupied.

And after the fall of France: "Only the imperialists of London and Paris and their social democratic and bourgeois democratic allies are to blame for the continuation of the war." Not a mention of the invading Germans!

Again, later in the year, when the aerial Battle of Britain was at its height:

> The English imperialist bourgeoisie continues the war. It still announces that this war is "for democracy", "for freedom", "for the independence" of the English people. Nothing is more shameful than this lie. The English imperialist bourgeoisie is saving its imperialist booty.

German propaganda, like Moscow's, was never questioned:

> The most recent revelations of the *German White Book* eloquently unmask the shameful and perfidious game of the Anglo-French imperialists and of their "democratic" and "social democratic"

lackeys... The Communists were therefore completely in the right when they attacked from the first day of the imperialist war the Anglo-French imperialists as aggressors.[13]

Ljubo Sirc, who was a student in Slovenia at this time and would later join the Partisans, recalled in his memoirs, *Between Hitler and Tito*, how his communist colleagues

> had been taxing our patience for some time. We had had running battles with them because they were always denigrating the Army, protesting against the partial mobilization of the reserve and resisting measures everybody knew were needed to withstand the mounting German pressure on Yugoslavia... At the beginning of 1941, the underground Communist Party of Yugoslavia had issued a resolution attacking the English and French imperialists who "had helped to kindle the new war conflagration, not in order to defend freedom, democracy and independence of small peoples, but in order to defend their colonial empires and hegemony". In the very same resolution, the Soviet invasion of Poland and the Baltic States in alliance with Hitler's Germany had been hailed as the "liberation of 23 million working people from the national and capitalist yoke".

Hugh Seton-Watson, a respected historian of the Balkans, says that "during the period of alliance between the Soviet Union and the Third Reich the Yugoslav Communists had directed their main hatred against Britain".[14] Djilas reveals in his *Memoir of a Revolutionary* how Tito went to great lengths after the war to conceal this anti-British and pro-German stance on the grounds that "it was 'embarrassing today'".

Although these were dramatic times, Tito did not hurry home. The Comintern kept him in Moscow until the end of 1939. He went on to Istanbul, where he stayed four months, ostensibly awaiting forged travel documents. He had become infatuated with a 26-year-old Slovenian, Herta Haas, whom he had met in Paris in 1937. He was enjoying the ritzy lifestyle, staying in luxury hotels, eating at expensive restaurants and wearing fashionable clothes, which his high salary from the Comintern now allowed. He was never to lose his taste for "good living"! Herta returned with him to Zagreb in April 1940 when, at the Comintern's behest, he purged yet more dissidents within the Party. Those unwilling to back the Germans wholeheartedly, or who even faintly favoured the British stance, were included. As most of the older members had by now been eliminated, it was a much younger party. Tito, 48 in 1940, had become a sort of father figure to many of his comrades.

The Yugoslav Party was undoubtedly stronger than before. Its numbers, though, about 6,600 in October 1940, were still miniscule. They were mostly townspeople and intellectuals, with very few peasants or workers. At least half were Croats. Crucially Tito had given it cohesion by establishing party cells throughout most of the country. It was now poised to take advantage of whatever the coming war would bring. Even so, it could never have attained national power if that war, and more particularly the brutal German occupation, had not wrecked the country's social and political framework, thereby creating an administrative vacuum.

CHAPTER TWO

Germany Occupies Yugoslavia

"start a Partisan war
behind the enemy's lines"
STALIN

FACED DURING THE LATE 1930s with the expansionist ambitions of Germany and Italy, the Serb-dominated Yugoslav Government in Belgrade had sought belatedly to unite the country by appeasing the perennially embittered Croats. Autonomy was granted them in internal affairs over an expanded province amounting to almost a third of the country. Although agreed in August 1939, this self-government was not due to come into full effect until the coming of age of the young King Peter II in September 1941 when fresh elections were planned. It was hoped that by then a new federal constitution for the whole of Yugoslavia, including similar Slovenian and Serbian autonomous provinces, would be in place. Meantime it merely irked the more militant Serbs, Slovenes, Macedonians and Montenegrins, and swelled their discontent with Prince Paul's administration.

As regards outside help, Serbia had long enjoyed social and cultural connections with France. These were carried over after 1919 into Yugoslavia. For a while France appeared to be offering a sort of guardianship through the Franco-Yugoslav pact of friendship and understanding of November 1927. It was meant to reassure Yugoslavs at a time when Italy was pressing for border adjustments in her favour. Military protection was never offered explicitly, though there were close links between the French and Yugoslav armies regarding training and equipment. During the 1920s France had also promoted the "Little Entente" between Yugoslavia, Czechoslovakia and Romania, but again without any military backbone. This had been followed in 1934 by a wider Balkan Entente embracing Yugoslavia, Romania, Greece and Turkey. It was intended to deter Hungary and Bulgaria from seeking the return by force of the territories lost in the

First World War rather than to provide viable protection against German and Italian military ambitions. Such protection could effectively come only from major powers like Britain and France (who now had more pressing problems closer to home and were not all that interested in the Balkans) or from the Soviet Union (which *was* interested in the Balkans though not necessarily to the advantage of the countries concerned).

Italy's invasion of Ethiopia in 1935, which Britain and France did little to oppose, revealed the weakness of the League of Nations. It was followed by Germany's reoccupation of the Rhineland in March 1936 and her takeover of Austria two years later, which again the British and French made no attempt to prevent. Then the Czechs lost out to Germany at Munich in September 1938, although they had a treaty with France. All of this made the Yugoslavs realise that they could not count on British or French support, let alone protection. They would have to fend for themselves against any aggressor. At best they could hope to buy time by remaining neutral; at worst by appeasing Germany and Italy. Their fears were further inflamed when the Germans occupied Prague in March 1939 and, only days later, Italy invaded Yugoslavia's southern neighbour, Albania.

Insecurity among the Balkan nations reached fever pitch in August 1939 with the signing of the Hitler-Stalin Pact, which suggested that the Soviets were now in cahoots with an expansionist Germany. Further confirmation followed when Poland was quickly partitioned between the two signatories. Stalin also grabbed Latvia, Lithuania and Estonia, as well as great chunks of Romania. A neutral stance became difficult to maintain after the German armies' sweeping successes in the West during 1940 led to France's speedy collapse and Italy's entry into the war on Germany's side. Desperate for friends, two days after France's surrender the Yugoslavs established diplomatic relations with the Soviet Union – hitherto unthinkable for the anti-Bolshevik Yugoslav royal dictatorship. The British were not best pleased. Prepared to countenance German interests in the Balkans, London had long been determined to keep the Soviets out of the area at all costs.

Seeking to woo Italy away from Germany, Britain had been reluctant to show favour to Yugoslavia in case Rome thought it provocative. But after the Italian declaration of war British policy changed. When it looked likely Italy might invade Yugoslavia, London hinted to Belgrade about possible military aid, though it is difficult to see how it could have been spared when Britain was herself threatened with invasion. Luckily London's bluff was not called. Italy did not invade. Hitler vetoed it, anxious not to provoke Stalin too soon. Italy instead moved against Greece later in the year.

The Yugoslav Regent, Prince Paul – the real power in the country – was thought to be pro-British. He had been educated at Oxford and was married to the sister of the wife of the British King's younger brother, the Duke of Kent. The future George VI had been best man at his wedding and was godfather to his eldest son. One of Paul's closest friends at Oxford had been the Conservative politician and diarist "Chips" Channon, with whom he later shared a house in London. They kept in touch with each other for the rest of their lives. Channon's only son, who was to become a Conservative Member of Parliament too, was named after Paul. In his diaries the elder Channon maintains that Prince Paul was strongly pro-English and anti-German:

> They all talk English amongst themselves, read *The Tatler*, barely understand Slovenian and Serb, and dream of their next visit to London ... he gave me his solemn oath that in the event of war he will never do anything – anything to hurt England. At worst, he will be neutral, as he would not dare to come in on our side, as both Germany and Italy would at once squeeze his country to death ... he hates the Huns![1]

But the British Foreign Office had never been convinced of Prince Paul's hatred of the Huns. They had noticed his increasingly friendly disposition towards things German after Hitler came to power. The then senior British diplomat in Belgrade had commented to London in 1936 that Prince Paul "looks upon the Nazi regime as the bulwark against Bolshevism", preferring "to see Yugoslavia dominated by Germany than overrun by Italy via Albania or delivered over to the tender mercies of the Communists".[2] Paul certainly shared Hitler's abhorrence of communism. But he was also terrified of Germany's strength, especially after its annexation of Austria, which brought the Nazis to Yugoslavia's northern borders. Churchill used to refer derisively to Paul as "Prince Palsy", dismissing him as an "amiable and artistic personage". Even though he had cracked down heavily on Tito's communists during 1940 and early 1941, when they instigated strikes in munitions factories which they maintained breached Yugoslavia's neutrality. Tito was certainly diligent in his discharge of Moscow's diktat that the Germans be not provoked in any way!

Stephen Clissold, who was to become a liaison officer with the Partisans, was working in Zagreb then. He quotes in his biography of Tito, *Whirlwind*, published in 1949, a secret directive issued at this time in which Tito urged Party members who might be called up for military service to

> disorganise the resistance of the Yugoslav Army by creating confusion among officers and men so that defeat appears to be the result of the incompetence of the officers' corps whose authority will be destroyed once and for all.

Tito also encouraged his colleagues to

> render any assistance necessary to the Ustase, Macedonian, Albanian and other nationalist organizations, in so far as they may contribute towards the speedy overthrow of the present regime. Help should also be given to the Montenegrin Separatists if they adopt an anti-royalist line in Montenegro.

After the fall of France, those Yugoslav newspapers controlled by the regime – by far the majority of them – simply printed without comment the Axis propaganda line in their coverage of the war. Also, despite shortages at home because of bad harvests, Belgrade fulfilled all Hitler's demands for food and minerals. Germany, Austria and Italy had long been the main buyers of Yugoslavia's minerals, taking between them almost two-thirds of her exports. Yugoslavia in turn had become heavily dependent on those same countries' manufactured goods. By 1941 Germany was far and away Yugoslavia's best customer as well as her biggest supplier, taking well over half of her exports and furnishing a similar proportion of her imports. It was a dangerous dependence which the Nazis did not hesitate to exploit. Yugoslavia was already providing Hitler with 90 per cent of his tin, 40 per cent of his lead, 10 per cent of his copper, plus substantial amounts of antimony and, together with Greece, more than 45 per cent of his aluminium. All were vital to the German war machine.

German financial investments in the country had grown too. Within Yugoslavia there was a vigorous half-a-million strong *volksdeutsche* community, people of German nationality and descent who were enthusiastically pro-Hitler. They became a worrying factor in undermining Yugoslavia's resistance to the German diplomatic onslaught. Owning much of the country's most fertile land, they controlled a large part of Yugoslavia's food production. As the Yugoslav economy increasingly reflected Germany's dominant influence – and with German troops now on most of her borders – it was hardly surprising, under Yugoslavia's authoritarian regime, that criticism of Germany was discouraged if not directly banned.

This prompted the British to step up their intelligence and espionage activities inside Yugoslavia, subsidising and even financing anti-German political groups. Churchill had established the Special Operations Executive (SOE) in July 1940 after the fall of France "to set Europe ablaze". Commandos were to raid the Continent while resistance movements in the occupied territories would sabotage and subvert. SOE became particularly active in Yugoslavia. Among its agents there was Julian Amery, son of Leo Amery, a member of Churchill's cabinet and one of the British Prime Minister's closest friends. Arms and wireless transmitters were smuggled into Yugoslavia in diplomatic bags, and contacts were made with Serb nationalists. Should the Balkans fall into German hands, they planned to mine the Danube and sink barges loaded with cement in the narrow gorge called the Iron Gates on the Yugoslav-Romanian border. In this way they hoped to impede the supply of Romanian oil vital for Hitler's *Luftwaffe* and panzer divisions, as well as the delivery of other crucial minerals to Germany

Hitler had long had his sights on expanding Germany's influence eastwards at the expense of the Balkans. It was an essential part of his *Lebensraum* (living space) policy for the German peoples. More immediately, he needed for his war machine the oil, chromium, manganese, nickel, lead, tin, bauxite and copper that were abundant in the Balkans. He had successfully wooed the rulers of Romania, Bulgaria and Hungary. Now it was the turn of the Yugoslav Regent, Prince Paul. Paul had already made a state visit to Berlin in June 1939 when he had resisted Hitler's pressure for him to join the recently signed Pact of Steel between Germany and Italy, known as the Axis.

In early March 1941 Hitler invited him again, this time to Berchtesgaden, his mountain retreat in southern Bavaria. Hitler had even more urgent matters on his mind. He needed to transport his troops through Yugoslavia to go to the aid of the Italians in Greece. Their invasion of Greece from Albania five months earlier had met stiff resistance. Indeed Mussolini was in danger of being ignominiously defeated, especially as on 7 March the British had intervened on the side of the Greeks. Hitler planned to attack Russia later that spring and did not want to be delayed by an Italian debacle in Greece. Nor did he want British troops and planes within striking distance of his Romanian oil supplies, an essential ingredient in his war plans against Russia. Hence his anxiety to clear up as speedily as possible what he termed this *Schweinerei* (pigs' mess)!

Although Yugoslavia and Greece had previously been allies, Paul, whose wife was Greek, had straight away declared his country's neutrality. London interpreted this as denying transit rights through Yugoslavia for Germany's troops. Berlin, needless to say, thought differently and exerted all possible diplomatic pressure on the Yugoslavs to permit such passage. The bait proffered was the Greek port of Salonika, through which much of Yugoslavia's trade with the outside world was conducted. The British in turn again hinted at military aid were the Yugoslavs to assist Greece. But Paul must have realised that, with Britain fighting alone, such promises were impractical. London even dangled the prospect of border changes in Yugoslavia's favour after the successful conclusion of the war. They were to include those Adriatic islands and parts of Istria and Dalmatia ceded to Italy in the 1920s.

Paul knew only too well how vulnerable Yugoslavia was. Hitler would inevitably have his way. This seemed particularly so after the Romanians had invited the German Army into their country during October 1940. A month later they had, along with the Hungarians, joined Hitler's alliance with Italy and Japan, the so-called Tripartite Pact. Early in March 1941 the Germans had occupied Bulgaria without resistance. Yugoslavia was now ringed, except for Greece, by countries closely linked to Germany and Italy. To appease Hitler, Paul cracked down on pro-British demonstrations. He even relaxed police harassment of Tito's communists, perhaps as a desperate sign to the Soviets that *their* intervention would be welcome. Little did he know the Soviets were negotiating secretly with the Italians for the latter to recognise Bulgaria and the Dardanelles as Soviet spheres of influence in exchange for Soviet acceptance of Yugoslavia as an Italian sphere of influence!

To the British, as John Colville, one of Churchill's secretaries, confided to his diary on 5 March 1941, the day after Paul's secret visit to Berchtesgaden, Yugoslavia appeared "weak and vacillating".[3] But they did not understand the Serb mentality, with its penchant for ambiguity. The British were used to candour and straightforwardness. The Serbs, during centuries of Turkish occupation, had acquired the craft of evasion and delay – the need on occasion, when faced by an irresistible enemy, to appear to comply under pressure to unbearable demands, and then to dally in discharging them. Such was being Byzantine – a dirty word in the British diplomatic lexicon.

Meeting with the American Ambassador on 20 March, Paul found no understanding from him either. Nor was he offered any material support. Pressed to stay neutral, he replied: "You big nations are hard. You talk of our honour but you are far away."[4] Churchill had earlier commented, somewhat uncharitably: "Prince Paul's attitude looks like that of an unfortunate man in a cage with a tiger, hoping not to provoke him while steadily dinnertime approaches."[5]

Dinnertime for Paul was 25 March 1941. Having run out of pretexts for further delay and, more to the point, having been given an ultimatum by Hitler, he too adhered to the Tripartite Pact. The head of the British Foreign Office, Sir Alexander Cadogan, wrote in his diary that evening: "Yugs are signing – silly, feeble mugs."[6] Two days later Paul was ousted. Peter was proclaimed King, though still a minor, in a mainly Serb anti-German uprising. The coup was kindled by the British Secret Service with Churchill's full knowledge. Julian Amery had even got his father, who spoke Serbo-Croat, to appeal via the BBC to Yugoslavs, on the evening of 26 March, "to choose the path of honour rather than capitulation".[7] When told of the putsch, Paul merely commented "We're finished, in a week or two Germany will roll over us." He was sent into exile, to Greece, and eventually to Kenya. Churchill, well pleased, uttered his much-quoted, "Yugoslavia has found its soul," though it appears he filched it from Cadogan![8]

Churchill then tried to get the Turks to make "common cause" with the Yugoslavs, offering territorial concessions at the expense of Bulgaria, but to no avail. He attempted, too, to persuade the new Yugoslav regime to move its million-strong army against the "demoralised and rotten Italians" in Albania, claiming "masses of equipment" would fall into their hands.[9] But, afraid of provoking the pro-German Croats in their midst, they would not even allow the British Foreign Secretary, Anthony Eden, to visit Belgrade. Dithering over whether or not to renounce the signing of the Pact, they ended up in the worst of all possible worlds, having annoyed both Hitler and the British. Tito reported to Stalin that, although it had released some communists from prison, a weakness of the new government was that it contained "several explicit Anglophiles".[10] Djilas says that Tito "attacked 'Anglophile elements' and 'provocateurs' who demolished the German Tourist Bureau, the centre for Hitler's propaganda in Belgrade, and burned the German flag."[11]

Tito was later to claim he had instigated the coup, though he was not even in Belgrade at the time. He and his politburo were clearly surprised by the putsch. It had popular backing, especially among the young, who were chanting, "Better war than the Pact, better a grave than a slave; there can be no war without the Serbs." Some of the younger members of Tito's party joined in the anti-German rallies. They were discouraged by their elders, who cautiously awaited instruction from Moscow.

Nor were Tito and his comrades responsible for the conclusion of a "Friendship and Non-Aggression Pact" between the Soviets and the Yugoslavs on the very eve of Hitler's invasion. Of no material help to the Yugoslavs, it simply angered Hitler all the more. They had hoped for a stronger "of Mutual Assistance" pact. Moscow had initially promised it but renegued in the last minute, fearing to provoke Hitler. Stalin repudiated the Pact immediately after Yugoslavia's defeat so as not to offend Hitler further. He expelled its diplomatic representatives from Moscow on the grounds that their country no longer existed. Ominously, the coup had not been welcomed in Croatia. It was, though, in some parts of Slovenia, especially the capital Ljubljana.

Feeling humiliated – the torching of a swastika flag outside the wrecked German tourist office in Belgrade had been especially mortifying – Hitler demanded swift revenge. His generals were ordered "to smash Yugoslavia militarily and as a state".[12] He told the Hungarian minister in Berlin, "We will burn out for good the festering sore in the Balkans."[13] Without issuing an ultimatum or declaring war, but alleging Serb atrocities against the *Volksdeutsche*, German bombers raided Belgrade on 6 April, just ten days after the coup. Tito was in Zagreb, which was spared any bombing. The destruction in the capital was appalling and the casualties high. At least ten thousand are thought to have died. That same day the German army launched a blitzkrieg across Yugoslavia's borders, codenamed "Operation Retribution". The choice of label indicated Hitler's wrath.

Mobilisation had begun just three days earlier. Not wishing to provoke Hitler by issuing a public rally to arms, the troops had been sent individual call-up notices. Relying still on horses and oxcarts for transport, the poorly equipped and ill-trained Yugoslav army was no match for Hitler's motorised panzers. Within ten days it had surrendered. A similar fate befell the Greek army before the end of the month. The Germans lost just 166 men in capturing Yugoslavia. Hitler had overestimated the Yugoslav army's morale and effectiveness. It was a pale shadow of the Serbian army that had resisted so resolutely in the First World War.

The new Yugoslav government, with the young king, fled the country. Churchill was dismayed. He had expected them to remain and become a focus for some form of national resistance. He signalled, on 13 April, the British diplomat with them:

> We do not see why the King or Government should leave the country, which is vast, mountainous and full of armed men. German tanks can no doubt move along the roads and tracks, but to conquer the Serbian Armies they must bring up infantry. Then will be the chance to kill them. Surely the young King and the Ministers should play their part in this.[14]

The British intelligence agents fled too, some to Istanbul, which became for a while SOE's base for operations within the Balkans, before locating at Cairo. The only sabotage they had been able to carry out before their hurried departure was to put sand and other abrasives in the axle-boxes of some railway engines and wagons bound for Germany.

It was a bad time for the British all round. They had been forced to quit Greece somewhat ignominiously and had disastrously lost Crete. The Germans had come to the rescue of the Italians in North Africa, pushing the British troops back with what seemed surprising ease, through the Western Desert towards the Egyptian border. The German forces there had been led by General Rommel, whose *Afrika Korps* was to become a menacing spectre on the Mediterranean scene.

A small remnant of the Yugoslav army under Colonel Draza Mihailovic did take to the hills and forests to resist the Germans. Numbering no more than a few hundred, they eventually based themselves in a relatively inaccessible area known as Ravna Gora (Flat Mountain), a high plateau a hundred miles or so south-west of Belgrade. Mihailovic, aged forty-eight, a year younger than Tito, had been trained in France. He had fought gallantly with the Allies during the First World War and been awarded the Military Cross by the British. Serving thereafter as a military attaché in various legations, he was known to the British and was probably at one time on the payroll of the British Secret Service. He was certainly known personally to at least two SOE members, Julian Amery and Alexander Glen, an assistant naval attaché.

Mihailovic had headed a small department within the Yugoslav Army General Staff responsible for studying and planning guerrilla warfare in the event of occupation. He had also lectured on the subject at the Military Academy in Belgrade. Though a Russophile, he was fervently anti-communist. He was known, too, to be anti-German, intensely loyal to the monarchy and a passionately patriotic Serb. His criticism of the army's defence plans had annoyed his superiors. They reprimanded him in 1938 for breaking up a pro-Nazi demonstration in Slovenia, and again in 1940 for making sympathetic remarks after Dunkirk to the British military attaché at an official function in Belgrade. For the latter he had been confined to barracks for thirty days, an unusual punishment for an officer of his rank. When Hitler struck Yugoslavia, Mihailovic was Director of Operations of the Yugoslav Second Army. Within the day he had become its Chief of Staff.

Churchill was certainly right that Yugoslavia, with its mountainous terrain, remote forested valleys, deep gorges and ravines, few roads and thinly spread population, was ideal guerrilla territory. An occupying force, inevitably confined to garrisoning the towns and cities, and faced with long lines of communication, would find it a monumental headache. Moreover, in Serbia at least, the occupiers would also face a hostile populace.

By contrast, Tito's communists remained in the towns. Many of them openly co-operated with the Germans. Some even denounced to the Gestapo those of their countrymen resisting the occupiers, especially if, like Mihailovic's supporters, they had been linked to the previous regime. Party leaflets dubbed the latter "lackeys of London" and called on the public not to help them in any way. Tito's line was still that the English "imperialists" had instigated the war by provoking Germany. Djilas says, "a decision was made to denounce the officers", that is Mihailovic's men, who were "hiding in the mountains of western Serbia, threatening to take over after the defeat of the Germans and 'save the country' from the Communists". It was straightaway resolved "to begin an armed struggle against them".[15] Djilas admits no attempt was made to resist the Germans who, perhaps constrained by the Hitler-Stalin Pact, did not go out of their way to hunt down known communists.

Croat units in the army had mutinied in support of the Germans. Many Croat soldiers had simply abandoned their positions; others had overpowered and even murdered their Serb officers. Just three days before the German invasion a Croat pilot had flown his plane to Austria, taking with him the locations of the Yugoslav military airfields and numbers of aircraft expected at each site. Tito's military chief later admitted that Croat communists had incited many of these desertions. There was an instance of some junketing Croat officers pausing to surrender their troops to the advancing Germans and then returning to their party "as if nothing untoward had happened".[16] Alexander Glen recalled to me that, when driving from Belgrade to the coast with his wife and some Yugoslav politicians in April 1941, they had been stopped near Mostar at a roadblock manned by Croat soldiers who were picking out Serb officers from the cars in their convoy and shooting them.

German troops were warmly welcomed in Croatia and, to some extent, in Slovenia, but not in Serbia. According to the war diary of one of the German army corps, their soldiers entered Zagreb on 10 April to the "jubilation of the civilian population", which was "indescribable". Croatian and Slovene troops captured by the Germans were released almost immediately. Serb soldiers taken prisoner, more than 180,000 of them, were shipped off to camps in Germany and Italy. Most of them, especially the officers, were never to return. A further 200,000 Serbs, dissident Croats and Slovenes were forced to work in Germany.

Yugoslavia was dismembered. In the north, Slovenia was divided between Germany and Italy. The Italians, like the Hungarians, had joined in attacking the Yugoslavs just days before the surrender. Most of Dalmatia was ceded to Italy and the remainder added to Croatia, which was further enlarged at the expense of Bosnia-Herzegovina. While occupied by both Germans and Italians, Croatia's internal administration was given over to Ante Pavelic and his fascist paramilitary Ustashi, who had returned from their refuge in Italy. Apparently Stalin considered recognising Pavelic's regime, putting out diplomatic feelers to that end. Nothing came of it. Perhaps he was put off by Pavelic's speedy declaration of war on Britain. Croatia subsequently declared war on the United States. There is no record of their having done so on the Soviets, but Croatian troops were sent to fight alongside the Germans on the Russian front. A Croat regiment was captured at Stalingrad. After what Moscow described as "re-education", it transmogrified itself into the Free Yugoslav Legion that fought with the Red Army in the later stages of the war. It even helped the Russians capture Belgrade in October 1944. With the blessing of the anti-British Grand Mufti of Jerusalem, Bosnian Moslems were recruited to SS Divisions in 1943. They became some of the most feared and fanatical members of those infamous units. The Italians also took control of Montenegro, and the Bulgarians of most of Macedonia. Other parts of Yugoslavia were given to Hungary and to Italy's vassal state Albania.

In August 1941 a pro-Nazi puppet government led by a Serb general, Milan Nedic, was installed in what was left of Serbia, which now came under direct German military rule. Nedic had been Mihailovic's superior. Little love was lost between them. Nedic had issued the reprimands against Mihailovic and had sought to demote him. He was allowed to recruit a state militia to police Serbia for the Germans. The Serbs were also required to pay Germany's occupation costs. Already considerable, they were to increase steadily as the war went on. Hitler's aim, as he informed the Italians, was "to reduce Serbia to the smallest limits to prevent ... conspiracies and intrigues". He was determined the Serbs should be made to "pay for Sarajevo" (presumably he meant the assassination there of Archduke Ferdinand in 1914, allegedly on Serbian orders), as well as for their part in the German defeat in the First World War. He wanted them destroyed as a nation. The German Army High Command was instructed "to treat them exceptionally badly".

Because the Serbs were Orthodox Christians, Hitler feared they might be potential allies of the Soviets. He did not relish their being in the rear of his troops about to invade Russia. Concentration camps were set up near Belgrade and a reign of terror began, with the help of the local *Volksdeutschen* who had taken part in the successful German invasion. At least thirty thousand of them, dressed in paramilitary uniforms, were said to have been engaged. All cultural life in the Yugoslav capital now came under their control. Grains, fats and meat were commandeered and sent from Serbia to Germany to the detriment of the local populace. Factories were dismantled and shipped to the *Reich*. Those not needed were broken up for scrap metal.

Hitler remained wary of the Serbs for the rest of the war. Because of Serbia's strategic importance, straddling crucial lines of communication between central Europe and the southern Balkans, and because it was the source of large quantities of minerals vital to his war effort, he made sure it stayed under German control. The Danube, the main transport route for Romanian oil and Balkan wheat to the *Reich*, passed through Serbia, as did the railway from Germany to Greece that was to be important for supplying his troops in North Africa.

Croatia witnessed the worst immediate atrocities. The Ustasha militia, in a barbaric orgy of medieval proportions, murdered, with knives, meat hooks, bludgeons or whatever weapons were to hand, thousands of Jews and gypsies, and hundreds of thousands of Croatia's Serbs. Their aim was to create an ethnically pure country. Whole communities were massacred and countless villages razed to the ground. Men, women and children were thrown alive into ravines. Mutilated Serb bodies were floated down the various tributaries of the Danube to the Serbian capital bearing the inscription "Meat for John's Market, Belgrade". A favourite Ustasha ploy was to corral Serb villagers, young and old, into their churches and then to torch the buildings. Serbian Orthodox clergymen were particularly targeted. By the end of the year only eighty-five remained of the six hundred or so there had been in Croatia earlier that spring. Most had been forced to flee, but at least two hundred, including three bishops, were murdered. Numerous Serb churches, monasteries and cemeteries were desecrated or destroyed. The Orthodox cathedral at Banja Luka was completely demolished.

Milovan Djilas describes in his *Wartime* memoirs how "nearly every Serbian village had its own ditch where the frenzied Ustashi had thrown their victims". He details a joint German and Ustasha offensive in Bosnia during 1942 that led to forty thousand Serbs being "sent to their death at Jasenovac, probably the most horrible of the camps of World War II". Jasenovac was seventy miles south-east of Zagreb, on the banks of the Sava River. Djilas adds:

> Hitler's invasion unearthed the long pent-up shadows of ages past and gave them a new dress, a new motivation: neighbours who might have lived out their lives side by side were now all of a sudden plundering and annihilating one another.

The Ustashi are believed to have exterminated nearly one hundred thousand Serbs, Jews and gypsies at Jasenovac alone. There were other, though smaller, concentration camps. Estimates of the total number of Serbs murdered by the Ustashi vary wildly. The Germans suggested four hundred thousand. A further four hundred thousand are thought to have fled or been deported from Croatia to Serbia and Montenegro. Three hundred thousand more are said to have been forcibly converted to Catholicism, though this did not prevent many being subsequently killed.

The Ustashi considered they were waging a crusade on behalf of the Roman Catholic Church against Eastern Orthodox Christians, Jews, Moslems and Bolshevik atheists. Jews were forced, as in Germany, to wear yellow armbands; Serbs were compelled to wear blue ones with the letter "P" for "Pravoslavac" (Orthodox). Most Serbs were Orthodox Christians. All schools run by the Orthodox Church were closed. Even the Cyrillic script was banned. The Catholic press in Croatia backed Pavelic and the Ustashi throughout the war. The Church hierarchy made no public protest or condemnation. The head of the Roman Catholics in Croatia, Archbishop Stepinac, blessed Ustashi in his cathedral and praised them in his sermons. So did most of the other Catholic bishops, some of whom participated in the massacring. Franciscan priests led many of the Ustasha units and openly propagandised on behalf of the Ustasha state. The Vatican voiced no public disapproval, although it knew full well what was happening in Croatia. The Pope in fact gave credence to the Ustashi by personally blessing Pavelic during a private audience in Rome and receiving a delegation of more than a hundred of his most fervent followers. By contrast, the head of the Serbian Orthodox Church was imprisoned and eventually shipped off to Dachau concentration camp.

The indiscriminate bestiality of the Ustashi shocked even the Germans, who were ordered not to interfere. Some Italian soldiers did intervene to protect victims and disarm the Ustashi. Others encouraged the Serbs to resist, often giving them the weapons to do so. In official military reports to Rome, the Ustashi were described as "a crowd of barbarians and cannibals". Italian officers on occasion even forcibly reopened Serb churches the Ustashi had closed. Many of the Serbs who took to the hills to avoid the Ustashi were fed and armed by the Italians. Thousands more fled to Serbia and Montenegro. In some areas the Serbs greeted the Italians as their saviours.

This was the beginning of Italian-Serb interaction. Historically Serbs had had few dealings with Italians. There was no tradition of animosity between them, as between Croats and Italians, or Slovenes and Italians, because of border disputes and the like. This co-operation led to constant friction between the German and Italian occupiers, and between them both and the Ustashi, all to the benefit of those resisting the occupation. There was further antagonism between Italians and Croats over Italy's annexation of coastal Dalmatia, including the ports of Dubrovnik and Split, which the new Zagreb authorities deeply resented.

The Yugoslav communists had always regarded the Ustashi as natural allies in the revolutionary struggle against the Serbian-dominated Yugoslav regime. They had helped them in various ways. Rankovic, a leading member of Tito's polituro and future head of his secret police, had struck up close friendships with many of the Ustashi leaders while in prison. On release, he had hidden one of them in his mother's house. Many communists in Croatia assisted the Ustashi in tracking down Serbs at this time. Tito's men certainly made no attempt to resist the Ustashi, seeing the benefit of their liquidating the Serb establishment. The Ustashi terror had provoked resistance within Croatia to them and to the Germans and Italians, but it was mostly a defensive action by local Serbs. Croatia was in a state of revolt from late May 1941 onwards. The near anarchy prompted Tito and his politburo to quit Zagreb for the relative quiet of Belgrade.

The German army was to blame the Ustashi for arousing resistance within Croatia. Because Hitler had given them his blessing when Pavelic visited Berchtesgaden in early June 1941, no senior German officer was prepared to protest publicly against their conduct. No doubt Hitler had recognised in Pavelic a like-minded racist who hated Serbs and Jews as much as he did. He was more than willing to grant the Ustashi free rein. That Pavelic was said to keep a wicker basket in his office full of human eyeballs gouged from Serb victims was perhaps only to be expected!

When he moved to Belgrade, Tito left Herta Haas behind, although she was about to give birth to their first baby, a son, Aleksandar-Misa, known as Misha. She was imprisoned and tortured by the Ustashi, as well as by the Germans. Tito did not see her again for two years. He would not see their son until 1948, when Misha briefly lived with him. Such was his need for women that, almost immediately after his arrival in Belgrade, he took as his mistress a twenty-year-old student, Davorjanka Paunovic, known as Zdenka. He had met her in Zagreb while she was studying radio-telegraphy there. Though never popular with his entourage, being prone to bouts of extreme temper, she stayed with him until 1944. Djilas hints in his memoirs that sexual promiscuity was prevalent within the Yugoslav communist leadership, whereas chastity was strictly enforced among the rank-and-file. He saw no hypocrisy in this. Promiscuity at the top and prudery at the bottom were to be carried forward into the Partisan Army.

The Yugoslav army's debacle and the humiliatingly speedy bolting of the king and government were clearly beneficial to Tito. The country's major institutions – the dynasty, the army and the political parties – were utterly discredited. Not being directly associated in the ordinary Yugoslav's mind with the catastrophe and, most crucially, remaining on the scene, the Yugoslav communists now had a unique opportunity to fill the political and spiritual void. It was as favourable a situation as they could have wished for in which to promote their revolutionary purposes.

Hitler's attack on Russia on 22 June 1941 was to change things even more dramatically for Tito. His first reaction was simply to applaud Stalin in the usual abject terms and to assure Moscow of his faith in an eventual Soviet victory. Such was his military naivety then that he assured his party comrades the Red Army would soon liberate Yugoslavia and they would be in power within months. The historian Mark Wheeler, in his contribution to Tony Judt's *Resistance and Revolution in Mediterranean Europe 1939-1948*, describes how Yugoslav communists established first aid stations in the Vojvodina to assist the expected Soviet paratroopers! Farmers were encouraged to mow their meadows earlier than usual to ease the landings. Tito sent envoys around the country to rustle up plans for resistance while he remained in Belgrade, no doubt to be on hand to greet the Soviet liberators.

Instead, Hitler's panzers swept the Red Army aside and were quickly on their way to Leningrad and Moscow. Stalin, finding himself in a life-and-death struggle, ordered Tito's communists to forget their revolution and begin fighting the Germans inside Yugoslavia. They were to, "without wasting a moment, organize Partisan detachments and start a Partisan war behind the enemy's lines ... and make him feel he is under siege."[17] The Russian guerrillas who had harassed Napoleon's retreat from Moscow in 1812 had been called partisans. Stalin was keen for Tito to co-operate with all anti-German elements within Yugoslavia, even if they were anti-communist. Clearly he had Mihailovic's forces in mind. They were obviously known to Soviet Intelligence.

Tito expected the Soviets to supply him with the wherewithal for such resistance. His messages to Moscow at this time pleaded for weapons and explosives and their arrival was awaited daily. Much time and effort was expended on arranging drop zones. Djilas was to learn, when he visited Moscow in 1944, that the help intended "was to take the form of Yugoslav émigrés who were in fact Soviet informers, rather than the munitions which were needed"![18] It was three years before any Russian aid reached them. Meanwhile they were told to rely on what they could filch from the German and Italian occupiers. Not all the Yugoslav army's weapons had been surrendered to the Germans. Large caches of military equipment had been hidden, of which Tito and Mihailovic were to avail themselves. As most of it was located outside Serbia, Tito was to benefit the more.

The communists had never been numerous in the countryside, where four out of five Yugoslavs lived. They were based almost exclusively in the towns and cities. In calling for immediate resistance, rather than for a revolution sometime in the distant future, their usual mantra, they were venturing into new waters. Inevitably mistakes were made. From the moment of the German invasion, the Party had split into national cliques: Croat, Slovenian, Macedonian, Montenegrin and Serb. There had been separate organisations for these since the mid-1930s.

Tito's communists were later to claim that they began the real resistance in Yugoslavia. The truth is different. Their first action, on 7 July 1941, a date fêted in Tito's day, as "The Day of the Uprising", was the killing not of Germans but of two Serbian policemen, admittedly working for the occupiers, at Bela Crkva! The first German soldier was killed twenty days later in an ambush on the road between Uzice and Valjevo, but not by a communist. It prompted instant reprisal. Eighty one local Serbs were rounded up and Serb gendarmes were ordered at gunpoint to shoot them. Many of the gendarmes straightaway deserted and joined Mihailovic's forces. He had not been responsible for the incident either. It had been a simple highway robbery that had, presumably, gone wrong. The soldier's belongings, including his boots and socks, had been stolen, but not his rifle.

That Stalin was impatient with Tito's slow reaction is evidenced by a Moscow broadcast on 10 August calling on the Serbian nation to

> disobey orders. Fall on German garrisons and kill soldiers and officers. Destroy railway lines for German transports. Blow up bridges, German munitions and oil. Cut telephone lines. Don't give a single grain of wheat to the Germans … Deal in the same measure that which has been dealt to you: for every fallen Serbian head, let one hundred Fascist heads fall. Be true to Serbian traditions and the warlike traditions of your ancestors.[19]

The first act of sabotage had been the wrecking of a bridge in late April by Mihailovic's forces. The German occupiers reported other incidents within Serbia, as did the Italians in Montenegro. Most were by loyalist Serbs. The Germans invariably referred to them as "communist bands" because in Nazi parlance this was their most abusive term. It was in the interests of the German propagandists to conceal the existence of any nationalist opponents to the occupation. Hitler's army chief, Field Marshal Keitel, is on record as saying, on 16 September 1941: "Each incident of insurrection against the German armed forces, regardless of individual circumstances, must be assumed to be of Communist origin."[20] What little opposition the *Wehrmacht* had met in its April 1941 invasion had come from Serb units of the regular Yugoslav Army. By German reckoning some 300,000 or so Serb troops were still at large. An early German military order after the Yugoslav surrender warned that "anyone found in Serbian uniform, if armed, is not protected by the usages of war and is immediately to be shot. The corpses of the shot are to be hung up and left to hang."

The Montenegrins had always allied themselves with the Serbs. They objected strongly to Italy's attempt to convert them into a satellite state like Albania, with a minor Italian royal as monarch. There was a full-scale uprising there in mid-July. Rebels took over the main towns and villages, apart from the capital, Cetinje. Several thousand Italian troops were killed or captured. Tito sent Milovan Djilas, himself a Montenegrin, to make sure the Partisans benefited from it. He was instructed to impose his authority on the uprising and, if necessary, to "shoot anyone – even a member of the provincial leadership – if he wavers or shows any lack of discipline."[21] Official Partisan historians claim Djilas started the uprising, but he admitted later it was already in full swing by the time he arrived. In any case the Italians, with the help of the Montenegrins' traditional foes, the Albanians and Bosnian Muslims, brutally suppressed it within weeks. This disillusioned many of the locals, who sought some form of accommodation with their occupiers in a spirit of "live and let live". Thereafter the Italian troops kept to the towns and were prepared to countenance armed bands in the countryside provided they did not attack them.

The communists made themselves unpopular among the Montenegrins by venting their frustration on the richer peasants – the kulaks in the Bolshevik lexicon – whom they felt had not supported the uprising with sufficient enthusiasm. They burnt their lands and pillaged their properties, to the delight of the Italians who preferred Montenegrins to fight each other rather than them. These richer peasants threw in their lot with Mihailovic's men, as did the merchants and professional classes. All of which increased the animosity between the communists and the non-communists, again to the advantage of the occupiers. The Serbs had been fighting for their lives in Croatia ever since Hitler's invasion. Many of them had taken refuge in Montenegro from the Ustasha terror. Because food was scarce, friction was frequent between the newcomers and the Montenegrin peasants. The communists sought to turn this to their benefit, as did the Italian occupiers.

Djilas maintains Tito tried to sack him in November 1941 for apparently organising too much resistance in Montenegro. In Tito's estimation this had led to unnecessary casualties among the Partisans there. Djilas believed it was Tito's suspicious nature, like Stalin's, that persuaded him that Djilas was "growing too independent". He was recalled to Tito's headquarters, expecting a rebuke. Instead he was given the task of denouncing in the Party's news sheets those deemed dangerous to their cause. His denunciations were usually a preliminary to their physical liquidation, he was to admit. Djilas was convinced Tito was so uncertain of himself at this time that he became afraid whenever his politburo colleagues were out of his sight!

Although subversion and sabotage would not decide the war, they were, until the Russians and, more particularly, the Americans, entered the scene, Churchill's only hope of making life difficult for the Germans occupying mainland Europe – along with bombing, blockading and the occasional commando raid. Hence his intense interest in SOE. To avoid it being swallowed up by the traditional espionage services, he had placed it within the Ministry of Economic Warfare, or "Ministry of Ungentlemanly Warfare" as he called it. Its head was Hugh Dalton, a Socialist. Almost immediately a turf war sprang up between it and the regular Secret Intelligence Service (SIS). The latter at times seemed more interested in doing SOE down than in beating the Germans.

SOE was beset from the start by interdepartmental rivalries and jealousies. Having been created, in Churchill's words, "to set Europe ablaze", the joke was that it was only Whitehall that felt the heat! Malcolm Muggeridge, who worked for MI6 (SIS) at this time, said in his memoirs, *Chronicles of Wasted Time*, "though SOE and MI6 were nominally on the same side in the war, they were, generally speaking, more abhorrent to one another than the *Abwehr* [the German Secret Service] was to either of them." SOE's official historian, William Mackenzie, put it down to "the old contrast between the polished product of tradition and the energetic but injudicious parvenu". He claimed:

Formally relations at the top were correct, though distant, in lesser matters the atmosphere was bad; there is plenty of evidence of the suspicion and dislike which existed between various branches of the two organisations, both in London and in Missions overseas.[22]

Mackenzie's account, though written shortly after the war, was thought too controversial for public exposure then. Publication was not permitted until the year 2000!

Mackenzie acknowledged: "From SIS's point of view SOE was an upstart organisation staffed by amateurs not one of whom understood the elements of secret work. It was invading SIS's territory with much sound and fury." Even so,

> they had been entrusted by the War Cabinet with a task of an entirely novel kind, which was of the greatest importance to the whole Allied strategy ... SOE complained that while they were called upon to reveal all their projects to SIS they got very little by doing so except discouragement: and there was no reciprocal attempt by SIS to put its cards on the table and invite the cooperation of SOE. In all practical fields – wireless communications, sea transport, the recruitment of personnel – SIS claimed absolute priority for intelligence: and its secretiveness could be as dangerous to SOE's agents as SOE's inexperience was to SIS.

Nor was SOE liked by the military chiefs or the Foreign Office. It had attracted buccaneering, oddball, raffish types not used to obeying rules or to working through normal channels. Army officers and diplomats tended to be conventional souls, abiding by traditions. It was hardly surprising they should not readily take to SOE with its unorthodox methods and viewpoints. The downside of the absence of mutual respect was their lack of enthusiasm when it came to allocating scarce resources, particularly aircraft for the crucial supply drops to resistance groups on mainland Europe. It did not help matters that clear lines of demarcation were seldom drawn – or, when tentatively drawn, were never kept to – between SOE and the other Whitehall warrior institutions. When things went wrong, and they often did, the opportunities to blame each other were boundless.

Bickham Sweet-Escott of SOE, in his memoir *Baker Street Irregular*, maintains:

> Nobody who did not experience it can possibly imagine the atmosphere of jealousy, suspicion and intrigue which embittered the relations between the various secret and semi-secret departments in Cairo during that summer of 1941, or for that matter for the next two years ... It was not quite Hobbes's war of every man against every

man. But certainly every secret organisation seemed to be set against every other secret organisation.

Professor Hugh Seton-Watson, a Balkan expert and a member of SOE in Cairo, was to say later:

> SOE was an upstart organisation, inevitably viewed with suspicion and jealousy by all existing departments. From the beginning it was given impossibly ambitious tasks and denied the resources for them. When the tasks were not achieved, it was easier to blame the upstarts than to find remedies.[23]

Leo Marks, in charge of SOE's codes, recalled, in his memoir *Between Silk and Cyanide*, visiting SOE's Cairo headquarters "in Rustom Buildings, a large grey-pillared block in the centre of an otherwise respectable residential area. Every taxi-driver in Cairo knew the address and charged double for reaching it." To most it was known simply as "the secret building"!

Julian Amery, working then for SOE in Cairo, wrote to his father, a close friend and cabinet colleague of Churchill's, on 15 August 1941 about "something like a general insurrection" which was underway in Serbia and Bosnia. As "the peasants there and in Greece" had not yet been fully disarmed by the Germans, a golden opportunity seemed to be being missed "to launch a general revolt in the Balkans" which would "help the Russians to hold out and thus help preserve the first glimmer of a chance of victory since the War started."[24] Leo Amery passed the gist of the letter to Churchill. Dalton, at Churchill's behest, later that same month discussed the Yugoslav situation with the Yugoslav government-in-exile as well as with British diplomats and military chiefs. While welcoming resistance, especially if it deterred the Germans from reducing the strength of their occupation force, they jointly decided against encouraging "any attempt at large-scale risings or ambitious military operations, which could only result at present in severe repression and the loss of our key men." Instead the guerrillas in Yugoslavia should be helped to prepare "a widespread underground organisation ready to strike hard later on, when we give the signal."[25] This was in keeping with SOE's policy of encouraging the formation of "secret armies" in the occupied countries that would rise up when Allied troops returned to continental Europe.

The British had known of Mihailovic's existence since mid-June. The Soviets probably knew earlier, through their embassy in Sofia. Regular radio contact with him was established only in mid-September. His aim, he told London, was to recruit, train and arm an underground resistance movement ready to attack the Germans when the moment seemed propitious – such as when the Allies invaded the Balkans. For that, he would need weapons, supplies and money, which he hoped would come from Britain. He argued that it was pointless, if not suicidal, to waste their manpower and puny resources on attempting to fight the vastly superior Axis armies. They clearly could not liberate Yugoslavia on their own. SOE, who had set up a base in Cairo from which to organise operations in the Balkans, made contact with Mihailovic and got £20,000 in gold to him by courier from Istanbul early in September to buy food and arms for his forces. Julian Amery had wanted a full-scale British military mission sent immediately to Mihailovic. But that was going to take a little longer.

Concerned more with their campaign against the Russians, the Germans quickly withdrew the cream of their troops, reducing their garrisoning of Yugoslavia to the bare minimum. While they concentrated on holding the important cities and main lines of communication, responsibility for the occupation elsewhere was left largely to the Italians, Bulgarians and Croats. The Bulgarian troops were never popular with the Serbs because of their historic enmity towards each other.

Half of Germany's oil, all of its chrome, 60 per cent of its bauxite, 24 per cent of its antimony and 21 per cent of its copper were procured from Balkan sources at this time. Apart from Norway, Yugoslavia was the only source in Europe of molybdenum, used to armourplate warships and tanks. Much of these supplies were carried on the Danube and the strategic railway linking Germany and Greece which passed through Belgrade and Serbia. The largest copper mines in Europe were in Serbia. Hence for Berlin Serbia was always Yugoslavia's most important region. Its security was always a German and not an Italian responsibility. Serbia was, of course, where Mihailovic was based. Tito's Partisans did not operate there after the autumn of 1941, so their eradication was never such a pressing necessity for Hitler. Tito for most of the time functioned in more remote areas under the control of the Italians or Croat militias. He was to survive by resisting only when attacked and then quickly moving out of harm's way: so-called fighting retreats. The Partisans were never a major threat to the Germans, only a nuisance. Because he was in German-controlled Serbia, and closer to

Hitler's vital lines of communication, Mihailovic's was always the hotter seat.

When faced with sabotage in Serbia – however sporadic and unco-ordinated – the Germans, lacking the luxury of numbers to deal with it effectively, terrorised the populace into submission with brutal reprisals. They announced that a hundred Serbs would be executed for every German killed and fifty for every German wounded. Every house from which shots were fired at German soldiers would be destroyed and its male inhabitants older than fifteen put to death. Hitler had charged his local commander with "securing in Serbia the traffic arteries by the most severe means". Between 19 and 21 October 1941 2,778 young Serb men, many mere schoolboys, were seized randomly in Kragujevac, an industrial city of some 35,000 inhabitants about forty miles south of Belgrade. They were shot in reprisal for the killing in the vicinity of twenty-three German soldiers and the wounding of others in various acts of sabotage earlier that month.

Alexander Petrovica, a Serb living in London, told me fifty years later how he had been one of those schoolboys in Kragujevac seized by the Germans. He had been freed because his teacher had pleaded he was too young to die. He remembered fleeing in terror and hearing throughout the night machine-gun fire, and the next morning the screams and wails of mothers when they found the bodies of their sons. "It was a terrible experience hearing the whole town crying at the same time," he said. "The community was shattered. Complete generations had disappeared overnight."

Already 2,100 male Serbs had been shot in reprisals at Leskovac and elsewhere on 2 October. A further 1,755 were executed at Kraljevo later that same month, as well as 1,200 in Belgrade itself and several hundred at Krupanj. Many peasants' homes, and even entire villages, were destroyed. According to German sources, 21,809 Serbs were executed in reprisals for the killing that autumn of 203 German soldiers and the wounding of 378. Hostages were even held in advance.

When news of this reached London, the Yugoslav government-in-exile ordered Mihailovic to lie low and avoid Germans while they awaited events. He was told to disband most of his forces, said by then to have increased to several thousand, though not all were armed or fully trained. The principal event awaited was an Allied invasion of the Balkans, but this was unlikely to happen for some time, if at all. British military chiefs agreed with this, as did the diplomats. The Foreign Office's official historian of the Second World War, Sir Llewellyn Woodward, was to say:

> British policy towards local resistance in Yugoslavia as elsewhere was based on the sound view that premature attempts at insurrection should be discouraged since they would have little military result and would merely add more savage reprisals to the miseries which the peoples under enemy rule had to endure.[26]

Mihailovic was himself determined to avoid useless sacrifice. While sending most of his men home, he encouraged others to join Nedic's State Guard so that he might access their weapons when the moment was opportune. He always expected Nedic's forces to support him when the Allies invaded. Meanwhile he considered them an ideal source of intelligence about German troop movements. He had not of course envisaged that, when he contacted these "agents", his communist opponents and, more surprisingly, their British supporters, would consider it treacherous collaboration.

Mihailovic was forever conscious of the enormous suffering of the Serbs in the First World War – there were a million casualties in a population of just four and a half million. Mindful of how near they had come to annihilation as a nation, he was anxious to avoid another catastrophe on such a scale. The preservation of Serbia, and in particular of the Serbs as a nation, coloured his behaviour, especially his dealings with the British. He feared, too, for any diminution of the Serbs' numerical superiority within Yugoslavia. None of these concerns was ever really appreciated by the British, certainly not by Churchill and his immediate circle. The Germans understood them and did everything in their power to increase his anxiety in that regard.

Determined to safeguard the Serb nation, and therefore giving a higher priority to saving Serb lives than to killing Germans, it was unthinkable Mihailovic would consider having any long-term truck with the Axis. He had studied *Mein Kampf* sufficiently to understand Hitler's true feelings towards slavs in general. *Temporary* arrangements, however, were not ruled out. "Using the enemy" was how such deals were described in the Balkans. Meaning using one enemy (say the Germans or Italians), to help fight another (in Mihailovic's case, Tito's communists) when it was seemingly in *both* their interests to do so – finding a way to obtain supplies openly from your enemy in order to endure; buying time or bolstering survival, probably both. Such deals could only be short-term. Mihailovic and the Axis occupiers knew that eventually they would have to fight each other to the death. That was the way of things in the Balkans. Churchill and his circle never appreciated this. What looked like treachery to the Western mind was to the Balkan a subtle, momentary siding with the invader in order to facilitate the elimination of a domestic opponent. Roosevelt used to quote a Balkan proverb to explain the United States' apparent friendliness during 1941 towards the quisling Vichy administration in France: "In times of grave danger you may walk with the devil until you have crossed the bridge."

Both Tito and Mihailovic were to make tactical and limited accommodations with the local enemy when it suited them. Resistance groups elsewhere would do the same. It was an accepted tactic of guerrilla warfare. Tito called his contacts "mere consultations", but those of Mihailovic "treacherous collaboration". Collaboration, by any definition, has a political connotation. It implies a permanent, systematic alliance between collaborator and occupier through the pursuit of common goals, not just military objectives, and usually over a wider area than the immediate locality.

Most of the temporary arrangements between Mihailovic's forces and the Italians were anti-Partisan rather than pro-Axis or anti-Allies. They were simply defensive measures against Partisan marauding. They stemmed from Italian troops intervening to protect Serbs from the murderous Croat Ustashi. Later, when SOE, most often for logistical reasons, could not supply Mihailovic, they gave him money with which to buy ammunition and weapons from the Italians, as did the Yugoslav government-in-exile in London. They were open about it. His accommodations with the Italians were sanctioned to that end!

Contact between Mihailovic's forces and the Germans had no such precedents. This was why much was made of the revelation that Mihailovic and three of his lieutenants had met a German delegation on 11 November 1941 in the town of Divci, near his Ravna Gora stronghold. Desperate for weapons and ammunition to ward off Partisan attacks, Mihailovic had evidently hoped to convince the Germans of his anti-communist credentials and so obtain arms unconditionally. He was rebuffed. The Germans kept a transcript of the encounter, in which Mihailovic said:

> I am neither a communist nor do I work for you. But I have attempted to alleviate and hinder your terror... [The communists] wish to see the greatest number of Serbs killed in order to ensure their own later success. No agreement can be made with them...

I intend to continue the fight against the communists which began on 31 October... We need ammunition. This need brought me here... I ask you in the interest of the Serbian people, as well as in your own interest, to supply me, if possible, with ammunition this very night... Otherwise, if I am not given any ammunition, the communists will again obtain sway over Serbia.

He was told the German delegation was empowered only to accept his unconditional surrender, to which he replied: "I do not see any sense in your invitation to come to the meeting if this is all you had to say. You could have done it through the middlemen."[27]

Whether Mihailovic ever convinced himself communist control was a worse evil than German occupation, as Tito apologists have maintained, is a moot point. Certainly there must have been moments when the differences seemed minimal. But he was too much of a Serbian patriot to tolerate a permanent German occupation. The western Allies were to underestimate the fears of the land-owning Serbian peasantry for the Bolshevisation of their country. Some of them considered occupation by the Germans the lesser of two evils. Alexander Glen, who met Mihailovic before the war, but during the war was involved more with the Partisans, insisted to me:

I'm absolutely satisfied Mihailovic was never a traitor. To be a traitor you have to be a traitor to your own loyalties and I don't think he was. He remained loyal to what he believed the interests of his country demanded, and his king.

Tito, a Croat, was less squeamish about reprisals, especially to Serbs, an attitude that never endeared him to the Serbs of Serbia. It was a reason why he was not able to gain a foothold there until the Red Army created one for him in October 1944. He felt the communists, as a revolutionary party, had to be seen to be active. His movement thrived on the anarchy that was Ustasha Croatia in 1941 and 1942. Also he was being pressed by Moscow to cause havoc in the German rear, to deter the Germans from releasing their occupation forces to fight the Soviets. That his actions might lead to the loss of innocent life clearly never troubled him. The reprisals produced ready recruits. Many were anxious to wreak vengeance on the Germans for the murder of loved ones, or because they had been rendered homeless by the razing of their villages by the Ustashi.

These recruits were the toughest and most fanatical of fighters. They had little to lose. Their singleminded lust for revenge made them readily accept the role of dedicated communists – the merciless discipline and the absolute devotion to narrow doctrine. With no families or homes to go back to, they remained loyal to Tito wherever he moved within Yugoslavia. Mihailovic's forces were always keen to return to their farms to help with the harvest and to protect their wives and children. They were reluctant to stray far from their Serbian base. They were loath to do anything that might put their families and properties at risk from the occupying forces.

Djilas was to admit that the Partisans specifically chose, as locations for their attacks on the Axis forces, those villages or towns where the local populace was antagonistic towards them or unduly indifferent to their aims. The intention was to draw down enemy reprisals and thereby radicalise them. Mostly it worked. Anger and a desire to avenge the Axis drove many survivors to join the Partisans. It was important politically for the Yugoslav communists to have a standing army. They were in effect putting down a marker for future power in Yugoslavia.

Tito was later to welcome into the Partisan ranks former Ustashi, no questions asked. With their guilty past they were that much easier to control, and keener to prove their fervour. When it became obvious that the Germans were not going to win the war, the Croatian Army and the Ustasha militias became important recruiting pools for him. It would have been unthinkable for Mihailovic to have recruited Croats and Ustashi. Tito had begun with a communist core in the summer of 1941, but thereafter attracted non-communist anti-German Serbs, Croats and Slovenes. Whereas in 1941 and 1942 most Partisans were Serbs, by October 1943 Croats were in the majority.

As a revolutionary, there were clear advantages for Tito in the civil chaos resulting from the wrecking or weakening of existing administrative structures. Destroying municipal offices, with their tax and landholding records and other archives, made it all the more difficult for the old regime to be restored. Tito's aim from the start was to turn the war of liberation against the occupying forces into a civil war against the Yugoslav ruling class. The Partisans were not remiss, when the opportunity arose, in settling old scores with those associated with the previous Serb-dominated regime. Policemen, village chiefs and other local functionaries would have wanted to resist the establishment of communism.

Initially the Partisans were under strict instructions from Moscow to avoid clashing with Mihailovic's forces. The Soviets did not want to antagonise the British, on whom they were then dependent for aid. But soon Mihailovic and Tito were fighting each other far more than they were fighting the occupiers. For one thing, such combat did not incur reprisals from the Germans. The clashes were principally about territory. Mihailovic was determined to keep the Partisans out of Serbia. The Partisans were equally determined to get a foothold there. The most important and most populous province of Yugoslavia, it held the key to post-war control of the country.

As Milovan Djilas bluntly put it in his *Wartime* memoirs, "Serbia, along with Montenegro, was of decisive importance: [Mihailovic's forces] had to be beaten on their own breeding grounds." The Germans and Italians realised this too and used rumour and disinformation to fan the flames of the fratricidal struggle. While the Partisans and Mihailovic's men were fighting each other, the task of the occupiers was eased. The German propagandists depicted the Partisans as sinister agents of Red Terror and Mihailovic's forces as deluded handmaidens of the perfidious British. They also exploited the antagonism between SIS and SOE. The latter considered Yugoslavia their domain, and Mihailovic their man. This SIS resented.

Ljubo Sirc recalled how, in Slovenia, the communists undermined their political opponents by spreading false rumours

> supported by slogans written on walls and in underground newspapers. Very often the "activists" doing this sort of job were caught and sent to prison, but nobody seemed to care. They were soon replaced by others equally willing to be sacrificed. The leadership appeared to welcome the arrests which they saw as cementing the solidarity of the population and strengthening their resistance. The accepted slogan was: "There must be victims!"

He mentions how the communists

> called for action at any cost and for people to join the Partisans, regardless of whether they had arms and were able-bodied. Anybody who advised taking only calculated risks was branded a traitor. Warfare for the Communists was an extension of political propaganda and they wanted victims so as to gain support from the dead men's relatives... "Liquidations", that is the murder of people whom the Communist Party disliked (hardly ever the invaders) had become common practice at the end of 1941.

He claims a thousand people, out of a population of just 300,000, were killed in this way in Italian-occupied Slovenia alone during the first year of the war: "The Communists murdered them because they considered them opposed to the aims of the Communist Party."[28]

*

The Yugoslav civil war had begun on day one of the German occupation, though everyone denied it. Either side blamed the other for its start. The Axis forces quickly became the secondary enemy. Few realised then what a terrible fratricidal bloodletting there was to be. Unequalled anywhere else in occupied Europe, it was characterised by exceptional savagery. Estimates of the numbers killed run into hundreds of thousands. Certainly more Yugoslavs were killed by each other than by Germans. And they killed more of each other than they did Axis occupiers. It is believed a million Yugoslavs, about half of them Serbs, died as a result of the war. Of these less than 100,000 were killed by the occupiers. Djilas noted: "In a divided nation the traitor is simply the person who betrays one's own side. There is immeasurably more bad blood in a fratricidal war than in any war between countries." Americans, with memories of their own "brother against brother" Civil War, would say Amen to that.

Djilas detailed how seldom prisoners were taken from the Mihailovic forces, except to be tortured for information. After torture, execution inevitably followed. He witnessed many such executions. In time they became commonplace. Of one he says:

> They were typical mountain people – rawboned, with their heads swathed in scarves, so that one could only see moustaches covered with frost, and little eyes which stared in disbelief into the rifle barrels. I felt sorry for them as I turned in my saddle and saw them fall. But I felt no pangs, rather the terrible compulsion which had mindlessly and irrevocably joined our destinies.

He continued:

> Even more horrible and inconceivable was the killing of kinsmen and the hurling of their bodies into ravines – less for convenience than to avoid the funeral processions and the inconsolable and fearless mourners. In Herzegovina it was still more horrible and ugly: Communist sons confirmed their devotion by killing their own fathers, and there was dancing and singing around the bodies.

Of other executions he witnessed, Djilas comments: "As usual, no effort was made to bury them properly: their legs and arms stuck out of the mound. Civil war has little regard for graves, funerals, requiems." It was a Party rule that, if any member surrendered to the enemy, whether German, Italian or Mihailovic supporter, he should be executed if found later, regardless of the circumstances. He admits that the Partisans resorted to reprisals themselves. Apparently Tito told them: "Well, all right, we can burn a house or a village here and there." They did not hesitate to loot villages known to be pro-Mihailovic. Djilas acknowledges, too, the destruction of Serbian churches and monasteries, some containing rare books. Serbian priests did not readily yield to the communist demands. The Partisans were to kill 153 Serbian Orthodox clergymen and 355 Roman Catholic priests.

Justice was rough and ready on both sides, but the struggle was not simply between Tito and Mihailovic. The Partisans murdered more than 2,000 anti-communists in Slovenia in the first eighteen months of the war. The White Russian community there was a particular target. Djilas says 7,000 of them were killed in just four days during September 1943.

In hindsight, it was a mistake on Mihailovic's part to lie low and not show his face around Serbia and the rest of Yugoslavia. It meant he never had much sway outside Serbia, or indeed outside Ravna Gora. He was not averse to exaggerating the extent of his authority to impress the British and his own government in London. In truth his control over his subordinate commanders was remote and only spasmodic. They acknowledged his authority only because of his links to the Yugoslav government-in-exile and to the Allies, which legitimised them in the eyes of their followers. Tito's communists had a single organisation and were ruthlessly disciplined. Mihailovic was never able to curb the excesses of, for instance, the Chetniks in Montenegro, who operated independently. He tolerated the situation because they were as fervently anti-communist as he was, and protected his flank from the Partisans. Their numbers helped to make his influence appear nationwide. Their excesses, however, antagonised non-Serbs and were to prove his undoing. As were their open accommodations with the Italians, which he could not afford to denounce or admit.

They called themselves Chetniks after the nineteenth-century term for the patriotic Serb irregulars who fought for their national identity against the Turkish occupiers and were a sort of unofficial home guard or militia. Sometimes spelt *Cetniks*, the word meant members of a *ceta* or company of soldiers. Usually they let their hair grow long and had flowing beards. It was the custom among male communicants of the Serbian Orthodox Church to refrain from shaving and cutting their hair for forty days following the death of a loved one. In this case the loved one was their native land. The more extreme among them vowed not to shave or cut their hair until the last occupier had been driven out. They armed themselves with curved daggers and ornate pistols, and wore tall sheepskin caps bearing the royal coat of arms.

In those areas where the Serbs were in a majority, the name Chetnik was esteemed, but it had also been espoused by fanatically nationalistic Serb veterans from the Great War. The Yugoslav authorities occasionally used them as police auxiliaries in regions where the Serbs were in a minority, such as Croatia, Bosnia and Slovenia. These auxiliaries earned a reputation for extreme brutality, as the Black-and-Tans did in pre-independent Ireland last century. Thus the name Chetnik had a gruesome connotation in many areas where the Serbs were not in a majority. A further complication is that those Serbs who had willingly thrown in their hand with the puppet government running Serbia for the Germans, becoming gendarmes and policemen, also called themselves Chetniks. The Germans dubbed them "legal Chetniks".

Mihailovic had originally called his forces The Ravna Gora Movement but the name was changed on the instructions of the Yugoslav government-in-exile to The Royal Yugoslav Army in the Field. Later they became known as The Yugoslav Army in the Homeland or simply The Yugoslav Home Army. Some sympathetic to Mihailovic used the term Loyalists; Churchill referred to them initially as patriots. Those less well-disposed towards him, particularly Tito's communists and their Soviet masters, and in time Tito's British supporters, always dubbed them Chetniks, meaning the term to be pejorative, almost a form of abuse. The name stuck, to his undoubted disadvantage. By the end of the war it was universal in the Western press and even in Allied documents, as it usually is to this day. Tito's men were hardly ever called communists, but instead anti-fascists or, more usually, Partisans, a sympathetic, praiseworthy description. Similarly the Partisan Army described itself as the National Liberation Movement, in contrast to Mihailovic's Royal Yugoslav Army with its reactionary undertones. Any who opposed Tito's communists were dismissed as fascists or enemies of the people. Labels are important in a propaganda war, most certainly in a civil war. In choice of nomenclature the communists were always streets ahead of their political opponents. Witness how after 1945 they commandeered the term "peace" to describe their anti-capitalist, pro-Soviet stance!

While Tito was a politician turned soldier, Mihailovic was a soldier who had to become a politician. He never quite made the transition. His misfortune was that he was, in many ways, a simple regular officer with no ambition to assume a political role. He was loyal to his king and to his government, a fierce traditionalist rather than an adventurous radical. His movement was predominantly military while Tito's was always political. Somewhat limited in outlook and lacking in charisma, Mihailovic was simply not fitted to become a power politician. He had scant political guile or acumen. Nor had he a clear political agenda, other than to restore the *status quo ante.* Not even every Serb favoured this, particularly as the regime's political leaders had run away, leaving the people to the cruel mercies of the occupiers. Certainly very few, if any, Croats, Slovenes, Macedonians or Bosnians wanted to restore the old Serb-dominated set-up. Mihailovic's association with the former government became more and more of a handicap for him. He was not helped in his relations with the British authorities by the machinations of the politicians-in-exile in London. Above all, he lacked the ruthless singlemindedness and relentless determination of his rival, Tito.

At a time when occupied Europe was beginning to turn politically to the left, after Hitler's devastating defeat of the old order, and its peoples were seeking a radical alternative to that which had failed them in their hour of need, Mihailovic had no revolutionary purpose. He did not realise a revolution was underway. He wanted simply to rid his country of the occupiers. Nor had he much flair for organisation or decision-making. Something of a bumbling bureaucrat, he had scant control over his scattered followers, who looked to their immediate commanders for leadership. Slight in stature and wearing steel-rimmed glasses, introverted with a somewhat retiring nature, he was hopeless at public relations. He was outmatched in every way by the aggressive propaganda of the communists. They portrayed him to non-Serbs as the bearer of Serbian vengeance and to Serbs as an agent of British imperialism seeking to exploit them. To the Allies he was depicted as a traitorous collaborator with the occupiers. That all anti-communists and opponents of the Partisans were characterised as collaborators went unchallenged! He had no propaganda machine himself, no ready means of countering the negative and destructive image of him put about by Tito's and Moscow's agitprop merchants. The London Yugoslavs were slow to contest the anti-Mihailovic propaganda. When they did, they were unconvincing. Nor was he helped by the BBC's initial fulsome praise of him and his forces. It raised expectations that could not reasonably be met.

Good news was at a premium for the Allies that summer and autumn of 1941. This is why Mihailovic was so idolised in Allied newspapers as the man who first raised the flag of resistance against

Hitler in occupied Europe. *Time* magazine in the USA put his portrait on its cover. The Yugoslav government-in-exile promoted him to General. Little was immediately expected of him. In a world that had begun to believe Hitler invincible, it was enough in simple propaganda terms that he existed. Claims he had 100,000 men under arms were not challenged.

Churchill enthused. Guerrilla warfare appealed to his romantic nature. On 14 October he charged "the Chiefs of Staff to consider as a matter of urgency what could be done to help on the revolt".[29] They replied the next day: "From our point of view revolt is premature, but patriots have thrown their caps over the fence and must be supported by all possible means."[30] Churchill on 4 November was insisting, "everything possible must be done to keep the rebellion going and to send in the arms, equipment and supplies which were vital to the rebels."[31] The Foreign Secretary, Anthony Eden, complained on 13 November at the delay in sending such help but was more pragmatic in his enthusiasm. Mihailovic's resistance, he had told the defence chiefs on 31 October, allowed us "to assure the Soviet Government that we are doing everything possible to create a second front in the Balkans which they desire".[32] This over-praising of Mihailovic was to lead to his undoing. When he failed to live up to his early promise the disappointment was bitter.

While he remained in Serbia, Mihailovic had the backing of the local peasantry and the bourgeoisie. These groups were strongly opposed to communism and determined to keep Tito out of Serbia. But Mihailovic's holeing up in Ravna Gora made it easy for Tito's communists to get a grip on the rest of the country. Forever moving around, in the face of pressure from the German and Italian occupiers, they became better known to people. Wherever they went they were able to fan the flames of revolt. They benefited, too, from the anti-Serbian feeling of non-Serbs in Bosnia-Herzegovina and Croatia. The occupiers were thinner on the ground there. Provided they kept away from the Danube valley and the main Zagreb-Belgrade-Salonika railway, the Partisans were likely to be left undisturbed by the Germans.

CHAPTER THREE

Early Resistance

"Partisans, prepare your machine-guns
to greet the king and Englishmen"

HAVING HITHERTO RUN his resistance from a well-appointed villa in a fashionable suburb of Belgrade, Tito left the Yugoslav capital on 16 September 1941. By scheduled train and taxi he made his way to Uzice, a bustling market town of some 12,000 souls in the western Morava valley. Here he set up his headquarters, a hundred or so miles south of Belgrade, and a mere thirty miles from where Mihailovic had already established himself. An area from which the Germans had recently withdrawn, it was populated by small peasant landholders who were far from enthusiastic at having communists in their midst, particularly when some of them were murdered for alleged antagonism to the Partisan cause. In retaliation, hundreds of Tito's supporters were killed later that autumn when a bank vault converted into a factory making rifles and small arms was blown up. The communists were always less at ease with country folk than with those living in the bigger towns and cities.

Styled the Uzice Republic, it was intended to signal the start of the communist revolution within Yugoslavia. Milovan Djilas describes in *Wartime* how, when he joined them from Montenegro in mid-November,

> the men were not in strict uniform but well dressed, nearly all wearing garrison caps – the Serbian military caps worn by the Royal Yugoslav Army. The only exception was Tito. He had a Soviet *pilotka* made for himself, a pilot's cap which was later dubbed a *titovka*, and became the regulation cap in the army of the new Yugoslavia... Everybody had red stars of thick fabric sewn on his cap, while Tito wore an enamelled Soviet star with a hammer and sickle which came from who knows where and had been presented to him as a gift.

The top echelons ate apart, waiting deferentially until Tito joined them before commencing. Tito usually had better food than the rest, because, Djilas claims, his followers insisted he should. Wherever possible he had a separate cook and even a cow to provide him with fresh milk. Djilas says "hierarchical precedence grew with the revolution, and apparently became as important and necessary to it as fervour and egalitarianism". He remarked that, after his experiences in Montenegro, he "found this hierarchical and official decorum shocking".

Djilas' memoirs illustrate how bureaucratic the Partisans soon became. The pages are littered with mentions of committee meetings. Nearly everything, it seems, required decision by a committee. Djilas referred to the double standards he had noted earlier: "the leading men in the Central Committee – Tito, Zujovic, and Rankovic – were followed about by pretty young secretaries who were obviously more intimate with them than their duties required". He felt

> there was something ugly about all of this, though perhaps not because these comrades had new mates: no one is sentenced to live out his whole life with the same wife or husband. Rather it was because among the troops the strictest Puritanism was practiced in every respect.

Sexual liaisons among ordinary partisans were forbidden. Partisan women who became pregnant were, it was said, instantly shot. Partisan men caught *in flagrante delicto* were similarly eliminated.

Tito had no qualms about living off the countryside. He relied on the locals for food and shelter. Sometimes they were paid in promissory notes meant to be honoured after the Germans had been defeated. Very few were ever redeemed. Usually supplies were simply filched. He did not yet feel the need to curry local favour. Survival was his paramount concern. Arms and weapons were pinched from the occupiers or the Ustashi. He had hoped for help from Moscow, but because of the Soviets' military problems, that seemed improbable in the foreseeable future. He was suspicious of the Western Allies, assuming strings would be attached to any support from them. As he gained confidence, he became less wary of the British. He realised they could easily be manipulated for his own ends.

Tito met Mihailovic on 19 September. It was the first of a series of encounters that autumn which many hoped would lead to some form of co-operation. Nothing came of them, as their aims were diametrically opposed. Mihailovic was convinced Tito was a Russian and reported so to London. Suspicious of the Soviets, a

Serb nationalist at heart and pro-British, Mihailovic remained loyal to the Yugoslav government-in-exile in London. Tito, a Croat, hated that government and was anti-British as well as fervently pro-Soviet.

At least one joint action did take place: the capture of the two-hundred-strong German garrison at Gornji Milanovac on 28 and 29 September. That Mihailovic kept the prisoners, as an escaped British officer, Captain Christie Lawrence, was to testify, suggests his forces played the major role. There were four other British officers also with Mihailovic then. All, like Lawrence, had jumped from trains carrying them through Serbia as prisoners-of-war from Crete, where they had been captured earlier that summer.

But it was not long before the Partisans and Mihailovic's forces were fighting each other. Each blamed the other for firing the first shot in anger. Tito is on record as claiming the killing of "several hundred" Mihailovic supporters near Uzice on 2 November, including the local commander.[1] Anthony Eden cabled his Ambassador in Moscow on 16 November:

> The position is now complicated by the fact that a form of civil war appears to have broken out between patriots in Serbia under Colonel Mihailovic and guerrilla bands in Montenegro with varying degrees of Communist colour.

The Ambassador was to ask the Soviets "to urge the Communist element in Yugoslavia to put themselves unreservedly at the disposal of Colonel Mihailovic as the national leader".[2]

Djilas concedes Mihailovic at this time had far more men under his command than Tito had. The Germans had no firm knowledge of the Partisans' strength and assumed Mihailovic ran all resistance within the country. They did not distinguish then between the two forces. To the Germans anyone opposing them was a bandit and resistance was usually described as "bandit activity". This confused the Enigma decoders who did not always know to which camp to ascribe the resistance mentioned in German signals. Enigma was the German machine-cipher that the British cryptanalysts at Bletchley Park had broken in 1940. The BBC at that time reported only Mihailovic's activities, as did the Comintern's Radio Free Yugoslavia when it began broadcasting in Serbo-Croat early in November 1941. Based in Russia, though purporting to come from inside Yugoslavia, it lauded the Yugoslav people's "continuing fight against the fascist invaders under Mihailovic's brave leadership".

Radio sets were few in Yugoslavia at this time outside the main towns, though most villages had at least one. Their numbers were to increase as the war went on. Radio Free Yugoslavia of course had Soviet interests at heart, praising Mihailovic only when they needed to curry favour with the Allies to get supplies. Once Moscow established regular contact with Tito it was used from mid-1942 onwards to promote the Partisan movement and to denigrate Mihailovic. Djilas admits one of his main tasks then was to feed Radio Free Yugoslavia with propaganda for their cause. The BBC's news reports in Serbo-Croat, so-called Radio London, were initially considered more reliable. That was to change, especially in Serbia. Mihailovic listened to London daily whereas the Partisans preferred Radio Moscow. Later they too favoured the BBC when it began belittling Mihailovic and glorifying Tito.

With the Germans nearing Moscow, Stalin was continually urging Churchill that autumn of 1941 to open a second front – anywhere – to threaten Hitler's rear and relieve the pressure on the Red Army. His repeated demands irked Churchill and his advisers. Some felt Stalin needed reminding it was his own policies that had put him in this predicament, as well as crippling Britain. Following the Molotov-Ribbentrop Pact of August 1939, the Soviets had diligently aided Hitler's military machine and sought to impede the Allied war effort, so that Britain was in no position to comply with Stalin's request.

Many around Churchill saw the resistance in Yugoslavia as an alternative to this second front. They suggested encouraging Mihailovic, and whoever else was defying the Germans there, to greater efforts. At the very least, it was thought, some supplies should be sent to them. There were others who argued such resistance was premature, that it was bound to fail and end in needless casualties and suffering. They reasoned that supplies were already overstretched and could not be spared. The compromise reached was that everything possible should be done to aid the resistance, provided it did not interfere with British operations in the Middle East.

The Yugoslav government-in-exile had been lobbying Churchill to send a mission to Mihailovic. He was also being prompted to do so by his cabinet colleague Leo Amery, whose son Julian had been urging SOE to mount a mission. SOE now agreed. They were also keen to know whether other groups were resisting within Yugoslavia and elsewhere in the Balkans. During the night of 20 September 1941 Captain Bill Hudson was put ashore by submarine on the Montenegrin coast near Petrovac, occupied then by Italians. Thirty years old, he had worked in western Serbia before the war as a mining engineer and was fluent in Serbo-Croat. He had already participated in other covert SOE and SIS operations. With him were two Yugoslav officers and a wireless operator, all Montenegrins.

En route to Ravna Gora, Hudson and his group came in contact with Montenegrin nationalists who were still resisting the Italians. They also met some Partisans, including Milovan Djilas, who were at first suspicious of their motives. Eventually they were taken to see Tito at Uzice on 23 October. Tito was not interested in British supplies as he was expecting help from the Soviets. Hudson was embarrassed when his wireless operator insisted on staying at Tito's headquarters with the wireless transmitter which Tito was to use in contacting Moscow! The wireless operator remained with Tito until he was killed in May 1944 in a surprise German attack.

Hudson and the other Montenegrins went on to Ravna Gora. Mihailovic wanted aid as quickly as possible and the first airdrop occurred on 9 November. It did not amount to much, but was a morale boost, not least as regards his standing with Tito's Partisans. With typical Serb exaggeration, the story soon spread that more than a hundred air-loads had been landed! Mihailovic had been fore-warned of Hudson's arrival but was narked he had visited Tito first. He was annoyed, too, that the wireless operator had stayed with Tito. However, the two Montenegrin officers were to remain with Mihailovic to the bitter end. Mihailovic was never totally convinced of Hudson's loyalty and this distrust was to colour their relationship. Hudson's youth and low rank did not help.

Hudson soon became aware of the bitterness and distrust between Mihailovic and Tito. He offered to mediate to prevent it deteriorating into full-scale civil war, having already witnessed fighting between them. In a radio message to SOE Cairo on 13 November, using Mihailovic's transmitter, he urged such mediation but received no encouragement. However, the British Foreign Office, having already insisted to the Yugoslav government-in-exile that Mihailovic stop fighting other Yugoslavs, pressed Moscow to use its influence on Tito for him to do so too. It appeared to have some effect as Tito agreed an armistice on 21 November. Tito's official biographer, Vladimir Dedijer, quotes him as saying at the time: "We must see to it that we do not cause the Soviet Union any foreign policy diffi-culties."[3] Stalin was anxious not to annoy the British and Americans unduly as he was dependent on them for aid. On 28 November

Churchill urged his military chiefs to help the guerrilla fighters in Yugoslavia: "Everything in human power should be done."[4] But no substantial aid was forthcoming. The war was not going well for the British in North Africa.

In late November the Germans, reinforced with troops spared from France, drove Tito and his Partisans out of Uzice in some confusion. Hudson was visiting them, hoping to recover his wireless transmitter. He escaped back to Mihailovic, managing to bury the bulky transmitter en route. Miraculously, it was recovered and returned to him the following May. Djilas says the Partisans were almost routed at this time. Less than 2,000 of them escaped. The Germans claimed at least 1,400 were killed and about 400 taken prisoner. The real losses were thought to be much higher. Only 11 Germans were killed and 35 wounded. Determined to show the local Serb peasants the folly of aiding resistance, the Germans burnt houses, destroyed cattle and uprooted crops.

Such was the shambles, with most of their weapons, ammunition, vehicles and equipment left behind in the panic, that Tito offered to resign as leader of the Party. Djilas maintains the chaos of the flight and the extent of the reversal could be laid at Tito's door. He had displayed a "lack of resourcefulness and vision."[5] Djilas insists Tito had little talent as a military leader, being "oftentimes rash and nervous" with "an overwhelming concern for his personal safety". After Uzice it was noticeable Tito relied much more on his other military commanders.

The Germans went on to attack Mihailovic, causing him heavy casualties and compelling his forces to disperse. Frustrated at not capturing him, they wrecked neighbouring villages, killing or taking hostage many of the local chiefs thought to have housed Mihailovic's men. That the Germans feared Mihailovic's forces then is indicated by the report on 3 December to Berlin of Felix Benzler, the German Foreign Office's representative with the German army in Yugoslavia. He maintained Mihailovic was a threat while he remained "a rallying point for all insurgents with nationalist feelings".[6] German soldiers were promised six weeks leave if they took Mihailovic dead or alive. Civilians were offered 200,000 dinars (about £800 at 1941 prices) for his capture. As yet there was no price on Tito's head. Many of Mihailovic's companions were caught and shot. His wife was arrested and subsequently died in prison. Hudson was forced to flee. Nothing was heard of him for more than five months. SOE Cairo presumed he had been killed or captured and sought to replace him. Constantly hunted by the Germans, he survived the bitter winter with the help of friendly peasants.

Following up their success at Uzice, the Germans forced Tito's Partisans out of Serbia entirely. Pushed into remoter and more mountainous Montenegro, then under Italian control, they were not to return until the final months of the war. The Italians were less thorough in their occupation. Provided they were not attacked, they were prepared to turn a blind eye to roving bands of rebels.

Among the rebels operating in Montenegro were groups of Serbs, independent of Mihailovic, calling themselves Chetniks. Many had local agreements with the Italian occupiers to leave each other alone. They resented the Partisans invading their patch. Consequently there was more fighting between Partisans and Chetniks than between either of them and the Italians – which the Italians encouraged. Told of this, the British again pressed Moscow to use its influence on Tito to stop the disputes, though this time without effect. They had already insisted to the Yugoslav government-in-exile that Mihailovic order the Montenegrin Chetniks to desist. He maintained they were not under his control.

Tito's communists and their Moscow allies quickly magnified these truces with the Italians into full-blooded treacherous collaboration. That the Partisans were ready themselves to conclude pacts with the occupying forces when it suited them was never given wide publicity. The fact was that both sides turned to the occupying forces whenever they needed help. If it suited those forces, as it often did, they got that help.

Local German and Italian commanders, in their operational reports, did not always distinguish which group they were dealing with; they tended to dub all rebels Chetniks. By now the Bletchley code-breakers were reading those reports. Thus Mihailovic, more than Tito, came to be identified with such "collaboration". The German army, on strict instructions from Hitler, was seldom happy about colluding with Serbs. On 11 November 1941 the German command in Belgrade instructed officers on no account to carry out "negotiations with the Chetniks ... especially the Mihailovic people". They were to insist "that they turn over their arms and enter German custody".

That winter, comforted by news from Moscow that the German advance had been halted, Tito in a propaganda gambit named his surviving band of Partisans the First Proletarian People's Liberation

Brigade. Numbering about twelve hundred, they were proletarian only in name. At this stage most of the Partisans were either party activists or from the urban middle classes. The date chosen was Stalin's birthday, 21 December! Tito planned other such brigades. Four more were named during the following year. So-called "shock troops", thoroughly indoctrinated in the Party line, they were intended to deliver the communist revolution in Yugoslavia. Tito insisted on such indoctrination. He was determined to instil in these units the strictest possible discipline by constant political instruction. Discipline was always harsh within the Partisans. Those less than enthusiastic for the cause were dealt with summarily. As in the Red Army, each unit had its political commissar responsible for ideological correctness. In Djilas's phrase, "ideology commanded the rifle".[7]

Ironically, Stalin was not thrilled with the gesture. Nor did he approve of the Partisan uniform including a cap with a five-pointed red star, as worn by the Red Guards during Russia's own civil war. He complained that the Partisans seemed to be "acquiring a Communist character". Tito was reminded that "the immediate task is to unite all anti-Hitler elements and defeat the invader". Stalin had criticised the naming of a "Red Republic" at Uzice. Tito never repeated the mistake. Thereafter he described his movement as "anti-fascist" or "national liberation". Stalin was clearly reluctant to annoy the British and Americans in any way at this stage. He dismissed, too, Tito's allegations of Mihailovic's collaboration with the Germans, in particular that Mihailovic was doing it with the full knowledge of the British and the London Yugoslavs: "It is difficult to agree that London and the Yugoslav Government are siding with the [occupiers]. There must be some misunderstanding."[8]

Stalin was probably also not best pleased his name was being linked with Tito's in the new marching songs and poems the partisans favoured. "With Tito and Stalin, two heroic sons, not even Hell will confound us" ran one. Already a personality cult of Tito was being created: lyrics extolled him in lines like "Comrade Tito, we swear to you we shall not deviate from your path" and "Comrade Tito, little white violet, all our youth cries hail to thee". Other songs berated the British and Mihailovic as "class enemies". When an Allied landing was thought imminent on the Dalmatian coast – it would be more to Mihailovic's advantage than to Tito's – jingles urged, "Partisans, prepare your machine-guns to greet the king and Englishmen"!

Milovan Djilas confirms in his *Wartime* memoirs that Stalin was concerned not to alarm the British and Americans. The Partisans were equally anxious not to "complicate the Soviet government's relations with Britain. [This was] important for us, in view of our ideological dependence on Moscow." Stalin was forever warning Tito to be careful the West did not catch on to any hint of Soviet orchestration of Partisan activities. Contacts between the Partisans and the Soviets had been close and continuous from the start of hostilities, despite Moscow's denials. At first they even claimed not to know who Tito was. When asked to press Tito not to fight Mihailovic, they hid behind the excuse that the Partisan-Chetnik dispute was an internal Yugoslav affair in which they did not wish to become involved.

With the better news from Moscow, Tito no longer felt the need to engage in sabotage, and he was not pressed to do so by the Soviets. He largely ceased offensive action against the Axis forces occupying the country, except when seeking food and ammunition. He concentrated on eliminating his political opponents. The civil war in Yugoslavia was his paramount concern; defeating the Axis was the responsibility of the Allies. Determined to conserve his military strength, he withdrew when attacked. This was classic guerrilla warfare. The winning of territory does not count. Preserving one's force does.

By Christmas Day 1941 the Partisans had been driven out of Montenegro. Forced across the mountains into Bosnia, they suffered heavy casualties from frostbite and typhus. Food was scarce. At times they were reduced to eating their horses. Nor were they welcomed by the villagers along the way. Most wanted to be left to cultivate their land. They were already living in terror of the occupiers. To them the Partisans were troublemakers, bringing problems rather than easing them. Vladimir Dedijer in his *War Diaries* mentions them fleeing from a pincer movement on 18 January 1942 and releasing "Germans after negotiations". This suggests an exchange of prisoners or some form of truce. A week later barely a thousand of them reached Foca in the remote south-eastern corner of Bosnia. Here they managed to stay a few months. Dedijer says that by 7 April 1942 nearly 13,000 party and youth members had been killed. This did not stop Tito boasting to Moscow he had 200,000 fighters at his command. There was no way such a number could have been fed, housed and hidden amid such barren mountains, as the Soviets must have realised. The peasants themselves could barely eke out a living. He claimed Mihailovic's forces, with the help of the British, were harrying him more than were the Germans. Moscow could only offer sympathy, not material assistance.

Tito was at this time neurotically suspicious of the British, almost to the point of paranoia, as were most of his colleagues. Djilas maintains they

> had inherited an ideological intolerance of "English imperialism", and were particularly mistrustful of the [British] Intelligence Service ... [which] had been often mentioned in the so-called Moscow trials: we believed – or forced ourselves to believe – that many leaders of the Russian Revolution had been led astray by the clever English.[9]

Stephen Clissold, in his 1949 biography of Tito, quotes a long letter from him to the Central Committee of the Communist Party in Croatia dated 8 April 1942. It includes the following:

> We have now certain proof that the British, through their agents in Yugoslavia, are working not to remove, but rather to intensify, the differences between ourselves and other groups such as the Chetniks. England is supporting different Chetnik bands just as the Germans are doing and egging them on to attack us. We have proof that British policy aims at sabotaging and compromising the struggle for national liberation so that when the situation is favourable and Italy leaves Hitler and comes within their grasp, the British will land troops in Dalmatia and elsewhere and appear as "liberators" to save the country from chaos. To this end about ten so-called "military missions" have already arrived and are doing their dirty work in different parts of Yugoslavia ... You must be on your guard against this happening in Croatia. If any missions arrive, see that you are not taken in by them. Find a way of denying them direct access to the people and keep them well under your own control.

The Germans issued another demand in April for Mihailovic and his top commanders to surrender. They followed this up by incarcerating some of their relatives in the newly established concentration camps in Serbia. An attempt was made to kill Mihailovic by delivering an explosive device disguised as a British supply parcel. He was forced to decamp to Italian-occupied Montenegro in early June, where Hudson joined him.

In May 1942 the Germans, Italians and Ustashi returned in force to Foca and drove the Partisans out. Numbering about three thousand, they marched northwards some one hundred and fifty miles, keeping to the heavily forested mountainous watershed. About forty miles inland from the Dalmatian coast, this was the boundary between the German and Italian occupation areas in Yugoslavia. Frequently bombed, hiding by day in caves and forests, they suffered appalling casualties. Dedijer relates in his *War Diaries* how they lost more than four hundred in a single skirmish with Ustasha and Italian troops. Much of their food, weapons, ammunition and medical supplies were obtained from the Ustashi and Italians. Sometimes they had to attack them in their heavily guarded strongholds. Dedijer mentions several prisoner exchanges and truces were occasionally agreed with local enemy garrisons.

Eventually, in November 1942, they reached Bihac, a railway town of fifteen thousand inhabitants in northwest Bosnia, seventy miles south of Zagreb. Here they overcame the Ustashi garrison and were able to stay for a while. The attention of the Germans and Italians had been diverted elsewhere. This trek of 115 days became compared in Partisan mythology to the Long March of the Chinese Communists under Mao Tse-tung in 1934!

Tito's more militant lieutenants were constantly reminding him that they should be in Serbia, rather than in Croatia or Bosnia. To control Yugoslavia they needed to control Serbia. Djilas mentions in *Wartime* how they kept coming back in their discussions to "the separation from Serbia, without which it was impossible to win, or even to preserve the movement from disaster". But Serbia was where the Germans were in force. Survival was Tito's main priority. To outlive his political opponents he needed to avoid trouble. Dedijer admits in his *War Diaries* that there were very few Partisans in Serbia at this time, and they were becoming fewer by the month. Tito was helped in his survival by the chaos in Ustasha-run Bosnia and Croatia. Many young Croats and Bosnians had taken to the hills themselves to escape being conscripted to fight against the Russians on the dreaded eastern front. They were ready recruits to Tito's Partisans, whose numbers began to swell.

The Partisans set about politicising the peasants, spreading the gospel of communism. As many of them were intellectuals, schools were set up and villagers, young and old, were encouraged to attend. There had been no schools since the German invasion, so the teaching was welcome. That it included lessons on Marxist-Leninism, as well as reading, writing and arithmetic, seemed a small price to pay. That the pre-war ruling classes were denounced and the old regime ridiculed was perhaps barely noticed. They had never been popular in this part of the former Yugoslavia.

Because of the lack of news about the Partisans, Mihailovic and the British thought they had been wiped out! On 26 November 1942 Tito established the Anti-Fascist Council of National Liberation of Yugoslavia, intended as a rallying-point for "all true Yugoslav patriots". He had wanted to set up an alternative government to the Yugoslav government-in-exile in London but the Soviets dissuaded him. They were reluctant still to offend the British. Stalin had recently agreed to the Yugoslav legation in Moscow being raised in status to an embassy. Tito was told not to give the impression that he intended establishing a Communist state in Yugoslavia after the war. He was to speak of free elections and protecting private property, and to duck the issue of the future of the monarchy. Radio Moscow now began reporting Partisan operations in detail.

CHAPTER FOUR

The London Yugoslavs

"a government on sufferance
– legitimate but irrelevant"

MARK WHEELER

THE YOUNG Yugoslav King Peter and his government had reached London on 21 June 1941. They received a warm welcome, owing more to the popularity of the 27 March anti-Hitler coup in Belgrade than to the ignominious way in which they had fled the country. They basked in the glory surrounding exaggerated reports of Mihailovic's resistance against the Germans. Even so, the honeymoon was short-lived. They quickly became a source of exasperation to their British hosts because of their constant bickering. Vane Ivanovic, a Yugoslav who had dealings with the exiled government at this time, says the British Foreign Office eventually came to regard the London Yugoslavs "with little short of contempt".[1]

The eighteen-year-old king, a godson of George V and a great-great-grandson of Queen Victoria, was dispatched to Cambridge to continue his education. A spell later in the Guards or the Royal Air Force was intended. He turned out, however, to be more of a playboy than a statesman-in-waiting, preferring fast cars and making merry in nightclubs with his aides-de-camp. He was somewhat immature for his age, shy and inhibited. Uninterested in affairs of state, he had had no real training for kingship. Having just escaped his mother's apron strings, he fell straightaway into the clutches of Princess Aspasia of Greece and her daughter Alexandra, whom he eventually married. Machinations over the marriage were to occupy most of his time and efforts, and to a large extent those of his government, during their years in exile.

Although not all his ministers were Serb, his government was inevitably Serb-inclined and Serb-dominated. That domination grew after reports filtered through to London of the Ustasha atrocities against Serbs in Croatia. This made the position of the few Croatian ministers virtually untenable, particularly as they were reluctant to recognise, let alone condemn, those atrocities. Sir George Rendel, the luckless British diplomat delegated to look after the Yugoslav government-in-exile, maintains in his memoirs, *The Sword and the Olive*, that the atrocities

> split the Yugoslavs in London ... The Serbian and Croat Ministers would hardly meet. I begged the Croat Ministers to issue some clear and unequivocal statement condemning and repudiating the atrocities perpetrated by the Ustashi. But, with what seemed typically short-sighted obstinacy, they refused to be either wise or generous, and continued to flog the dead horse of Croat grievances in and out of season.

Surprisingly, the BBC played down the Ustasha butchery in their broadcasts. Much more was made of far smaller massacres in France and Czechoslovakia.

It soon became clear to the British diplomats that Croatia could never be accepted as a credible partner in a post-war united Yugoslavia. The Yugoslavia of old could not simply be resurrected. Croatia and Serbia would need to be separated. Alternatively the two might form part of a larger federal state than the previous Yugoslavia, perhaps embracing Bulgaria and Greece. A Foreign Office memo of 14 November 1941 said:

> In dealing with this internal crisis we can, I think, safely disregard the future of both Yugoslavia and the Serbian dynasty: on present showing, neither are likely to survive the war, in their present form at any rate.[2]

Consequently, despite the pleas of the Yugoslav government-in-exile, the British, and in time the Americans too, refused to guarantee Yugoslavia's territorial integrity after the war. This was to be a continuing bone of contention with the London Yugoslavs. The British did recognise King Peter and his ministers as the legitimate government of Yugoslavia, as did the United States, but they could not get them to agree a blueprint for a future Yugoslavia. As time went on more and more British diplomats became convinced the lead could come only from the contending parties within Yugoslavia itself. This was to Tito's advantage. By the end of 1942 many of them had washed their hands of the Yugoslav government. It had become, in their eyes, to quote Mark Wheeler, "a government on sufferance – legitimate but irrelevant".[3]

The London Yugoslavs were fractious over what the British, with a life-and-death struggle on their hands, considered frivolous details. Whitehall, and Churchill in particular, grew ever more weary of them. Because Mihailovic was closely associated with the Yugoslav government, this clearly influenced Churchill in his eventual decision to favour the apparently less bothersome Tito. In January 1942 Mihailovic was appointed King Peter's Minister of War and later that year Commander-in-Chief of the Yugoslav Army of the Homeland. Sir George Rendel confided to his memoirs:

> The British Government, intensely preoccupied with the major issues of winning the war, rightly resented being worried with petty personal quarrels of this kind, which showed a total lack of understanding of the gravity and immensity of the real issues with which the whole world was faced. The prestige of the Yugoslav Government steadily sank in consequence, and the foundations were laid of that lack of confidence and respect for the exiled Yugoslav politicians which made it possible for us, and for the bulk of the Yugoslav people themselves, some two years later, to abandon them with hardly a qualm, and to acquiesce in Tito's anti-monarchical revolution.

For Britain in 1942 the situation was still desperate, despite her no longer fighting alone. The Japanese attack on Pearl Harbor in December 1941 had at last brought the Americans into the struggle, but the first nine months of 1942 saw the nadir in British fortunes when Hong Kong, Malaya, Singapore and most of Burma fell to the Japanese. The loss in June of Tobruk in North Africa to Rommel threatened Egypt. Most of SOE's files in Cairo were destroyed in panic. To the inhabitants of the Egyptian capital 1 July 1942 became known as "Ash Wednesday" because of the amount of paper burnt that day! On the Russian front the *Wehrmacht* reached the Volga at Stalingrad and threatened the Caucasus. The fear was of a gigantic German pincer movement from Africa and Russia linking up in Iran or Iraq, sources of Britain's oil.

It was not until late autumn, with Rommel's defeat at El Alamein and the successful Anglo-American landings in Morocco and Algeria, that the tide could be said to have turned in the Allies' favour. An invasion of southern Europe from North Africa could now be seriously considered. The Italians in Yugoslavia became ever more demoralised and hence less and less interested in hunting down resistance fighters whether Partisans or Mihailovic's men. They were increasingly ready to agree truces and accommodations, to the intense annoyance of the Germans.

Initially the Soviets favoured restoring the *status quo ante* in Yugoslavia with perhaps some territorial extension westwards at the expense of Italy. They had renewed diplomatic relations with the Yugoslav government-in-exile on 28 August 1941 and wanted to send a military mission to Mihailovic inside Serbia. This the London Yugoslavs would not countenance. Stalin also wanted to establish in Moscow a Yugoslav National Committee with the aim of raising a force of Yugoslavs, armed and equipped by the Soviets, to fight the Germans. He had already done it for the Poles and the Czechs. The London Yugoslavs became even more alarmed, fearing it would undermine their authority. They were relieved when the Soviets were dissuaded. Until the German advance on Moscow had been halted in December 1941 the British had not taken the Soviet viewpoint seriously. Many in London had been convinced the Red Army would not hold out against the *Wehrmacht*. Bruce Lockhart, Director General of the Political Warfare Executive (PWE), confided to his diary on 26 October 1941 that "no one serious" had expected Russia to last more than a few weeks![4]

When the Red Army had not been routed as anticipated, British diplomats began worrying about possible Soviet expansionism. They thought they could accommodate most of the territorial gains the Soviets would expect after the successful conclusion of the war. The Baltic states of Latvia, Lithuania and Estonia, plus Romania's Bessarabia and northern Bukovina, had already been secured through secret clauses of the infamous 1939 Hitler-Stalin Pact, but they envisaged trouble with Moscow over the future of eastern Poland. They feared, too, that the Soviets, fortified by their ethnic links with the slavs, would want to fill the vacuum in Eastern Europe left by Germany's defeat. They worried that Hungary, Romania and Bulgaria might fall under Soviet sway. This might make it difficult for Greece and Yugoslavia to remain independent. A phrase common in Foreign Office memos at that time describes the Soviets as "fishing in the troubled waters of the Balkans".

Alarm bells rang when the Soviets tried to woo the Yugoslav government-in-exile with the offer of a five-year mutual assistance pact. The British Foreign Office thought this a likely preliminary to turning Yugoslavia into a Soviet protectorate. When London insisted that the duration of such a treaty be limited to that of the war, the Soviets turned truculent. They began openly attacking Mihailovic and the Yugoslav government-in-exile in their propaganda. Hitherto the Soviet-controlled Radio Free Yugoslavia had been even-handed in its reporting of resistance within Yugoslavia. In April 1942, no doubt at Tito's behest, it alleged some of Mihailovic's commanders were collaborating with the Germans. Thereafter it became ever more one-sided in its chronicling of Yugoslav affairs, lauding the Partisans and denigrating Mihailovic. It relied for its information on Tito, with whom it was now in continuous contact. In March 1942 Tito had been told he had the Comintern's "complete, unbreakable confidence". In July Moscow declared its full support for the Partisans. When it became evident the Soviets, not the western Allies, would most likely liberate the Balkans, British leverage in seeking a political solution there post-war diminished. In the end it virtually disappeared.

SOE Cairo did not know much about what was going on inside Yugoslavia during early 1942. It had lost contact with Hudson and was riven with internal rivalries – not just between it and the traditional secret service (SIS), but also with its own London headquarters. In addition, the attention of the military chiefs was concentrated on events in North Africa, particularly the ebb and flow in the fortunes of the British forces facing Rommel's *Afrika Korps*. They also had to cope with the United States' entry into the war and the changes that brought to attitudes towards operations in, for instance, the Mediterranean.

SIS, in contrast, was now better informed about Yugoslavia, through the Enigma intercepts and from agents they had parachuted into the country. There had been seven successful and only two unsuccessful Anglo-Yugoslav missions during the early months of the year. All three missions SOE had mounted to replace Hudson had been unsuccessful. SIS now knew of resistance in Slovenia, hitherto thought a passive pro-German province. The snag was that SIS and SOE were not exchanging information. There was also a shortage of aircraft for airdrops to the resisters.

Many of the Allied military chiefs, particularly the Americans, had serious doubts about the value of sustaining resistance inside Yugoslavia. They argued that because supplies were so scarce, they could be better used elsewhere. The prevailing view in London was that at best the resistance should remain low-key. PWE, the propaganda arm of the intelligence services, maintained "the aim is to encourage resistance and boost Mihailovic without instigation to revolt". Enigma decrypts revealed there had been another abortive attempt by the Germans to capture Mihailovic.

Hudson had been incommunicado from late November 1941 to

April 1942; Mihailovic had often been silent for weeks on end between December and early May. In March he had complained that the Partisans were still hindering his activities and that the Germans, Italians and Ustashi were aiding them in this. He implored London to demand the Russians order the Partisans to stop. When Hudson finally came back regularly on line in June 1942, he reported the Chetniks in Montenegro and Herzegovina were receiving weapons from the Italians. In July he signalled that Mihailovic had strengthened his position in Montenegro around Mount Durmitor, and in general sounded much more optimistic. He had been promoted to Major and awarded the Distinguished Service Order. Sixteen sorties were flown to Mihailovic between 30 March and 3 June 1942.

King Peter and his prime minister visited Washington that June. President Roosevelt's spokesman praised "the fine achievements of General Mihailovic and his daring men" that were "an example of spontaneous and unselfish will to victory". A report to Churchill by the Director of Military Intelligence on 2 June maintained Mihailovic rather than Tito's communists should enjoy the Allies' exclusive backing on political grounds. Churchill minuted "good" on the report but took no further interest in Yugoslav resistance until the year's end.

On 16 June General Sir Alan Brooke, Chief of the Imperial General Staff, Churchill's most important military adviser, urged that everything possible be done to increase the level of aid to Mihailovic. During August Military Intelligence estimated Mihailovic "will have ready for action when the day comes a force of 60-80,000 of the best type of Serb fighter". Meantime, "in our opinion it would be dangerous to risk reprisals severe enough to cause estrangement among potential supporters."[5] The Foreign Office agreed, minuting on 24 September that Mihailovic's "potential value, both military and political, at a later stage of the war" justified continuing British support.

But Radio Free Yugoslavia had intensified its criticism of Mihailovic on 6 July 1942, denouncing him personally as a traitor and a collaborator. The claims were taken up for the first time by the official Soviet news agency Tass on 19 July. They were given wider publicity later that month by a Swedish Communist newspaper *Ny Dag*, and by the *Daily World* in the United States, in reports based entirely on the broadcast. The British Foreign Office protested to the Soviets, who replied on 7 August with what they described as details of the alleged collaboration. The 12 August issue of *Soviet War*

News maintained Tito, not Mihailovic, was the real leader of Yugoslav resistance.

The Yugoslav government-in-exile retaliated later that autumn by itemising for the Russians the misdeeds and atrocities against Mihailovic's forces perpetrated by the Partisans. Eden in his reply to the Soviets on 20 August dismissed the allegations of Mihailovic's collaboration as Partisan propaganda which could not be taken as "objective and accurate evidence". He requested that Moscow cease attacking him.[6] The Soviets did not respond and London did not pursue the matter. The Red Army was in trouble. The Germans had reached Stalingrad and were threatening the Caucasus oil-fields. Stalin increased his pressure on the British and Americans to open a "Second Front".

Following Eden's visit to Moscow at the end of 1942, the British Foreign Office changed its stance. Instead of refusing to accept Mihailovic had ever "collaborated", they claimed that if he had then it could be justified. He was still the horse to back in the political stakes for the future of Yugoslavia. Other Whitehall warriors, though, now favoured establishing contact with the Partisans and even sending a mission to them. In October the BBC, hitherto mentioning only Mihailovic's forces, was authorised to refer favourably to the Partisans. Meant perhaps to stir Mihailovic into action, it merely infuriated him. Shortly afterwards, however, he did organise more acts of sabotage.

Sir George Rendel, British Ambassador to the Yugoslav government-in-exile, observes in his memoirs, *The Sword and the Olive*, how "the full weight of left-wing influence in England was ... thrown on Tito's side". London's Ealing Studios made a movie lionising the Yugoslav resistance movements, particularly the Chetniks. As a result of a vigorous campaign by the *Daily Worker*, claiming it was unfair to the Partisans and even anti-Soviet, the title was changed from "Chetniks" to "Undercover". Favourable references to Mihailovic were mostly excised.

Himmler's representative in Serbia, SS-Gruppenfuhrer August Meyszner, was asked by Hitler in August 1942 to assess the strength of resistance in the event of an Allied landing in the Balkans. Ironically he reported to Berlin without mentioning the Partisans or Tito: "The Mihailovic movement covers a whole area of Yugoslavia. In the Serb areas it is enlisting the population, raising detachments." Himmler himself, in a letter that same month to one of his officials in Yugoslavia, maintained:

The Serbian people are a people who have been in armed resistance for centuries and are trained for it ... Anything that would in any way contribute to the strengthening of the Serbian government and thus of the Serbian people must be avoided.[7]

Earlier, on 17 July 1942, Himmler had signalled a subordinate: "The basis of every success in Serbia and in the entire south-east of Europe lies in the annihilation of Mihailovic." It was a remark Hitler was often to repeat. The German Commander-in-Chief South-East, General Kuntze, had reported to Berlin on 12 July that "the most dangerous opponent" in Serbia was Mihailovic, whose influence he claimed was spreading. Hitler became more and more convinced Mihailovic was merely biding his time to strike at the occupiers. The Germans estimated Mihailovic's strength then at about a hundred thousand!

SOE sent more money to Mihailovic in early August 1942. The courier was Captain Charles Robertson, who was in fact a Canadian-Yugoslav by the name of Dragi Radivojevic posing as a British officer. He had probably been recruited by William Stuart or William Deakin (see next chapter) when professing to be a trained ship's wireless operator. Although he had been with the International Brigade in the Spanish Civil War, he claimed he was no longer a communist. It had been intended to drop him to Tito's Partisans: William Mackenzie says there were at least nine unsuccessful attempts to do so between April and August 1942. It seems it was a hasty last-minute decision to send him instead to Mihailovic. That he spent much of his time praising Tito and trying to persuade Mihailovic and his men to decamp to the Partisans suggests it was a mistake! That he was meant to be Hudson's wireless-operator replacement did not help Hudson's relations with Mihailovic. Eventually he debunked to the Partisans, taking with him a British officer newly attached to Mihailovic, Major Neil Selby. Selby was captured by the Germans and later shot when allegedly trying to escape. The Partisans were to execute "Robertson" for what they claimed were his "Trotskyist" beliefs. Prior to his parachuting into Yugoslavia, he had been looked after in Cairo by James Klugmann, of whom more shortly.

Other couriers reached Mihailovic during September with large sums of money in gold and Italian lira. Because SOE Cairo could not supply him directly, it was suggested he use the cash to buy weapons and ammunition from the Italians. As Mihailovic was convinced Hudson too was a Tito spy, the Foreign Office and SOE London decided that month to bite the bullet and replace him. Their choice was Colonel Bill Bailey, a 37-year-old metallurgist fluent in Serbo-Croat, who like Hudson had been resident in Yugoslavia before the war. They had worked for the same company and had both been involved in secret service activities. Bailey had been SOE's boss in Belgrade and later in Istanbul. Before moving to Cairo, he set up a broadcasting station in Jerusalem transmitting misleading information to the Axis forces in the Balkans which purported to originate from inside the region – so-called "black propaganda". He had also visited Canada for SOE.

While in Cairo, Bailey incurred the enmity of many of the exiled Yugoslav senior military officers there, so the Yugoslav government in London did not welcome his assignment to Mihailovic's headquarters. Almost immediately after his appointment he contracted malaria and did not reach Mihailovic until Christmas Day 1942. His was certainly a curious appointment, particularly as he had been responsible, while in Canada, for recruiting Croat-born Canadian Communists to be parachuted into Yugoslavia to make contact with the Partisans. Now he was being sent to the headquarters of the Partisans' main opponent in Yugoslavia as chief liaison officer for the British!

Bailey's instructions were to urge Mihailovic to increase his sabotaging of the Axis lines of communication through Serbia. But just before Bailey arrived in Yugoslavia, Hudson had signalled Cairo that, because of the threat of reprisals, Mihailovic was reluctant to initiate substantial sabotage prior to an Allied invasion. He had assured Hudson, though, that once that invasion occurred "no blood would be spared". Because he depended for supplies on the Italians, who shared his antagonism towards the Partisans, Mihailovic was unwilling to attack them. He believed that, when they quit the war, which he expected to be soon, they would hand over their equipment and weapons to him. These could then be used against the Germans on the Allies' behalf.

Whereas Hudson understood Mihailovic's position, Bailey was anxious to change the situation radically so as to impress his superiors in SOE. His early signals to Cairo included comments such as Mihailovic "must be made to realise we can make or break him. In return for the former we demand frank and sincere co-operation." It is hardly surprising that his relations with Mihailovic were never warm. No doubt the London Yugoslavs had forewarned Mihailovic of Bailey's activities in Canada. He must have learned, too, of the misgivings of the Cairo Yugoslavs and felt doubly suspicious of

Bailey and resentful of the British. That some of the airdrops reaching him included anti-snake-bite serum not needed in Serbia would not have improved his relations with Bailey. Nor did the children's-size shoes, left-footed pairs of boots, grenades without detonators and Italian East African Occupation lire overstamped "Ethiopia". It is easy to see why Mihailovic became convinced the Italians, in the short term, were a more reliable source of supply than the British.

General Alexander, the newly appointed Commander-in-Chief, Middle East, telegraphed Mihailovic on 22 September 1942 to request he attack the Belgrade-Salonika railway along which supplies were being delivered to Rommel. This was in the run-up to the battle for El Alamein. Mihailovic replied that he had recently sabotaged this line, as well as coal mines and other vital installations – which Enigma decrypts were to verify. He would continue doing so but did not want any publicity, particularly via the BBC. His actions had already provoked heavy reprisals, he did not wish to risk yet more.

Felix Benzler, the German Foreign Office's Plenipotentiary in Serbia, reported to Berlin on 27 September that Mihailovic continued to be "a serious danger". Hundreds of Mihailovic's supporters were arrested that month, largely as a result of the Germans having broken his radio codes. Most were immediately executed. The Lisa antimony mine near Kraljevo, the largest in the Balkans, was damaged in mid-October. Many of the Germans guarding it were killed. Instant reprisals among local Serbs resulted. Axis shipping on the Danube was also attacked. A call for civil disobedience in Serbia during November was partially successful. Peasants delayed supplying the occupiers, miners slowed down production and many state officials absented themselves from work. That Mihailovic's plea for secrecy had merit was shown when the Germans in retaliation shot more than fifteen hundred Serb hostages in Belgrade alone during December, plus a further two hundred and fifty in Petrovac and a hundred at Ljutovnica.

The official policy of both SOE London and the Yugoslav government was still to discourage Mihailovic from undue activity, so as to conserve his forces for a possible invasion by the Allies. The BBC included such instructions in their broadcasts throughout November 1942. That month Tito suggested to the Germans that they collaborate in destroying Mihailovic's forces prior to such a landing. Like the Germans he feared the mass uprising of Serbs that was expected to coincide with an Allied invasion. Unfortunately for Tito, Hitler had just instructed his army to eliminate both the Partisans and Mihailovic's men in an operation planned for early 1943.

Hitler never stopped worrying about an Allied invasion of the Balkans. The likelihood of it grew after the British Commonwealth's victory at El Alamein in November 1942. This was why he stationed such a large force in the Balkans, especially in Greece, the expected location of any landings. He summoned Mussolini to a meeting in East Prussia in December 1942 to discuss this concern. Mussolini was too ill to attend and sent instead his Foreign Minister, Count Ciano, who reported back to Rome the German anxieties. Evidently Hitler had

> stressed again the utmost importance of the pacification of these regions in face of an eventual British front in the Balkans. Every measure must be taken to prevent the outbreak of fire in our rear in case an Anglo-Saxon landing takes place.

Hitler had also reminded the Italians of the vital importance to his aircraft industries of the copper, chrome and bauxite of the area. It was crucial that the railway line to the *Reich* through Serbia was kept open: "If this was lost the Balkans were finished for the Axis. The recent blowing up of a bridge had shown how disagreeable such a disruption of traffic could be." The bridge in question was the Gorgopotamos which a British-led group of Greek partisans had destroyed earlier that autumn.

> The enemy must therefore be prevented from continuing with their partisan war against Axis communications, otherwise a catastrophic situation would arise. The partisans, with Mihailovic at their head, were working closely with England, whence they received material from submarines at night on the Dalmatian coast, and also inform-ation and gold from parachutists.

Hitler felt the Italians were not being aggressive enough against Mihailovic's forces in their areas of occupation. More "resolute and ruthless action" was called for. He deplored their friendly relations with the Chetnik leaders. Ribbentrop suggested to Ciano they should exploit such relations "to lay a trap for Mihailovic and to hang him as soon as he fell into our hands".[8]

Hitler's worries over a landing in the Balkans were to dog him for the rest of the war. The Allies exploited them, to divert his energies from more important concerns. He returned to the subject in mid-February 1943. His intelligence chief, General Reinhard Gehlen, had claimed Mihailovic was backed by 80 per cent of the Serbs. Hitler reiterated his belief that the Italians were not being sufficiently belligerent towards Mihailovic. The military situation in North Africa had worsened for the Axis. There had been, too, the disaster at Stalingrad – three hundred thousand troops surrendered there on 3 February.

Ribbentrop was sent to Rome to tell Mussolini "the bands must be destroyed, men, women, and children, because their continued existence endangered the lives of German and Italian men, women and children". Hitler was apparently convinced the Partisans and Mihailovic's forces were really one entity under the direction of the British General Staff. It was, he said, "high time we exterminated this movement if we do not want to incur the risk of being stabbed in the back the moment the Anglo-Saxons land in the Balkans."

According to Ribbentrop, Hitler's "gravest concern" sprang from his fervent conviction that the final Allied assault would come from the south-east as a sort of personal revenge on Churchill's part for the Dardanelles fiasco of 1915.

> This was the historic invasion route into the heart of Europe, and the obvious point of concentration for the Allies. An enemy landing in the area, backed by local nationalist and Communist uprisings, might lead to the rapid control of the whole region, and the worst nightmare of all, to the exposing of the German southern flank in the East and an eventual gigantic turning movement – a joint Anglo-American-Russian enterprise – into Germany itself.[9]

Hitler was at it again in April 1943 when he met Mussolini near Salzburg. He once more pressed the Italians to eliminate both Mihailovic's forces and the Partisans. But the Italians saw Mihailovic as a counterbalance to the Ustashi and the Partisans. Hitler's military representative in Rome, General Rintelen, continued the pressure the following month with the Italian High Command, giving them a letter from Hitler saying unless order was restored in Yugoslavia "a crisis as grave as that of North Africa must ensue".[10] But he too could not stir Mussolini's generals to decisive action.

A Yugoslav government crisis occurred that autumn of 1942 over the appointment of an ambassador to Washington. The nominee was thought too anti-Croat by the Croat ministers in the Government. Churchill became involved when King Peter and his mother Queen Marie came to see him on 9 December. They sought his advice on the crisis and urged more support for Mihailovic. Churchill had a soft spot for royalty, especially descendants of Queen Victoria, and Queen Marie was a great-granddaughter. He put them on to Eden, who lunched the two on 11 December. The encounter prompted Eden to send a report to Churchill on 17 December regarding resistance in Yugoslavia. In it he criticised Mihailovic for not bothering the Germans enough. He said he intended threatening Mihailovic with reducing or even ending aid to him. Clearly he did not realise that up to then barely thirty tons of supplies had been sent to Mihailovic! Eden maintained that, while there might be short-term advantages in aiding the Partisans too, it was in Britain's long-term interests "to go on supporting Mihailovic in order to prevent anarchy and communist chaos after the war".[11] Churchill merely noted in reply, "good; I agree". Eden felt he could not protest because of the effusive tributes Mihailovic had recently received from the War Office. The BBC had ceased criticising Mihailovic and SOE Cairo had just started a new propaganda service that was praising him fulsomely.

On 19 December the Joint Intelligence Sub-Committee of the British Chiefs of Staff, in a briefing paper for Churchill, suggested support for the Yugoslav guerrillas should be concentrated on Serbia and Montenegro where "General Mihailovic already has an organization". In addition, according to Sir Harry Hinsley in his official history of British Intelligence in the Second World War, Enigma decrypts at this time showed that

> the Germans increasingly disliked what they learned of Cetnik-Italian collaboration, suspecting a secret understanding between the two, and that far from collaborating with the Cetniks themselves, they remained determined to eliminate Mihailovic's organisation.

SOE Cairo's Chief of Staff, Colonel Keble, reported on 28 December:

> It is quite useless repeat useless sending any strong or other message from His Majesty's Government to Mihailovic with a view to spurring him to further activities when we lack almost entirely means of supporting him.[12]

Eden opted instead to contact the Soviets to see if they could persuade Tito to join forces with Mihailovic. As the British Ambassador to Moscow was then in London, it was not until early March 1943 that the approach was made. It was rebuffed on the grounds that reconciliation between Tito and Mihailovic was an internal matter for the Yugoslavs themselves. Events elsewhere, however, had moved on apace, making these concerns no longer pertinent.

CHAPTER FIVE

A Decisive Year

"could even be called the Klugmann period
and it changed a great deal"
BASIL DAVIDSON

THE YEAR 1943 was to be decisive in the fortunes of both Yugoslavia and Tito. The strategic position of the Allies changed dramatically for the better, particularly in the Mediterranean. The Axis forces were being conclusively cleared from North Africa. "Fortress Europe" could now be assaulted, though how and where was still a source of dissension between the British and the Americans. The Americans favoured a strike across the English Channel from Britain itself. Churchill preferred to attack "the soft underbelly of the Axis crocodile", Italy and the Balkans. In the immediate afterglow of the El Alamein victory the previous November, the Anglo-American military planners had been inclined to carry the war to the Balkans rather than land in Italy. Enigma decrypts indicated the Germans would give defence of that area priority over occupying Italy, should the latter collapse. The German war machine depended heavily on Balkan raw materials.

Politically, Churchill was anxious the British and Americans should reach central Europe before the Russians. He was eager to bring Turkey into the war as a base from which to strike, through Bulgaria. This did not enthuse the Americans. But at the Casablanca Conference in January 1943 Churchill got Roosevelt's agreement to invade Sicily that summer. The hope was that it might hasten Italy's exit from the war. To assist it, the Allied military chiefs were keen to deter the diversion there of German divisions from the Balkans. With that in mind Churchill renewed his interest in an Allied landing on the Adriatic coast of Yugoslavia, which Mihailovic eagerly awaited. Tito feared it. It would alter the political balance in Yugoslavia in favour of Mihailovic and the Serbs, on whose uprising Churchill was relying. Such a landing would have needed American co-operation, especially regarding air-cover and landing craft. This was unlikely to be forthcoming.

There were many on the British side who felt the Americans became somewhat unhinged whenever the Balkans were mentioned. According to the American historian Richard M. Leighton,

> the area to the east of the Adriatic was regarded by American strategists with something akin to the superstitious dread with which mediaeval mariners once contemplated the unknown monster-infested reaches of the Western Ocean.[1]

Julian Amery saw a less mystical aspect to the American reluctance to be drawn into the Balkans. He thought they suspected the British had imperialist interests there to do with protecting communications with India and the Orient, and so were wary of any British wish to invade there. These were suspicions Stalin was to exploit whenever the subject came up at conferences with Roosevelt and Churchill. Once an Allied landing was not on the cards, Mihailovic was doomed. It meant the Balkans would be liberated by the Soviets. As Tito was Moscow's man, the Partisans would inevitably end up in power in Yugoslavia.

The Americans had their eyes firmly focused on a cross-Channel invasion of France. To them all this manoeuvring in the Mediterranean was a needless distraction. This did not stop the British from trying one deception after another to convince Hitler an Allied landing in the Balkans was a possibility, that he should never relax his guard there. And Hitler fell for the deceptions hook, line and sinker. There were rumours of a non-existent British 12th Army being fitted out and trained in Egypt during 1943 for an invasion of the Balkans and the famous Operation Mincemeat, known to filmgoers as "The Man Who Never Was". A corpse purporting to be that of a British staff officer killed in a plane crash was washed ashore on the Spanish coast on 30 April 1943. He bore a letter to General Alexander indicating that the Allies were planning an invasion of Greece and that the rumoured landing on Sicily was merely a subterfuge.

Enigma decrypts showed that the deception so convinced Hitler that he increased the number of German divisions in the Balkans from eight to eighteen between March and July 1943. He more than doubled the number of German fighter-planes in Greece and Crete, and transferred a group of motor torpedo boats from Sicily to the Aegean. He ordered Rommel to Greece on 25 July 1943 to head a new Army Group there, only to recall him before he arrived, having heard of Mussolini's fall from power, and to send him instead to Italy. The Japanese Ambassador reported in early October that Hitler thought a Balkan invasion much more likely than an attack on the Italian mainland. The Germans were still convinced in January 1944 that the Allies would invade the Balkans and moved further scarce naval forces there. Fears of such an invasion were fanned again that spring, deterring a planned transfer of troops from the Balkans to France and the Russian front.

Unlike the diplomats at the British Foreign Office or the White-hall warriors at SOE's London headquarters, the military chiefs were not concerned with long-term political considerations. They were now prepared to release aircraft to supply the resistance movements in the Balkans on a greater scale than before, provided they got value in terms of keeping as many German troops as possible out of Italy and Western Europe. Whether that value came from communist partisans or anti-communist loyalists in Yugoslavia was immaterial to them. Moreover, since Stalingrad, admiration for the Soviet war effort had diminished their hostility towards communists in general.

SOE London remained sceptical about the strength of the Partisans but was keen to know more about them. Moscow was pressing Eden to recognise them. The Soviets had found new political vigour with their successes on the battlefield. SOE Cairo thought the guerrillas in Croatia and Slovenia might not be communist and might have no connection with Tito's Bosnian Partisans. They could be worth pursuing in their own right. SOE Cairo was especially keen now to contact Tito.

En route to Turkey to try again to persuade the Turks to join the Allies, Churchill dropped off in Cairo. He lunched privately on 28 January 1943 with Captain William Deakin, a young Oxford history don who had helped him research his *Life of Marlborough*, published in the 1930s, and later *A History of the English-Speaking Peoples*, then unfinished. Churchill had maintained a close and warm relationship with Deakin. Martin Gilbert, Churchill's official biographer, mentions Churchill lunching previously with Deakin on 6 August 1940. Deakin wrote to Churchill on 18 October that same year: "please do take every care of yourself in these trying days".[2] Churchill had encouraged him to join SOE, which he duly did, initially being sent to North America on its behalf.

Deakin was now based in Cairo. In what clearly was a well thought out and ably rehearsed gambit by him and his SOE Cairo colleagues, he pressed Churchill during the lunch to take more notice of Tito's efforts. A similar approach to their superiors in London had recently been rebuffed. On this occasion the stratagem was successful. Later that day Deakin's boss, Colonel (soon to be Brigadier) Mervyn Keble, SOE Cairo's Chief of Staff, met Churchill and was asked to prepare a report. According to Martin Gilbert, this was

> about the respective fighting abilities, regions and objectives of the Serb resistance leader General Mihailovic, whom Britain was currently supporting, and the forces in Croatia and Slovenia under the command of the partisan leader Josip Broz Tito, which were receiving no outside help, and which the Germans were declaring to be Communist.

In Gilbert's estimation "Churchill's meetings with Deakin and Keble were to be decisive for British policy towards the resistance forces in German and Italian occupied Yugoslavia."[3]

Keble's report was delivered to Churchill two days later, while he was still in Cairo. It claimed Tito's forces, being more widely spread, were pinning down more enemy divisions than Mihailovic's. It denied Tito's forces were all communist. Many were school teachers, students and skilled workers "who are politically extreme left". The rank and file included "peasants, deserters from the Italian and Croat armies, and refugees whose homes have been destroyed, and who are not necessarily politically minded". It was "not accurate to adopt the German technique of branding the whole movement as 'Communist'". If resistance in Croatia and Slovenia was to be "raised to a level sufficiently effective to be of real military value to the Allied war effort, aid must be organised independently of the existing programme regarding General Mihailovic". Mihailovic was containing three German and six Bulgarian divisions in Serbia. A further six Italian divisions were being contained in Montenegro by forces favourable to him. "Other resisting elements" not under Mihailovic's command were, it was claimed, tieing down thirty Axis divisions in Croatia and Slovenia.[4]

The report recommended SOE be allowed to contact these other resisting elements so as to co-ordinate the aid to all guerrillas within Yugoslavia. It accepted there was no direct evidence Mihailovic was collaborating with the Germans. As for his collaborating with the Italians, it repeated that some of his subordinate commanders had concluded local arrangements. They were mutual non-aggression pacts and agreements to co-operate against the Partisans. The report stressed the need for sufficient aircraft to drop the supplies; only four were currently available. Liberator bombers with their longer range would be the most suitable. Eight of them would be ideal. SOE Cairo was anxious that the job of aiding these other resisting elements be given to them rather than to the conventional secret services (SIS) – and least of all to their SOE colleagues in London. Churchill took the point about sufficient aircraft and tried to persuade Eisenhower, whom he met in Algiers on his way home, to release more, but without success.

The report was most probably written jointly by Deakin, his section chief Basil Davidson, a former journalist with experience of the Balkans in a secret service capacity, and their assistant James Klugmann. While Deakin was new to Yugoslav affairs and to Cairo, having just arrived the previous month, and Davidson had been there only since October 1942, Klugmann had already served almost a year in the section. An able linguist, he outshone everyone on the staff in his knowledge of Serbo-Croat. A workaholic, he was responsible for preparing the section's intelligence digests and situation reports. As well as briefing military personnel and visiting VIPs on the situation in Yugoslavia, he came in time to handle all the raw intelligence material reaching the office concerning that country. He decided in what form to pass it on to London and elsewhere. These were chores his more easy-going colleagues were only too eager to leave to him.

Klugmann owed his job to the old-boy network. He had been appointed by a senior intelligence officer, Terence Airey, from his old school, Gresham's in Norfolk, when they had met by chance in Cairo. A low ranker in the Royal Army Service Corps at the time, within weeks he was commissioned as an officer. Basil Davidson clearly admired him. In his memoirs, *Special Operations Europe*, he writes that this period "could even be called the Klugmann period and it changed a great deal". Davidson's own sympathies then lay more with the Partisans than with Mihailovic. He describes himself as "a well-marked Partisan supporter" and gives the firm impression that Deakin felt that way too. Davidson describes the Keble memo as "shrewdly composed". By contrast, Deakin in his memoirs, *The Embattled Mountain*, does not mention Klugmann or Keble, or even meeting Churchill in January 1943.

Documents released in May 2002 to the Public Record Office (PRO) in London, now styled the National Archives, disclosed that Klugmann, who died in 1977 at the age of 65, had joined the Communist Party in 1933. He had been suspected by MI5 thereafter of working for the Soviets, and for the Communist International (Comintern) in particular. Tito had of course worked for the Comintern. Klugmann's MI5 file, released then too, includes an incriminating transcription of a bugged conversation on 8 August 1945 with Bob Stewart, a senior member of the executive committee of the Communist Party of Great Britain. In it Klugmann admits serving Moscow since his student days. He reveals he had convinced his SOE commanding officer to let him continue handling highly sensitive communications between the Middle East, Yugoslavia and London despite concerns expressed by MI5. He was said, too, to have had links with the Egyptian communist party who were in radio communication with Moscow throughout the war.

Klugmann had achieved a double first in modern languages at Trinity College, Cambridge. His friends there included Kim Philby, Guy Burgess, Anthony Blunt, Donald Maclean and John Cairncross, the infamous Soviet spy ring of Cambridge-educated traitors. Known first to their Moscow masters as simply "The Five", in 1960, with the popularity of the Western movie *The Magnificent Seven,* they were apparently promoted to "The Magnificent Five"! Klugmann was said to have encouraged many of them to become communists, especially Maclean, with whom he had been at school. Blunt (later Sir Anthony Blunt, Director of London's Courtauld Institute of Art and Surveyor of the Queen's Pictures) admitted as much in an article, "From Bloomsbury to Marxism", in the November 1973 issue of *Studio International*: "It was primarily [Klugmann] who decided what organisations and societies in Cambridge were worth penetrating [by the Communists] and what were not." Miranda Carter, in *Anthony Blunt: His Lives*, says that when Blunt left MI5 in October 1945 he told his Soviet masters,

> MI5 knew about James Klugmann's espionage activities. On the microphone hidden at the CPGB's [Communist Party Great Britain's] headquarters, Klugmann had been overheard saying he'd passed secret documents to Tito's Communist partisans in Yugoslavia.

The top KGB defector Vasili Mitrokhin, in *The Mitrokhin Archive*, which he wrote with the Cambridge historian Christopher Andrew, discloses that Klugmann had been recruited as a Soviet spy in 1936. He and the young Marxist poet John Cornford were considered

> the two most prominent Communist Party activists in Cambridge. Though Cornford was killed in the Spanish Civil War in 1937, just

after his twenty-first birthday, Klugmann went on to become head of the Party's propaganda and education department, a member of the political committee (in effect its Politburo) and the Party's official historian.

The Labour Cabinet Minister Denis Healey had been a friend of Klugmann's at Cambridge. He records in his autobiography, *The Time of my Life*, that Klugmann, while with SOE in Cairo, was "simultaneously an agent of the Comintern, for which he had started recruiting spies in Cambridge in 1934". Christopher Andrew, too, in his earlier *KGB: The Inside story of its Foreign Operations from Lenin to Gorbachev*, which he published with Oleg Gordievsky, himself at one time KGB's head of station in London, describes Klugmann as an "active Soviet agent" throughout the war.

Klugmann may well have helped to recruit some of the Magnificent Five as Soviet spies. Mitrokhin maintains it was certainly true of John Cairncross, another first class honours graduate in modern languages at Trinity. Cairncross entered the Foreign Office in 1936. During the war he was private secretary to the minister overseeing the intelligence services. All the secret cabinet papers passed through his hands, including those regarding Britain's atomic bomb project. Later he worked at Bletchley, where he had access to the top Enigma decoded intercepts. He was awarded one of the highest Soviet decorations, the Order of the Red Banner. Mitrokhin says Klugmann often acted as courier for Cairncross and his local Soviet controller in London. Klugmann most probably recruited other Soviet spies like Michael Straight. Mitrokhin claims the Soviets used him as a "talent-spotter".

He had also helped to recruit volunteers for the International Brigade in the Spanish Civil War at the time Tito was doing so. There has been speculation as to whether the two met or were in communication then with each other. Klugmann had not been vetted when he joined SOE. They had been more interested in his aptitude for languages, which included colloquial Arabic and Serbo-Croat. Initially a private, it was only when he was commissioned as an officer in February 1942 that he was vetted: then the MI5 dossier was revealed. MI5 strongly advised against his continuing to work for SOE. They were overruled by his immediate bosses in Cairo, who promoted him to captain in May 1943 and to major a year later. He was the sole staff officer involved in policy, intelligence and operational briefings who remained in SOE Cairo's Yugoslav section throughout its existence. His was a pivotal position. He dealt daily with the British liaison officers in the field, arranging their supplies, handling their signals and summarising their reports before passing them on to London. It was a situation in which he could easily exert leverage.

Klugmann was never charged with espionage. Chapman Pincher, in his *Too Secret Too Long* exposé of British intelligence outfits, says Klugmann was one of John Cairncross's "most important field officers... Between them they provided the KGB with a continuous reading of Allied plans concerning Yugoslavia, and Klugmann helped to change them in Moscow's interests." Pincher claims:

> Klugmann did all he could to induce SOE headquarters in London to dump Mihailovic, who was anti-communist, and switch all support to Tito, a partisan leader who wanted a communist Yugoslavia after the war. He saw to it that pleas for food, weapons and other supplies from Mihailovic's forces were suppressed or, if any action was taken, that the supplies were diverted to Tito.

Peter Kemp, a member of SOE, describes in his memoirs, *The Thorns of Memory*, arriving in Cairo and being surprised

> to find my Cambridge contemporary James Klugmann, once the secretary and inspiration of Cambridge communists, now established in this headquarters as intelligence officer of the Yugoslav section. Having been required, like other recruits to SOE, to sign a document affirming that I had never been a member of any fascist or communist organisation, I was astounded to find Captain Klugmann in such a responsible and confidential post.

According to Kemp,

> Major Basil Davidson made no attempt to hide his antipathy to the Cetniks and to those who supported them in London. He even suggested I sign a paper to the effect that I had been subjected in London to indoctrination on behalf of Mihailovic; I firmly refused, but it showed the sort of feeling that was to embitter relations between British officers both at headquarters and in the field.

Hugh Seton-Watson, then special adviser to SOE Cairo on Yugoslav and Bulgarian affairs, shared an office with Klugmann, whom he described as "a Soviet sympathiser" like him. Seton-Watson had spent time in Belgrade before the war. Later he became Professor of Russian History at London University. On 9 November 1942 he had produced a paper on Yugoslav internal politics between the wars and how they were likely to work out under the occupation. It had been circulated within SOE. On the file copy that has survived,

Keble had noted: "the attached is an excellent appreciation, written, I should say, by a Communist and one who is definitely anti-Mihailovic"![5]

Just two days before Deakin's fateful lunch with Churchill in Cairo, Seton-Watson published an article in *The Spectator* attacking Mihailovic. He accused the Serbs of exaggerating the Ustashi atrocities. Later that year he and Klugmann were closely involved with Frank Thompson, a school chum of Seton-Watson's at Winchester and a known communist, in a scheme to organise a Bulgarian resistance group. The ploy came to nothing when Thompson was captured and shot by the Bulgarian police. Others parachuted in had also been caught and executed. Scarce supplies dropped to them were picked up by partisan groups friendly to Tito operating in Macedonia. They were used against Mihailovic's forces there, as Michael Lees, a British liaison officer with them, was to testify. Vladimir Dedijer, in his *War Diaries*, says that when a delegation of Partisan leaders came to Cairo in December 1943 Seton-Watson advised them to be sure to tell the British journalists, about to interview them, that the Partisans really cared for animals: "If you have any kind of picture with a dog or cat, you would gain the favour of many people in England".

Malcolm Muggeridge, a wartime member of the British Secret Service, described SOE Cairo's Yugoslav section in his memoirs as a left-wing organisation. John Eyre, who was also working in SOE's Balkans section in Cairo, was proved later to have been a Soviet agent. The novelist Anthony Powell, then working in a branch of military intelligence in London, recalled in his memoirs reading "reports circulated on the situation applauding the Yugoslav Communist irregulars in a tone more suitable to an adventure story in the *Boy's Own Paper* than a sober appreciation of what was happening". He thought the advice based on those reports "dubiously reliable".[6] Joan Miller, a former secretary in MI5 working at Bush House for the BBC during the War, records in her memoirs, *One Girl's War*, catching an army major passing messages about the Middle East to the Soviets. She was enraged when he was not punished.

Michael Lees told me how, when he decided in 1986 to write his memoirs, he went to the PRO in London to see whether any of his signals to Cairo from inside Yugoslavia had survived. A few had. He was appalled to find that, when passed on to London or précised and included in more general SOE appreciations of Yugoslavia, they had been doctored to show Mihailovic's forces in an unfavourable light. When he mentioned this to colleagues who had been with Mihailovic they disclosed that many of their reports had been doctored too. Briefs critical of Tito's Partisans and laudatory mentions of the anti-communist Mihailovic forces had not found their way to Churchill and the other decision-makers. They had been mystified as to why they had been ordered by SOE Cairo not to sabotage enemy installations like railway bridges, airfields and power stations. Supply drops had often comprised office equipment, toilet rolls, single left-footed boots and raw onions that were plentiful in Serbia, rather than the explosives and weapons requested.

More particularly, they had been infuriated by the BBC ascribing to the Partisans much of the sabotage carried out by Mihailovic's forces. They mentioned only Tito's being the subject of a wanted poster throughout Yugoslavia with a price on his head, 100,000 Reichsmarks in gold, whereas there had been a similar one concerning Mihailovic. Although this was pointed out to them, the BBC never issued a correction. All of this led them to believe there was a concerted plot by SOE Cairo to demoralise the liaison officers with Mihailovic. Bill Hudson was also to complain that his reports to Cairo had been unduly edited within SOE.

In August 1999 Sir Ian Fraser wrote a letter to *The Spectator* about his colleague at Lazards merchant bank during the 1970s, Jasper Rootham. A liaison officer with Mihailovic's forces, Rootham had been invalided out of Yugoslavia to Italy in 1944. He was directed to Klugmann's caravan for instructions. Klugmann was lunching at the time. Rootham noticed on Klugmann's desk his latest situation report, which, he said to Fraser, had been

> "edited" so as to be almost unrecognisable. He rummaged around in the caravan and found several other reports of his own and his mission colleagues, similarly "edited". The effect of the changes was to present Mihailovic and the Royal Army as German collaborators and to attribute these assessments to the British colonels who commanded the mission. In this form the reports went to London.

According to Fraser, Rootham "had attempted to protest to a higher military authority but the doctors ordered him to hospital straight-away, and before he left hospital he found that he was posted back to London."

SOE Cairo also prevented Italian troops surrendering to Mihailovic but allowed them to do so to the Partisans. The BBC hailed these as victories for Tito and further instances of Mihailovic's inactivity. Bill Hudson, the longest standing British liaison officer with Mihailovic, let rip to Cairo in a signal dated 22 September 1943:

> I have been waiting one and a half years for battle dress blouse size 6 feet, waiting at least 7 months for boots size 11 and riding breeches size 6 fit and large greatcoat. All repeatedly asked for. It was not funny last year when in lieu of above you sent me my tennis trousers and silk pyjamas, nor this year when you sent your stunted five foot five outfits. In fact ever since you sent me in from Cairo with bum W/T equipment your supply dept has been just plain lousy.[7]

On his return from meeting Deakin and Keble in Cairo, Churchill lost little time in instructing the head of SOE London on 12 February 1943 as "a matter of the greatest importance to establish the desired closer contacts" with the other resisting elements in Yugoslavia, such as the communist Partisans. It was April, though, before the first exploratory missions were parachuted into Croatia. For Basil Davidson, "The Cairo 'partisans' had won." He says: "SOE London blew its top and the Foreign Office wavered; even the chiefs of staff, hearing their cries of anger or their doubts, tried to limit the consequences." Nevertheless, for him,

> the thing was certainly done ... we "partisans" in the office, knowing that all might yet depend on broadening the breach and shoving men through it before fresh obstructions could be raised, gathered in support.

Davidson in his memoirs details attempts to court martial him over the loss of a secret file that was eventually found in one of the senior colonel's cupboards. When the finger of suspicion was pointed at Klugmann "Keble pushed James into a lavatory and said that security was after him, but that he, Keble, would protect him".

SOE London remained unenthusiastic about establishing contact with Tito. They disputed Keble's claim that the Partisans were tieing down thirty Axis divisions. The War Office agreed, maintaining there were seventeen Axis divisions in the Partisan areas and fourteen in Mihailovic's.

Bailey reminded Cairo that Mihailovic had received only two airdrops between late October 1942 and late February 1943. SOE London estimated he needed at least twenty-eight drops a month to function adequately. They also pointed out that the BBC's excessive lauding of Partisan activities was not helping Bailey in his attempts to influence Mihailovic. A broadcast on 21 February had particularly irritated Mihailovic when it said:

Recently we have begun to receive at last in London more certain news of the action of the Yugoslav partisans. Until a few months ago, such information was incomplete, confused and very scarce and, therefore, we were not able to refer regularly to the important and courageous front of the Yugoslav partisans which represents the only organized military force now fighting in Occupied Europe.[8]

Despite Churchill's urging, the military chiefs were reluctant to grant SOE extra aircraft. The Liberators were needed for strategic bombing in Europe or hunting U-boats in the Atlantic. They also questioned the necessity of aiding both Mihailovic and Tito. When challenged on 4 March, they said that, politically, Mihailovic was perhaps the better bet "since he could provide some organisation and control whereas under the Partisans chaos would probably ensue when the Axis forces were defeated".[9] A Foreign Office briefing for Anthony Eden on 8 March declared, "our long term interests demand continued support of Mihailovic in order to prevent anarchy and communist chaos after the war".[10]

The Germans shared the British diplomats' and military chiefs' continuing high regard for Mihailovic. The head of German Military Intelligence in Eastern Europe, General Reinhard Gehlen, reported to Hitler on 9 February 1943:

Among the various insurgent movements which increasingly cause trouble in the area of the former Yugoslav state, the movement of General Mihailovic stands in first place with regard to leadership, armament, organisation and activity... [His followers] come from all classes of the population and at present comprise about 80 per cent of the Serbian people ... their number is continuously increasing.[11]

Told the Italians had been co-operating with some of Mihailovic's forces, Hitler angrily wrote to Mussolini on 16 February:

Mihailovic's aim is to get arms and supplies for his own purposes by pretending to help your troops to pacify the country. In this way his formations are getting everything they need so as to be able to start fighting us when the time comes ... I consider it desirable, in the interest of our common aims that your Second Army should regard Mihailovic and his movement as bitter enemies of the Axis powers and I request you, *Duce*, to issue orders in this sense to your military commanders.[12]

The Italians replied they would willingly give up their collaboration with the Chetniks once the Partisans had been liquidated. The Bletchley decoders knew the Germans had been reading Mihailovic's signals to his commanders since July 1942. Their decrypts revealed he intended turning the Italian weapons against the Germans. Hence the latter's exasperation with the Italians and their instruction to their own troops that "no Cetnik formations whose leaders were proved to be in touch with Mihailovic are to be spared".[13]

The Germans had launched, in mid-January 1943, their largest offensive to date against the Partisans in western Bosnia, thought then to number nearly twenty-five thousand. Called Operation *Weiss*, it embraced tanks, bombers and about sixty-five thousand troops. Confusingly, the Partisans numbered these operations against them the Second Offensive, Third Offensive and so on, as though they were their own offensives. To a certain extent they became so in Partisan mythology: that they survived them could rightly be adjudged a success. Guerrillas win by not losing. The arduous and heroic nature of these retreats from the German pincer movements created binding comradeship. Tito always avoided direct battles with the Germans, knowing he could not possibly win them.

If there was a choice between fighting Germans and fighting Mihailovic's forces, the Partisans always preferred the latter. Not just because they were an easier foe – they were far less disciplined and motivated than the Partisans – but because in their eyes they were the *real* foe. Tito had been planning a breakthrough that spring into Montenegro and southern Serbia, Mihailovic territory, which the German offensive now prevented. Hitler wanted to relieve the pressure on the Ustashi and Italians in Croatia by ridding them of the Partisans, or at least pushing the Partisans into the more remote south. He hoped thereby to release further troops for the Russian front.

Bailey reported to Cairo on 3 February 1943 that Tito's situation in western Bosnia seemed desperate. He had already been driven from Bihac. His defeat was thought imminent. Bailey hinted this might be "the best solution for our long-term policy".[14] The Partisans were retracing their steps in the "Long March" of the previous year. Steadily pushed back by the Germans, they had to fight their way through the Italians and Ustashi in front of them. It was an unusually harsh winter, with waist-deep snow and sub-zero temperatures. They slept in the frozen forests by day and moved only at night because of the incessant bombing. Casualties were heavy. The plight of the wounded was pitiful. There were already four thousand of them by mid-February, being transported in great discomfort on bullock carts. Typhus was prevalent and lice were everywhere. Medical supplies were soon non-existent.

Vladimir Dedijer maintains in his *War Diaries* that they were kept going only by the news of the Red Army's victories. He would have us believe their usual greetings to each other were "Long live our Russian brothers", "Every bomb that falls on us is one less on Russia", "Long live comrade Tito – he never forgets us" or "Comrade Tito demands this of us – the Germans will not pass. They will be stopped and thrown back"! He says there were popular poems with lines like "Comrade Tito, you are a son of the people. They sing to you from love. Without you, we would not exist". He claims that to sustain morale party meetings were held en route and even courses on "The People's Liberation Struggle", taught by Djilas among others. Occasions such as the 25th anniversary of the founding of the Red Army on 23 February 1943 were meticulously observed. Food was scarce as the countryside they were retreating through was desolate. They relied for supplies on what they could capture from the Italians who were the source, too, of much of their weaponry and ammunition.

For a time, the Partisans were surrounded within the narrow gorge of the Neretva River in western Bosnia and were forced to jettison their heavy weapons and slaughter their horses. Most of the wounded had to be abandoned, many preferring to kill themselves with grenades rather than fall into enemy hands. The Ustashi were notorious for giving the wounded short shrift. With the Germans behind them, their only escape was to cross the fast-flowing Neretva River. On the other side were Italians as well as Mihailovic's forces, determined to prevent them invading their territory. The Germans were relying on this. The crossing points were under constant fire day and night. But cross the river the Partisans did, on 7 March, suffering appalling casualties in the process. The Italians had quietly withdrawn, leaving behind the weakly armed Chetniks, many of whom fled when surprised by the Partisans. After this the Chetniks' fighting spirit declined rapidly. Only about ten thousand Partisans escaped across the Neretva and Drina rivers. These crossings became part of the Partisan legend and were the subject of numerous propaganda films and other fictional works.

Djilas tells us, "this was the only time during the entire war Tito didn't shave every day". Apparently Tito would always shave himself, whereas the battalion barber shaved the others twice a week. Djilas recalls:

> Tito exhibited nervousness, even rashness, in issuing commands. While he was confident in determining strategy that was more political than military in character, as a commander he reacted too quickly

to the changes so inevitable in war, and as a result frequently changed his orders. Temperamental by nature, with an exceptional sense of danger and a keen, quick intelligence, in battle he didn't have the necessary detachment, and often moved large units to protect himself and the Staff.

Djilas admits their reporting of battles was not always precise: "Sometimes we exaggerated and sometimes we passed over things in silence, but always from our viewpoint and for our cause."

Reports reaching SOE London on 28 February suggested the Partisans had been virtually eliminated. The Germans claimed they had suffered more than 12,500 killed and about 2,500 captured. That same day Mihailovic accused the British of seeking to wage war to the last drop of Serb blood, bought with a trivial trickle of arms. This was at a christening in the Montenegrin village of Gornje Lipovo, where he was temporarily headquartered. Bailey, who was present, admits much plum brandy was consumed by everyone. Mihailovic said he would never be a party to such a "shameful commerce typical of traditional English perfidy". Worse was to follow. He declared, Bailey reported, that his enemies were the Partisans, the Ustashi, the Moslems and the Croats – in that order. Only when he had dealt with them would he turn to the Italians and the Germans. Even then he would be reluctant to tackle the Italians whom he called "his sole source of supply". He was incensed by what he described as "the BBC's new policy of advertisement for Tito", maintaining "the BBC with revolting cynicism had dropped its support of the sacred Serbian cause, and its functions now consist of publicising a band of terrorists".[15] No doubt Mihailovic was exasperated too at the way his battle with the Partisans was going. The outburst fractured relations between him and Bailey. They did not talk to each other for six weeks.

Clearly Bailey had been stung by what Mihailovic had said, but in reporting the speech at such length rather than accepting it as the drunken tantrum of a tired, frustrated, elderly, sick (Bailey had already reported Mihailovic suffered from vertigo), defeated soldier, he must have realised it would be used in evidence against him. He knew how many enemies Mihailovic had in Cairo and London and that they would welcome the ammunition he was now providing. Hence it is not easy to understand Bailey's motives in the matter, other than a pedantic wish to inform London of everything happening in the Mihailovic camp. Certainly he was diligent in his telegraphing. Djilas in his *Wartime* memoirs, describes

Mihailovic's outburst as one "not even we Partisans could have written for him".

The timing could not have been worse for Mihailovic, coming so soon after Churchill had given SOE Cairo the green light to approach the "other resisting elements". That Mihailovic had recently reminded London he had had only two airdrops of supplies since Bailey arrived on the scene was conveniently forgotten in the ensuing brouhaha. He had complained that, without a further five airdrops immediately, he could not regard the British as serious supporters. SOE's official historian, William Mackenzie, maintains Mihailovic's outburst

> had some justification: the British had only sent in three tons of stores since Bailey's arrival, a trifling amount compared with what could be extracted from the Italians by intrigue, bribery and blackmail. In addition, the BBC had (since about October 1942) been indulging in a rather ill-coordinated campaign of advertisement for Tito, which infuriated Mihailovic without coercing him.

Despatches concerning Mihailovic usually did not find their way quickly to Whitehall. But Klugmann made sure Bailey's report about Mihailovic's outburst was passed speedily on to SOE London, the Foreign Office and Downing Street. It was a turning point in the future prospects of Mihailovic and Tito. The Foreign Office was naturally annoyed. Too late Bailey thought fit to add that Mihailovic also had a heart complaint brought on by overwork and the harsh conditions in which he had been living in the mountains and forests during the past two years. In his defence, a Foreign Office memo of 2 March to PWE pointed out that in BBC broadcasts "during the first three weeks of February Mihailovic was only mentioned once, whereas the Partisans were referred to seven times and 'patriots' twice". In the broadcast of 11 February there had been a formal tribute "to the heroic struggle of the Yugoslav Partisans and their many successes which are making a vital contribution to the Allied fight against the enemy." All of which led the diplomats to conclude that Mihailovic, in complaining, had "a *prima facie* case".[16] On 12 March, SOE London complained to the Foreign Office that

> in their endeavour to build up the Partisans [the Soviets] openly attack Mihailovic, call him a traitor and demand his extermination. We, on the other hand, have not only refrained from attacking Mihailovic's opponents, but in the last few months we have actually boosted them.[17]

Nevertheless the Foreign Office insisted the Yugoslav government rebuke Mihailovic. This duly happened and prompted the riposte:

> with the weapons so far received by air, I could not even equip 200 men, and I had still not been sent any explosives. Yet we were being requested to destroy public objects which, however much they were willing, units of the Yugoslav army could not carry out. I deny the suggestion that I have any kind of connection with the Italians. Some of our units have simply succeeded in fooling the Italians, and in this way extracting a greater quantity of weapons from them. I said in my speech to Colonel Bailey that he would do well, in his report to London, to stress that we were ourselves using these weapons against the Italians.

Churchill, too, was annoyed and warned the London Yugoslavs that if Mihailovic did not curb his language British support might be dispensed elsewhere. However he also reminded the Foreign Office on 29 March that, while Mihailovic's attitude was intolerable, it was perhaps understandable in the absence of real assistance:

> He is certainly maltreating us, but I believe he is also double-crossing the Italians. His position is terrible, and it is not much use preaching to the "toad beneath the harrow". We must not forget the very little help we can give.[18]

Four days later Churchill sent a note to the Chiefs of Staff Committee: "I believe that, in spite of his present naturally foxy attitude, Mihailovic will throw his whole weight against the Italians the moment we are able to give him any effective help."[19] By contrast, Bailey recommended SOE Cairo cease further supply drops to Mihailovic. Klugmann and his colleagues were only too eager to concur. They were resumed only after Mihailovic had submitted to a further chastisement from his London masters.

News was beginning to filter into London, via Enigma intercepts, of negotiations with the Germans, set in train by the Partisans in early March, ostensibly to secure an exchange of prisoners. Djilas says Tito told them to describe the negotiations as merely "an exchange of the wounded".[20] Tito himself was to call them "consultations", as have the more respectful Yugoslav historians ever since. Vladimir Dedijer details in his *War Diaries* several previous prisoner exchanges during 1942. Djilas mentions in his *Wartime* memoirs an even earlier exchange in November 1941 between the Partisans in Montenegro and the Italian occupiers there. He also tells of a prisoner exchange in August 1942 between the Partisans and the Germans. The Germans themselves recorded negotiations with the Partisans in November 1942 that led to an exchange of prisoners and "a sort of armistice". The latter was to allow the Partisans to withdraw to an area held by the Italians where they were to be left undisturbed provided they attacked no Axis troops and allowed the free transport of minerals and supplies to Hitler's forces. There had also been an exchange of prisoners with the Ustashi in September 1942, for which the Soviets had reproved Tito. This did not discourage him from negotiating a further exchange in January 1943, abruptly ended by the German offensive.

A much more disquieting aspect of the March 1943 negotiations was that the Partisans had sought respite from the German encirclement so as to attack Mihailovic and hopefully push him back into Serbia. According to the German summary of the proceedings,

> the delegation sees no reason to fight the Germans since they want to fight only the Cetniks. They are an independent national movement, labelled communistic because they wanted to have no connection with London ... The People's Army of Liberation want to join in a war against England in case of a landing [in the Balkans] ... The question of an armistice was cautiously indicated.

Apparently the Germans were told that, because Mihailovic was their mutual enemy, there was no reason for them to fight each other. It was suggested that they agree respective territories of interest. In exchange for a truce the Partisans offered to cease sabotaging the Belgrade-Zagreb railway. Dedijer says Tito had already sent orders to the Party's provincial committee for Bosnia and Herzegovina "not to take action against the Germans since this would not serve the interests of our present operations". His motive became clear when he also indicated to them:

> Our most important task is now to annihilate the Chetniks of Draza Mihailovic and smash their administrative apparatus which constitutes the greatest obstacle to the spread of our national-liberation struggle.

Wilhelm Hoettl, a senior officer in the German Secret Service in Yugoslavia at this time, maintains Tito had promised that

> if the Germans would undertake not to attack him inside a certain reserve territory to be agreed upon, he would refrain from extending

his revolt to other parts of the Croat State. As an earnest of his good faith he was prepared also to abstain for an agreed and specified period from all acts of terrorism and sabotage.[21]

The Partisan negotiators were Milovan Djilas, Koca Popovic (commander of the First Proletarian Brigade and perhaps the most anti-British of Tito's generals) and Vladimir Velebit (a lawyer and close friend of Tito's who spoke German extremely well, having been educated in Vienna). Djilas and Popovic both spoke German too. Djilas did not disclose his name to the Germans for fear he would be marked down for instant execution. The negotiations lasted from 11 to 30 March. They took the Partisan leaders to the German headquarters at Sarajevo and to Zagreb, where Djilas was allowed to visit a girl friend and Velebit to see his parents.

What the British did not know then, and was revealed only long afterwards, was that the Partisans had proposed joint action with the Germans to oppose an Allied landing on the Yugoslav coast. Wilhelm Hoettl confirms this. Djilas says, "we didn't shrink from declarations that we would fight the British if they landed".[22] Nora Beloff maintains, in *Tito's Flawed Legacy*:

> It was to fend off this risk that in November 1942 Tito put out his first feelers to discover whether the Germans would accept an arrangement which would allow him to concentrate all his forces on wiping out the Cetniks before the Allies arrived.

The Germans did not think the time then ripe, they did though in March 1943 when their military situation had dramatically worsened with their defeat at Stalingrad the previous month. Hitler feared the Allies might threaten his rear with a landing in the Balkans. Mihailovic looked forward to such a landing, which would trigger his Serb uprising and hence increase his stature with the Allies; Tito feared it. If Yugoslavia were to be occupied by the British and Americans, it would be difficult, if not impossible, for him to carry through his communist revolution.

To stir things up between Moscow and London, and perhaps to divert Soviet attention from his "consultations" with the Germans, about which they were already suspicious, Tito had signalled Stalin:

> On Mihailovic's staff there are now some twenty-five English officers who dress in Serbian national costume ... Their senior, a colonel, claims to represent the English government ... Mihailovic and the English officers often meet with representatives of the Italian administration ... Among not only our soldiers but also the whole

population, hatred is growing against the English for not starting a second front in Europe.[23]

There is no record of whether Stalin took this signal seriously or even replied to it.

The prisoner exchanges did occur. They included Tito's wife, Herta Haas, though the Germans did not realise who she was. Vladimir Velebit says she was deeply hurt to discover Tito had taken a mistress immediately after leaving her behind in Zagreb two years before when she was about to have their baby. She never forgave him for this and took the opportunity to join another Partisan unit in Slovenia. She married again after the war, had two daughters and maintained contact with Djilas through his second wife. Tito wanted to give her a medal on her sixtieth birthday, but it was refused.

The Partisans were granted their requested respite from German attack while they fought Mihailovic and the Montenegrin Chetniks. The *de facto* truce lasted more than six weeks. According to Djilas

> the Germans indicated that they would cease operations as soon as we stopped our raids on the railroad line in Slavonia... Tito immediately ... stopped the operations of the Slavonian Partisans, particularly on the Zagreb-Belgrade railroad.[24]

Djilas maintains Tito told his forces:

> Do not fight Germans [as] your most important task at this moment is to annihilate the Chetniks of Draza Mihailovic and to destroy their command apparatus which represents the greatest danger to the development of the National Liberation Struggle.

Djilas says the agreement with the Germans did not give him "any pangs of conscience ... military necessity compelled us".[25] It was the same reason Mihailovic's commanders had given for their temporary compacts with the Italians, which Partisan propaganda branded as treacherous collaboration!

When told by Djilas that the Germans had treated him well, Tito apparently replied: "Yes, it seems that the German army has kept something of the spirit of chivalry".[26] The March 1943 "consultations" were to lead to further exchanges of prisoners. There was certainly another later that year, and one in March 1944. Between then and the end of the war there were at least forty meetings between Partisan representatives and the Germans, leading to the release of more than six hundred Partisan prisoners. In July 1944, when an Allied landing on the Istrian coast was rumoured, the Slovene Partisans offered the Germans an armistice.

Some local German commanders did favour temporary agreements with the Partisans to help them eliminate Mihailovic's forces. They argued that publicising such arrangements would help undermine the morale of resistance movements elsewhere in occupied Europe. Hitler, though, vetoed any idea of a long-term truce with what he dismissed as "communist bandits", saying, "I don't parley with rebels – I shoot them".[27] Ribbentrop produced a further reason when he wrote, on 21 April 1943, to the German Ambassador with Pavelic's administration in Zagreb who had advocated the March truce. He reminded him that Hitler had recently demanded Mussolini end his agreements with the Chetniks: "I must point out that it is not for us to play off the Chetniks and the Partisans against each other by clever tactics, but to destroy them both." Siegfried Kasche, the ambassador in question, had evidently told Ribbentrop: "in all of the negotiations with the Partisans to date ... [the] reliability of Tito's promises [was] confirmed".[28] This suggests there had been other agreements between the Germans and the Partisans.

Bailey's report of 22 March, outlining these recent negotiations without giving damaging details, was held up in Cairo and not received in London until 22 May, two months later. Most likely James Klugmann was responsible for the delay. Bailey's signals were transcribed in his office before being passed on to SOE London. But London had already heard through Enigma intercepts in mid-March that negotiations were taking place, though they did not know the incriminating particulars. They suspected that the Germans might have armed the Partisans in their successful fight against Mihailovic:

> If it is confirmed it would show that the Italians and Germans are arming both sides so as to exploit their mutual hatred and divert attention from themselves ... it would also show that the Partisans are no better than Mihailovic.[29]

By mid-April SIS was reporting that the German offensive had fizzled out. The Partisans had survived, albeit severely battered, while Mihailovic's men seemed to have suffered "a major reverse".[30] The Chetniks had been pushed back into Montenegro and Serbia and never re-emerged. Chetnik morale was devastated by the Neretva defeat. Thereafter Mihailovic became weaker, the Partisans stronger. Any prospect of his eliminating them militarily had vanished. Politically, however, it was still in his interests to maintain a sufficiently large force for him to be reckoned a serious contender at the peace-treaty table. His main task now was to survive, in the hope that his fortunes might change. But once a Balkan invasion by the western Allies was no longer likely, Mihailovic was effectively doomed.

Bailey complained to Cairo on 9 April about "errors of fact" in recent BBC broadcasts. It had been claimed that the Partisans had resumed the initiative in Bosnia and that the Bosnians were now "enthusiastic for the Patriot Army of Liberation". He pointed out that, as the Partisans' "principal fighting is against Chetniks and most people in this part of the country know that, it is senseless to talk of Patriots assuming the initiative in Bosnia". He reminded Cairo that there was little love lost between the Bosnian Muslims and the Serbs. He also reiterated that

> factual inaccuracies greatly weaken BBC prestige, which is one of our best weapons, and when the inaccuracies concern controversial matters grave misunderstandings are liable to ensue, and we cannot afford them.[31]

Mihailovic was caught in a cleft stick over BBC publicity. He liked it, but it brought German attention to his activities and hence reprisals. Without it, he was in danger of being dismissed as inactive and, more critically, a non-runner in the Yugoslav political stakes. He worried about the BBC's admiration for the Partisans. SOE London continued to insist that, while both resistance movements in Yugoslavia should be encouraged, there was not the "slightest possibility of running the two movements in double harness". Mihailovic was still their man.[32]

SOE Cairo thought differently. Therein lay the difficulty. They controlled the supplies to Mihailovic and so could determine the level of support to him. It was clear too that SOE London and the Foreign Office were fighting a losing battle against the exclusive backing the BBC seemed to be giving the Partisans. The German propagandists, relishing the BBC's pro-Partisan stance, were keenly persuading the Serbs their interests were being sacrificed to Britain's need to conciliate the Russians.

Ever more daringly unrepentant, the BBC broadcast on 11 June a thinly veiled comparison between Mihailovic and the cartoon character Colonel Blimp. Mihailovic's inevitable objection was dismissed by PWE as "hypersensitiveness".[33] Other BBC "transgressions", including further claims of Chetnik collaboration, prompted Mihailovic to complain again to the Yugoslav government in London on 19 July:

The propaganda over the London Radio is provoking greater and greater revulsion among the people ... All the shootings in Serbia and other Serb provinces are not announced over the London Radio, neither does it take the part of our people there. The people interpret this as being deliberate and that the Serb sacrifices are in vain.

By way of an explanation, Bailey signalled on 27 July: "In late June members of one of our Missions blew a bridge on a dead end of no practical importance near Vrnjci for demonstration purposes. 80 persons were shot at Kraljevo on 26 June in reprisal." He added that a hundred and twenty schoolboys between the ages of fourteen and seventeen had also been shot there that same day for belonging to a youth organisation affiliated to Mihailovic.[34]

To his credit, Bailey unfailingly reported to Cairo on reprisals. One of his earliest signals, dated 21 January 1943, stated:

In reprisal for demolition of railway-bridge between Petrovac and Pozarevac on 13 December 1942, 50 hostages were shot. The Germans attribute sabotage to Mihailovic's organisation and all shot are described as his supporters.

Again on 28 May 1943: "150 hostages shot 25 May in Kraljevo." Cairo was unmoved by the terrible retribution the Germans were wreaking on the Serb civilians. Their attitude was typical of the British military establishment at this time. Jasper Rootham, one of the liaison officers with Mihailovic, says in his memoirs:

To listen to an account of reprisals from the lips of a BBC announcer and from the lips of the woman whose house has been burnt or whose husband has been killed are two quite different things, as I myself can testify.

Bailey defended Mihailovic further when he telegraphed London on 27 July 1943: "the BBC is losing its reputation for dispassionate and accurate service owing to [the] predominantly Croat character of broadcasts ... [and the] undue prominence given ... to pro-Partisan propaganda."[35] Although PWE felt there was some truth in Bailey's strictures, they claimed they could do little as they had lost control over the content of BBC broadcasts. SOE's titular head, Lord Selborne, who had succeeded Hugh Dalton, had already complained to Eden on 8 July that the BBC's broadcasts for some time "had been unduly biased in favour of the Partisans and against Mihailovic".[36]

An attempt was made in August by the Foreign Office and the Ministry of Information to rein in the BBC and impose a superficial impartiality on its reports about Mihailovic and Tito, but with little effect. When the BBC did praise Mihailovic for an exploit, William Deakin, by then at Tito's headquarters, immediately telegraphed, apparently at Tito's behest, claiming it was a "deliberate and subtle lie". A correction was promptly broadcast. Mihailovic had just survived another kidnapping attempt by a strong German and Bulgarian force. Bailey's archive was captured. It contained details of his adverse comments on some of Mihailovic's commanders and his correspondence with Cairo concerning the BBC and the Partisans. The German propagandists had a field day.

Having gathered from Bailey and Hudson that Mihailovic had only loose control over his commanders in the field, SOE Cairo decided to send British liaison officers to those commanders in Serbia. They began arriving in April 1943, each with a wireless transmitter, and told to communicate directly with Cairo and not through Mihailovic's headquarters. Most of the supplies to Mihailovic now went directly to those officers, eventually seventeen in number. Requests from Cairo for sabotage and information were similarly routed to them.

The amount of sabotage increased sharply, though the input from individual Mihailovic commanders varied greatly. Some were keen to participate, others less so. A few were downright obstructive. Most of them continued to worry about reprisals. One of the liaison officers, Jasper Rootham, recalled in his memoirs, *Miss Fire*, helping to organise an attack on a German boat in the Danube on 25 October 1943. Its skipper, a German, was killed and traffic on the river temporarily disrupted. One hundred and fifty Mihailovic sympathisers in Belgrade were shot three days later. Rootham observed remorsefully: "for this sacrifice of innocent lives no military objective of comparable importance had been achieved and we knew well that it was we ourselves who had forced the action."

In March 1943 SOE Cairo decided to send missions of Croatian-born Canadian communists to Partisan areas. Many were former miners who had migrated to Canada during the lean years of the 1920s and 1930s. Some had fought in the Spanish Civil War. They had been waiting in Cairo since the beginning of the year, looked after by James Klugmann. Curiously enough, Colonel Bailey, helped by Tim Buck, secretary-general of the Canadian Communist Party, had recruited them in Canada during early 1942.

The recruitment probably began as a general trawl by SIS of *émigré* Yugoslavs willing to engage in subversion against the Germans, before being taken over by SOE. SIS's man in North America then was Charles Ellis, whom Peter Wright in his *Spycatcher* exposé names as a Soviet agent. Another SIS senior staffer in North America at that time was Cedric Belfrage, who in 1953 fell foul of Senator McCarthy's communist witch-hunt and was forced to leave the USA. Elisabeth Bentley later identified him as a fellow Soviet spy. The head of SIS Security in London then was of course Kim Philby. In charge of SIS's Yugoslav desk there was John Ennals; his Cairo equivalent was James Miller. All three had been friends of Klugmann at Cambridge. They were known Soviet sympathisers, if not spies – certainly so in the case of Philby. Ennals was eventually to parachute into Yugoslavia. Moscow knew what was happening and no doubt put Tito in the picture.

A special SOE training centre, called Camp X, had been set up in Canada near Toronto, on Lake Ontario. The Yugoslav government-in-exile in London was not told. Of the hundred or so initially recruited, thirty were chosen for the final training which began during late July 1942. Among them was Nikola Kovacevic, then in his mid-fifties, who had been sent by Tito in 1937 to contact Yugoslav *émigrés* in North America. He had settled in Canada illegally, assuming the name Karko Sikic, a *bona fide* resident who had recently died in an accident. Kovacevic claimed in the Belgrade newspaper *Borba* in 1982 that Colonel Bailey, when asked why he was recruiting only communists, although there were many more pro-royalist Yugoslavs in Canada at that time, had replied that only the communists were fighting Germans. Bailey was helped in his recruiting by Captain William Stuart. Stuart had been employed by SIS from the outbreak of the War to work in Yugoslavia under the cover of being Britain's vice-consul in Zagreb. He had been detained by the Italians after the German invasion but had managed to escape to Britain. Born in Yugoslavia, he had been educated there, as well as in Hungary. His mother was Hungarian and his father Scottish. They had migrated to Canada during the 1920s. He had become a Canadian citizen in 1933. He spoke Serbo-Croat, German and Hungarian.

According to David Stafford, in his history of Camp X, Tim Buck told the recruits before they left Canada that they were not to do anything "against the interests of the Party and the progressive movement". They were given the names of Communist Party contacts in Cairo. Vane Ivanovic, a Yugoslav serving with British Intelligence, maintains William Deakin was also involved in the recruitment while working for SOE in North America. Deakin does not mention in his memoir, *The Embattled Mountain*, that he was in North America then. He does say he briefed the Canadian Croats while they were in Cairo:

> One evening in late April 1943, I went to the villa outside Cairo where the Croat group were isolated and tense. After briefing them on the details of our planning and on the latest local picture which had been pieced together, I gave them a firm assurance that our headquarters would only issue final technical instructions if it was considered that the realistic chances of success were high. I remember using the phrase "60-40".

Two separate groups were parachuted by SOE Cairo on 21 April into Partisan areas in eastern Bosnia and western Croatia. They soon made contact with the local Partisans and were evidently warmly welcomed. Tito was clearly expecting them. He indicated so to one of the local Partisan chiefs who had had doubts about their credentials. David Stafford says this chief was told to give the Canadians "necessary information about Chetnik treachery and/or enemy forces but no information about our forces". The Canadians reported that the Partisans would welcome British aid, were well armed with captured weapons and were active against the Axis along its lines of communication. SOE London thought these reports were not impartial, coming as they did from known communists. SOE Cairo believed them totally. The Canadians were to remain with the Partisans until the war's end.

On 26 April SOE Cairo claimed the Partisans were on the verge of eliminating the Chetniks entirely and that the Yugoslav civil war might soon be over. Such "information" could only have come from the Canadian Croats. Apparently Tito let it be known he was ready to receive a British mission, which SOE Cairo was now keen to send. No doubt he had been informed of the Allies' exasperation with Mihailovic, presumably by Klugmann, and was eager to take quick advantage of it. He realised his chances of determining Yugoslavia's future political structure depended upon the attitude of the Allies towards the Yugoslav resistance groups during the war. If the Allies continued aiding the anti-communists, then Mihailovic might still prevail in a post-war Yugoslavia, even if the Soviets were to dominate the rest of south-eastern Europe. Shorn of Allied military aid and political support, Mihailovic could perhaps be eliminated by the Partisans, if not by the Axis. If Tito were to get that aid and support *exclusively* then eliminating Mihailovic would be all the easier.

Even so, Tito was not to know in the spring of 1943 how easy it would be to win that *exclusive* Allied support, how gullible the Allies would be when faced with his blandishments. He was about to pull off *the* confidence trick of the war. Djilas says Stalin was surprised that Tito's clear intention of liquidating Mihailovic and of ruling Yugoslavia post-war met such little resistance from the Allies. The increasing demoralisation of the Ustashi in Croatia and Bosnia-Herzegovina undoubtedly helped Tito. It encouraged Croats and Bosnians to join the Partisans, especially those within the militias who knew they would not be welcomed by Mihailovic's mainly Serb forces. The Comintern suggested Tito contact anti-Bulgarian groups in Macedonia. For historic reasons they were wary of the Serb-dominated Mihailovic forces. He also contacted the communists in Albania under Enver Hoxha. Tito had helped to establish the Party there in November 1941. Hoxha, like Tito, was more interested in eliminating his political rivals than in fighting Germans and Italians.

William Deakin, then aged thirty-one, was chosen to head the British mission to Tito, meant to test the waters prior to sending a full-scale one later in the year. He dropped into Tito's headquarters near Zabljak in Montenegro on 28 May 1943, together with Captain William Stuart, who had helped recruit the Canadian Communists. Stuart was apparently to represent the interests of military intelligence. With them were two radio operators, Walter Wroughton and Corporal Rose, and a marine sergeant who was both cipher-clerk and bodyguard, plus one of the Canadian Croats who was to interpret for Deakin. Rose's real name was Peretz Rosenberg. A Palestine Jew of German origin, he had been planted on SOE Cairo by the Jewish Agency with the aim of finding out what he could about the plight of Jews in Yugoslavia. The Jewish Agency's objective was to create a Jewish state in Palestine. He survived the war and became head of the clandestine radio service of Haganah, the Jewish insurgent organisation dedicated to forcing the British out of Palestine.[37] Deakin does not mention in his memoirs whether he knew of Rosenberg's real mission at the time, though he does admit to visiting him in Israel after the war.

Before he left Cairo, Deakin wrote to Churchill informing him of his mission. Churchill asked to be kept apprised of its progress. SOE Cairo sent Churchill at this time two memoranda on Yugoslav affairs that, according to Deakin, "implied a clear departure from existing policy of exclusive support of Mihailovic". Desmond Morton, Churchill's special assistant on intelligence matters, intervened at the behest of the Foreign Office to delay the memoranda reaching the British Prime Minister, but it was only a temporary hold-up. Thereafter Deakin reported directly to Churchill. Cairo tried to persuade the Foreign Office on 23 May to denounce, via the BBC, three of Mihaolovic's subordinate commanders for allegedly collaborating with the Italians. It was meant, so it was said, to ease Deakin's acceptance by the Partisans. The Yugoslav government was not to be told in advance. No doubt James Klugmann was behind this, but he was unsuccessful.

Deakin arrived in the middle of a massive German offensive against the Partisans, known as Operation *Schwarz*. Involving five German and three Italian divisions, plus some Bulgarian and Croatian formations – 117,000 men in all – it had first been launched on 15 May against Mihailovic. Taken by surprise, his casualties had been heavy – 3,764 captured and 17 killed according to Enigma decrypts. The Germans were to claim far more against the Partisans – 13,000 dead or taken prisoner. The Enigma decrypts put the German losses at 583 killed, 425 missing and 1,760 wounded.

According to the official Enigma historian, Sir Harry Hinsley,

> the Enigma decrypts contained no evidence of Cetnik collaboration with the Germans. On the contrary, they showed that though the Germans had long been aware of the existence of complex rivalries between Mihailovic and non-Mihailovic factions among the Cetniks, they were becoming increasingly alarmed about the collaboration of Mihailovic's forces with the Italians – and so much so that when planning Operation *Schwarz* they were determined to override Italian objections to the rounding-up and disarming of Mihailovic's bands. They initially insisted in the face of Italian opposition that all Cetniks should be rounded up and on Hitler's orders took measures to withhold the plan from the Italians for as long as possible. In reply to Italian demands for exemption at least for Cetniks outside the fighting area, they then warned the Italians that they had Sigint [Signal Intelligence – the general term for the processes of interception and decryption and the intelligence they produced] evidence that the Cetniks were playing off Germany against Italy and instructed their own forces that "no Cetnik formations whose leaders were proved to be in touch with Mihailovic are to be spared".

Vladimir Dedijer, in his *War Diaries*, says Tito delayed escaping the German encirclement to await Deakin's arrival, such was the importance he placed on the mission. Dedijer complained: "Every hour wasted costs us dearly." Deakin was soon wounded in his foot by shrapnel from the same bomb that hurt Tito's shoulder and killed both Captain William Stuart and the commander of Tito's bodyguard. Stuart's death meant Deakin was now effectively on his own. Not speaking the language, he would have to rely for interpreting on his Canadian Croat companion who was of course a communist. He was very much at the Partisans' mercy for information.

Hitherto an academic, this was Deakin's first experience of war. The circumstances of his wounding and the shared dangers bonded him powerfully to Tito in a personal and permanent way, as he was later to admit. According to some of his colleagues, he thereafter thought of Tito as a blood brother. Deakin states in his memoirs, *The Embattled Mountain*, that during the Partisans' terrifying retreat from Mount Durmitor, "I had taken on by stages a binding and absolute identity with those around me". Fitzroy Maclean's biographer Frank McLynn relates how "Deakin soon became an enthusiastic advocate for the Partisans. His reports ... provided more nails for Mihailovic's coffin." His early signals were glowing in their estimates of the Partisans' strength and morale. He claimed they were a much bigger annoyance to the Germans than was previously thought. Needless to say these signals were passed with unusual speed to Churchill.

Djilas by contrast described the Partisans at this time as a disorganised rabble. They fled from the Germans across the many ridges and peaks of Mount Durmitor, and over the Piva, Tara, and Sutjeska rivers with their deep gorges. They hid in caves in the canyon walls by day, escaping the incessant bombing and machine-gunning of the Stukas and Dorniers, yet suffered horrendous casualties. Beset by disease, especially typhus, they had little food and scant medical supplies. They were forced to eat their horses, abandon their wounded and execute their prisoners. Thereafter neither side took prisoners.

Vladimir Dedijer's wife Olga, a surgeon who had been in charge of one of the medical units, was killed in the crossing of the Sutjeska River. This was another of the escapes from German encirclement which became a Partisan legend and even a Hollywood film with Richard Burton playing Tito. Djilas recalls, in *Wartime*, revisiting the crossing site five years later and noticing remnants of the slain still lying there. He says "they took steps to have the bones collected properly: with the Sutjeska legend there also arose the need for its material enshrinement".

Djilas maintains the losses "were enormous: around 7,000 picked men, or almost every other comrade". The Germans were particularly ruthless to civilians encountered en route. Few buildings were left intact. More than fifty villages were razed to the ground. Deakin observes: "The scattered dead lay, spilt in heaps, as if by a giant hand, across this landscape of the moon." But the Partisans had again survived. Tito now moved his headquarters back into Bosnia, to Jajce, where Deakin arranged for a British army surgeon to be parachuted in with much-needed medicines and bandages. Other supplies and additional liaison officers were flown in as well. That Deakin and his entourage had also survived says much for their bravery. Djilas describes Tito as looking drawn and gaunt after the escape from Zabljak, having lost so much weight. Exasperated at the failure of their latest offensive, in mid-July 1943 the Germans spread posters around Bosnia and Serbia of both Tito and Mihailovic, offering rewards of 100,000 gold marks each for their capture, dead or alive. The BBC mentioned only the poster of Tito, as have most histories of the period since.

Churchill hoped Tito would place himself under the overall command of the British military chiefs, and perhaps even consider co-operating with Mihailovic. Deakin was soon disabused. SOE London was shocked there was no mention in Deakin's directive of any attempt at peace making between the Partisans and the Chetniks. Bailey had been ordered to seek such co-operation at Mihailovic's headquarters. The Foreign Office had secured Mihailovic's agreement to obey the directives of the Commander-in-Chief Middle East in all operational matters. He had little alternative; otherwise he would receive no aid. As a replacement for Stuart, Flight Lieutenant Kenneth Syers was parachuted in to collate intelligence material on behalf of SIS and to act as Deakin's deputy. Deakin came to rely on Syers for information regarding Partisan activities, as did Fitzroy Maclean when he joined them at Tito's headquarters. Maclean's biographer Frank McLynn identifies Syers as a communist. According to Vladimir Velebit, the main liaison between Tito and the British mission, Syers was "relatively active after the war in the British Communist Party".

Michael Lees, in *The Rape of Serbia*, quotes Velebit as saying:

> One of my most important tasks, as I conceived it, was to convince [Deakin] that the Cetniks, the Mihailovic people, not only did not fight the enemy but they actually collaborated with him in many various and different ways. My system of indoctrinating Deakin was to take him to a stream nearby, very nice cool and fresh water, where we used to bathe in the whole afternoon: I took always a bunch of

captured documents with me, and I read them to him and translated them and I gave him many transcripts for his own use. I think this course of indoctrination, if I may call it that, worked very well because Deakin got more and more convinced that the Mihailovic movement was really no good at all, and was really a kind of fifth column supporting the enemy rather than a resistance force.

Djilas says Deakin was well aware at this time that the Partisans were executing Mihailovic's supporters.

By mid-1943 a Balkan invasion by the Allies was no longer likely. The Americans were dead set against it and the British could not have mounted it on their own. Yugoslavia would be freed by the Red Army who would favour Tito's Partisans. Julian Amery, in *Approach March*, commented:

> There is in our national character a strong urge to find a moral justi-fication for political decisions. Instead of admitting that we had failed to get our strategy accepted and that it was therefore no longer practical politics to support Mihailovic, we made a virtue of neces-sity and turned the man who had been our friend into a scapegoat for our own impotence. This hypocrisy, and it was nothing less, was accepted by British opinion while a more realistic admission of our true motives would have been profoundly shocking. But few people outside were taken in.

Hitler, however, still worried about an invasion of the Balkans. He told the assembled generals and admirals at his so-called Naval Conference in May 1943 he "could not believe that a primary objec-tive of the Allies would not now be the strategically vulnerable, econ-omically vital, Balkan peninsula". He had on 14 May declared to his military chiefs:

> If the worst comes to the worst, the Italian peninsula can be sealed off somehow. It is of decisive importance for us to hold the Balkans: oil, copper, bauxite, chrome, above all security, so that there is not a complete smash there if things get worse in Italy.

According to the eminent Cambridge historian Ralph Bennett (himself an Enigma decoder), in his *Ultra and Mediterranean Strategy*, carefully planted Allied rumours in the autumn of 1943 of a Balkan invasion

> were, for the time being at least, doing more to focus Axis attention on the Balkans than the activities of either Tito or Mihailovic. Fears that the Allies might be contemplating a seaborne descent upon

Greece, the Aegean, or the Dodecanese persisted long after the landing in Sicily.

Because of these rumours Hitler moved divisions from the Russian front and Western Europe into Greece and elsewhere in the Balkans. As late as the summer of 1944 he still worried about a Serbian uprising coinciding with an invasion which he told his staff "could produce catastrophic results".

General Warlimont, Deputy Chief of the Operations Staff of the *Wehrmacht*, observed in his memoirs, *Inside Hitler's Headquarters*, that Field Marshal von Weichs, Commander-in-Chief in Southeast Europe, came to Hitler's headquarters on 22 August 1944. He sought permission to arrange a combined operation with the Chetniks against the Partisans. Hitler refused. He maintained that the Serbs were "the only real people in the Balkans", hence Germany must "determinedly resist all plans for a greater Serbia". Warlimont's boss, Colonel-General Jodl, summarised Hitler's point of view as: "a Serbian army must not be allowed to exist. It is better to have some danger from Communism."

Hitler was undoubtedly also concerned about Italy, whose people yearned for an end to the war and whose soldiers had not much fight left in them. Mussolini had been given a virtual ultimatum from some of his senior generals to sue for peace. He had met Hitler on 17 July 1943 to discuss the matter but Hitler refused to countenance any thought of the Italians making a separate peace. When Mussolini reported back to his generals, they took the matter out of his hands, persuading the Italian king to sack him on 24 July. Three weeks later negotiations were opened in Lisbon with the Allies and Italy capitulated on 9 September. But by then enough German troops had been poured into Italy and her possessions in the Balkans to meet Hitler's security needs.

SOE Cairo had sent Bailey a mischievous signal on 29 May to be passed to Mihailovic. Emanating no doubt from James Klugmann, it suggested that, because his forces were so weak following the recent German offensive against them, he should seriously consider withdrawing to south-eastern Serbia. This would leave the rest of the country to the Partisans, who "represent a good and effective fighting force in all parts whereas only the Quislings represent General Mihailovic". The Foreign Office was appalled when it found out and demanded the signal be rescinded. It eventually was, though not before harm had been done. Bailey had passed it on to Mihailovic who, needless to say, had been furious.

Michael Lees, one of the British liaison officers with Mihailovic, reminded me before he died that it was just three days after this signal had been sent that SOE Cairo had parachuted him into Mihailovic's area to work with one of his commanders. If SOE Cairo really thought these commanders were quislings, why, he asked, were they risking his life so wantonly? Eight other missions like his were sent to Mihailovic at that time. They were all located within sabotaging distance of such key targets as chrome, copper, lead and zinc mines, as well as the strategic north-south railway line. Lees also said that, when he and the other liaison officers were parachuted into Serbia, they were not briefed in any detail about Tito and the Partisans. Nor was there any mention of Deakin's mission, although they departed from the same airport, Derna, apparently on the very same evening.

SOE Cairo was clearly influencing the generals. On 8 June 1943 the Middle East Defence Committee declared in a telegram to London: "The Partisans are now the most formidable anti-Axis element in Yugoslavia and our support of them is therefore logical and necessary". Churchill agreed. He pressed for supplies to be dispatched to the Partisans immediately and additional aircraft released for the purpose. "This demand", he told his Defence Secretary, General Ismay, on 22 June, "has priority even over the bombing of Germany."[38] The air resources needed to send up to five hundred tons a month of arms and equipment to the Yugoslav partisans from 30 September onwards would be "a small price to pay", Churchill told the Staff Conference the next day, "for the diversion of Axis forces caused by resistance in Yugoslavia". Every effort should be made, he said, "to increase the rate of delivering supplies... It was essential to keep this movement going."[39] Churchill says in his memoirs that that summer "the Balkans, and especially Yugoslavia, never left my thoughts".[40]

Churchill was impressed by the Enigma decrypts at the time of Operation *Schwarz* that spring, which seemed to indicate that thirty-three Axis divisions were operating in Yugoslavia. However, according to the official Enigma historian Sir Harry Hinsley, the number of German divisions in the whole of the Balkans had increased between March and 10 July from eight to only eighteen, largely in reaction to the British deceptions. Nevertheless Churchill telegraphed his Commander-in-Chief, Near East, General Alexander, on 22 July that he was sending him a full account which I have had prepared from "Boniface" [Churchill's cover name for Enigma decrypts] and all other sources, of the marvellous resistance put up by the so-called partisan followers of Tito in Bosnia and the powerful cold-blooded manoeuvres of Mihailovic in Serbia ... Great prizes lie in the Balkan direction.[41]

Although more planes were promised, it took further interventions by Churchill before the airdrops increased. SOE's official historian, William Mackenzie, maintains "there is no doubt that in this crucial phase of its development SOE and the Resistance movements which it led were sustained very largely by the personal influence of Mr Churchill."

As a result of Deakin's enthusiastic messages, Churchill now decided to send a full-scale mission to Tito. It was to be led by a brigadier who would prepare an in-depth study of Yugoslav resistance as a whole. He would also have a political adviser. Lieutenant-Colonel Fitzroy Maclean, a thirty-two-year-old Conservative MP who spoke Russian, had been summoned to London by the Foreign Office with a view to appointment as that adviser. Maclean had so far had an adventurous war with the Special Air Services (SAS) in Iraq and Libya. Previously he had spent some time in the Soviet Union as a diplomat, so was experienced in the ways of the Foreign Office. Mihailovic's mission, too, was to have a new head: forty-six-year-old Brigadier Charles Armstrong, a regular soldier of twenty-five years' experience and a veteran of Dunkirk and North Africa. His political adviser was to be Colonel Bailey. Both missions were to have American observers.

Maclean got himself invited for the weekend to Chequers, the British Prime Minister's country home, where he talked Churchill into giving *him* the job of leading the Tito mission. It helped that his father had been with Churchill at Sandhurst and that he was a close friend of Winston's only son, Randolph. They had been at Eton together. He had previously supped with the Churchill family, and for a time had dated Winston's niece Clarissa, who was eventually to marry Anthony Eden. Churchill wrote to Eden on 28 July that he wanted Maclean – "a man of daring character with Parliamentary status and Foreign Office training" – to head the mission with the rank of brigadier and to be his own political adviser. "What we want", Churchill insisted, "is a daring Ambassador-Leader with these hardy and hunted guerrillas".[42] Maclean was certainly a high-flyer. In just two years he had leapt in rank from lieutenant to brigadier! His cousin Michael Lees claims the clinching factor was Maclean's offer to take Churchill's troublesome son Randolph along with him and thus get him out of his father's hair.

It so happened that, during the evening Maclean was at Chequers, news came through that Mussolini had been toppled. Maclean says Churchill took him aside and said:

> This makes your job more important than ever. The German position in Italy is crumbling. We must now put all the pressure we can on them on the other side of the Adriatic. You must go in without delay.[43]

Maclean was to report directly to Churchill and to consider himself Churchill's "own personal representative with the Partisan command". To that end, according to Basil Davidson, "he provided himself with a separate and secret radio link, by wavelength and code, between himself in Yugoslavia and General Wilson in Cairo, as well as with the Prime Minister in London".[44] He could bypass SOE and the Foreign Office.

Michael Lees is on record as saying ruefully that

> the British liaison officers with Mihailovic had no imprimatur from Churchill. We were on our own with hosts who were being deceived, betrayed, and denounced as enemies by our own headquarters. Our requests and our signals were being ignored. Our successes were being attributed to the Partisans, not to our hosts, the Loyalists.[45]

Maclean is similarly on record as saying he asked for a communications system separate from SOE as "various friends of mine who had been dropped into Greece and elsewhere had told me that large numbers of their most important signals had been either lost or deliberately suppressed."[46] While each of the British liaison officers with Mihailovic's forces communicated directly with Cairo, and not through Mihailovic's headquarters, those with Tito communicated with the outside world via Maclean himself. It meant there was no supervision from Mihailovic's headquarters. SOE wished to oversee its officers in the field directly and to co-ordinate their operations. But Maclean did not see himself as part of SOE. He had a different agenda.

Maclean's instructions from the Foreign Office dated 11 September were

> to endeavour to bring about the co-ordination of the military activities of Mihailovic and the Partisans (and any other resistance elements in Yugoslavia) under the direction of the Commander-in-Chief, Middle East ... to endeavour to reconcile all such groups to

each other and persuade them to subordinate the racial, religious and ideological differences which separate them today, so that Yugoslav unity may be preserved and the political, economic and constitutional problems which today confront the country may be settled by the free will of the people. It is also the hope of His Majesty's Government that King Peter will return as the constitutional monarch.[47]

Maclean says he sought further clarification from Churchill of these instructions and was told:

As the whole of Western civilisation was threatened by the Nazi menace, we could not afford to let our attention be diverted from the immediate issue by considerations of long-term policy. We were as loyal to our Soviet allies as we hoped they were to us. My task was simply to help find out who was killing the most Germans and suggest means by which we could help them to kill more. Politics must be a secondary consideration.[48]

Such an over-simplification of motives was to cause much rancour within the London intelligence community. SOE's Bickham Sweet-Escott recalled in his memoirs: "The conflict between our short-term military objective and our long-term political aims which some of us had been afraid of for so long had now become much more than a theoretical possibility."

Basil Davidson parachuted into Tito's headquarters in Bosnia on 15 August. His task was to contact Hungarian resistance groups currently inside Yugoslavia and eventually to establish himself in Hungary. He had run a news service there before the war, while working for the British secret service. The intention then had been to train anti-Nazi Hungarians for sabotage operations should the Germans occupy the country. He had had to flee when Hungary joined the Axis in April 1941. His mission on this occasion proved unsuccessful too. He remained, though, for more than a year with the Partisans in the Vojvodina, the flat, fertile area between the Danube and its tributary the Sava.

Five days before Davidson arrived at Tito's headquarters, ranks had been introduced into the Partisan army. Milovan Djilas says Tito felt it necessary to meet the British brigadiers and colonels on an equal footing. Overnight the members of the politburo all became generals. Intriguingly, Vladimir Dedijer recollects, in his *War Diaries*, meeting on 18 August an English mission in a town called Prekaja: "A few people from this mission are behaving oddly. They salute with the clenched fist. One of them asked… 'How can I join the Communist Party?'"

Mussolini's fall had renewed Churchill's interest in the Balkans. On 14 September he was rebuking his Chiefs of Staff for not exploiting

> the highly favourable possibilities now offered to us without in any way prejudicing the build-up in Italy. We should certainly try to obtain some seaports on the eastern side of the Adriatic and excite and sustain the patriot activities to the utmost.[49]

He raised again the issue of a Balkans campaign with Eden who was in Moscow on 20 October. The Americans and the Soviets were still against it.

On 18 November he again berated his military chiefs for not having exploited the confusion in the Balkans following Italy's capitulation: "after the initial shock of Italy's surrender, the Germans seemed to have recovered themselves and to be pressing back the Partisans at almost all points".[50] Two days later he was complaining that a "complete neglect to do anything effective has taken place in this extremely important Balkan theatre".[51] He was still lamenting the following January: "We are letting the whole of this Dalmatian coast be sealed off from us by an enemy who has neither the command of the air nor the sea."[52]

Italy's exit from the war on 8 September had eased the harassment of the Partisans and the Germans could no longer spare divisions to mount the massive encircling movements of old. This meant that much military booty, including ammunition, tanks, heavy weapons, vehicles and food, was up for grabs. Tito was able to obtain much more of it than Mihailovic – six divisions' worth – as he was in the Italian occupation area. Nevertheless he complained to Deakin about not having been told an Italian armistice was in the offing. He moved swiftly into Dalmatia, taking over enough arms and equipment from the Italians to double the size of his field army, and enlarged considerably the territory he controlled. His supporters in Slovenia were equally quick to grab Italian spoils before the Germans could. The Italian collapse was a psychological boost for the Partisans as well as a practical one. It made possible control of Yugoslavia's Adriatic coastline – the point of entry for any Allied invasion – though such control was to be intermittent until late 1944.

The Partisans speedily used their new weaponry to wipe out many of their political opponents, especially in Slovenia. Mihailovic was furious when Colonel Bailey barred him from disarming in late September the nearly fifteen-thousand-strong Italian Venezia

Division then occupying much of Montenegro. Allegedly the Allied Commander-in-Chief preferred the Italians to keep their weapons and to come under his jurisdiction. Mihailovic's forces had moved into the area where the division was based, killing at least two hundred Germans and putting several hundred more to rout, but the BBC attributed this success to Tito's Partisans. When eventually the Partisans came on the scene, they did not feel bound by Cairo's restraints and straightaway disarmed the Italians. The weapons were then used to destroy most of Mihailovic's forces in Montenegro. Bailey, again on Cairo's orders, had dissuaded Mihailovic from strengthening his forces there.

The Italian debacle, in particular the Partisans' acquisition of most of the Italian equipment, tilted the balance of strength firmly in their favour. It was the undoing of those Chetnik groups who had relied on the Italians for supplies, and in some cases protection from Partisan harassment. The Partisans were able the more easily to pick them off, which they promptly proceeded to do. Western aid to the Chetniks diminished; that to the Partisans rose dramatically. The Red Army's successes against the Germans that autumn were a further boost for the Partisans, and a setback for Mihailovic. They made it even more certain Yugoslavia would be liberated by the Soviets. His contribution to that liberation was no longer necessary.

Nevertheless Mihailovic was to remain convinced to the end that the British and Americans still needed him for political reasons. According to the American-Croat historian Jozo Tomasevich:

> The Chetnik leaders, and Mihailovic in particular, were confident that the Western Allies because of their opposition to the possible spread of Communism would never allow the Russians to acquire a decisive influence in the Balkans. The Chetniks made the erroneous assumption that they were indispensable to the Western Allies and therefore must be supported by them. In his telegram of 7 November 1943, to his commanders, Mihailovic put this idea in a nutshell: "England can never relinquish the Balkans to Russian influence, because in that case it loses the Mediterranean – this is clear to everybody".[53]

Within Croatia itself the Italian collapse led to further confusion among the Ustashi. Many now joined the Partisans, who were more than willing to forget their previous misdemeanours. As the war went on, Croatia became more and more a German dependency. The Allies were slow to take advantage of the Italian debacle. The Germans were allowed to re-occupy the areas in the Balkans formerly garrisoned by their Axis partner, notably the islands off Yugoslavia's Dalmatian coast that held the key to supplying by sea either the Partisans or Mihailovic's forces. Vladimir Dedijer, in his *War Diaries*, says of the Italian surrender: "That Mussolini has fallen, that Italy has been ousted from the war, thanks must be given primarily to the Red Army. It was the one which buried all hope that the Axis forces had for a victory in the war." So much for the Anglo-American successes in North Africa, or for the invasion of Sicily. It shows where Partisan loyalties lay that autumn of 1943.

CHAPTER SIX

Enter Fitzroy Maclean

"we could only report about
the partisans"
JOHN HENNIKER-MAJOR

FITZROY MACLEAN dropped into Tito's headquarters at Jajce in Bosnia on 18 September 1943. With him, as his deputy and chief military adviser, was Colonel Vivian Street, twenty-nine years old, a regular officer. He had had a spell as a prisoner-of-war when captured by the Italians; he was eventually to become a major-general. Accompanying them were Sergeant Duncan, an SAS orderly who had been with Maclean on several of his previous exploits, and an American, Major Linn Farish. Deakin was not there to greet them. He was on his way to Split on the coast to help organise the surrender of the Italian forces there. Three days later there parachuted in Major John Henniker-Major, twenty-eight years old. Like Maclean he had spent some time in the Foreign Office. He was later to become the British Ambassador to Jordan, and then to Denmark. Also Major Peter Moore, a demolitions expert, already awarded the DSO and MC; two other sappers, Major Michael Parker and Lieutenant Donald Knight; and Major Gordon Alston who had been David Stirling's intelligence officer in the SAS and was now to represent the SIS at Tito's headquarters. Major Robin Whetherly, a cavalryman, Corporals Dickson and Andrew, and two wireless operators made up the rest of the party.

Henniker-Major, in his memoirs *Painful Extractions*, says their brief

in Winston's inimitable style was short and clear: find out whether partisan or Chetnik was the best resistance group to support; find out Tito's agenda; endeavour to mediate between Tito and Mihailovic; gain Tito's support for the return of the King; supply resistance groups; co-ordinate resistance operations with our own in Italy; evacuate their wounded.

But their

first task, given personally by Winston to our mission, was to discover which of the resistance movements was fighting and killing the
most Germans. This was really the sole criterion on which the government, in the person of Churchill, would decide which group to
back and, of course, *we could only report about the partisans* [my italics].

Deakin returned after a few days to find Maclean already enthusing about the Partisans. Within forty-eight hours of arriving he was
sending Cairo and London reports of Partisan territorial claims and
divisional strengths. These were even more glowing than the reports
Deakin had sent shortly after his arrival in Yugoslavia. His source of
information could only have been the Partisans themselves. According to Henniker-Major, Maclean never mastered Serbo-Croat but
communicated with Tito in Russian. Neither did Deakin speak
Serbo-Croat, while Henniker-Major spoke only some German.
Shortly after their arrival, the western open-palm salute was substi-
tuted among the Partisan leadership for the communist clenched
fist. Associated with the International Brigades of the Spanish Civil
War, Djilas says it had hitherto been the accepted greeting. Evidently
the change was at the behest of the Soviets who were anxious to
minimise overt communist symbolism. Perhaps through force of
habit, most young Partisans continued to prefer the clenched fist, as
the Allied liaison officers with them were to vouch.

Vladimir Velebit was assigned by Tito to liaise with Maclean's
group: in particular, as he admitted later, to see they did not stray
from headquarters. Shortly after arriving, Maclean received an
instruction from the Foreign Office to dissuade Tito from attacking
Mihailovic's forces. Maclean refused to do so: it might damage his
relations with Tito at this early stage; it was well known Tito was
determined to "liquidate" Mihailovic. The diplomats had thought it
a good moment to exert leverage on Tito to end the civil war in
Yugoslavia: clearly he wanted supplies and perhaps needed the Allies
more than they needed him. The Soviets were in no position to help
him. Eighty tons of supplies were dropped to Tito while Maclean was
initially with him. Maclean says he had been promised three times as
much. Even so, it was far more than Mihailovic had received during
the previous two years!

Mihailovic was forever being pressed by the liaison officers with
him, as well as by SOE Cairo, to stop fighting the Partisans. The
Foreign Office and War Office files of the period confirm this. There
is no evidence of similar pressure being exerted on Tito by the liaison officers at his headquarters to stop him attacking Mihailovic.

Maclean is on record as saying he did not pay "all that much attention" to impressing upon Tito "the advisability of coming to terms
with Mihailovic".[1] Michael Lees, one of the liaison officers with
Mihailovic, mentions in his memoirs numerous occasions when he
and his British colleagues prevented Mihailovic's forces attacking the
Partisans, even when the Partisans were ambushing them or hamper-
ing their sabotage operations. It is evident from Maclean's own
memoirs that he sided with Tito in the Yugoslav civil war.

The supplies to Tito were most certainly given with the proviso
that they were not to be used against other Yugoslavs, such as
Mihailovic. Tito never for a moment hesitated in either making this
promise or breaking it. Maclean and his colleagues knew this but did
nothing. The liaison officers with Mihailovic's forces accompanied
the active units and took part in sabotage operations, on many occasions leading those operations. The liaison officers with Tito never
participated in planned actions. They were kept at arm's length by
the political commissars and prevented from interviewing individual
partisans or talking to local villagers.

Eli Popovic, one of the American liaison officers at Tito's headquarters, told me he was never allowed to move freely, he had always
to walk under escort. He never saw any action against Germans,
though he did see some against Mihailovic's forces. He and his
British colleagues with the Partisans relied entirely on what the Partisans told them. They had no independent sources of information
and very few of them spoke Serbo-Croat; he did, but Maclean and
Deakin certainly did not. Evidently Tito did not like the liaison officers with him to be proficient in Serbo-Croat, particularly if they
were Americans of Serbian ancestry. He took the first opportunity to
have Popovic recalled home. Peter Solly-Flood, a liaison officer with
Mihailovic and later a senior British diplomat in Washington, was to
complain that he and his colleagues seemed to be operating to one
set of rules and those with Tito to a completely different set.

It was shortly after Maclean's arrival in Yugoslavia that Tito successfully persuaded the BBC to use the term "National Liberation
Army" rather than Partisans. King Peter had already been cajoled
into making two broadcasts containing complimentary references to
the Partisans. When, in Cairo, he made an appeal for an end to
family quarrels and for all those resisting in Yugoslavia to obey
Mihailovic, the Political Warfare Executive (PWE) refused its re-
broadcast from London, citing technical difficulties. Michael Rose of
the Foreign Office minuted on the file in question: "The failure to

give King Peter's broadcast was a trick on PWE's part ... quite inde-
fensible".[2] When the Foreign Office suggested the London Yugoslavs
be granted broadcasting facilities in Italy, PWE found further technical reasons to prevent it.

In early October PWE directed the BBC to report Partisan operations in all parts of Yugoslavia except Serbia and Macedonia, where
there were few Partisans. They were to report Mihailovic activity
only when "confirmed news of any considerable successes".[3] As confirmation usually lagged behind initial reports, giving time for Tito to
claim Mihailovic's actions as his own, this in effect meant a ban
on mentioning any Mihailovic success. Later that month PWE
instructed its practitioners "to treat the Partisan movement as a military organization, not as a political movement".[4] By early November
the BBC was directed to report Partisan activities in Serbia and
Macedonia, though not to exaggerate their extent.

That Maclean had immediately taken to Tito is indicated time
and time again in his memoirs. No doubt Tito in turn recognised in
Maclean a man as ambitious as he was. Maclean was also a man in a
hurry.

By 5 October, after scarcely two weeks at Tito's headquarters,
Maclean felt he had enough information to write his report. He left
for the Dalmatian coast with Street, Henniker-Major and Duncan to
reconnoitre landing sites for the Royal Navy to ship in supplies.
Street was sent back to Jajce before they reached the coast. Maclean
explained in *Eastern Approaches*:

> The Germans were firmly established across our route and the only
> way of reaching the coast was to get through their lines at night ... we
> should look very foolish if both Vivian and myself were taken
> prisoner. I accordingly decided to send Vivian back to Jajce with the
> bulk of the kit, and to go on to the coast myself, taking with me John
> Henniker-Major and Duncan.

They visited the islands off the Dalmatian coast, in particular
Korcula, where later Maclean was to own property. They also made
contact with the Royal Navy before returning briefly to Jajce to see
Tito. Maclean then made his way back to the islands, this time to Vis.
Here he was picked up and ferried to Bari in Italy, where SOE Cairo
had established itself, and thence by plane via Malta to Cairo.
Curiously Deakin, who was at Tito's headquarters throughout this
period, does not mention in his memoirs Maclean's second visit to

Tito. He says simply that Maclean left on 5 October "to travel over-land to the coast now held in part by Partisan forces since the Italian surrender, and thence by sea to Italy".

Maclean is intriguingly vague about dates. Nowhere does he indicate exactly when he left for Italy or Cairo. His biographer, Frank McLynn, does not throw light on the matter either. However, Donald Hamilton-Hill states in *SOE Assignment* that he flew from Cairo to Brindisi in Italy with Maclean on 15 October and dined with him the following evening in Bari, together with Major General Colin Gubbins, Head of SOE. While there is no mention of this encounter in Gubbins' own biography, there is a reference to Maclean being in Bari on 3 November and then accompanying Gubbins to Malta.

What is certain is that Maclean had been away barely a month and had witnessed hardly any action – in his memoirs he says he saw no warfare – and so had been unable to judge for himself the fighting capability of the Partisans. Like Deakin, he had made no effort to contact Mihailovic or to talk to any of the liaison officers with experience of Mihailovic's forces, although an assessment of their effectiveness was part of his brief. He preferred to rely on information the Partisans pushed his way. Apart from journeying to and from the coast, he saw nothing of the country. He did not visit Serbia, the most populous Yugoslav province and the pivotal battleground in the war against the Germans, bestriding as it did the vital north-south rail and road links between Greece and the *Reich*. However, he was now in the unique position of being the first British liaison officer to come out of Yugoslavia! As his biographer Frank McLynn indicates: "We should not discount the 'being there' factor. Bailey and the others sent out their reports by cable; Fitzroy flew out from Bari with his and accompanied it through the corridors of power in Cairo."

Maclean completed his report within days of his departure from Yugoslavia. Dated 6 November, it was apparently received in Cairo much earlier by Ralph Stevenson, who had taken over from George Rendel as ambassador to the Yugoslav government-in-exile. Rendel, realising Mihailovic was to be dumped, which he found personally distasteful, had asked to be released. It reached London on 12 November and was instantly dubbed "The Blockbuster" by Whitehall insiders. Issued from Churchill's office as a "Special Paper" and circulated to the Commonwealth Prime Ministers, it was even couriered to Roosevelt and the State Department in Washington. The

Chiefs of Staff speedily received copies too, as did all the members of the War Cabinet. Churchill scrawled "most interesting" on his copy. The head of the Foreign Office's Southern Department, Douglas Howard, thought it "wretched". He minuted,

> I am not at all sure that it is in our long-term interest to assist the Partisans to control the whole of Yugoslavia. It may be that they will find themselves in that position as a result of their own efforts, but I am not sure that we should assist them to that end.[5]

The Report[6] contained much that, to say the least, was and still is controversial. It certainly has not stood the test of time. It compares with the infamously dodgy dossiers of Anglo-American intelligence material put out by the British Government in the run-up to the war over Iraq in 2003. Their various claims, although eventually disproved, were politically influential in decision-making at the time. As Michael Lees puts it in *The Rape of Serbia*:

> In about 5,000 words of effusive praise Maclean presented the Partisan claims and pretensions far better than their best public-relations men could have done. In flowering Foreign Office prose he laid out the Partisan case without any wheretofores, howevers, or notwithstandings. He put their case without any serious consideration of any other viewpoint. He assumed the role of Tito's ambassador. But, even more, he assumed the role of Tito's prosecuting counsel in the case against Mihailovic.

Elisabeth Barker, then head of PWE's Balkan section, claimed the Report "gave a big shove to the movement towards dropping Mihailovic which was gathering momentum throughout November and the first half of December 1943".[7] An American commentator was to say: "it is doubtful that Tito himself would have changed a word".[8]

Maclean's opening sentence states: "The Partisan Movement, which now dominates the greater part of Yugoslavia..." but he could not have verified this first-hand. He had not travelled around the country. He had not set foot in Serbia, Yugoslavia's largest province, and neither had Deakin. He and Deakin had not talked to any of the British liaison officers in Serbia and Macedonia. He must have relied solely on what the Partisans told him.

The Foreign Office official deputed to study Maclean's report minuted:

> Brigadier Maclean's information on the predominantly Mihailovic areas (i.e. Serbia proper and parts of Macedonia) cannot be regarded

as reliable, since it can only have been obtained from the Partisans themselves, and their only interest is to make themselves out as strong as possible... Two recent reports from Stockholm ... both state that 75 per cent of the inhabitants of Serbia are pro-Mihailovic, and we have no evidence at present to refute these assertions. If this is in fact the case, we cannot accept the concluding section of Brigadier Maclean's report as a basis for the formulation of our future policy. For example, his statement that if we were to drop them (i.e. Mihailovic and the Chetniks), the leaders would fade away and the rank and file join the Partisans, has as far as our evidence goes no basis in fact and is merely wishful thinking on the part of the Partisans. On present showing, the leaders would not disappear, but would be more likely to join up wholeheartedly with Nedic and the Germans. That might in effect be a solution of our problem, but hardly one which we could justify before the eyes of the world. In effect if we were to drop Mihailovic, we should merely be assisting the Partisans to enforce an authoritarian and unpopular regime on an unwilling Serbian people... Recent reports from Mihailovic leave no doubt that he intends to resist Communism to the last, and if it came to civil war, he would certainly have the full and unqualified support of all those who are at present backing the quisling regime of General Nedic. By throwing up Mihailovic, we should not therefore avoid civil war, but merely take sides in it and irrevocably compromise ourselves in the eyes of the Serbian people.[9]

That Serbia was the key to the whole situation, and that it had not yet been won by the Partisans, is confirmed by Milovan Djilas in *Wartime*:

The Chetniks knew they weren't lost as long as they didn't lose Serbia, just as we knew that we wouldn't win unless we won in Serbia ... Tito indicated ... that the penetration into Serbia was their most important task.

Similarly, the American liaison officer with Mihailovic telegraphed his superiors in Washington on 5 September 1943, saying the British

would think that Mihailovic was not a good boy [and] would give all their support to the Partisans. This straight simple military approach sounds OK till you get here and find that Mihailovic virtually controls all the operations in Serbia proper, Sanjak and part of Montenegro. The Allies cannot ditch Mihailovic here, because they would not find a substitute. The Serbs look to Mihailovic and will follow no other. The Partisans and communism have absolutely no appeal in Serbia ... if the British drop Mihailovic they will have no resistance group in this vital area.[10]

Having been tipped off about this signal – SOE Cairo were reading all the American signals – the British Minister of State in Cairo telegraphed the Foreign Office in London two days later to warn them of the attitudes of the American officers with Mihailovic: "One such officer has been at Mihailovic's headquarters for some time and seems likely to cause trouble owing to tendency to branch out on a line of his own"![11]

Djilas was later to observe how surprised they were that Maclean quickly became a mouthpiece for Tito, even helping him draft replies to messages from London. Maclean admits in *Eastern Approaches* that he did this. Henniker-Major, in his memoirs, confesses that he and Maclean were "perhaps occasionally being a bit too credulous of the partisan gloss on their actions". The chief American observer with Maclean's mission was blunter. He told Washington that the Yugoslavs he had been in contact with "love intrigue and gossip, and are the most profound liars I have ever met".[12]

Maclean in his Report went on to maintain that the Partisan movement "disposes of an Army of some 26 divisions" numbering 220,000 troops of whom "50,000 are said to be in Bosnia, 15,000 in the Sanjak, 20,000 in Croatia, 10,000 in Slavonia, 60,000 in Slovenia and Istria, 25,000 in Dalmatia, 10,000 in the Vojvodina and 30,000 in Serbia and Macedonia".

Such a figure would have put the Partisan strength at more than double that of the Germans in Yugoslavia! Noticing this, a Foreign Office official minuted that, if true, why had the Partisans not driven the Germans out of Yugoslavia long before now, let alone liquidated Mihailovic? Major Linn Farish, the senior American officer at Tito's headquarters, in his own report submitted to Washington at the same time, states: "their present strength is given by them as 180,000 men which are included in 18 divisions". Vladimir Velebit, Tito's main liaison with Maclean, admitted to me that Maclean's figure was an exaggeration. He said no one knew then how many Partisan supporters there were in Yugoslavia, other than those with Tito in Bosnia. There was no way such numbers could be fed, clothed, armed and hidden with the resources the Partisans then had.

By the time Maclean came to write *Disputed Barricade* in 1957, he halved the Partisan figure to 110,000 based, he said then, on a German estimate in December 1943. Stevan Pavlowitch, in his *Yugoslavia* published in 1971, gives an estimate of 60-80,000 made by a correspondent of the London Roman Catholic weekly, *The Tablet,* who in April 1945 had analysed the Partisan and German communiqués during the autumn of 1943. William Deakin in his memoirs quotes a figure of 75,000 but gives the game away by saying "at no time were we in a position to acquire professional and detailed information as to a conventional order of battle of the Partisan forces". The true strength was more likely between 44,000 and 65,000 – about the same number as Mihailovic's force, although Maclean claimed in his Report that the Partisans outnumbered Mihailovic's men by ten to one. The official Yugoslav military encyclopaedia published in Belgrade in 1964 put Mihailovic's strength in Serbia alone in December 1943 at 60,000 – and Mihailovic could call upon more than a quarter of a million Serbian peasants, who were armed, partly trained and standing by to rise up once the Allies began liberating their country. Tito had no such reserve.

As regards Maclean's claim of 30,000 Partisans in Serbia and Macedonia, he was to admit, in his memoirs *Eastern Approaches* published in 1949, that even by the spring of 1944 the Partisan strength in Serbia "was to all intents and purposes an unknown quantity". He also declares in those memoirs that, when his subordinate John Henniker-Major was sent to Serbia in April 1944, "he had found the Partisans neither numerous nor well equipped" and repeats that by September 1944 "the Partisans in Serbia were still to some extent an unknown quantity". Maclean reported to London on 29 September 1944:

> At the beginning of this year Partisan forces in Serbia were limited to a few scattered, ill-equipped detachments of a few hundred men each, who were all that had been left to carry on the struggle after the Partisan defeat and withdrawal of 1941. Owing to inadequate communications these were out of touch with each other and with Partisan GHQ.[13]

Major Dugmore, a member of Maclean's staff, is on record as saying there were no more than 1,700 Partisans in the whole of Serbia in January 1944. Michael Lees, who was a British liaison officer in Macedonia during the autumn of 1943, maintains there were never more than 500 Partisans there at that time. Vladimir Velebit admitted to me there were very few Partisans in Serbia and Macedonia during 1943 and early 1944 and that they had perhaps exaggerated when briefing Maclean! Vladimir Dedijer, in *Tito Speaks*, quotes Stalin as saying in November 1944: "I know those Partisan figures. They are always exaggerated."

Maclean claimed that, unlike the anti-communists, Tito was killing Germans – five for every Partisan lost, he asserted. Both

Velebit and Milovan Djilas assured me this statistic was absurd. The Partisan losses were always far heavier than those of the Germans. According to German records, in their June 1943 offensive against the Partisans, which Deakin experienced and which immediately preceded Maclean's arrival, they suffered 583 killed, while inflicting 7,500 deaths on the Partisans. Djilas puts the Partisan losses for 1943 alone at 25,000 killed and for the whole war at over 300,000 – some twenty to thirty times more than the Germans suffered.

It is now believed that, prior to the Red Army's entry into Yugoslavia in October 1944, the Partisans killed at most about 5,000 Germans and Mihailovic's forces nearer half that number. Whether such numbers shortened the war, or changed its direction in any substantial way for the better from the Allied point of view, is a moot point. That the relatively small disparity in the numbers decided the ditching of one lot of resisters and the promotion of another at such expense and with such shattering political consequences is even harder to justify. As SOE's official historian William Mackenzie indicates: "It was not understood that sometimes it costs too much to 'kill Germans', when the cost is reckoned in terms of British policy, not simply of British and Allied dead."

That Churchill could be crudely bloodthirsty was indicated by Michael Carver (Field Marshal, Lord Carver) in his contribution, "Churchill and the Defence Chiefs", to Robert Blake and Roger Louis's *Churchill*, published in 1993. He cited Winston's complaint to General Wavell over the British withdrawal from Somaliland in 1940. Churchill compared the British casualties of 260 dead with the Italian 1,800 and called for the dismissal of the British commander, General Godwen-Austen, as well as for an official enquiry. In rejecting both, Wavell, Godwen-Austin's superior, ended his telegram: "a big butcher's bill is not necessarily evidence of good tactics". Carver says this "not unnaturally infuriated Churchill even more". Churchill never forgave Wavell for the remark and took the first opportunity to sack him.

Maclean alleged in his Report that Tito had "the wholehearted support of the civil population" and hence could unite the country after the war. It beggars belief how he could possibly say this, having seen so little of Yugoslavia. British liaison officers and American airmen in Serbia at the time said it was certainly never true there. Maclean of course never set foot in Serbia; neither did any of his liaison officers until well *after* he had completed his Report. Again he could have relied only on information from the Partisans in making this claim. Michael Lees, who was in Serbia from June 1943 until May 1944, recalls he never once heard people there "expressing support for communism or for the Partisans. They were Royalists to a man; and they swore total support for 'Uncle Draza' Mihailovic."[14]

Maclean implied in his Report that Tito's Partisans were pinning down fourteen elite German divisions. This point, William Deakin maintained to me, over dinner at his, club Brooks in London's St James's in December 1991, most impressed Churchill's military advisers. They were anxious that as many top German divisions as possible be kept away from Western Europe in the run-up to the June 1944 Normandy landings. Deakin said the generals were far more interested in the number of divisions being tied down in the Balkans than in any crude calculation of who was killing the most Germans. When Churchill stated to Stalin at the Teheran Summit in late November 1943 that Tito's men were containing thirty German divisions in Yugoslavia, Stalin corrected him, saying that according to his information there were only eight German divisions there. Stalin's information appears right.

According to Sir Harry Hinsley's official *British Intelligence in the Second World War,* the Joint Intelligence Sub-Committee of the British Chiefs of Staff estimated at the time of Italy's capitulation in September 1943 that the Germans had sixteen divisions in the Balkans, of which six and a half were in Yugoslavia. As a result of the capitulation, the number in the whole of the Balkans rose to 21 by November 1943 and to 22 by the end of February 1944. However, the new divisions were not all entirely German but included Croats and Bulgarians. Hinsley maintains:

> Reports from the liaison officers at Tito's HQ and elsewhere in Yugoslavia were usually received less promptly than the [Enigma] decrypts, and the information they gave about the enemy, especially about his movements and intentions, were almost without exception either imprecise or (as Sigint showed) inaccurate.

Research at the Imperial War Museum in London in 1992 revealed that German troop strength in Yugoslavia during the period in question, September to November 1943, never exceeded eight divisions. These were invariably under-strength and composed either of relatively inexperienced men or those exhausted and recently transferred from the Eastern Front for recuperation. They were certainly not "elite" formations, and so unlikely to have been transferred to north-western Europe to meet the Allied invasion except in the most dire circumstances. In addition, these divisions were coping not just with the Partisans but with the other resistance forces too. They were in Yugoslavia principally to protect the German strategic lines of communication, which passed through Mihailovic's territory, not Tito's, as well as the sources there of minerals vital to Hitler's war effort. They were also there to deter Turkey from entering the war on the Allied side, and to deter an Allied landing on the Yugoslav coast or in Greece. Hitler remained convinced of this likelihood almost to the end. Continuing British deception schemes aimed at keeping him convinced probably played a bigger role in pinning down German divisions in the Balkans than the exploits of the resisters, however valiant. As one of the British liaison officers then in Yugoslavia graphically put it to me, "If Tito and all his forces had disappeared into a black hole in the ground, not one of those divisions could have been taken away."

The then Professor of Modern History at Oxford, Norman Stone, writing in *The Sunday Times* in 1992, agreed with our research, saying he had reached the same conclusion regarding the small number of German divisions in Yugoslavia during the period in question. In fact he put the figure lower, at only six divisions in August 1943:

> Of these, two were manned by Croats, with German officers. Of the others, three contained elderly territorials – *Landsturm* – and there was one really serious division, the *SS Prinz Eugen*. So can we please hear no more of the supposedly vast force pinned down by "the partisans"? ... There were very few real German divisions, most of them were under strength, and they consisted of wheezing Dad's Army types, dragging beer bellies up hill and down dale.

A year later, in a letter to *The Times Literary Supplement*, Stone quoted Glaise-Horstenau, the German general on the spot, who said there were just "two 'usable' divisions" of Germans in Yugoslavia in September 1943. Stone added: "there were others, making up the numbers, but they were useless in [Glaise-Horstenau's] opinion. They consisted of poor old territorials, under strength." The military historian Albert Seaton had earlier, also in *The Times Literary Supplement,* quoted Field Marshal Freiherr von Weichs, Commander-in-Chief Group F, which covered both Yugoslavia and Greece. He recorded in his diary journeying to Rastenburg on 24 September 1943 (six days after Fitzroy Maclean parachuted in to Tito's headquarters) to warn Hitler that he held 5,000 kilometres of frontage with what he euphemistically termed "ten divisions, some of which were of poor quality". Seaton had been stung to write by a letter the previous week from a former member of SOE Cairo, Gordon Fraser, who claimed the Balkans, and Yugoslavia in particular, was awash with hundreds of thousands of top-notch German troops that autumn of 1943. Seaton concluded: "I trust that SOE's political intelligence was more accurate than its military intelligence from whatever sources it came."[15] The military historian Sir John Keegan, in his massive single volume *The Second World War*, published in 1989, maintainsd "strategically, estimates of Tito's diversion of forces from Hitler's main centres of operation are now seen to be exaggerated".

Maclean hinted in his Report that Tito would allow the Yugoslav people a free choice of government after the war, including a democratic decision over the monarchy. Yet, within weeks of Maclean delivering his Report, and before Churchill had made his decision, Tito on 29 November 1943 formally repudiated the Yugoslav government-in-exile. He forbade the king from returning to the country unless a post-war referendum endorsed him doing so. He set up the Partisans as a provisional government with him as premier. He even promoted himself to marshal, thus putting himself on a par with Stalin and the other Allied leaders. The 29 November pronouncements were not disclosed to Churchill, although Deakin and other members of Maclean's mission had attended the gathering at which Tito had made them. Being unfamiliar with the language, they may not fully have understood what was happening!

Tito had not sought Stalin's permission for any of this, which annoyed the Soviet leader. Djilas says Stalin viewed it "as a stab in the back", occurring as it did when the Teheran Conference was in session.[16] Stalin felt sure the Allies would object, particularly to Tito's creating a provisional government, and was evidently very surprised when they did not. Djilas, in *Wartime*, maintains Maclean told Tito that Britain would not "insist very much on the King and the government-in-exile". Maclean, in *Eastern Approaches*, was to say that when he visited Serbia in September 1944, "Most of the Serbs with whom I talked were monarchists (even the Communists admitted that in Serbia over 50 per cent of the population were in favour of the monarchy)."

Maclean claimed in his Report that religious toleration prevailed among the Partisans. When Evelyn Waugh, a devout Catholic, went to Tito's headquarters he reported very differently. He was to detail the closing down of churches, the slaughter of priests and the compulsory indoctrination of Marxist-Leninist atheism. Maclean accepted that the Partisans were bent on exterminating Mihailovic's supporters, but he said he could not "find evidence of mass arrests or executions [by the Partisans] on the lines of those perpetrated by the Ustasi and Cetniks". Djilas maintains Maclean knew full well the Partisans shot Chetnik prisoners out of hand. In *Wartime* he relates numerous instances of such executions during the time of the Maclean mission.

Maclean also asserted in his Report that, while the Partisans fought the Germans, Mihailovic's men either helped the Germans or did nothing. He claimed they were "set in their collaborationist ways" and that Mihailovic was "thoroughly discredited in the eyes of most of the population". Once again, Maclean could not have known anything first-hand. He had not talked to anyone outside Tito's head-quarters, certainly to no one in the Mihailovic camp. He had relied solely on what Tito's people told him. This did not stop him declaring there was "irrefutable evidence" of some of Mihailovic's commanders having collaborated with the Axis occupiers. The official Foreign Office historian of the Second World War, Sir Llewellyn Woodward, observes:

> It is, on the whole, fairly safe to assume that evidence about General Mihailovic coming from Marshal Tito or his entourage is as unreliable as evidence from the side of General Mihailovic about the Partisans.[17]

Maclean's opposite number with Mihailovic, Brigadier Armstrong, signalled Cairo on 16 November:

> Mihailovic may have many faults but a desire to collaborate with Boche not one. Mihailovic most indignant apparently received signal British saying Mihailovic duped, etc., collaborating Boche. When you do this, heaven's sake give me warning. Even then I am on a bad wicket without proof.[18]

Wilhelm Hoettl of the German Secret Service, based for some time in Yugoslavia, says of these claims in his memoirs, *The Secret Front*:

> The obvious differences between the Cetniks and the Communists made it easier for the German Secret Service to establish contact with the former. I can testify that Mihailovic himself rejected every approach.

Hoettl also cites instances of temporary accommodations between the Partisans and the Italians:

The longer the guerrilla warfare lasted, the more frequent became deals in arms and munitions between Italian units and the partisans. Things reached such a pitch that there was a fixed and recognised price for all weapons, from a rifle to a piece of field artillery, and the partisans, as can be well imagined, made handsome use of this market.

Apparently in 1942 the German military police captured a Partisan courier on his way to the Italian Commander-in-Chief's headquarters. Interrogation established that his taking such messages was a common occurrence. Hoettl mentioned, too, prisoner exchanges between the Partisans and the Germans, especially in 1943. One involved Hoettl himself as a go-between and was intended by Tito to lead to a truce, but Hoettl's masters turned down the deal. On another occasion Tito offered to co-operate with the Germans in the event of an Anglo-American landing on the Adriatic coast. This approach was passed to Berlin, who again turned it down, having evidently consulted Hitler.

According to Franklin Lindsay, a senior representative with Tito from the Office of Strategic Services (OSS), forerunner of the CIA,

> Tito used the charge of collaboration against Mihailovic as a political tool to deter the British and the Americans from providing even psychological support to Mihailovic. He could only justify to the British and the Americans his armed attacks against the Chetniks by making the charge that Mihailovic was a German collaborator. Therefore, Tito argued, his attacks against the Chetniks were the same as attacks on the Germans. Also it would be harder for the Allies to defend their support for Mihailovic if he was a collaborator than if he was simply curbing his attacks to minimize German murder of Serb peasants.[19]

Julian Amery suggested to me that, in order to justify the decision to drop Mihailovic, "we sought to blacken his reputation by alleging he was treacherously collaborating with the Germans". To our shame, "we allowed ourselves to vilify him".

Enigma decrypts during September 1943 showed that the Germans at the outset of their campaign to disarm the Italians had arrested many of Mihailovic's senior officers in Croatia, Slovenia, Bosnia and Serbia. One decrypt, on 1 October, drew attention to the fact that, if the Chetniks took over the arms of the Italian Venezia Division, the German position in the border area between Serbia and Montenegro would become untenable. This makes it all the more bewildering why SOE Cairo would not allow Mihailovic to disarm the Venezia Division – unless of course it was James Klugmann at work again. Earlier Enigma decrypts, according to Sir Harry Hinsley, "far from providing evidence of Cetnik-German collaboration, continued to leave no doubt that at least at the highest level the Germans remained set on Mihailovic's destruction".[20] Ralph Bennett, in his *Ultra and Mediterranean Strategy*, says of the Enigma decrypts regarding Mihailovic that, even by the end of 1943, "there was still no proof from what was by now the Allies' largest and most reliable source of intelligence that Mihailovic was personally involved in any act of collaboration".

Describing anyone they did not like or who opposed their point of view as a fascist or treacherous collaborator was a common communist gambit. Those who opposed Tito's communists were invariably classed as fascists and collaborators. But, in not distinguishing just who was a fascist or a collaborator, many of the British officers at Tito's headquarters at best condoned and at worst connived in helping Tito achieve his political aims.

Ironically, at the very moment Maclean was delivering his Report, Tito's Partisans were successfully negotiating a deal with the Germans to obtain some horses in return for refraining from sabotaging the Belgrade-Zagreb railway! But then Maclean did not mention anything about the Partisans' own "consultations" with the enemy. Particularly those in March that year, which, from the Allied point of view, were a much more treacherous act than any of the temporary accommodations Mihailovic's commanders had contemplated. Joining forces with the Germans in opposing an Allied landing on the Adriatic coast would almost certainly have led to Allied deaths and casualties.

Neither Mihailovic nor any of his commanders had ever considered *killing* Allied troops – which the Partisans were clearly prepared to do! They had obviously not told Maclean of their undertaking not to sabotage German military installations or harass German troop movements – the price of their truce while they attacked Mihailovic's forces across the Neretva River to push them back into Montenegro and Serbia, their heartland. Vladimir Velebit and Milovan Djilas have given chapter and verse on this. Velebit admitted to me that the Germans considered Mihailovic an undoubted enemy. They did not trust him and hence could never have collaborated with him in any true sense. Hitler was almost paranoid on the subject. As late as the summer of 1944 he worried about a Serbian uprising coinciding with an Allied invasion of the Balkans.

In reply to allegations of Mihailovic's collaboration, Michael Lees says that during his time with Mihailovic's forces, from June 1943 until May 1944, Axis troops were repeatedly attacking him. He never felt they were on his side! His remarks were echoed by other liaison officers with Mihailovic and by the downed American air-crews he was sheltering. As the latter were to point out, even after the British had dropped him Mihailovic continued to give sanctuary to more than five hundred Americans who had bailed out or crashed over Serbia when returning from bombing raids in central or eastern Europe. None of them ever came to harm in Mihailovic's hands. By contrast there were many complaints about their treatment from those airmen who had dropped over Partisan territory. When the time came for the evacuation of the American airmen, scattered over thousands of square miles of Serbia, they were safely passed between friendly villagers to the departure point, even though by then the Allies were arming Mihailovic's enemy.

Jasper Rootham, in *Miss Fire*, describes how, when they were ordered to withdraw from their base in eastern Serbia to rendezvous at Mihailovic's headquarters with the other British liaison officers for their departure by air, their "journey to the west [was] more of a triumphal progress than anything else. Everywhere we were met, escorted, fed and housed" by Mihailovic sympathisers. Michael Lees recalled to me his shame when reading, at the Public Record Office in London, a signal from Fitzroy Maclean in which he outlined the procedure for the evacuation in May 1944 of the British liaison officers with Mihailovic. Their safe conduct through Partisan areas was to be guaranteed by Tito but any others of Yugoslav origin accompanying them were to be handed over to the Partisans. It was clear what was in store for them.

While Maclean and Deakin were at Tito's headquarters, Archie Jack, a liaison officer with Mihailovic, demolished in late September and early October 1943 five bridges on the Belgrade-Sarajevo railway. They included the 450-foot single-span river bridge near Visegrad. The line was out of action for many months. He had done this with the help of Mihailovic's men and in the presence of Brigadier Armstrong, the newly arrived head of the British mission to Mihailovic. Incredibly, the BBC broadcast that the sabotage had been carried out by the Partisans. Asked by Armstrong to correct the mistake, they never did. Archie Jack told me, when I visited him in France before he died, that he had counted in the files at the Public Record

Office in Kew more than seventy reports to Cairo from liaison officers with Mihailovic's forces detailing sabotage operations between August and December 1943. He had been unable to discover whether any of them had been passed on to London. He said that when he had requested replenishments for the explosives expended in blowing up the bridges at Visegrad, Cairo had refused on the grounds that the supplies could be better used elsewhere in Yugoslavia.

Armstrong had earlier complained, again without success, when the BBC had described as Partisan victories the killing and capture of Mihailovic forces and the taking of towns from them. Yet when the BBC had the previous month credited Mihailovic with a Partisan operation, William Deakin had immediately protested. The BBC not only issued a correction but informed him in advance exactly when it was to be transmitted so he could alert his Partisan complainers to listen in. They did and evidently then joined Deakin in sending a signal of thanks to the BBC!

Michael Lees records that his very first sabotage operation, on the night of 30 September 1943, in which a section of the vital Belgrade-Salonika railway was demolished with the help of Mihailovic's forces was also attributed by the BBC to the Partisans, although he had reported his success to Cairo forty-eight hours before the broadcast in question. On another occasion a successful wrecking of the same railway line, again with the help of Mihailovic's men, was credited by the BBC to the Partisans, who had in fact tried to ambush Lees and his men when they returned from the operation. Thereafter, apparently, the expletive "You lie like London", became commonplace amongst Mihailovic's forces.

The liaison officers with Mihailovic were told to report to Cairo only those operations they had themselves witnessed or been able to confirm by checking on-site or interviewing witnesses. The liaison officers with the Partisans, who never saw action themselves, could report only what they had been told by Tito's headquarters. This difference in reporting procedure prompted Brigadier Armstrong to send a tongue-in-cheek reminder to Cairo on 9 November 1943:

> We would like to know if Partisan BLO [British liaison officer] statements are based on eye witness observations or merely circumstantial reports from local Commands. Here we try to be impartial. Hope BLOs with Partisans do same.[21]

He knew full well they did not.

Michael Lees complains in his memoirs of being restrained in his sabotaging of railways and other military installations not by Mihailovic but by SOE Cairo. They were constantly either not sending the demolition materials requested or delaying permission for the sabotage, so that the opportunity for carrying it out was often missed. In August 1943 he reconnoitred and planned, with the help of Mihailovic's men, the destruction of a bridge on the important Belgrade-Salonika railway which the Germans were using to transfer troops from Greece to Italy to face the Allied invasion there. He was ordered not to go ahead at the last minute by SOE Cairo, without any explanation. On withdrawing they were ambushed by Partisans, who had clearly been tipped off about their presence. These Partisans spent their time canvassing political support among the peasants and did not trouble the Axis occupiers in any way. They ambushed him on several occasions and hindered his sabotage operations. When he sought to mediate with them, they tried to take him hostage.

Lees states the Partisans were disliked intensely by the Serb villagers because they requisitioned food from them, sometimes forcibly. Mihailovic's people always paid for their victuals. He claims the Partisans there never sabotaged anything. During the autumn of 1943 Mihailovic's men carried out at least two train derailments under his instructions. Although reported immediately to Cairo, they were not heard about in London until the summer of 1944. He reported many other successful sabotage operations along this important railway and suggested they could keep it permanently cut if given the necessary support. His signals were ignored.

He is adamant Cairo could have been in no doubt about their extensive activity that autumn along that crucial railway line and of their willingness to increase the activity. His signals to SOE Cairo during October and November 1943 for permission to sabotage German installations elsewhere in Serbia, that he had fully reconnoitred with the help of Mihailovic's people, were similarly ignored. He recalls in particular requesting permission to sabotage an important power station feeding an armaments factory in Serbia. The constant ignoring of his signals at first puzzled and then exasperated the Mihailovic forces with him. It led to their doubting his authority with Cairo as well as Cairo's sincerity. He says other liaison officers with Mihailovic had similar experiences. He recalls, too, being ordered by SOE Cairo to operate only in uniform. If he had done so it would have put his life at risk and prevented him from undertaking any close reconnaissance.

Lees was particularly rueful when Mihailovic was ditched. He records in his memoirs:

> it effectively stopped our nascent sabotage action on the vital Salonika-Belgrade railway line in the Morava valley just as we were getting going. Nothing was done against the Axis on that line throughout most of the important winter of 1943-44, while the Partisans concentrated on gathering their forces and equipping them with British arms in order to bring their civil war to Serbia.

Bored while waiting to be evacuated from Serbia in the spring of 1944, he derailed a train on the Belgrade-Salonika railway just north of Leskovac, only to be chastised by his superiors in Cairo for doing so!

The American historian David Martin, in *The Web of Disinformation*, lists actions by Mihailovic's forces that autumn of 1943. He discovered them while studying, in the Public Record Office in London, the SOE Operational Log of incoming messages from British liaison officers in Yugoslavia.

> Most of the actions described in the compendium are relatively small ones – blowing up bridges, tearing up tracks, wrecking trains, killing 40 Bulgarians here or 16 Germans there – but there are many of them. There are also some half-dozen large-scale actions – very large-scale by guerrilla standards – where the enemy death toll ran from 200 to 300.

Interspersed sadly, are references like:

> as reprisals Huns burnt village ... 420 houses and killed all male population who did not escape ... Huns shot 35 hostages ... burnt 18 houses ... reprisals followed. All village burned, women and children taken away ... Huns take 200 hostages ... Bulgars burned village and killed 15 villagers ... all males over 15 years being removed by Huns ... 150 persons were shot ... Bulgar reprisal activity ... Huns have imprisoned 90 Serbs ... villagers irrespective age and sex shot at all places.

I researched the Log too and found other messages from these same liaison officers that autumn:

> 4 bridges destroyed at Mokragorac... Blew one kilometre east railway... line will be out of action for ten days, was pulling fifty trains per day, troops, tanks, arms to Greece ... train derailed and number of Hun victims ... Train derailed on line Pristina-Pec ... three miles of railway line torn up by Mihailovic forces ... Visegrad Rugatica under Mihailovic control... Mihailovic forces occupied Zvornik after

fighting Huns and beat off two counter-attacks, thereafter taking large amount arms and ammo ... Mihailovic forces attack Hun and Ustashi, near Tuzla, inflict losses ... Mihailovic forces destroy train full of Huns and explosives in tunnel ... line at Dobrun, seven kilometres east Visegrad destroyed many places ... near Uzice Mihailovic forces destroy 4 locomotives and 70 freight cars by explosives. Huns take 200 hostages Uzice.[22]

I found also a German proclamation of 3 October 1943 announcing the shooting of 385 Mihailovic sympathisers in Belgrade and Cacak in retribution for sabotage.

The Operational Log is littered with pleas, clearly being repeated for the umpteenth time, for airdrops of explosives and other supplies required for long-planned sabotage operations. There are numerous complaints about poor quality or insufficient quantity when, belatedly, supplies were received, and on occasion sheer bewilderment at having been sent unrequested items like office equipment, when warm clothing and mail from home were sorely needed. There are gripes too about the expected planes not turning up or else flying overhead too high to see the flares that had been carefully lit.

Nor was the frustration with SOE Cairo confined to the British liaison officers. The American Lieutenant George Musulin planned an attack on the important Lisa mine near Dragacevo, Hitler's biggest source of antinomy, used in tempering steel for shells, bombs and other weapons. When he signalled Cairo for permission to proceed, he was told not to do so and no reason was given.

The head of the Foreign Office's Southern Department, Douglas Howard, was forever complaining about the activities of SOE Cairo. His memo of 9 September 1943 is typical:

> The fact is, I am sure, that SOE Cairo (plus the minister of state) do not *want* us to come to a satisfactory arrangement with Mihailovic. We have been on the verge of doing so many times, but on each occasion a spanner has been thrown in to prevent us. I recall the following occasions. We sent Bailey the directive. For various reasons or excuses it did not reach Mihailovic for many weeks. Just when Mihailovic was about to reply, Glenconner [head of SOE Cairo] sent his famous "bludgeoning" telegram. It took weeks to get that straight again. Mihailovic then replied to the directive (satisfactorily in our view and that of SOE here). Before we could reply to that effect, Bailey sends in his ultimatum. Mihailovic replies, again satisfactorily, but SOE Cairo find it unsatisfactory and now suggest another "showdown", on the grounds that he will probably refuse to cooperate with

us. Would it not be more normal to tell Mihailovic that we accept his reply and will do our best to support him. If *then* it proves unsatisfactory, and he fails to carry out his promises, we should reconsider our policy; but to do so on the *assumption* that he will not do so, seems to me a typical SOE way of doing things.[23]

Brigadier Armstrong delivered to Mihailovic, on 24 September 1943, a letter from General Maitland Wilson, the Allied Commander-in-Chief, Middle East, in which he said: "It has now become logistically possible for me to send you military supplies on a much larger scale." When it was decided to send the two brigadiers into Yugoslavia the intention was that they should receive equal supplies until they had reported to Churchill. However just two days earlier SOE Cairo had signalled all the missions with Mihailovic:

> Programme of flying disorganized this month due (1) Demands on our aircraft for other purposes owing to fall of Italy, (2) Initial bad weather, (3) Very bad start Bizerta which will have repercussions sorties. Realise delicacy your position and doing best see no mission suffers out of proportion. Unwilling give any figure for remainder period. We regret very much.

Two days before that signal, which had not been sent to Maclean's mission with Tito, Maclean had reported on his initial meeting with Tito:

> Regarding supplies, I told Tito that he could count on a minimum of sixty sorties next month. He said that the quantities promised hitherto have no relation to those actually received and this and other questions were further complicated by apparent absence of reliable communication with Cairo. I replied that sixty was a firm figure and that steps were being taken to establish satisfactory communications.[24]

Tito got his supplies. Mihailovic did not get his.

The BBC became noticeably more pro-Partisan that autumn of 1943, and not just in attributing Mihailovic successes to Tito. The German propagandists spotted the change in emphasis. They lost little time in fomenting matters by suggesting the duplicitous English imperialists were again up to their tricks, sacrificng Serbian interests in a wish to mollify the Soviets. Armstrong wearily complained to Cairo about actions carried out by Mihailovic's men that had been witnessed by Bailey and yet credited to the Partisans by the BBC. On 16 November he signalled:

If you want to get the best out of Mihailovic you must give him a fairer press and broadcasts. Bailey was with Mihailovic forces when [they] took Priboj and Bijelopolje and Berane. I saw capture Visegrad, destruction bridges, and know Ostojic took Rogatica. Mihailovic never credited with any [of] these, although reported to you. On other hand, when Partisans drove his forces out, Partisans credited on BBC [with capture of these places from enemy]. Show this to comrade Fitz [Roy Maclean].[25]

Despite further pleas from Armstrong and his American colleague Colonel Seitz, the BBC never issued a correction. Armstrong cited another incident when the BBC praised Tito for capturing the town of Priboj, although on the day in question one of his Serb colleagues had been shopping there and had not noticed any Partisans! He complained to Ralph Stevenson on 20 November "that the BBC broadcasts to Yugoslavia are causing intense bitterness and mistrust".[26] Jasper Rootham, a liaison officer with Mihailovic's forces, recalled sabotaging three coal mines in Serbia during the autumn of 1943. He informed Cairo but the BBC never mentioned them. He maintained the "BBC's service in Yugoslavia over the last 9 months steadily contributed towards lowering British prestige in the part of Yugoslavia [Serbia] in which I was serving".[27]

Major Erik Greenwood, another British liaison officer with Mihailovic's forces, signalled Cairo on 30 November 1943: "We are so surrounded by lies and contradictions and so lacking true information that we have lost faith in everything except our ultimate victory, inevitability of which we hammer into Serbs constantly."[28] Jasper Rootham, in his memoirs *Miss Fire*, says that after the Visegrad incident

Mihailovic personally asked that no further mention of his own troops or their activities should be made in the BBC's European service, and stuck to his point in spite of attempts by British officers on the spot to dissuade him. It was perhaps not unnatural that, thereafter, the influence of the "pro-action" and "pro-British" party at Mihailovic's headquarters declined, and that he fell progessively more under the sway of those elements which were urging him to concentrate on preserving his resources for what they regarded as the inevitable show-down with the Partisans.

That autumn Allied planes bombed Nis, a railway town in Serbia, killing at least three hundred civilians and wounding hundreds more. Jasper Rootham recalled the Germans made much of this first bombing raid by the Allies, publishing photographs of the civilian damage with the caption, "This, Serbians, is your reward ... for your loyalty to Great Britain in her hour of trial". He said the Germans never lost an opportunity

> to fan the flames of civil war, and at the same time, by representing one party as the sinister agents of the Red Terror and the other as the deluded hangers-on of the impotent and perfidious Anglo-Americans, to sow the greatest possible doubt about Allied community of purpose.

Rootham maintains that while they never "were able to persuade anybody to feel for Germany and Germans anything but bitter hate", for some there grew "the conviction, that there might even, after all, be something worse than a German occupation – a Revolutionary Terror". Thus were the Germans able to establish in the Serb mind the idea that Yugoslavia had been consigned to the Communists. Bailey was to claim BBC broadcasts had been "by far the most important" factor in spreading political bewilderment throughout Serbia and Montenegro.[29]

Armstrong corroborated this in a brief signal to Ralph Stevenson, the British Ambassador to the Yugoslav government-in-exile, on 21 November 1943. He maintained the BBC was "entirely discredited and few listen". He sent a longer signal the next day, in which he reported:

> The biased tone of the British BBC propaganda and the paucity of material support during the past four months has raised serious doubts in most local commanders' minds as to British intentions towards Yugoslavia and Serbia. They may well feel, that abandoned as they are by the British, their sole hope rests in continued loyalty to Mihailovic in order to maintain his organisation as a compact force with which to protect Serb interests against powerful internal enemies.[30]

Knowing Churchill's admiration of Lawrence of Arabia, Maclean had included a reference to him in the very opening paragraph of his Report: "As Lawrence wrote of the Arab revolt: 'We had won a province when we had taught the civilians in it to die for our ideal of freedom. The presence or absence of the enemy was a secondary matter.'" Churchill had an emotional bond with the Balkans, forged perhaps by his Dardanelles involvement in the First World War. Also his Boer War experiences made him interested in guerrilla warfare *per se*. As Yugoslavia was the only war theatre then with substantial guerrilla activity he became absorbed in that country. The accounts by Deakin and Maclean of the seemingly reckless heroism of the Partisans clearly beguiled him. He was adventurous by nature, hence the appeal of adventurers like Fitzroy Maclean. This led him in turn to be fascinated by Tito, "the great guerrilla" in his lexicon, "hardy and hunted". He was a figure seemingly out of a feudal past, living in caves and forests, perpetually on the move, achieving deeds of derring-do. Deeds he would have liked to be doing himself, but as a desk-bound warrior could not. And an increasingly frustrated one as the Americans and Russians came to dominate affairs.

Churchill had always been drawn to mavericks and buccaneers. He had a romantic enthusiasm for the unorthodox and the quirky, for people who defied convention. He delighted in the irregular. He had a life-long interest, too, in military intelligence. Cloak-and-dagger operations appealed to his vivid imagination. He enjoyed meeting secret agents. His eagerness for the unconventional some-times carried him away, to the alarm of traditional army types like his long-suffering military chief, Sir Alan Brooke. He was also an impa-tient man, hence his irritation with Mihailovic for wanting to wait until the Germans were on their knees before issuing his call to the Serbs to rise up against them. Churchill was always for immediate action at all costs.

Maclean was also fascinated by Lawrence of Arabia. He perhaps saw himself as Lawrence of Yugoslavia, blowing up bridges and trains, leading the south Slavs out of their German bondage. Bruce Lockhart, Director-General of PWE and a former colleague of Maclean's in the Foreign Office, is on record as saying "he longs to be a Lawrence". Maclean's biographer, Frank McLynn, confirms this. Lockhart felt, however, that Maclean "has great qualities of persist-ence and determination, but has more courage, guts, in his long frame than brains!"[31] He said Anthony Eden "did not think much of Fitzroy either as a man or as a politician".[32] Ironically, as Djilas indicated in his *Wartime* memoirs, the Yugoslav Communists "saw in Lawrence of Arabia not an idealistic hero, but the perfidious, arrogant champion of an empire"!

As well as recommending "support of Mihailovic should be discon-tinued" and "our aid to the Partisans should be substantially increased", Maclean somewhat darkly urged that "BBC broadcasts and other publicity should be kept in line with the policy of His Majesty's Government." Such a suggestion was beyond his military brief. If carried through, it could only be to the benefit of the Partisans politically. The BBC in its promotion of Tito was to exaggerate his exploits in much the same way as it had exaggerated Mihailovic's in the dismal days of 1941. The difference was that now the villain of the piece was not Hitler but Mihailovic.

Simon Trew, in *Britain, Mihailovic and the Chetniks, 1941-42*, says of that earlier promotion:

> having built Mihailovic up to such dizzy heights, the sense of disillusionment was all the more acute when it became obvious that he was not quite what he seemed. Ultimately, of course, the British were to be even more disappointed in Tito, whose Army of National Liberation was neither the efficient military machine which it pretended to be, nor the politically-moderate mass movement which the British hoped they might be able to influence. However, having made one mistake and admitted it, it proved impossible in the end to acknowledge a second of yet greater proportions. The victor's history was written, and Mihailovic was cast in the role of collaborator and villain. He was in fact neither, but given the complexities of war in Yugoslavia, and Britain's sorry role in determining her fate, it is perhaps easy to see why he needed to be.

Maclean got his way with the BBC. Tito was able to hog the airways while Mihailovic got only negative publicity, if any. Thereafter the Foreign Office and PWE files are full of directives to this effect as the BBC became ever more openly pro-Partisan. PWE directed on 31 December 1943: "do not mention the Yugoslav War Minister [Mihailovic] except when the news demands it ... praise the Partisans' military successes, but say as little as possible about their political aims."[33] A further directive of 14 January 1944 to the BBC stipulates: "Do not mention the Cetniks ... quote reports of Partisan activity in Serbia briefly, be careful not to exaggerate their importance since Partisan activity is obviously still on a small scale." On 21 January: "No mention should be made of Mihailovic until further notice"; 28 January: "Show unobtrusively that the majority of Partisan forces is Serb";[34] 25 February: "Give Tito his title of Marshal".[35] Later directives became even more blatant, typically on 27 May: "Stress that Tito has sunk his Communist aspect in his Yugoslav patriotism, and has disclaimed the intention of reversing the Serbian property system."[36]

David Garnett, in *The Secret History of PWE*, cites a broadcast in January 1944 by the "Man in the Street", who turned out to be the BBC's own Director of European Broadcasts, Noel Newsome. Tito was linked favourably with the 27 March 1941 coup although he had taken no part whatsoever in it. This prompted SOE's head, Lord Selborne, to complain to the Foreign Secretary of the broadcast's "continuous left-wing propaganda to all Europe, frequently not in line with HMG policy". Eden called for the script and minuted: "it deserved all the harsh things Lord Selborne had said. Historically it was disgracefully inaccurate and the BBC should tell the truth." Garnett's official history, although written shortly after the War, was not published until 2002: the Cabinet Office had considered his judgements of PWE personnel too scandalous!

Newsome was a controversial figure. He joined the BBC's European Service from *The Daily Telegraph* just after the War started. He was the European News Editor until promoted in the autumn of 1941 to the new post of Director of European Broadcasts. Michael Stenton, in his masterly study of the BBC's wartime propaganda role, *Radio London and Resistance in Occupied Europe*, reveals that Newsome, in his unpublished memoirs,

> records that his "two touchstones" for judging the fitness of people to produce broadcasts to Europe were soundness on the USSR and acceptance that victory and peace depended on the overthrow and reform of "all the Fascist States: Italy, Japan, Hungary, Rumania, Bulgaria, Yugoslavia and Greece, Spain and Portugal".

Apparently Newsome "did not relish the awkward reality of alliance with something like the *ancien regimes* of Poland, Yugoslavia and Greece". He

> was ferociously Russophile ... if Stalin was a dictator, so was the Viceroy of India ... [he] admired Stalin's regime, and even the Terror, because it had strengthened Russia and tamed the Revolution. When others hesitated, he found it a pleasant duty, as "The Man in the Street", to assure listeners that Britain and the Soviet Union were, constitutionally, moving towards the "same goal" and were destined to "meet on common ground", and to boast that British and Soviet views about the coming settlement were so "fundamentally identical" that all contrary assertions were "pernicious nonsense".

No doubt the BBC's admiration for Stalin enhanced his prestige throughout Europe and helped facilitate the acceptance of communism there.

Hubert Harrison, the BBC's Balkan Editor, who had previously been the Belgrade correspondent for Reuters and the *News Chronicle*, also did not conceal his dislike for Yugoslavia's pre-war regime or the

Yugoslav government-in-exile. The Foreign Office files for 1943 are full of complaints about him. Stenton maintains:

> In the support for the Yugoslav Partisans cynicism, ingenuousness, and honesty were whisked together in a bewildering flurry of pragmatic bravura. If the BBC failed to lift the Earth it may be that they missed a place to stand on.

Elisabeth Barker, who headed PWE's Balkan Section during the war, considered the BBC "very unmanageable".[37] The German propagandists, realising the importance of the BBC broadcasts, occasionally transmitted fake ones, interspersing misleading information with authentic news reports. They even had a phoney Churchill voice!

Asa Briggs, in his monumental official history of the BBC, glosses over the shenanigans at the Yugoslav Service (the name was changed from the Serbo-Croat Service in January 1943). He devotes only a few paragraphs to it. Apparently Newsome was well thought of within the BBC; the London Yugoslavs were considered a pain.

Vane Ivanovic, a Yugoslav who was with the Political Warfare Executive (PWE) in Bari, mentions in his memoirs meeting Vladimir Velebit there in early 1944 and discussing Maclean with him. Evidently Velebit said: "To us it seems that for Fitzroy Maclean there is first of all Fitzroy Maclean." Ivanovic observed of Velebit and the other Partisan leaders:

> They well knew – and some of them told me so – on what absurdly slender knowledge of the situation Maclean's appraisal had been made. They themselves were by no means as sanguine of their ultimate success as Maclean was.

Apparently they took comfort that Maclean, having coupled his career to their locomotive, now had a vested interest in seeing they reached their political destination!

SOE's official historian, William Mackenzie, observes:

> Tito and his staff were very clever men ... the British Liaison Officers were largely innocents abroad, who knew nothing of guerrilla warfare and very little of Yugoslav language or history or politics. Their reports were at this stage almost without exception more lyrical and less realistic than those of the old warriors Hudson and Bailey; and in part for that very reason they were more influential at home. Hence arose most naturally the widespread conviction that the Partisans were "not really Communist", and that Tito could in due course be tamed to co-operate in a new "national" government of Yugoslavia,

Tito, August 1942

Draza Mihailovic, 1943

recognising the legitimacy of King Peter. All Yugoslav history and the whole political character of the movement made this impossible; no middle course was open.

Maclean and Deakin had going for them their ready contact with Churchill, which their opposite numbers with Mihailovic lacked. Maclean's biographer, Frank McLynn, quotes the historian Mark Wheeler arguing to him that Mihailovic's liaison officers, such as Bailey, were not in the same league:

> These people didn't have access, hadn't been to the right schools, were not part of the Establishment. A class interpretation is possible. Bill Bailey was Emmanuel School, Wandsworth; Deakin and Maclean were Winchester and Eton products.

Deakin went to Westminster but it does not weaken Wheeler's point! Brigadier Armstrong had apparently tried to turn down his appointment as head of the mission to Mihailovic when he found it was to involve politics. He had no background in Balkan affairs and said later he received no briefing on the political situation in Yugoslavia before setting out. Strictly a military man, he had little influence in Whitehall and no experience of diplomacy.
Vane Ivanovic maintains in his memoirs:

> I cannot, especially writing today, dismiss this evidence that the military evaluation so made by Deakin and Maclean (through which the meanest intelligence staff officer could have driven a coach and four) was, or could have been, the *sole* ground for the acceptance of the Partisans as a fully fledged allied force.

He was not alone in being surprised the figures and claims in Maclean's Report were not subjected to a rigorous general staff analysis. Ivanovic was convinced Churchill's decision to back Tito and to drop Mihailovic was taken before Maclean's mission to Yugoslavia, that Churchill was merely looking for some justification for it. He was not alone in that assessment.

Others argue that Churchill's closest military adviser, the Chief of the Imperial General Staff, Sir Alan Brooke, let his boss have his way over Yugoslavia in order to divert him from invading Norway, a pet project of his at that time. Most of the military chiefs considered it rash, if not foolish in the extreme. Reading his diaries, it is clear Lord Alanbrooke, as he became, was forever endeavouring to dissuade Churchill from his more adventuristic schemes, as witness an entry for 30 August 1943:

[Churchill] has an unfortunate trick of picking up some isolated operation without ever really having looked into it, setting his heart on it. When he once gets in one of these moods he feels everybody is trying to thwart him and to produce difficulties. He becomes then more and more set on the operation brushing everything aside, and when planners prove the operation to be impossible he then appoints new planners in the hope that they will prove that the operation is possible.

It is significant Alanbrooke did not figure in the decision-making over Tito and Mihailovic!

CHAPTER SEVEN

The Fateful Decision

*"Naturally to Maclean Tito is all white
and Mihailovic all black. I have a suspicion that
grey is a more common Balkan colour"*
ANTHONY EDEN

SUCH WERE MACLEAN'S high-level contacts that on 4 November 1943, having just flown into Cairo from Bari, he was dining with the head of the Foreign Office, Sir Alexander Cadogan, and Anthony Eden's private secretary, Oliver Harvey. Both were on their way back from Moscow where the American, British and Soviet foreign ministers had been preparing for the Stalin-Churchill-Roosevelt summit in Teheran later that month. The next day he saw Eden himself. He pushed his recommendations and suggested flying in a delegation of Partisan leaders to meet Churchill and the other decision-makers in Cairo. Eden initially agreed, but he later changed his mind, insisting it was purely a military team, meeting only military people and not politicians. Maclean said he would return to Tito's headquarters to arrange it all. Oliver Harvey recorded in his diary:

> Fitzroy is sure that Tito represents the future government of Yugoslavia, whether we like it or not, a sort of peasant communism, and we should be wise to come to terms and try to guide them. This also has been more or less agreed upon.[1]

Eden remarked to his colleagues that Maclean was very pro-Tito. Ralph Stevenson, the British Ambassador to the Yugoslav Government-in-exile, reported to London on 5 November that the Partisans were clearly on their way to becoming masters of Yugoslavia.

Maclean even dined with the Yugoslav king at Stevenson's house on 10 November. Apparently Peter was willing to meet Tito, but Maclean and Stevenson advised against it. They thought Tito would probably not want to. Suggesting it, they felt, might harm Maclean's relations with him. During the next days Maclean busied himself in

Cairo promoting his Report, managing to see most of the main decision-makers there. He dined again on 25 November with Cadogan, who was en route to Teheran for the Big Three Conference. The following morning he once more met Eden to discuss his Report. Later that same day he met the military chiefs on the Middle East Defence Committee, persuading them to step up supplies immediately to the Partisans. In his memoirs *Eastern Approaches* Maclean says his report "caused something of a stir, and I was under instructions to return to Cairo in a few weeks, when, I gathered, Mr. Churchill himself would be there".

SOE Cairo prepared a report itself on 19 November entitled "Appreciation regarding the military situation in Serbia so as to determine what in the future should be our military policy". Almost certainly written by Klugmann, it reiterated Maclean's claims regarding Partisan strength and included selective complaints from liaison officers with Mihailovic. It similarly sought to denigrate Mihailovic, claiming his movement was "associated in the minds of the majority of the Serbs with the corrupt and pro-Fascist circles who brought their country to disaster".[2] Like Maclean's, it recommended ending support for Mihailovic and withdrawing the liaison officers with him. Widely and speedily circulated within Cairo circles, it was discussed the very next day by the Special Operations Committee.

Ralph Stevenson, the British Ambassador to the Yugoslav government-in-exile, took upon himself to prepare a note for that same Committee, dated 29 November, entitled "Political Aspects of a Change of Policy towards General Mihailovic". He claimed: "it is an established fact that for some time General Mihailovic has been a bad investment for us." Mihailovic, he maintained, "is more interested in the post-war political situation in Yugoslavia than in helping the United Nations to defeat the Germans" – as if Tito himself were not similarly *more interested*! Stevenson did warn, though, that a break with Mihailovic "would involve us in the internal affairs of Yugoslavia and would in fact be assisting to fasten a movement on Serbia which we have no sufficient ground to believe would be welcome". He also admitted, "we are not in possession of enough information regarding the Chetnik movement and its hold on Serbia to make up our minds on the matter" and felt a decision should be deferred until Colonel Bailey was able to report.[3] Bailey had been expected to do so in person in Cairo that month, but SOE Cairo claimed logistic problems prevented this.

*

SOE London had asked Armstrong and Bailey to prepare a report similar to Maclean's, which they duly did. Dated 18 November, it did not reach London until 1 December. Sent by cipher from Yugoslavia in 92 separate sections, it took three days to signal to Cairo. There its deciphering and transcription were given no priority. Some sections went missing. It was not discussed at the Foreign Office until 10 December, the very day Churchill made his fateful decision in Cairo. It was not delivered to any of the main decision-makers until long afterwards and was given a much less extensive distribution than Maclean's Report. By this time it was too late for it to have any influence. Unfortunately, too, it was a rambling and incoherent document, in stark contrast to Maclean's precise and persuasive prose.

It revealed Mihailovic's conviction that the Red Army would get to Serbia before the British or Americans and his now rooted distrust of the British on account of the BBC's favouring the Partisans: "*Perfide Albion* attempting to purchase strategic benefits with Serb blood." He believed it had already been agreed that Yugoslavia should be under Soviet influence after the war:

> Greatest mistrust and apprehension, however, derive from the conviction of all Yugoslavs here that the present 100 per cent support of Partisans by BBC, including gross misrepresentation of known facts, plus minimum mention of Mihailovic's activities, plus greater material support he believes we give the Partisans, plus fact that it is clear to him that a BLO with Partisans is always believed in preference to a BLO with his forces, all add up to mean that British have completely sold Yugoslavia down the river to the Russians.

He expected he would "have to fight his own battle with the Partisans after the war without material, moral or political support from us".[4] Even so, Armstrong and Bailey recommended that both Mihailovic and Tito be supplied, and some form of accommodation sought so that Yugoslavia could be divided between them.

The Foreign Office official Philip Nichols, assigned to analyse it, minuted his opposite number at SOE London on 10 December:

> Armstrong's and Bailey's proposals are certainly a brave effort to solve our Yugoslav problem. They are, however, based on the assumption that the Partisans will be prepared to collaborate in some way or another with Mihailovic. It seems to us that Maclean's report has put this possibility quite out of court. That being so, Armstrong's proposals rather fall to the ground. Furthermore ... we are now convinced it is necessary to get rid of Mihailovic.[5]

There is no evidence Churchill knew of the Armstrong-Bailey Report, let alone read it!

Churchill was not due back from Teheran until early December. Maclean meanwhile arranged the flying in to Cairo of a delegation of Partisan leaders, brow-beating an air vice-marshal into releasing an RAF plane for the purpose. It took several attempts, including, sadly, some British and Yugoslav fatalities, before William Deakin and the Partisan group were flown out on 3 December from a landing strip newly prepared near Tito's headquarters. James Klugmann looked after the delegation, which included Vladimir Velebit, while they were in Cairo.

The British Prime Minister arrived in Cairo on 2 December from the Big Three Summit with Roosevelt and Stalin, where they had agreed to increase support for Tito "to the greatest possible extent".[6] He had argued that the Balkans was an area "in which we could stretch the enemy to the utmost and give ourselves relief from the heavy battles which lay ahead".[7] Roosevelt had not shared his enthusiasm for the Partisans. Stalin had been surprised at Churchill's exaggeration of their strength and his high regard for Tito. Stalin disputed the number of Axis divisions in the Balkans the Partisans were allegedly tieing down, as Churchill later admitted in his memoirs. Tito assumed Stalin had persuaded Churchill to back him and was astonished when he was told that it was the other way round!

Churchill had proposed that the Anglo-American army, then in Italy stop half-way up the peninsula, cross the Adriatic to Yugoslavia and make for Vienna through the Ljubljana Gap in the eastern Alps. Stalin and Roosevelt had vetoed this, Stalin because he wanted to keep the British and Americans out of the Balkans, Roosevelt because his military chiefs had their sights firmly fixed on a cross-channel invasion of France and did not want any more Mediterranean sideshows to delay it.

Maclean and Deakin met Churchill at 10am on 8 December. According to Maclean, Churchill was

> installed in a villa out by the Pyramids. He was in bed when we arrived, smoking a cigar and wearing an embroidered dressing-gown. He started by telling us some anecdotes about the Teheran Conference and his meeting with Stalin. This, it appeared, had been a success. Then he asked me whether I wore a kilt when I was dropped out of an aeroplane, and from this promising point of departure, we

slid into a general discussion of the situation in Yugoslavia. He had read my report.[8]

In reiterating the report's main points to Churchill, Maclean apparently stressed his belief that weapons given to the Partisans would be used solely to kill Germans. In fact he knew perfectly well he could not control Tito's use of them; he must have realised they would be used to kill political opponents. He repeated, too, his conviction that Mihailovic was irredeemably compromised by collaboration. Knowing Churchill's weakness for the Yugoslav monarchy, he argued that King Peter's only chance of regaining his throne would be to dismiss Mihailovic and back Tito. Tito would then be responsive to British advice. Supporting the Partisans, he maintained, would help remove Soviet suspicions of the West's intentions in the Balkans.

A grand working dinner was held that evening at the British Embassy, hosted by Churchill. Yugoslavia was very much on the agenda. Among those present were Field Marshal Smuts, the South African Prime Minister (and one of Churchill's closest friends and advisers), Eden, Cadogan and Sir Miles Lampson, the British Ambassador to Egypt; as well as Maclean, Deakin, Randolph Churchill, and Julian Amery. Amery had expected to be sent to Greece to help reconcile the communist and royalist guerrillas, but Churchill had decided against reconciliation, plumping instead for the royalists. He suggested to Amery, by way of compensating for his disappointment, that he should join Maclean's mission in Yugoslavia. But Maclean would not have anything to do with Amery, believing him too pro-Mihailovic. At Randolph Churchill's prompting, they did discuss the matter. Amery says in *Approach March*: "I did not want to become involved in breaking with Mihailovic and this had become Fitzroy Maclean's main objective."

Two days later, on 10 December, Churchill held a working lunch with Maclean, Deakin and General Colin Gubbins, head of SOE, during which he made his fateful decision to accept Maclean's recommendations in full: to back Tito wholeheartedly and to drop Mihailovic completely. Although Churchill did not announce his decision publicly until 22 February 1944, he wrote and told Tito of it in early January, assuring him Mihailovic would receive no more aid. He went further and agreed to accept the Partisans as co-belligerents with the Allies, as Tito had requested. This gave them enormous prestige and credibility among those Yugoslavs who had hitherto wavered between backing Tito or Mihailovic. It also brought the Partisans within the Geneva Conventions regarding the conduct of war. No other guerrilla group then on the European continent was so protected.

Apparently a map of Yugoslavia showing the various areas claimed by Maclean to be held by the Partisans and the forces of Mihailovic respectively played an important part in Churchill's decision. Michael Lees suggests it was probably the one to which Desmond Morton, Churchill's intelligence aide, had referred to in his memo to Churchill dated 2 December 1943:

> SOE Cairo has given me for you a copy of their *most secret* map show-ing the disposition of the Partisan forces and Mihailovic's as at 8am this morning 2 December... This map shows the position much better than the one which you receive daily in London. The London version suggests that the Germans hold most of the country with the Partisans hiding in inaccessible districts. Cairo's operational map, which is corrected daily from the large number of operational telegrams which they receive from the field, shows almost the reverse to be the position. The Germans are holding all the main lines of communications but the greater part of the country is in Partisan hands. The Cairo map also shows the very small districts now held by General Mihailovic.[9]

The London maps were put together from the Enigma decrypts and other intelligence information, whereas Klugmann was respons-ible for compiling the Cairo maps. He was effectively in sole charge of SOE Cairo's Yugoslav desk at this time. Basil Davidson had left in August, Keble had been transferred elsewhere on 27 November and Deakin did not return until 4 December. Moreover Deakin, as he admits, was heavily engaged, as soon as he returned to Cairo, in com-posing a memo for Maclean and Churchill on Mihailovic's alleged collaboration.

There was trouble later over other maps compiled by Klugmann, as Michael Lees relates in his memoirs. When he and the other liaison officers with Mihailovic were flown out of Yugoslavia in the spring of 1944, they had to travel a hundred and fifty miles across Serbia to the evacuation point, and they did not encounter a single Partisan unit. Yet when they arrived in Bari, Italy, where SOE Cairo was then located, the maps in the offices showed the areas they had passed through to be firmly in Partisan hands. One of his colleagues, Major Jasper Rootham (later a top official in the Bank of England), was so incensed he struck the pins from the map. Thereafter he and the other liaison officers who had been with Mihailovic were forbidden access to the SOE map room! Also, the American Lieutenant-Colonel Robert McDowell in his November 1944 report on the Yugoslav guerrilla scene to Washington, says that on the eve of his departure to Serbia in the summer of 1944

> he examined a situation map [in Cairo] prepared by the British from Partisan sources. This showed much of Western Serbia where the mission was expected to land as Partisan "liberated territory". After landing [he] diligently sought for evidence of Partisan liberated areas between the Morava and the Drina [rivers] but found that there were none and had been none.

Deakin, in his memoirs *The Embattled Mountain,* says of the 10 December meeting with Churchill: "As I talked I knew that I was compiling the elements of a hostile brief which would play a decisive part in any future break between the British Government and Mihailovic." He recalls being interrogated by Churchill for nearly two hours

> as the officer mainly concerned with interpreting the evidence derived from captured German and Cetnik documents concerning the links between Mihailovic and his commanders with the Italians and the Germans.

He does not mention that those "captured" documents had come mostly from the Partisans. Nor does he appear to have questioned their veracity, which is surprising for a professional historian. He had of course never met Mihailovic or any of his commanders, and hence had no first-hand knowledge of them. Neither had he talked to any of the liaison officers who had been with Mihailovic. Also, as he admits in his memoirs, he never sought to interrogate Chetnik prisoners. He relied in the main on what the Partisans told him. In his obituary of Deakin for *The Independent* newspaper in London in January 2005, the historian Sir Michael Howard stated: "as a young officer in the Special Operations Executive it was largely his experience and advice that persuaded Winston Churchill to support the Communist partisans in Yugoslavia," a point of view firmly endorsed by the obituarist in *The Times* who declared:

> It was largely as a result of Deakin's reports of the partisans' effectiveness and perhaps, too, of the faith which Churchill personally had in Deakin's judgement, that the British Government decided to withdraw its support from the Cetniks and to concentrate on helping the partisans.

That Tito might want Mihailovic eliminated, not for the better pursuit of the war but for purely political reasons, seems never to have troubled Deakin. Tito was later to say how surprised he had been to find Deakin and Maclean such willing tools in his desire to liquidate his political opponents. He honoured Deakin in 1969 with the Partisan Star First Class "for special services in the People's Liberation War". Deakin had already been awarded the Russian Order of Valour in 1944. By then Maclean had been deluged with much higher awards. According to *The Times* obituary of him, he had been given by Tito a "summer home in Korcula, a Croatian Adriatic island, which Tito allowed him to own despite foreigners being forbidden to possess property in communist Yugoslavia". It comprised two small Venetian seventeenth-century palaces. The Maclean family still own them.

Deakin relied on information passed to him by the Partisans. As a professional historian he must have realised it would be partial and needed to be supported by other, less subjective sources. He relied, too, on extracts from reports by British liaison officers with Mihailovic's forces, no doubt selected by Klugmann. Ironically, most of the liaison officers in question, many of whom I have since interviewed, were extremely sympathetic to Mihailovic. They maintain their comments were taken out of context, or else had been made when they were deeply disillusioned at the lack of supplies from Cairo and consequent reluctance on the part of some of Mihailovic's commanders to undertake sabotage.

Jasper Rootham, one of those officers, recalls in his memoirs *Miss Fire*, that he and Erik Greenwood, another liaison officer, received a signal from SOE Cairo on 29 November 1943 asking whether any of Mihailovic's commanders had to their knowledge received orders from Mihailovic to collaborate with the Axis. This suggests, even at that late stage, Klugmann was still scratching for "evidence". Not only was their answer no but Rootham mentions the execution in December 1943, by his local Mihailovic commander, of a subordinate "for treating with the enemy". The subordinate had replied to a letter from the Germans who were threatening to burn down a nearby town in retaliation for an attack in which thirty Germans had been killed. He had, truthfully or untruthfully Rootham does not say, disclaimed responsibility for the raid. Rootham says he quoted the story "to show that, in Eastern Serbia at any rate, there was up to the end of 1943 no question at all of collaboration with the Germans".

While perusing official files at the National Archives in London I came across a letter from Major E.C. Last to J. Reed of the Foreign Office dated 4 August 1944, typical perhaps of many such, accompanying the testimony of a British Liaison Officer recently evacuated from Mihailovic territory:

> On the vexed subject of Collaboration by the Cetniks with the Germans and Bulgars. He was in Southern Serbia from May to December of last year [1943] ... He states, "I did not discover any reason to suspect that there was any collaboration in my area between the Cetniks and the Germans or Bulgars, whilst I was there, and I have no reason to suspect so now".

Major Last adds, somewhat wearily (he had clearly interviewed many such liaison officers):

> Of course a good deal depends on one's definition of "collaboration", but at any rate it seems pretty clear that this particular officer saw nothing in the way of direct relations between the Cetniks and the enemy.[10]

One would expect Deakin, as a professional historian, to offer by way of balance similar evidence concerning links Tito and his commanders had with the Italians and the Germans. Yet there was no mention at all to Churchill of the March 1943 negotiations between the Partisans and the Germans, or, for instance, of the prisoner exchanges of August and November 1942, the gist of which had been revealed by Enigma decrypts. The March 1943 parleying could well have led to substantial Allied casualties, a circumstance Mihailovic's commanders never intended in their temporary "accommodations" with the Italian occupiers.

Deakin appears to have been unwilling to give any weight to the "reprisals" argument when considering Mihailovic's attitude to sabotage, in particular Mihailovic's concern not to furnish the Germans with an excuse to exterminate the Serbs. Indeed Churchill and his advisers seem not to have worried much about reprisals against Serbs, though they were concerned about retribution against the French. The *Maquis* were often enjoined to avoid civilian casualties by not killing Germans. There are very few references to reprisals in Deakin's memoirs, *The Embattled Mountain*. Nor in any of his writings does he dwell on the impact of the Ustasha massacres on the Serbs, leading to their enhanced suspicion of Croats in general, especially after the Croat treachery during the April 1941 German invasion. This was in line with Churchill's own attitude then.

Erik Greenwood, a liaison officer with Mihailovic, told me how his Serb colleagues were forever talking about the Ustasha massacres. All discussion of Serbo-Croat relations was clouded by the million or so Serbs they were convinced had been massacred by Croats. He claimed London made bigger noises about much smaller massacres in France and Czechoslovakia. My only conversation with Deakin, in December 1991, certainly confirmed these impressions. There was an interesting incident during dinner at Deakin's London club, Brooks, when a Tory grandee the worse for drink lumbered over to our table and insisted on introducing his equally inebriated guest, to Sir William: "Meet the man most responsible for the f***ing mess Yugoslavia now finds itself in!"

One of the instances of Mihailovic's alleged collaboration cited by Deakin involved a November 1943 report from two British liaison officers with Mihailovic's subordinate commander, Radislav Djuric. Apparently Djuric had been ordered by Mihailovic to contact the Germans in Belgrade directly. When I located the signal in question at the National Archives at Kew, I noticed a member of the Foreign Office had written on the outside of the file, "another nail in Mihailovic's coffin".[11] However, it turned out it had been merely suggested to Djuric that he infiltrate young volunteers into the pro-German Serbian state guard in Belgrade with a view to obtaining intelligence of German troop movements. The aim was also to gain access to their weapons and ammunition in the event of a general uprising when the Allies were about to liberate Yugoslavia.

The liaison officers in question were new to Yugoslavia. Not understanding Serbo-Croat, they had relied on an interpreter, who had clearly misled them. Their report to SOE Cairo had been eagerly seized upon, presumably by Klugmann, and copied to SOE London, the Foreign Office and Churchill himself, who passed it on to President Roosevelt and some of the Commonwealth premiers. Although the mistake was discovered *before* Deakin's decisive discussion with Churchill, there is no evidence that he was told or that any attempt was made by SOE to issue a correction.

That there was mischief-making behind the incident was made clearer when it was learned later that the subordinate commander in question had long been jealous of Mihailovic. Seeking to take his place in Britain's favour, Djuric had a motive for denigrating him. Djuric absconded eventually to the Partisans, eluding arrest by Mihailovic who suspected him of treachery. He had taken as his mistress a notorious ex-Gestapo spy and former communist who had previously been the mistress of a German general! Tito had evidently welcomed him and promptly gave him a post in the Partisan army. He further rewarded him after the war. Fitzroy Maclean in his memoirs mentions meeting Djuric in September 1944:

> This amusing, somewhat cynical character seemed to have been received by the Partisans with open arms, although in the past he had always been known, even amongst the Cetniks, for the ruthless brutality with which he had waged war against them.

Michael Lees in his memoirs records how Djuric, whom he describes as "the ultimate nasty bit of work", prevented him on many occasions from sabotaging the important north-south railway passing through his area, which was used by Hitler to transport strategic materials to the *Reich*.

Sir Harold Hinsley in his official history, *British Intelligence in the Second World War*, cites instances of Mihailovic's alleged collaboration reported to SOE Cairo by a Captain Robertson, then attached to Mihailovic's headquarters. Clearly no one told Hinsley that "Robertson" was in fact the communist spy Dragi Radivojvec, a Canadian-Yugoslav apparently controlled by James Klugmann. He debunked from Mihailovic's headquarters to Tito's in controversial circumstances and was eventually executed by the Partisans for his alleged Trotskyist beliefs! It could well be that Deakin used him as a source too.

Churchill had asked Deakin to convey to the Yugoslav monarch, then in Cairo, his decision regarding Mihailovic and Tito. King Peter says in his memoirs, *A King's Heritage*, that he found Deakin "very 'anti-Mihailovic'" and "rather naïve", particularly as he felt "the Partisans were not virulently Communist". He found "his knowledge of the Serbian language was very elementary". Peter also records how, when his prime minister Bozidar Puric asked Churchill for proofs of Mihailovic's collaboration, the reply was, "I have no proofs, but I am satisfied that he is collaborating."

Prior to Deakin's decisive meeting with Churchill, Ralph Stevenson, the British Ambassador to the Yugoslav government-in-exile, had cabled the Foreign Office in London from Cairo on 3 December 1943. The Special Operations Committee, in considering future relations with Mihailovic, had, he said,

> agreed that, *as most of the evidence regarding Mihailovic's collaboration with the enemy could not be published*, it was desirable to strengthen the case against him by calling upon him to carry out by a given date

some specific operation known to be within his power, *in the certain knowledge that he would fail to do so* [my italics].[12]

Stevenson signalled the Foreign Office five days later that the Committee had decided what operations (there were now to be two) Mihailovic was to carry out. They were to be detailed in a message Brigadier Armstrong was to deliver to Mihailovic. Armstrong was not to give the impression it was in any way a test; Mihailovic was simply being asked to confirm his sincerity to the Allied cause. However, "a final decision as to future policy towards Mihailovic may in fact depend upon the extent to which Mihailovic complies."[13] The message, in the name of the Commander-in-Chief, Middle East, General Maitland Wilson, went off on 13 December to Armstrong. It specified the demolition of two designated bridges on the Belgrade-Salonika railway and asked for Mihailovic's "agreement by 29th December".[14] SOE Cairo amended this to "compliance by 29th December".[15] Many commentators have since chosen to interpret this as requiring the sabotage to be *completed* in full by 29 December. But the message Armstrong actually delivered to Mihailovic said: "Your agreement requested by 29th December."

Although Armstrong passed the directive on to Mihailovic's headquarters as soon as he received it, he was unable to discuss it in person with Mihailovic until several days later. Before then Ralph Stevenson, who did not now hide his antipathy towards Mihailovic, indicated on 16 December to Armstrong: "Wish to make it clear to you that decision to break [with Mihailovic] is being considered on its own merits irrespective of Mihailovic's attitude towards these operations."[16] Churchill had apparently told Stevenson on 10 December that he wanted Mihailovic removed before the end of the month. Many in the Foreign Office wondered what would happen if Mihailovic carried out the directive. One of the British liaison officers with Mihailovic, code-named Field, wired SOE Cairo on 16 December that he had seen the previous day a signal from Mihailovic to Keserovic, one of his more capable commanders, ordering him to carry out the sabotage in question.

Not waiting for Mihailovic's reply to the directive, SOE Cairo had already, on 13 December, signalled the British liaison officers with the seventeen Mihailovic sub-missions to prepare to leave Yugoslavia or, if possible, to join the Partisans:

During the next few days His Majesty's Government may decide to drop Mihailovic which would involve evacuation all British personnel from Mihailovic HQ and areas. Burn this signal after reading. Only method evacuation is through Partisan territory. Tito has guaranteed safe conduct for all British entering Partisan areas from Mihailovic areas ... Treat this as a warning order. Will signal when decision made. Be prepared to move 15th, repeat 15th, if journey to Partisans considered possible.[17]

That Tito had given a guarantee implies he must have been told of the evacuation plan.

Armstrong reacted angrily to this message being sent without his knowledge. He cabled Cairo the next day indicating that a safe withdrawal could only be accomplished with Mihailovic's co-operation. Cairo remained silent. Some of the liaison officers were already preparing to leave, which made the Serbs under their command deeply suspicious. Concerned for their safety, Armstrong took the matter into his own hands and approached Mihailovic, who pledged his help. This let the cat out of the bag. Mihailovic realised Wilson's bridges directive was insincere. He had replied on 27 December to the effect that, though he thought the time-scale too short and he lacked the appropriate weapons for attacking pillboxes, he was nevertheless prepared to do his best. He assured Armstrong the sabotage would be carried out by mid-January at the latest. However, the targets were exceptionally well defended, because of their strategic importance to the Germans, so "success of operations may prove problematical".[18]

SOE Cairo refused to supply any of the explosives needed to blow up the bridges, saying Mihailovic must already have sufficient. But there had been no airdrops for some time. Nor were they prepared to guarantee replacing Mihailovic's stocks after the sabotaging: "There can be *no* [original italics] question of replenishment after the battle. Sorties are too scarce. They are better deserved, and bring better results elsewhere."[19] Clearly there were people in Cairo and London worried they might be put on the spot by Mihailovic's compliance with General Wilson's directive. They wished now to deter him. Archie Jack told me he had reconnoitred and planned in detail an attack on one of the bridges but had been forbidden to proceed by SOE Cairo. He had been prepared to sabotage the antimony mines nearby, too, but was ordered by Cairo to desist.

Without waiting for the 29 December "deadline" to expire, Stevenson cabled the Foreign Office in London on 28 December that he thought it unlikely Mihailovic would comply:

We are, therefore, fully justified, despite his statement that he will carry out the operations requested sometime during the first half of

January, in taking a decision now to withdraw our support from him. That decision, as stated in my telegram number 212, is based on his attitude of non-cooperation over a long period and on the fact that he has approved collaboration of his subordinate leaders with the enemy.

Eden replied the same day, and copied his reply to Churchill, pointing out the dilemma they might face if Mihailovic did pass this "test of his good faith". He added: "do you propose to ignore the fact and adhere to your advice of breaking with him at once?"[20]

That Eden's colleagues in the Foreign Office had not been swayed by this advice was evident from a memo written by Armine R. Dew on 30 December:

> I cannot help feeling that Cairo is making up a case for the immediate break with Mihailovic in order that this may smooth the way with Tito. But if Tito won't play on the other issues then we shall have broken with Mihailovic without any *quid pro quo* and may drive Mihailovic into the arms of the Germans and alienate all those with him.[21]

Sir Orme Sargent, the number two in the Foreign Office, commented the following day:

> I agree with Mr Dew that we ought for tactical reasons to go slow over Mihailovic ... It is essential therefore that our evidence of his treachery should be unanswerable: it is not enough merely to denounce him for not having attacked the Germans more vigorously or as vigorously as Tito. In that aspect he after all is no worse than have been the Greek guerrillas during all these months of civil war. Nor can we condemn Mihailovic because he fights the Partisans. It would be impossible to prove that Mihailovic was the first to attack ... Lastly we come to the unfortunate test operation. Here, as I foresaw, we have got ourselves into difficulty, for Mihailovic has not refused, as Mr Stevenson hoped he would, but has merely asked for a fortnight's grace in order to make his plans ... On the strength of this reply Mr Stevenson says we are fully justified in taking a decision now to withdraw our support from him: I beg to differ. I think it makes it increasingly difficult and is an additional reason for putting off our decision for the time being, in the hopes of some fresh development.

Anthony Eden's note in the margin, dated 1 January 1944 reads: "There is force in all this."[22]

But Stevenson kept at it and telegraphed the Foreign Office on 4 January:

President Tito with Prime Minister Winston Churchill in London, 16th March 1953

Tito, President of Yugoslavia, circa 1975

Brigadier Armstrong has reported that British Liaison officers are being sent out to watch attacks which Mihailovic forces may possibly carry out on two bridges during the first fortnight of January. Even if operations are carried out this will not in my opinion entail obligations to Mihailovic for reasons which I have already reported.[23]

And again on 7 January:

We do not expect that Mihailovic will in fact make a serious attempt to carry out the operations successfully. But in the unlikely event of his doing so, our attitude will have to be that we cannot regard last minute repentance as being sufficient to outweigh Mihailovic's record of two years' inactivity.[24]

Stevenson could have relaxed. Churchill, Maclean and Deakin had already decided to ditch Mihailovic regardless. Churchill was committeed: he had promised Tito so in a letter dated 8 January which Maclean was to deliver personally. Armstrong effectively drew a line under the affair when he signalled on 24 January that the operations had been compromised as the defences and local garrisons had been increased. The bridges, he said, were now guarded by tanks. Clearly the Germans had been tipped off. Mihailovic reported that the detachments designated to sabotage the bridges had been attacked by Partisans! Armstrong and Bailey continued to challenge the decision to drop Mihailovic, reminding London that Tito had little or no support in Serbia, Yugoslavia's heartland. But of course to no avail.

Maclean says he warned Churchill during their discussions in December 1943 that, as Tito was an avowed communist, Yugoslavia would most probably become a communist country if he gained political power there. Churchill, according to Maclean, replied: "Do you intend to make Yugoslavia your home after the war?" "No Sir." "Neither do I. And that being so, the less you and I worry about the form of government they set up, the better. That is for them to decide. What interests us is, which of them is doing most harm to the Germans."[25]

Churchill was of course under great pressure when he made his fateful decision to back Tito. His colleagues had long been concerned about his punishing schedule. Field Marshal Smuts complained on 30 October 1943 to Churchill's secretaries that they "let the PM work much too hard and much too late at night. We must remember Mr Churchill was not young any more." Churchill had had pneumonia in

February that year and had been confined to his bed for more than a week. His doctors had told him to take things easier. It was advice he ignored, despite the pleadings of his wife.

He had not been well enough to preside over the Cabinet on 11 November. The next day he left by train for Plymouth to sail in the battleship *Renown* for Egypt. He recalled in his memoirs *Closing the Ring*: "I was feeling far from well, as a heavy cold and sore throat were reinforced by the consequences of inoculations against typhoid and cholera. I stayed in bed for several days." When they reached Malta on 17 November, Churchill went ashore still feeling unwell and spent most of his two days there in bed. He telegraphed Eden on 18 November: "I am laid up with a sore throat for the moment and am remaining here today and probably tomorrow."[26] The sore throat persisted through the Teheran conference, as Alanbrooke noted in his diary for 28 November: "PM has bad throat and has practically lost his voice. He is not fit and consequently not in the best of moods." Churchill was again unwell immediately after Teheran, as Cadogan noted in his diary on 4 December: "PM not too well, and cried off dinner."[27] It was thought to be merely a stomach pain.

Martin Gilbert, in his official biography of Churchill, says that at this time

> Churchill submitted to a punishing schedule of talks and appointments. On December 8 his first meeting, at ten in the morning was about aid to Tito's partisans ... Shortly after midday Churchill called on King Farouk, then lunched with Eden and the King of Greece. Following his afternoon sleep, he had talks first with General Wilson, then, once more, with Harold Macmillan. At dinner at the British Embassy the guests included Field Marshal Smuts, General Brooke, Maclean, Deakin, Lord Jellicoe ... After dinner, there was a further discussion with Macmillan. "Winston was in great form and holding forth to a circle of these young men", Macmillan noted. But Smuts had formed a different impression of Churchill's condition, pulling Brooke aside while Churchill was presiding over the conversation "to tell me", as Brooke noted in his diary, "that he was not at all happy about the condition of the PM". Smuts told Brooke that he considered Churchill "worked far too hard and exhausted himself", and added that "he was beginning to doubt whether he would stay the course; that he was noticing changes in him".[28]

According to Lord Alanbrooke's fuller diaries, Smuts, one of Churchill's closest friends, went on to say Churchill, when tired, "had to rely on drink to stimulate him again".[29] Alanbrooke records he too

had noticed at lunch that same day, 9 December, the eve of his decision to back Tito, that Churchill

> was looking very tired and said he felt very flat, tired and had pains
> across his loins ... He kept on harping back and repeating details
> which were of no consequence and I saw that it was useless in his
> tired state to discuss the larger issues.

Churchill, in *Closing the Ring*, admits he "had not been at all well"
at this time: "I noticed that I no longer dried myself after my bath,
but lay on the bed wrapped in my towel till I dried naturally." He had
not felt so exhausted since the war began.

Gilbert says, on 10 December:

> Churchill had another busy schedule. In the morning there were
> meetings with both King Peter of Yugoslavia and the Regent of Iraq,
> followed by a Press conference. At lunch Yugoslavia was the issue,
> with the head of SOE, General Gubbins, Brigadier Maclean and
> Major Deakin being invited to the discussion of future support for
> Tito. Greece was the theme in the afternoon, with several Greek
> statesmen to see. There followed dinner at the British Embassy, at
> which Smuts, Eden, Cadogan, Casey and Randolph Churchill were
> among those present ... That night at 1am, Churchill left Cairo for
> the westward flight to Tunisia, the prelude, as he hoped, to a visit to
> the British troops in Italy.[30]

Alanbrooke noted in his diary for 11 December that, after the
eight and a half hour flight, "PM very tired and flat, he seems to be
in a bad way. The conference has tired him out and he will not rest
properly and insists on working." That night, at Eisenhower's villa
near Carthage, Churchill felt a pain in his throat and hardly slept.
In the morning he was found to have a temperature of 102 degrees.
A portable X-Ray machine was brought from Tunis. It showed a
shadow on his lung. He had pneumonia; pleurisy, too, was feared.
He was immediately given the new antibiotic sulphonamide, made
by May and Baker, and put to bed. His condition worsened on
14 December. His doctor Lord Moran told Harold Macmillan, the
future British Prime Minister, the next day that "he thought the PM
was going to die last night. He thinks him a little better as regards
the pneumonia, but is worried about his heart."[31] He had had a heart
attack. Various specialists were called from Cairo, Italy and London.
His wife and children were summoned to his bedside. He had
another heart attack on 18 December, but he began to pull through.
On 27 December he was able to move to Marrakesh in Morocco to
convalesce. He was there almost three weeks and did not return

to London until 18 January 1944. Some of his closest companions maintained he was never again as vigorous or as sprightly as before his illness.

Like their London colleagues in SOE, British diplomats in the Foreign Office, Churchill's Foreign Secretary Anthony Eden in particular, had played little part in the decision to drop Mihailovic and back Tito. By and large they had been mere spectators. As Churchill and Maclean between them had taken over British policy towards Yugoslavia from December 1943, they had become ever more distant observers. London had suggested the two main liaison officers with Mihailovic, Brigadier Armstrong and Colonel Bailey, be flown out of Yugoslavia for the Cairo meeting with Churchill. SOE Cairo had said it was not possible logistically, although a delegation of Partisan leaders was got out. They were trotted around to see the military and political chiefs and to make their influence felt.

The Foreign Office was concerned that dropping Mihailovic meant abandoning King Peter and the Yugoslav government-in-exile. They worried that the obsession with immediate military needs would lead to future political problems – as was to be the case. Eden wrote to Churchill on 19 January 1944, when he had finally read Maclean's Report: "Naturally to Maclean Tito is all white and Mihailovic all black. I have a suspicion that grey is a more common Balkan colour."[32] Eden was to say later that he never even knew about the Armstrong-Bailey Report.

Churchill telegraphed Eden on 20 December 1943 – two days after his heart attack – that he felt the time had come to press King Peter "towards procuring the dismissal of General Mihailovic", which he thought "a most necessary step". Churchill's son Randolph, about to join Maclean at Tito's headquarters, had been urging on him the "immediate repudiation" of Mihailovic by the British Government, "and if possible" by King Peter.[33] Eden, however, complained to Ralph Stevenson in Cairo on 28 December that he had as yet no conclusive evidence of Mihailovic's collaboration; if such evidence existed would he please forward it "by fastest available means".[34] Eden replied to Churchill the next day:

> I am doubtful whether we should tell Tito now that we are prepared to have no further dealings with Mihailovic. First, because we here at any rate have not yet got conclusive evidence of his misbehaviour, and secondly because tactically it would seem better to keep this up our sleeves as a concession to Tito if he is prepared to discuss working with the King at all.[35]

Eden telegraphed Churchill again two days later on 1 January 1944:

> As regards Mihailovic, I do not recollect any decision in Cairo to demand his dismissal before the end of the year. Maybe this was after I left. I still feel that it would be a mistake to promise Tito at this moment that we will break the man, not merely by depriving him of supplies, but by forcing the King to dismiss him ... I think Tito would look upon it as a sign of weakness on our part to volunteer this promise to him ... If we have a public and spectacular breach with Mihailovic our case against him for treachery must be unanswerable. I am still without evidence of this.[36]

Churchill replied the next day, when convalescing in Marrakesh:

> There is no doubt in my mind whatever that Mihailovic is in collaboration with the enemy. This was confirmed not only by people like Deakin who have come back from Tito's forces but by many of the officers now serving in the Mihailovic area. I have been convinced by the arguments of men I know and trust that Mihailovic is a millstone tied round the neck of the little King, and he has no chance till he gets rid of him ... Once Mihailovic has been dismissed, I believe that Maclean and Randolph will have a chance to work on Tito for a return of the King to his country.[37]

As regards millstones, it could be argued that, with their tedious machinations and endless squabbles which had long exasperated their British hosts, the king and his government had become a millstone around poor Mihailovic's neck!

Churchill again telegraphed Eden on 6 January: "My unchanging object is to get Tito to let the King come out and share the luck with him ... and bring in the old Serbian core." By "old Serbian core" Churchill presumably meant Mihailovic's followers whom he mistakenly thought were devoted more to the monarchy than to Mihailovic. In bringing them in, Churchill continued to be convinced Mihailovic's dismissal was "an essential preliminary".[38] He went ahead and in a letter to Tito dated 8 January, which Maclean was to hand over personally, wrote:

> I am resolved that the British Government will give no further military support to Mihailovic and will only give help to you, and we should be glad if the Royal Yugoslavian Government would dismiss him from their councils.[39]

Maclean reported that Tito was "frankly delighted" to receive the letter, which must have been an understatement! Churchill had jumped the gun on this. He had not agreed it with his cabinet colleagues.

Eden was still saying on 9 January: "it would be unwise to back Tito and abandon Mihailovic". He argued further in a cable to Churchill on 19 January:

> I understand that reports from our Liaison Officers show that Mihailovic undoubtedly still commands wide support in Serbia, perhaps in most of Serbia. If Mihailovic is dropped, what will happen to the Serbs who now support him? Some might go over to Tito, but the majority would probably either continue inactive or follow Mihailovic or some of his henchmen possibly into the enemy's camp. Unsatisfactory though Mihailovic is, there are still two Bulgarian divisions looking after him.[40]

Ambassador Stevenson let the cat out of the bag when cabling London from Cairo on 18 January:

> It is generally agreed here that Mihailovic's behaviour over last two years and other evidence do not support pretension that Mihailovic potentially controls resistance in vital areas. There is therefore justi-fication for our assuming that there is no Serbian resistance organ-isation other than Partisans, to which with military advantage to ourselves, Serbs can turn in event of a break with Mihailovic. Nor for operational reasons do we wish unco-ordinated individual resistance or dubious mushroom nationalist organisations to be promoted as substitutes for Mihailovic. We have also good grounds for assuming that the Partisans would be hostile to such organisations as they have been to Chetniks.

On the file copy held at Kew a Foreign Office official had pencilled: "Surely what we want is resistance – we can't possibly insist that the only sort of resistance we want is Partisan resistance." Douglas Howard, head of the Southern Department at the Foreign Office, minuted in that same file:

> Stevenson tells us flat that even if Mihailovic were removed the Partisans would be equally hostile to any other resistance organis-ations which might be set up in Serbia. That shows clearly enough that Tito is only interested in having no other competitive resistance units in Yugoslavia.[41]

Eden was not to get the "Evidence against Mihailovic" requested urgently from Stevenson on 28 December 1943 until 21 January 1944. It turned out to be a very slim, unconvincing volume.[42] In putting it together the Foreign Office quoted Armstrong as saying:

> Mihailovic has great political influence with the people of Serbia, particularly the peasants. His organisation is predominant and

well-developed throughout that country. He also commands the real
affection of the masses, not only as a Serbian nationalist, but also on
account of his stand against Communism. The Serb peasant is at
heart anti-communist and this attitude has been enhanced by the
behaviour of Partisans during their 1941 campaign in Serbia.[43]

They also observed:

> Mihailovic's hold on the Serbian people was further emphasised by
> Brigadier Armstrong's opinion that we should have no chance of
> getting rid of Mihailovic by disgracing him since even if written
> proof of collaboration with the enemy were in our hands the popu-
> lation of Serbia would simply refuse to believe it.

Armstrong maintained:

> the elimination of Mihailovic from the Yugoslav Cabinet would have
> little effect on his movement in Serbia. His followers would probably
> feel that they had been abandoned by the British and that their sole
> hope rested in continued loyalty to Mihailovic in order to protect
> Serbian interests against its powerful internal enemies. This means
> that we cannot count on our withdrawal of support from Mihailovic
> to bring the majority of Serbs into the Partisan camp: it is more likely
> to have the effect of confirming them in their determination to resist
> the Partisans at all costs. Our desertion of Mihailovic would merely
> be attributed to Soviet machinations. It might even drive Mihailovic
> himself and his supporters into open collaboration with the Ger-
> mans, or at least with Nedic.

It is not clear how widely this "Evidence against Mihailovic" was
distributed, if at all. In any case, by 21 January minds had largely been
made up, especially within Churchill's entourage. It would have been
difficult, if not impossible, for them to have gone into reverse,
despite the continuing concerns of senior diplomats in the Foreign
Office.

On 9 February the Commander-in-Chief, Middle East proposed the
immediate withdrawal of the liaison officers with Mihailovic. He
maintained that otherwise Tito might be unwilling to accept the full
Allied missions which were essential if British and American support
for him was to be effective. The Supreme Allied Commander in the
Mediterranean concurred. After further pressure from Churchill, so
did Eden on 17 February. The British liaison officers were not all
finally withdrawn until the end of May, mostly by air from a strip
secured by Mihailovic's forces. A few of the American officers stayed

behind as Mihailovic continued facilitating the rescue of American airmen. He was not dismissed by King Peter until 16 May.

Some of the British liaison officers travelled nearly two hundred miles from their operational areas to the evacuation point. None saw any Partisans en route but Mihailovic's forces defended them from attacks by the Germans until the moment of their departure. Bill Hudson was evacuated in mid-March. He and the American Colonel Seitz were fired upon and nearly killed by a group of Partisans when they became involved in a skirmish with some Germans and quisling Chetniks. Seitz was convinced the shooting was intended to appear as if done by the Chetniks for political purposes. Colonel Bailey was evacuated in mid-February. The liaison officers were given the option of joining the nearest Partisan units and Robert Wade was one of the very few who did. He told me how different the Partisans were from Mihailovic's men:

> They were very cold. Every word you spoke they noted. I'm quite sure there was no joy there at all. They were glum and dull. They never laughed. Whereas the Chetniks enjoyed life and we had a lot of drinks together. It was fun.

He also recalled seeing the Partisans recruiting men forcibly: "If they did not want to come, they ran away and were shot."

Indicative of how bloody-minded the British attitude towards Mihailovic was at this time was the experience of Mihailovic's aide, Major Vojislav Lukacevic. He accompanied Colonel Bailey to London as he was representing Mihailovic at King Peter's wedding on 20 March. Bailey was to acknowledge how helpful Lukacevic had been in facilitating his evacuation. Lukacevic did not return to Yugoslavia until May, laden with letters to Mihailovic including one from the king, as well as other gifts from him such as golden cufflinks, a revolver and a sub-machine gun, all embossed with the royal insignia. He was stripped of everything by the British authorities in Bari – even his personal belongings and wristwatch – before being allowed on the plane to Serbia to bring out the last of the British liaison officers. On other occasions when Mihailovic despatched envoys to solicit help from the Americans they were invariably delayed in Italy by the British. Harassed and sometimes imprisoned, they were allowed to go on their way only when their plight came to the attention of the Americans. The British also prevented attempts by the Americans to send Mihailovic food and medical or other non-military supplies.

The United States had had liaison officers with Mihailovic since mid-1943. Captain Walter R. Mansfield, a lawyer in civilian life and later a leading federal district judge, had parachuted in on 18 August. He was joined by Colonel Albert Seitz. They toured Serbia extensively, with Bill Hudson as interpreter. Mansfield reported to Washington in March 1944:

> Mihailovic still has a great grip on the Serbian peasant. Everywhere Colonel Seitz and I traveled on our tour through north-central Serbia the people in villages who turned out to see us cheered him madly. In private conversations they talk of him as one would of the Messiah. Cetnik troops and peasants alike sing romantic songs about him, and Ravna Gora, his original hideout, has become very sacred to the Serbian people. To them, Mihailovic still stands as a symbol of their spirit of resistance against the occupator. He also stands for the things they want, King and democracy. They feel that he did not desert them in their greatest hour of need, immediately after capitulation, but stayed to organise their resistance and fought against the Germans in 1941 when the big nations were losing the war everywhere else.

Mansfield also reported that he had noticed no collaboration between the Mihailovic forces and the Germans. Instead he had witnessed many clashes between them and had seen villages torched in reprisal by the Germans. He remarked on the strained relationship between his British colleagues and Mihailovic, which he put down to the frailties of their communications with Cairo and the waywardness of the airdrops: "There is complete distrust of the British by Mihailovic and his leaders, who feel the British have now sold them down the river to Stalin." They were especially irritated by the BBC, which "devoted its time almost exclusively to Partisan news and ignored Mihailovic". Moreover "in many instances BBC falsely credited the Partisans with many operations in fact carried out by the Cetniks". He said his British colleagues had obviously been told not to be unduly co-operative with the Americans. They were denied access to most conferences between the British and Mihailovic and had a lower priority than the British regarding outward signalling. The British insisted on vetting all outward American signals but would not let the Americans read theirs.

Although he had seen few Partisans on his tour of Serbia, Mansfield was appalled by the conflict between them and the Chetniks. He felt the United States and Britain were obliged to stop it. His impression was that the people in Serbia do not favour the Partisans, and that they are against communism. Every peasant wants only his King and a democratic form of government. We heard this expressed thousands of times. The peasants fear and hate the Partisans, whom they represent as an enemy which will burn down their houses and take away all of their food.

He had observed Partisans burning down houses belonging to Mihailovic supporters. As a result of Mansfield's report Washington wanted to send a bigger mission to Mihailovic. They were prevented by the British. Roosevelt also wished to extend Lend-Lease aid to him but was dissuaded by Churchill.

Churchill met King Peter on 13 April 1944 and advised him to dismiss his government as a way of "automatically" sacking Mihailovic. Peter was urged to form a small administration of people "not particularly obnoxious to Tito but still preserving a certain relation with the Serbian nation". All of which he telegraphed the next day to Stalin's Foreign Minister, Molotov![44] On 18 April Churchill wrote to his son Randolph in Yugoslavia:

> The Serbians are a valiant and powerful race, accustomed to centuries of torment. They have a large peasant proprietary and there can be no united Yugoslavia without their willing accord. A Balkan State without a Crown is an unimpressive political unit. They will need all their united forces and powerful connections to keep their independence.[45]

Churchill was a devoted believer in monarchy for historical as well as emotional reasons. Anthony Eden was less sentimental. He favoured backing the Greek and Yugoslav kings simply because that might help Britain retain some influence in their countries after the war. Elisabeth Barker, head of PWE's Balkan Section 1942-1945, maintains that of all the kings who fled from south-east Europe the Greek King George II

> was the only one whom the Foreign Office – and Churchill – tried really seriously to put back on his throne; efforts on behalf of King Peter of Yugoslavia appear in retrospect as a peculiarly lengthy and elaborate face-saving device.[46]

CHAPTER EIGHT

Churchill has Doubts

" 'In future', our directive ran, 'Mihailovic forces
will be described not as patriots but as terrorist gangs;
we shall drop the phrase "Red Bandits" as applied to
partisans and substitute "freedom fighters" ' "

RICHARD CROSSMAN

FOLLOWING CHURCHILL'S decision in December 1943 to back
Tito wholeheartedly, military supplies to the Partisans were immediately stepped up. In just two nights that month they received as
much as Mihailovic had in the previous two years! Liberators and
Dakotas suddenly became available for airdrops. By the end of the
war the Partisans were to receive more than sixty thousand tons by
sea and almost fourteen thousand tons by air from British and American sources, compared with the two hundred tons Mihailovic had
received. The aid was not just important militarily to the Partisans,
though it was to prove decisive in the Yugoslav civil war during 1944.
Vladimir Dedijer, in his *War Diaries*, maintains: "It does mean a lot in
the political sense. The people can see our power. They can see that
the Allies have acknowledged us." Dedijer had earlier said of William
Deakin and Fitzroy Maclean's appearances on the scene: "The arrival
of the English mission is a great victory for us."

While the Partisans grew steadily stronger politically and militarily, Mihailovic's forces became ever weaker. What is certain too is
that, after Churchill's decision, large-scale resistance to the German
occupation by either the Partisans or Mihailovic's forces virtually
ceased. Vane Ivanovic claims:

> From the moment of their recognition by the Western Allies, the
> Partisan leadership abandoned any serious initiative against Axis
> forces. They concentrated their efforts from early 1944 on for the
> Partisan return in force to Serbia and Macedonia, without control of
> which, plus the capital of Belgrade, no ultimate Partisan victory in
> Yugoslavia was conceivable.[1]

There are many who saw this, and still see it, as an example of British double standards. The British had been reluctant to send arms to Mihailovic during 1942 and 1943, and indeed virtually stopped doing so, because it was claimed he used them against the Partisans. Yet they continued sending weapons to the Partisans throughout 1944 when everybody knew they were being used against their political opponents, and that they had stopped resisting the Germans except when attacked.

American involvement in Yugoslavia now increased, largely due to the determination of the Office of Strategic Services (OSS), the US intelligence body, not to be stifled by SOE. The first OSS mission to Tito was parachuted in on 21 August 1943. Captain Melvin Benson was that envoy. He was joined on 18 September by Major Linn Farish. Farish's report to Washington was as enthusiastically pro-Partisan as Maclean's, but unlike Maclean he admitted his information came only from the Partisans. He returned to Tito's headquarters in January 1944, staying two months, and went back again in mid-April, remaining until mid-June. When he finally came out, a colleague who talked to him in Italy before dropping into Yugoslavia himself remembered him being

> disillusioned and greatly depressed. In his first report he had been certain the Partisans were fighting and would continue to fight the Germans. Now he believed that both the Chetniks and the Partisans were committed to fight each other to the bitter end ... It was inconceivable to him that the combined strength and influence of the Soviet Union, Great Britain, and the United States could not put an abrupt end to the civil wars in Yugoslavia and guarantee the people a free election.[2]

In his second report, dated 28 June 1944, Farish related how earlier that month, in the company of colleagues, including a British doctor, he had

> arrived in the Kukavica Mountains in search of three wounded American airmen, whom we found in a former Chetnik hospital in the area where the fighting had taken place [This was a battle a few days previously between Partisans and Chetniks in which the Partisans, according to Farish, had used weapons and ammunition recently supplied by the Americans]. These airmen informed us that they had been rescued by the Chetniks, that Chetnik doctors had treated them as best they could, and that the people of the so-called "Chetnik villages" had done everything possible to make them comfortable. They stated that a Chetnik doctor came back through the fighting for three nights to dress their wounds. They further stated

that this Chetnik doctor had photographs of a great many American and British airmen whom he had treated and helped to escape from the country… What a very peculiar set of circumstances these facts bring out! Rifles stamped "U.S. Property" firing W.R.A. [Winchester Repeating Arms] Ammunition, flown [in] by American airmen in American aircraft, being fired at people who have rescued other American airmen and who were doing everything to make them comfortable and to return them to safety. If I am confused, what must be the state of mind of the people of Yugoslavia … They are a simple peasant type of people, strong willed, hot-blooded, with tremendous powers of endurance and great personal courage … I do not believe there is any tremendous urge for Revolution among them. They love their mountains, their small homes, their farms, and their flocks. They want something better, but, measured by our standards, what most of them ask is not a great deal, a good government, their King and their church, schools, more roads, shoes, clothing, a few modern conveniences … The senseless killing of these people by each other must be stopped.

A few months after submitting his report, Farish was killed in an airplane accident in Greece. His close colleague Eli Popovic says he had been upset over what he had written in his first report, praising Tito: "He realised he'd been taken for a ride." Donald Hamilton-Hill, in *SOE Assignment*, mentions meeting Farish, who had complained of "the atmosphere of intrigue, evasiveness in discussions and deviousness in planning" at Tito's headquarters which he had found "too complicated for his peace of mind". After writing his second report Farish had had a mental breakdown and had been confined for a while in hospital in Algeria. His superiors had wanted to send him home, but he had refused.

Franklin Lindsay, a senior OSS representative with Tito, maintains in his memoirs, *Beacons in the Night*:

> Tito was determined to keep from us the extent to which the Partisans were fighting the Chetniks rather than the Germans as well as the extent to which they were using Allied weapons to do so. This undoubtedly was one factor behind Tito's campaign to restrict our contacts and movements with his units and to bring the maximum pressure on us to withdraw all American officers from Mihailovic's forces. In contrast, even after Allied support was stopped in 1943, Mihailovic and his commanders allowed American officers complete freedom to talk with all ranks and with civilians.

Another OSS agent was to signal Washington: "There's one thing about working with the Partisans that may as well be made clear once and for all. There is no such thing as freedom of movement."[3]

The British liaison officers with Tito quickly became mere conduits and quartermasters for handling the massive supplies pouring in to him. They took his requests for aid, passed them on to Bari and London, and then co-ordinated their dispatch and arrival. They had no say in how the supplies were to be used, nor did they demand any such say. This is remarkable as hitherto SOE policy had been to control strategy. Mihailovic had been made aware from the start that strings were attached to the aid he received. No strings were attached to the aid to Tito. Maclean, of course, maintained his was not an SOE mission but one reporting directly to the Supreme Allied Commander in the Mediterranean.

Lindsay relates how

> each month Allied headquarters would advise Tito through Maclean of the number of sorties that could be flown during the following month. Tito's headquarters then allocated these sorties to each Partisan resistance group. The volume of supplies for each was thus determined by Tito's headquarters, although the composition of the loads would be worked out by each Allied liaison officer together with the Partisan command with which he was working. Tito's purpose was to ensure that the British did not allocate supplies to specific areas for their own political reasons, or limit supplies to other regions to minimise the strength and influence of the Partisans there. Tito was thus able to control the allocation of Allied supplies to meet his own political and military objectives.

Apart from their political opponents now receiving no aid at all, the Partisans benefited enormously from not having to cope with thousands of wounded once they began to be flown out of Yugoslavia to Italy and Egypt. More than four thousand were airlifted before the end of 1943 and a further eight thousand during 1944. According to Vladimir Dedijer:

> The taking of the wounded to Italy represented the greatest aid which we received from the allies during the war. This not only meant the saving of the lives of our wounded comrades, but also the unburdening of our units, which in this way became far more mobile. They did not have to give up comrades to carry the wounded, to guard them, but could now manoeuvre freely.

Mihailovic had never been offered such help.

By October 1944 there were forty OSS officers in fifteen different missions within Yugoslavia. It soon became apparent to them that

Tito was interested only in their aid and not in their advice – certainly not in their leadership. The OSS boss General "Wild Bill" Donovan tried to persuade Roosevelt and Churchill to make him Allied supremo of guerrilla initiatives throughout the Balkans. Roosevelt was keen but Churchill adamantly opposed it. He had insisted earlier that the Americans with Mihailovic be withdrawn, which Donovan had resisted. The compromise was that Donovan was allowed to send new officers to Mihailovic to facilitate the evacuation of American aircrews forced to bail out over Serbia when their planes were shot down as they returned from bombing raids in south-eastern Europe, most often on the Ploesti oil wells in Romania. These were Hitler's main source of fuel for his tanks and planes, and they were the most heavily defended target in German-occupied Europe.

Captain Mansfield's report of March 1944 was severely critical of the Partisans and of British policy towards Tito. Thereafter there was a distinct anti-Tito mood in Washington. Most military chiefs and diplomats there resented Roosevelt's acceptance of British responsibility for Allied policy in the Balkans. Their anger came to a head over Britain's prevarication over the rescue of the downed American airmen. The report of another American, Colonel Robert McDowell, later that year was even more critical. He had already been responsible for a study of intelligence material based on Partisan sources in which he had concluded there were "so many serious contradictions in Partisan claims as to require rejection of the communiqués as serious military documents".[4]

The main purpose of McDowell's mission was to prepare the way for the evacuation of the airmen by locating possible airstrips from which they could be flown out. Franklin Lindsay remarks that the OSS group sent with McDowell for this task

> were impressed with the care the Chetniks took of the downed airmen. Men without adequate weapons, clothing, food, and medical care would nevertheless fight the Germans and Partisans to rescue and protect the Americans. The OSS men became personally embittered when the evacuation planes arrived either empty or with clothing and food only for the Allied airmen awaiting evacuation. This, in their view (and in mine), was a shoddy way to treat the Chetniks for risking their necks on our behalf. The orders were to strictly observe the American commitment to the British and Tito that no support was being provided. At the same time Allied aircraft were regularly

dropping weapons to the Partisan forces close by, who without a moment's consideration used them to subdue their prime enemy – the Chetniks.

To a man these aircrew were to vouch for the warm, kind and friendly treatment they received from Mihailovic's people. When debriefed by US intelligence officers they were also to confirm that they had seen no collaboration between Mihailovic's forces and the Germans. In fact many had witnessed armed clashes between Chetniks and Germans. Some related how Mihailovic's people had saved them from being seized by the Germans when they were injured in landing. Others described how they had been rescued after capture by the Germans. Such rescues had often prompted reprisals against local Serbs, the aftermath of which they had observed. The Germans razed villages thought to have harboured Allied airmen.

One rescued airman, Richard Felman, told me how, before setting out on their flight to Ploesti in July 1944, he and his crew had been warned to avoid the Chetniks if they bailed out over Serbia. It was said they were likely to cut off the ears of American airmen before handing them over to the Germans! Another recalled his rescuers being attacked by Partisans while transporting him to the evacuation airstrip. He had watched an Allied plane drop supplies to these Partisans and worried that the Serbs with him might react unfavourably. Instead they had expressed bewilderment, which he shared. Yet another airman had witnessed the Partisans killing Serbs who had helped the Americans evade capture by the Germans. Others, injured when their planes had been shot down, described how their wounds had been dressed by the Serbs, using plum brandy as an antiseptic because they lacked the proper medicines. They had been nursed back to health by the villagers who had fed them well although they barely had enough to support their own families.

Some of the airmen had feared the villagers might have been tempted to hand them over to the Germans in exchange for food and medicines. When they had voiced these concerns the Serbs had been shocked that they could have contemplated such a thing. They remarked how much these peasants hated the Partisans. One pilot, Charles Davis, who had spent some time with Mihailovic, attested to how much he loathed the Germans. He was not bitter towards the British and Americans for ditching him, merely perplexed. Others recounted how the villagers had hidden them when the Germans had come searching for them. If they had been found the villagers would have been shot on the spot. One described how the Germans had killed a fellow crewman who was bailing out. They had caught the body and stripped it of its clothing and valuables. Mihailovic's people had retrieved it and given it a decent burial.

Between August and December 1944, 346 Americans and 71 of other nationalities were evacuated from airstrips in Serbia and Bosnia built by Mihailovic's forces. Others had been flown out earlier, before the Allied missions to Mihailovic had been withdrawn. Mihailovic's attempts to contact the Allies regarding the airmen in his midst had at first been ignored by the British. The excuse given later was that the radio messages were thought to have come from Germans posing as Mihailovic supporters. Eventually the airmen themselves found a way of reaching the American authorities, who promptly put in hand a rescue operation.

The British had initially opposed the evacuation in case it annoyed Tito! They were further embarrassed when it was discovered that the main landing strip used by the American rescue unit at Pranjani in Mihailovic territory was shown on British maps as being firmly under Partisan control. They had even tried to involve the Partisans in the evacuation. This was resisted by the Americans only after Roosevelt had interceded with Churchill. Even so, the British put every obstacle possible in the Americans' way, delaying maintenance on the aircraft to be used and even on occasion giving misleading map references to the pilots. As a result, some of the early rescue attempts had to be aborted.

In the end it became a purely American operation. The compromise was that the same aircraft would first drop supplies to the Partisans and then pick up the downed airmen from Mihailovic's airstrip. Against British wishes, some of the incoming planes brought medical supplies for Mihailovic's forces. The Americans had wanted two of the British liaison officers previously with Mihailovic, Erik Greenwood and Kenneth Greenlees, who had been airlifted out, to return to Serbia to help with the evacuation. The British authorities would not release them. Apparently they had promised Tito that no officer who had been with Mihailovic would be allowed back into Yugoslavia.

Intriguingly – it may well have been insisted upon by Maclean – during February 1944 Churchill ordered his staff to prevent messages to and from Maclean being read by American Intelligence. He wrote to Anthony Eden on 12 February:

> Care must be taken to make sure that Donovan's organisation [OSS]
> does not get hold of my Personal and Privates [signals] to Maclean. I
> should be grateful if you would give instructions to make sure that in
> the future we have a secret line of communication with our own *chef*
> *de mission*.[5]

On 26 February he minuted General Ismay, his Defence Secretary:
"I do not wish the Combined Chiefs of Staff or the United States
Chiefs of Staff to sit in judgement on my telegrams or the Foreign
Secretary's to Brigadier Maclean."[6] Churchill became quite paranoid
and wanted to stop all his communications being overheard by the
Americans. On 6 March he asked General Wilson, Supreme Allied
Commander in the Mediterranean: "Are you sure that my telegrams
to you through this channel never pass through American hands and
are kept strictly secret?"[7]

That Churchill was far from confident of America's continuing
support for his stance on Yugoslavia was shown by his reaction to the
news on 6 April that Washington was about to send an intelligence
mission to Mihailovic. This was when Churchill was trying to
persuade the London Yugoslavs to ditch Mihailovic in favour of Tito.
He ordered SOE in Cairo to delay "by every reasonable means"
the flight arrangements of the American Mission – "the greatest
courtesy being used to our friends and Allies in every case, but no
transportation".[8] He cabled Roosevelt that the dispatch of such a
mission

> will show throughout the Balkans a complete contrariety of action
> between Britain and the United States. The Russians will certainly
> throw all their weight on Tito's side, which we are backing to the full.
> Thus we shall get altogether out of step.[9]

Roosevelt replied that the mission had "no political functions whatsoever" but was simply "to obtain intelligence". He agreed to delay
sending it at that time.[10] Others in Washington persisted. The
reports of Colonel Linn Farish in June and, more particularly, of
Colonel Robert McDowell in November were devastating indict-
ments in American eyes of Churchill's decision to back Tito.

Fitzroy Maclean seethed and imputed all manner of Machiavellian
motives to McDowell, from disobeying presidential orders to spying
on behalf of American commercial interests. He even hinted
McDowell might not be quite sane! Having failed to prevent
McDowell's mission reaching Yugoslavia, Maclean prevailed upon
Churchill to pressure Roosevelt into ordering him home.

Harold Macmillan noted in his diary meeting McDowell on 6 November:

> A charming American professor dressed in uniform. Round the inno-
> cent head of this sweet old man has raged a tremendous storm. He
> has been the OSS mission to Mihailovic. The President agreed in
> August (with Winston) to withdraw him. But for various reasons –
> because he could not be found or because he could not find all his
> team or because he wanted to see Father Sava – he has only just come
> out. Broad (at Bari), Air Vice-Marshal Elliot and all the real Tito fans
> (urged on by Brigadier Maclean) have ascribed the most sinister
> causes to this episode. But I feel sure that the dear colonel was not a
> very mysterious or dangerous force. He likes the Serbs, got interested
> in talking to them, does not think much of Mihailovic and still less
> of the old government party in Belgrade ... The Serb peasants,
> according to him, are not particularly loyal to the King and certainly
> have no liking for the Belgrade people. But they are quite well off,
> with good land, and being strong individualists will oppose Commun-
> ism, collectivisation, etc., to the end.

Tito's British fans did not let up trying to demean McDowell. They claimed that while he was at Mihailovic's headquarters in September 1944 Mihailovic met a German envoy with a view to collaborating and as a result received five thousand German rifles. McDowell maintained it was he, with the agreement of his Washington superiors, not Mihailovic, who had initiated the meeting, intended to sound out a possible surrender of the German forces in the Balkans. No rifles were received.

McDowell had spent twenty-five years in the Balkans before the war, including working for British Intelligence. He was later to become a senior Soviet analyst at the Pentagon. Roosevelt had asked him to report on guerrilla activity in western Serbia and eastern Bosnia where Mihaolovic's forces were largely based. He confirmed that the Partisans were using Allied weapons against Mihailovic's forces and that they rarely attacked German troops or installations. He had seen Germans retreating unmolested, although Partisans were nearby. He had observed Partisans attacking Mihailovic's men while they had been fighting Germans, allowing the Germans to escape. He said the people around Mihailovic could not understand why they had been prevented from arguing their case directly with the British and American leaders. They had been, as they put it, "sealed off as thoroughly as Jews in a German gas chamber – and for the same end".

An earlier report from a member of McDowell's mission, Lieutenant Ellsworth Kramer, had claimed that the Partisans tried to assassinate him. Separated from the main mission while seeking intelligence, he had joined a group of Chetniks who were attacked by Partisans. Wishing to mediate between them, he sent a courier to the Partisans to explain who he was. The courier was beaten and told there was no American mission in Serbia. In a further attack some Partisans were taken prisoner who informed Kramer they had been specifically ordered to kill or capture "the American officer with the Chetniks".[11] Kramer also reported seeing German troops retreating within yards of Partisan units who made no effort to harass them.

Milovan Djilas recalled, in *Wartime*, seeing Tito again in November 1943, after an absence of four months, and noticing how much weight he had put on. This grossness was never to leave him: "he had suddenly become heavy, never again to regain that look of bone and sinew which made him so distinguished-looking and attractive during the war". Djilas confirmed how the recognition of the Partisans as co-belligerents in the Allied struggle against the Axis gave them greater credibility, especially in Serbia where it was interpreted as Allied backing for Tito in the Yugoslav civil war.

After receiving Allied recognition, Tito dispersed his forces as a way of "spreading the revolt" – showing his military power to as much of the country as possible. This left him vulnerable to sudden attack, as happened on 7 January 1944 when the Germans drove him out of Jajce. He ended up living in a cave above the little town of Drvar in the Dinaric Alps of western Bosnia. He was willing to take the military risk for the political benefits of displaying his might countrywide. Because the British were committed to him, he knew they would come to his rescue if the worst were to happen.

Djilas noted how hierarchical the Partisans had become. Central Committee members had been made lieutenant-generals! When asked "Why so high?" Tito had replied: "No one should outrank Central Committee members." There were now disputes over seating arrangements at dinners, "yet none of us had a single change of underclothing, and we all ate tasteless stews, were bombed every day, and lived in constant fear that we would be driven into the woods". Appointments were now needed to see party functionaries. He "once found Tito in the cave practicing his signature – as befitted his new role as a ruler, and the atmosphere of titles, honours, and idolatry".

Ljubo Sirc, a less exalted Partisan, recollected army life at a Corps headquarters later in the war:

> The hierarchy showed in everything, especially food. There were three different kitchens: one for officers senior to major served several courses – soup, meat, two vegetables, salad and sweets; a second for staff members, to which I belonged, qualified for risotto or dumplings twice a day; the third for the ranks left men hungry. In pre-war Yugoslavia, the privileges of Army officers were a permanent target of communist criticism. Now everything had changed. Officers no longer had "batmen", instead they had two or three "couriers" each, doing the same jobs.[12]

There was no lessening of the civil war. This suited the over-stretched Germans who chose to control the Dalmatian coast and to protect the mineral deposits and the main lines of communication, as well as garrisoning the towns and major villages. The rest of the country became the domain of the two resistance forces. As long as they were at loggerheads with each other the occupiers' task was eased. The Germans saw to it, through propaganda and other pressures, that the flames of hatred were well fanned so that Tito and Mihailovic fought each other rather than troubling them.

Tito had sent Churchill a goodwill message while he was convalescing, no doubt at Maclean's suggestion. Churchill replied on 8 January 1944 assuring Tito of his full support and of his desire that the Yugoslav government sack Mihailovic without delay. Meantime Britain would maintain "official relations" with King Peter whose titular authority Churchill hoped Tito would now accept as well as that of the government-in-exile.[13] Tito took a month to reply. Djilas says they were surprised at Churchill's "naivety" regarding the king: "what possible significance could the King have in a Partisan and Communist army?" They feared Churchill might trick them – "the hidden trap of the old imperial wolf" – and worried that recognising the king would expose their weakness in Serbia. One of their shock-brigades had recently been annihilated trying to get a foothold there.

When he did reply, Tito refused point blank to take back the king or recognise the authority of the London Yugoslavs. Further letters were exchanged. Tito insisted his administration be recognised "as the only Government of Yugoslavia"; the King must submit to its laws. Churchill nevertheless went ahead and pressured Peter to dismiss Mihailovic. The London Yugoslavs became alarmed. The Foreign Office intervened, trying to support King Peter and his government, but it was too late. The king looked to the Americans for favour, as Roosevelt had never shared Churchill's enthusiasm for Tito. The Yugoslav ambassador in Washington led a boisterous campaign, whipping up antagonism against the Titoites. It was of no avail. Roosevelt merely told the king to take Churchill's advice "as if it was my own".

Tito was allowed a representative in London, Vladimir Velebit. He arrived on 1 May 1944 and was housed in grand style at the Savoy Hotel. He had insisted on being funded directly rather than having to rely on British "charity", as he claimed had happened on his previous trip to Cairo. As the Partisans had no international funds, Tito turned to Moscow for help. Just minutes before Velebit was due to leave in an Allied plane for Italy, en route to London, a Russian plane arrived at the airstrip near Tito's headquarters with the necessary dollars. In exchange, the Soviets asked Velebit to spy for them. Tito agreed. They were anxious to know whether the British and Americans planned to land in the Balkans!

Velebit was wined and dined by such venerable Socialist figures as Sir Stafford Cripps, who had been Churchill's envoy in Moscow, Harold Laski, chairman then of the Labour Party, and Kingsley Martin, editor of the left-wing weekly magazine *The New Statesman*. Tito was keen for Velebit to meet Churchill, as this would imply political recognition of the Partisans. The Foreign Office, knowing the anxieties of the London Yugoslavs on the matter, were equally determined Velebit should not meet Churchill or any government minister. Nor would they allow him to broadcast to Yugoslavia via the BBC. However, Laski and Kingsley Martin at Velebit's behest, no doubt prompted by Maclean, approached Churchill's close friend Lord Beaverbrook, the newspaper tycoon, who fixed it. On 21 May 1944 Velebit got to meet Churchill. Maclean saw to it that the encounter was well reported in the British press, to the chagrin of the London Yugoslavs and the Foreign Office.

The Foreign Office and the London Yugoslavs had been fighting a losing battle. Once it had been decided to back Tito and drop Mihailovic, the Allied propaganda machine had swung into action. Richard Crossman, a Labour cabinet minister in the 1960s, who during the war was much involved in "black" propaganda at the BBC before becoming Eisenhower's Director of Political Warfare to the Enemy and Satellites, was to recall:

> We had a recognised nomenclature for distinguishing between good
> and bad terrorists, and sometimes we had to change the labels rather
> abruptly. I remember, for instance, the awkward moment when the

Government dropped Mihailovic and backed Tito. "In future", our directive ran, "Mihailovic forces will be described not as patriots but as terrorist gangs; we shall drop the phrase 'Red Bandits' as applied to partisans and substitute 'freedom fighter'". At the time I do not remember being shocked that the tap of moral approval could be turned on and off so abruptly by the Foreign Office and the Chiefs of Staff. After all, we were fighting a total war, and I assumed that the men far above me, who made the policy decision, were as cynical about the distinction between patriots and bandits as we were. Only later did the truth dawn on me that British Cabinet Ministers, Archbishops and newspaper editors actually believed our propaganda and took this moral doubletalk seriously.[14]

Significantly, Serbia was the only place in occupied Europe during 1944 where the Germans did not discourage listening to the BBC! Mihailovic invited newspapermen to his headquarters but SOE Cairo always forbade their going, arguing their safety could not be guaranteed. They had no such qualms about visitors to Tito's headquarters. From January 1944 onwards there was a steady stream of American and British journalists, as well as VIPs such as Evelyn Waugh, Lord Birkenhead and Churchill's son Randolph. This was just after Waugh had completed *Brideshead Revisited*. Churchill had penned Tito a personal note concerning Randolph, and added: "I wish I could come myself, but I am too old and heavy to jump out on a parachute."[15]

The import of Churchill's sending his only son was not lost on the Partisans. Henniker-Major says, in *Painful Extractions*, that Randolph, who arrived on 20 January 1944, was "specifically charged with handling propaganda", though he does not detail Randolph's efforts in this regard and there is no official record of them. Propaganda was strictly the province of PWE, with which Randolph had no connection. PWE eventually sent out Lord Birkenhead as their representative with Tito. That Birkenhead was Churchill's godson was perhaps not a coincidence!

Clearly Randolph Churchill was there because of his name rather than to do a job of work. It was a smart move on Maclean's part: it tied the Churchill family to Tito's cause. Randolph was an instant channel to the top. Maclean was able to pepper his signals with phrases like "Randolph well and sends his love", knowing they would immediately find their way to Winston. His competitors had already realised he had powerful friends at court. That they would be brought to bear in his favour was a bit of luck Tito could never in his wildest dreams have foreseen. For Churchill, having his son with the Partisans allowed him, as it were, to participate in guerrilla warfare by filial proxy.

Henniker-Major describes Randolph as "undisciplined" and hints that he was considered a pain in the neck. The Foreign Office head, Sir Alexander Cadogan, described him in his diary as "a dreadful young man". Harold Macmillan confided to his diary that Randolph's "manners are dreadful, and his flow of talk insufferable. He always manages to have a row or make a scene wherever he goes." Churchill's chum Oliver Stanley told Bruce Lockhart, PWE's Director-General, that Randolph "was now a real thorn in the flesh of his father who could not manage him".[16] Being with Tito got him out of his father's hair! Franklin Lindsay, an OSS colleague, says the Partisans were clearly flattered to have Churchill's son with them

> but they were put off when he told them what he thought of them, which was seldom flattering. He was one of the most aggressively rude men I ever met. He once told me that whenever anyone was rude to him he was immediately three times as rude in return. He was sure to win out. No one could possibly best him.

Djilas maintains Randolph

> soon enchanted our commanders and commissars with his wit and unconventional manner, but he revealed through his drinking and lack of interest that he had inherited neither political imagination nor dynamism with his surname.

Whenever Randolph visited a village the commissar accompanying him was instructed to organise a mass reception and to introduce him always as Winston Churchill's son, which impressed everyone. SOE's official historian William Mackenzie mentions finding in the files

> a sad note by Bailey in the spring of 1944 recounting how much the Prime Minister and Mrs Churchill seemed to be moved by Randolph Churchill's snapshots of the Partisans, and regretting that it had never occurred to him that evidence of that sort might have helped the unlucky Mihailovic.

Henniker-Major clearly did not take to Evelyn Waugh either. He arrived after Randolph and was described as

> a crashing snob. He professed to be interested in Yugoslavia, though he loathed the partisans because they were all anti-Catholic, communists and peasants ... Waugh was not much practical use to [Maclean] however, because he could not bring himself to talk to any of the partisans.

Waugh compiled a report on how the Catholics in Yugoslavia would suffer under a Tito regime that "threatens to destroy the Catholic Faith in a region where there are now some five million Catholics". However Henniker-Major reveals their true significance when he describes Waugh, Randolph and Birkenhead as "markers on the board" that "gave the mission prestige and a higher profile back home, and added to the impression that Fitzroy had a lot of people on his side."

Waugh's presence in Maclean's mission proved a double-edged sword because he never liked the Partisans. In the end he was expelled from Yugoslavia as a result of their pressure. He confided to his diary:

> They have no interest in fighting the Germans but are engrossed in their civil war ... they make slightly ingenuous attempts to deceive us into thinking their motive in various tiny campaigns is to break German retreat routes. They want Germans out so that they can settle down to civil war.[17]

Nor did he like Maclean, whom he thought "dour, unprincipled, ambitious, probably very wicked". Unlike Maclean and Randolph Churchill, Waugh quickly concluded that the Partisans were interested only in Communist domination of Yugoslavia and that their promises of free elections after the war were a sham.

Lord Birkenhead was later to report:

> Of humour in the Partisan movement there is none. The cause is too holy, and it is indecent to laugh in church. The usual dreary Party slogans are scrawled over the walls: "Zivio Drug Tito" (Long live Comrade Tito), "Smrl Fasizmo" (Death to Fascism). On public occasions the party bosses intone party clichés in interminable fashion, unillumined by a gleam of levity. One writhes on a wooden bench in an unheated hall while the gloomy catalogue of phrases rolls on: "The Fascist bandits", "Long live the Anti-Fascist Committee of Liberation of Croatia", "Zivio Drug Tito". Such speeches by the leaders are received in docile silence by the audience until the end when a dutiful but rather automatic burst of applause goes up, and an hour of anti-Fascist songs rounds off a jolly evening at 2 a.m.[18]

The favoured songs had verses such as, "Oh Comrade Tito, Oh Comrade Tito, white violet, you are followed by all the young", "Oh Communist Party, Oh Communist Party, sweet scented flowers, you are followed by all our people" and "Give me a rifle three metres long to kill King Peter"!

One of the Americans attached to Maclean's mission, Major (later Colonel) Richard Weil, whom Maclean's biographer, Frank McLynn, says Fitzroy "had a high regard for", confided to OSS headquarters in Washington at this time:

> We do not know whether Partisan reports about action against the enemy are accurate, exaggerated or utterly untrue. This is because for the most part we have taken the Partisans' word for what went on in enemy actions since we have seldom had our own observers with them to make independent observations and reports.

Earlier he had written: "The Partisans announced claim ... that they, by their sole efforts, are 'containing' 17 German divisions and well over one-half million enemy troops in their country, is unquestionably false."[19]

Even the Soviets at last got around to sending a military mission to Tito. It arrived on 23 February 1944, thanks to the RAF. Because its head, General Korneyev, had lost a leg at Stalingrad and so could not drop by parachute, an airstrip near Tito's headquarters had to be prepared for the mission to glider in, together with their supplies of vodka and caviare, as well as full-dress uniforms, including gold epaulettes and tight shiny boots! Tito was not best pleased with the Soviet mission. They drank a lot and grumbled about the discomforts of guerrilla life, especially the lavatory facilities! Their latrine did not conform to Soviet army specifications. Eventually they got one that did. Tito told Djilas how, a few weeks after the mission's arrival, "when they were left by themselves, General Korneyev drunkenly kissed him and cooed, 'Oska, Oska' the Russian pet name for Joseph".[20] That the mission included two generals, several colonels and majors, plus the inevitable NKVD (Stalin's secret police) representative, boosted Tito's status.

Djilas says the Partisans did not hide from the British mission their enthusiasm for the Soviets. Now they "were no longer alone with the British, and that the scales in the world at large were tipped in our favour".[21] Not long after the arrival of the Soviet mission Tito let it be known that he should now be addressed in the respectful second person plural form *Vi* instead of the comradely *Ti* – a step along the path of building up a personality cult around himself.

Tito was in turn allowed a mission to Moscow. He sent Milovan Djilas with a Partisan general and a few party functionaries. New uniforms had been specially made for them out of material captured from the Italians! They arrived in the Soviet capital on 12 April. They had taken with them for safe keeping in the Kremlin the Party's archives and Dedijer's war diaries, fearing British intelligence agents might want to hijack them. Throughout the flight, and during its various stops, one of the mission had stood guard over them! Stalin kept the mission waiting several weeks before granting an audience. Djilas, who spoke Russian well, recalled approaching Stalin "in an ecstasy of idolatry".[22]

Soviet recognition of the Partisans as the legitimate government of Yugoslavia was the mission's purpose, as well as seeking military aid. They secured a promise of aid but not recognition before returning in mid-June. Djilas records that another of their tasks was to arrange the manufacture in Russia of suitable medals for "the new Yugoslavia"! He took with him a sketch of "how Tito's marshal's uniform would be decorated".[23] Tito had designed his own insignia, a heavily embroidered wreath of oak leaves. Djilas remembered, too, that Stalin insisted they should not frighten the English, "by which he meant that we ought to avoid anything that might alarm them into thinking that a revolution was going on in Yugoslavia or an attempt at Communist control". Stalin apparently chided them for having red stars on their caps. He warned them to be wary of Churchill who, in his words, was "the kind of man who will pick your pocket of a kopeck [the smallest Russian coin]"![24]

Tito had worried that the Soviets might raise the matter of the March 1943 "consultations" with the Germans. Djilas had been primed to describe them as merely an exchange of wounded prisoners. But nothing was said on that subject. While refuelling in Teheran, the Soviets arranged a massive reception for Djilas at which, according to American agents present, he was grandiloquent in his praise of Stalin, prophesying the worldwide triumph of communism after the war.

Yugoslavia's most important region, Serbia, was still largely Mihailovic territory that spring of 1944. Tito sent five thousand Partisans there during late March and early April but the invaders met stiff resistance from Chetniks, Germans and Bulgarians in turn, and were almost wiped out. The battered remnant withdrew in some confusion two months later. The Germans then took the opportunity to transfer further troops from Yugoslavia to face the new Russian offensive that was bringing the Red Army to the frontiers of Hungary and Romania.

On the eve of the abortive Partisan offensive, Maclean had cabled London enthusing over its prospects of success. He anticipated Tito's ascendancy over the whole country, assuming it was in Britain's interests to have a "strong democratic and independent Yugoslavia". The Foreign Office thought his despatch read "too much like a company prospectus to be altogether convincing". Even the pro-Tito Ralph Stevenson, commenting on the despatch, admitted that opposition to the Partisans in Serbia remained "solid and uncompromising". He felt this fact should be given "due weight when estimating Tito's chances of sweeping the country". Eden agreed and promptly circulated in the War Cabinet two reports recently received from Bill Hudson and Colonel Bailey reminding London of the strong anti-Communist feeling prevalent in Serbia.[25]

That Mihailovic's popularity continued to hold up in Serbia, despite his having been dumped by the British, was indicated in a German intelligence report of 11 July 1944. This claimed the Chetniks were backed by 90 per cent of the population there. A further Partisan attempt to break into Serbia in late August and early September again met heavy losses. Although Maclean was assuring Churchill the aim of the Partisan invasion of Serbia was to harass the German retreat from Greece, Tito's order of the day to his troops on 5 September disclosed the real intention:

> Keep in mind that the basic aim of this whole operation is to liquidate the Chetniks of Draza Mihailovic and the Nedic forces, as well as their [political and administrative] apparatus. Do not allow Mihailovic to carry out his mobilisation and to take people with him. Arrest Chetnik headmen in the villages, because they are the chief pillar of Mihailovic's strength among the people.[26]

No doubt Churchill had hoped Tito would use his new weapons to kill Germans. But Tito was concerned solely with who would prevail in the country after liberation. The winning of the war was the Allies' responsibility, not his. This did not stop him and his propagandists in the West hiding the horrors of a particularly brutal civil war under the romanticised veil of a patriotic struggle for national liberation.

The received view of Yugoslavia's wartime history has been that Tito led the Partisans constantly and courageously against the Germans; that, unlike the rest of occupied Europe, Yugoslavia freed itself. But German records show that after December 1943, despite the massive Allied aid passed his way, Tito's harassment of

Wehrmacht strongholds was only occasional and peripheral. The German High Command's eventual decision to withdraw its army from the Balkans was dictated, not by the Partisans, but by mounting Allied pressure from the eastern and western fronts. From the Allied point of view the Partisans were disappointingly slack in disrupting the German retreat. The German lines of communication from Greece to Austria through Yugoslavia were not ruptured during 1944.

It soon became evident that the Partisans were not tieing down German divisions, as Maclean had claimed. Almost immediately after Churchill's decision to back Tito became known, Hitler transferred the 114th Jaeger division from northern Dalmatia to Cassino in Italy. Four other German divisions were switched from Yugoslavia to Hungary in March 1944. General Colin Gubbins, the head of SOE, complained in May 1944 of "Tito's very half-hearted efforts in Yugoslavia".[27]

Vane Ivanovic says when refugees from the Dalmatian islands found their way to Bari in Italy during the winter of 1943-44 and discovered

> there was a Yugoslav who was a Major in the British Army, my office was besieged by people begging me to move them away from Partisan control, of which most of these peaceful Dalmatians had had only a few weeks' experience. That, all of them said, was enough.[28]

Ljubo Sirc observed of his fellow Partisans in his memoirs:

> The Western allies were immensely popular amongst the population in the rank and file, but they were almost as unpopular, rather hated by the higher echelons, because the higher echelons feared that if the Western Allies succeeded in having any influence in Yugoslavia they would prevent them from taking power.

Churchill had already begun having second thoughts. The two main liaison officers with Mihailovic eventually got out in the spring of 1944 and reported to him. One of them, Colonel Bailey, confided to colleagues that Churchill had remarked he now felt he had been badly misinformed about the situation in Yugoslavia and perhaps knowingly misled regarding Tito. Anthony Eden read the account of Brigadier Armstrong's meeting with the deputy head of the Foreign Office, Sir Orme Sargent, on 14 June 1944 and minuted six days later:

> I find this report most disturbing. Brigadier Armstrong does not bear out the oft-told tale of Mihailovic's collaboration with the enemy. Yet

he was with him all the time, wasn't he? I have never understood on what our evidence against him and his associates rests, tho' I have asked a score of times.[29]

Armstrong told Sargent that the

BBC broadcasts were having a lamentable effect in Serbia and were simply playing the German game. They gave out as facts Partisan propaganda claims which were palpably untrue, and which every Serb knew to be untrue.

Eden dined with Armstrong on 28 June and afterwards noted:

Mihailovic was not pro-German and did not wish to collaborate with them, nor is there any evidence of his having done so ... he is definitely anti-Communist, and as such considers it his duty to his country to attack the Partisans because they are a Communist movement.[30]

When Bill Hudson finally got out of Yugoslavia in April 1944 he was surprised to find few interested in his experiences. He discovered rumours had been put about that he was mentally deranged as a result of his ordeal with Mihailovic! Churchill eventually invited him to Chequers for lunch and told him he knew Cairo had cooked the books, that signals had been wantonly tampered with or destroyed and that SOE was "a nest of intrigue". All of which Hudson was later to confide to Norah Beloff. Interestingly, when Churchill wrote to Tito on 17 May to inform him King Peter had at last sacked Mihailovic as Minister of War, he took the opportunity to remind him:

We do not know what will happen in the Serbian part of Yugoslavia. Mihailovic certainly holds a powerful position locally as Commander-in-Chief, and it does not follow that his ceasing to be Minister of War will rob him of his influence. We cannot predict what he will do. There is also a very large body, amounting perhaps to 200,000, of Serbian peasant proprietary who are anti-German but strongly Serbian, and who naturally hold the views of a peasants' ownership community.[31]

He had wanted to add six words to the final sentence, "contrary to the Karl Marx theory", but had been dissuaded by Roosevelt to whom he showed the draft!

When the Foreign Office prepared a paper for the War Cabinet on 7 June 1944 entitled "Soviet Policy in the Balkans", Anthony Eden declared in the introduction: "In recent months I have become disturbed by developments which seem to indicate the Soviet Government's intention to acquire a dominating influence in the Balkans." Later in the paper he admitted:

> If anyone is to blame for the present situation in which the Communist-led movements are the most powerful elements in Yugoslavia and Greece, it is we ourselves. The Russians have merely sat back and watched us doing their work for them. And it is only when we have shown signs of putting a brake on their movements (such as our continued recognition of King Peter and Mihailovic, and more recently the strong line taken against E.A.M. [the Greek Communist Party] ...) that they have come into the open and shown where their interests lay.[32]

Peter Kemp had been parachuted into Albania in August 1943 by SOE to contact the non-communist resistance movement there, which drew its support from landowners, merchants, teachers, professional men and the like who distrusted and feared the communist guerrillas under Enver Hoxha. He describes in his memoirs, *The Thorns of Memory*, how his mission took him to Kosovo. Known then to Serbs as Old Serbia, it had been absorbed into Albania when Hitler dismembered Yugoslavia in 1941. Most Kosovans were Albanian, not Serb, and preferred a German to a Serb occupation. They were not friendly towards the Allies, fearing an Allied victory would return them to Serbian rule. Nor were the communist partisans popular in Kosovo. Kemp quotes one of his contacts as saying "We have nothing against you English ... only we don't want the communists here; and so we collaborate with the Germans, who help us to drive them out."

In late January 1944 Kemp was ordered by SOE Cairo to "break tactfully" his connections in Kosovo. His activities were making an "unfavourable impression" with Tito, whose relations with SOE Cairo were now "of overriding importance". Kemp discovered later that few of his contacts survived the war. Tito gave moral and logistical support to the successful communist takeover in Albania as well as to the unsuccessful grab for power in Greece.

Following his return to Cairo in December 1943, William Deakin was promoted to lieutenant colonel and became head of SOE Cairo's Yugoslav section. When it was relocated to Italy during the spring of 1944 he was seconded to Harold Macmillan's staff. Macmillan was Churchill's political representative in the Mediterranean. Deakin also became an adviser to the "Balkan Air Force", an Anglo-American inter-service unit established in early June 1944, with headquarters in

Bari, to co-ordinate all operations within the Balkans. He was responsible for choosing bombing targets.

Because they could fly from bases in Italy, and provide air cover for the Partisans, the Force could now bomb Yugoslavia. Targets were always agreed beforehand with Tito. From early 1944 the Danube near Belgrade was regularly mined, severely disrupting and for a time paralysing, the river-borne movement of oil and other military supplies, as Albert Speer, Hitler's Production Chief, was to testify. The railway lines passing through Serbia were constantly being hit too.

The Allied Air Force's most controversial target was undoubtedly Belgrade, on the Orthodox Easter Sunday 16 April 1944. More civilians were killed than during the *Luftwaffe* bombing three years earlier. Although the American planes were allegedly aiming at armament factories in the suburbs, Djilas admits "not one military target was hit, except for the haphazard destruction of a group of Germans here and there."[33] The Serbs remain bitter about it, convinced it was a Tito ploy, in which the British connived, to terrorise the people of Belgrade into turning their backs on Mihailovic.

Jasper Rootham recalls in his memoirs seeing hundreds of bombers flying overhead. He assumed they were heading for the Hungarian capital, Budapest, and was aghast when he heard of the Belgrade bombing:

> As one who spoke later with men who had been in Belgrade at the time, I must record that the effect of this raid on the feelings of the people towards the Allies was deplorable ... As for the Germans ... it was of course the biggest propaganda windfall they had ever had. They did not fail to use it.

The Allies also bombed Montenegrin towns such as Niksic, Danilovgrad and Podgorica, again sometimes on Orthodox Church festival days. Montenegro was of course largely Chetnik country. Djilas, a Montenegrin, says Podgorica was bombed so many times that by the end "it resembled an archaeological excavation through which only one path had been cleared". Some American airmen who had to bale out nearby reported the reactions of the inhabitants: "The Partisans are using you to kill us. They know there are no Germans in the town, only Chetniks. But they have told your headquarters it is full of Germans and asked for the bombing."[34] The Allies also bombed ports like Split. The Russians never bombed Yugoslavia.

CHAPTER NINE

Game to Tito

"had the nerve actually to fool and
humiliate the British and Americans in
the most comical way"

HEINRICH HIMMLER

THE ALLIES GOT BOGGED DOWN in Italy during 1944. The
Germans recovered their poise in Yugoslavia sufficiently to retain
control of all the key towns. They were under no threat from guerrillas and had, according to SOE's official historian William Mackenzie,
"freedom of movement for strong bodies of troops along the main
lines of communication". They could again harass the Partisans. Tito
was almost captured on 25 May at Drvar by parachutists and glider-
borne troops. He was about to celebrate his fifty-second birthday in
the company of the Allied missions, including Randolph Churchill,
though not Maclean, who was in London. Maclean's deputy, Vivian
Street, had noticed a German spotter plane during the previous days.
He alerted the Partisans who thought it a prelude to bombing. As a
precaution, the British mission took to the hills; not so all the others.

The Partisan losses were heavy: almost six thousand killed or
captured, so the Germans claimed. All of their signals equipment,
headquarters paraphernalia and heavy weapons, were lost. The Partisan command structure for a while was in disarray. Tito had been
living in a wooden hut in front of a cave, through which ran a rivulet
that was dry at that time of year. The water had worn an opening
through the roof of the cave out of which, according to Milovan
Djilas, Tito escaped. Though not before dithering, as his mistress
Zdenka apparently became hysterical. A rope was lowered from the
cliff above the cave, which they scaled. For a considerable time Tito
was out of touch with his staff and there was much confusion amidst
the fierce fighting. The Germans vented their anger at missing him
by massacring most of the local villagers and destroying their houses.

They took away Tito's marshal's uniform and personal memorabilia, which were put on show later in Vienna.

The British mission had been able to inform Bari. To hinder the hunt for Tito, Allied aircraft flew bombing sorties over the area. Directed particularly at German airfields, they destroyed numerous planes on the ground. More than five hundred Allied aircraft were involved, including nearly three hundred bombers. British commandos mounted diversionary attacks against nearby Dalmatian islands and they suffered heavy casualties. The extent of the losses prompted an official report complaining at the lack of co-operation from the Partisans:

> On no occasion of a joint attack during this operation did the Partisans conform to what was understood to be their plans ... An unnecessary number of casualties were caused by cross-fire from enemy positions which should have been neutralised by Partisan attack.

It was the first, and only, joint operation between British Commandos and the Partisans.

When Tito was eventually found, the Soviets persuaded him to accept British protection by locating on the Yugoslav island of Vis, then in British hands. General Korneyev had had enough of the discomforts of guerrilla life! They were all flown out on 3 June, including the Allied missions. They went first to Bari in Italy, where Tito snubbed a welcoming party of British dignitaries and official press, preferring to be met by the local Russians. They whisked him away in one of their cars. He claimed later he had not wanted it known he had left the mainland. Indeed Allied propagandists tried to give the impression he was still there, gallantly fighting the Germans. They denied reports from neutral countries that he had fled. The BBC announced he had merely moved his headquarters to another part of Yugoslavia. Tito had insisted that the aircrew rescuing him were Russian. The plane was American.

It was a few days before a British warship was found to take them all, together with Maclean who had joined them at Bari, on to Vis. Some thirty miles off the Yugoslav coast, this was reached on 7 June. During the trip his naval hosts plied Tito with champagne and cigars. Vis now became his headquarters for the next three months. He located himself in a cave on the side of the island's highest peak. It was now easier for him to receive visitors. Among his early callers was the Hollywood actor Douglas Fairbanks. Tito's son Zarko, whom he had not seen for almost fifteen years and who had lost an arm while serving in the Red Army, now joined him. Tito also switched mistresses, sending Zdenka, whose tuberculosis had worsened, to a sanatorium in Russia for treatment.

Churchill was anxious to take the opportunity, while Tito "lies under our protection", to reconcile him with the London Yugoslavs. He hoped he might be chastened by his recent experience and in a more realistic mood. Churchill had suggested to Eden on 5 June that perhaps King Peter and Dr Ivan Subasic, the new prime minister designate of the Yugoslav government and a Croat like Tito, could "settle there" on Vis also. They had "as much right to do this as Tito ... it seems to me that we have some good cards in our hands at last if we play them well".[1] Tito told Maclean he was willing to "talk things over" with Subasic "if he would come to Vis".[2]

Churchill's plan was for King Peter to sack Mihailovic and appoint Tito in his place as commander-in-chief of the Yugoslav army. Randolph had apparently convinced him that getting rid of Mihailovic "might create an atmosphere in which the King's future could be advanced". The head of the Foreign Office, Sir Alexander Cadogan, was not so convinced and tried to caution Churchill: "It seems to me that we may be a bit rash in urging the King to throw over Draza Mihailovic, until we know whether the Partisans will have anything to do with him." Churchill thought Randolph's advice was "sound".[3] Randolph had a private audience with the Pope on 13 June, when he assured him: "the whole trend today is away from Communism and that private property and religious institutions are guaranteed and respected by the movement of national liberation"![4]

Fitzroy Maclean argued to Churchill: "the King's willingness to disown Draza Mihailovic is the only repeat only chance for the monarchy". The King hesitated in following Churchill's advice but this did not stop Winston announcing on 22 February 1944 in the House of Commons that aid for Mihailovic would cease forthwith. It had of course long since ended. Churchill hoped Tito would allow King Peter to join him. He wrote four days later to Tito: "If I judge this boy aright, he has no dearer wish than to stand at the side of all those Yugoslavs who are fighting the common foe."[5] Tito ignored the suggestion and Churchill did not press him.

To appease Tito further, Churchill persuaded King Peter to replace his Serbian Prime Minister with a Croatian. Tito in turn was expected to dissolve his own "administration". This, Maclean had already told Churchill, he was reluctant to do. It was hoped a coalition government might be formed from members of both groups. Churchill also hoped Tito would renounce his intention of establishing communism in Yugoslavia after the war and agree to hold free elections. Having secured Allied recognition, and being the exclusive recipient of Allied supplies, Tito had little need to make concessions. The Soviets stepped in, however, and urged him to meet Dr Ivan Subasic, the candidate for Yugoslav prime minister favoured by Churchill. Thought to be a liberal, Subasic had been governor of Croatia immediately before the war. Now living in the United States, he was quickly brought to Europe, wished on King Peter and taken to Vis to meet Tito on 14 June. Peter was not invited, though apparently Tito said he was willing to meet him "a little later on".

On 17 June Tito and Subasic announced an agreement whereby the two governments would work together. It was not all Churchill wished. The London Yugoslavs were to disassociate themselves from Mihailovic and recognise the Partisans as "the sole legitimate fighting force on Yugoslav soil". They were also "to help the Partisans to punish all traitors who had collaborated with the enemy". All political decisions regarding the future of the country, including the monarchy, were postponed until the ending of the war. Churchill had wanted Tito committed to the continuity of the monarchy. He wanted, too, a coalition government with the London Yugoslavs in the majority, rather than a Partisan one in which royalists would have some representation. Tito "solemnly assured" Subasic and Ralph Stevenson, Ambassador to the London Yugoslavs that he did not intend to impose communism on Yugoslavia after the war. Stevenson told London he thought Tito meant what he said!

The Foreign Office continued to worry about the exclusion of the Serbs. There were no Serb ministers in Subasic's new government. They reminded Churchill that Serbia was still out of bounds to Tito, who had little support there. Djilas says Tito feared that the Allies might be tempted to divide Yugoslavia into a western Communist part and an eastern royalist part. The Foreign Office claimed Maclean appeared to be exceeding his brief by encouraging Tito to extend the scope of his movement in Serbia. Official policy was *not* to help Tito impose his communism on the Serbs but to promote his co-operation with them. They urged Churchill to rein in Maclean.

General Wilson, the Supreme Allied Commander in the Mediterranean, invited Tito to visit him in Italy during July. Tito declined. Vladimir Dedijer, in his *War Diaries*, says Tito's colleagues felt "it was not seemly for the supreme commander and president of the

National Committee to go on his knees to visit the commander of an allied sector, as if he were subordinated to him". Maclean thought Tito was reluctant to go in case Wilson sprang a meeting on him with King Peter, who was in Italy then. Churchill was furious. He demanded that Maclean tell Tito it was better, given his present mood, that he should "go back to his mountains and get on with the fighting".

Apparently the Soviets stepped in again and persuaded Tito to go to Naples on 6 August to meet the Allied military chiefs. General Alexander took him up to the front line and Maclean arranged for him to visit Rome. General Wilson mentions in his memoirs, *Eight Years Overseas*, that when Tito was staying at his headquarters a dispute arose over the sleeping arrangements. Tito refused to bed down in a tent, insisting on "being between walls". He was put up in the anteroom of the Officers' Mess! On 12 August he met Churchill, who had brought Subasic with him.

Churchill was casually dressed in his siren suit. Tito wore his splendid new marshal's uniform, complete with gold leaves and umpteen decorations, which the Soviets had tailored for him in Moscow after the loss of his previous one. Djilas had taken Tito's measurements with him when he visited Stalin in April. Churchill joked to his chums how hot and bothered Tito had been in the Italian sun, perspiring profusely, trying without success to loosen his collar which was clearly too tight for him. Tito had obviously thought it necessary to impress Churchill. American bystanders ridiculed the uniform even more. It reminded them of those worn by Park Avenue doormen!

Pierson Dixon, Anthony Eden's principal private secretary, recorded in his diary:

> Tito was cautious, nervous and sweating a good deal in his absurd Marshal's uniform of thick cloth and gold lace. Fitzroy and I sat opposite. The P.M. pitched into Tito a good deal towards the end, and told him that we could not tolerate our war material being used against rival Yugoslavs. But Tito must have known that there was no real threat against him, since we have consistently done nothing but court him. But he evidently thought it politic not to turn a deaf ear to the appeal.[6]

According to the official minutes of the meeting, Churchill "suggested" to Tito "that the right solution for Yugoslavia was a democratic system based on the peasants; conditions in the peasant holdings being gradually improved". Tito replied that he had no desire to introduce the Communist system into Yugoslavia, if only for the reason that it was to be expected that most European countries after the war would be living under a democratic system from which Yugoslavia could not afford to differ.

When Churchill asked him to "reaffirm publicly his statement about Communism", Tito hedged. He was "reluctant to do so at this moment since such a statement might give the impression that it had been forced on him and weaken his position".[7]

At dinner that evening Churchill, who Pierson Dixon noted in his diary, "thought [Tito] was getting away with too much", asked Dixon to draft a memo to him. This Dixon did and showed it after dinner to Churchill, who "stiffened it with statements about the importance of the Serbs and the need for unity if our supplies were to continue". It was filled with high-flown phrases like

> His Majesty's Government expect Tito to make, not only a statement regarding his intention not to impose Communism on the country, but also a statement to the effect that he will not use the armed strength of the Movement to influence the free expression of the will of the people on the future regime of the country. If it should turn out that any large quantities of ammunition sent by His Majesty's Government are used for fratricidal strife other than in self-defence, it would affect the whole question of Allied supplies.

Dixon confided to his diary:

> It is a pity the P.M. did not use this sort of language with Tito in the early days. Now it is too late. Tito is essential now to our war plans, and knows it, and the Russian armies are nearer to Yugoslavia than we are; so Tito snaps his fingers at us and is conciliatory only to the extent necessary to make a show of helpfulness.

Next day Churchill met Tito with Subasic; meanwhile the two had got together. As Dixon observed, it soon "became apparent that Tito had swallowed" Subasic:

> Whenever he was asked for his opinion, [he] merely reiterated or embroidered Tito's views. Tito did, however, make certain concessions of form such as agreeing that the amalgamated navy should be called the Royal Yugoslav Navy and promised to meet the King.

When the moment came for the official photographs there was, according to Dixon,

> an embarrassing pause before the two leaders sat down, broken by Tito waving [Subasic] to the place of honour on the P.M.'s right, with

the remark, "[Subasic] must sit there, as we mustn't get Mr. Churchill into trouble with the Conservative Party".

Tito knew he had no need to concede anything of substance to Churchill. With Mihailovic dismissed, he had no political competitor on Yugoslav soil. Regarding meeting King Peter, he simply maintained it was not feasible in the foreseeable future. He denied the Partisan movement was divorced from the great mass of the Serbian people. As for Churchill's wish that he proclaim his intention not to impose communism on his fellow Yugoslavs, Tito did on his return to Vis issue a statement that the aim of the Partisans was "not the establishment of Communism, which our enemies attribute to us". Nobody of substance believed this. Churchill telegraphed Roosevelt and Stalin that he had told Tito and Subasic "we had no thought but that they should combine their resources so as to weld the Yugoslav people into one instrument in the struggle against the Germans".[8] However he confided to Eden on 17 August that Tito and Subasic seemed to be getting on too well together. Eden felt Subasic, a Croat like Tito, underestimated the Serb problem.

Apparently Tito had been reluctant to meet Churchill, believing he would be cornered into making concessions. He had feared for his life – his bodyguards were heavily armed, to the consternation of his hosts. Churchill recalls in his memoirs that Tito wanted to bring these "ferocious-looking bodyguards, each carrying automatic pistols" into the meetings "in case of treachery on our part". He was dissuaded from doing so "with some difficulty". The Countess of Ranfurly, one of the secretaries at the meeting, records in her diary that she had to give tea to the Tito party: "Marshal Tito, resplendent in a blue and silver uniform and surrounded by five ferocious-looking guards with tommy guns walked in. He was short and stocky and dressed to kill." Later, when Tito came to see General Wilson, he "demanded to take his five thugs and their tommy guns to the meeting which caused a delay and much amusement among us".[9]

Churchill wrote to his wife a few days later that his meeting with Tito had gone quite well, but added, "unhappily Tito is now using the bulk of the ammunition we gave him to fight the Serbs". An OSS report to Washington at this time complained of American supplies dropped under British command being used to kill Serbs: the "Partisans have almost ceased fighting Germans and are openly concentrating on the civil war against the Serbs".[10] Churchill minuted Eden on 31 August: "It would be well to remember how great a responsibility will rest on us after the War ends, with Tito having all the arms and being able to subjugate the rest of the country by weapons supplied by us."[11] According to the official Foreign Office historian, Sir Llewellyn Woodward,

> Mr Eden noted on this minute that the Foreign Office hardly needed a reminder of this danger, and that the Prime Minister had persistently "pushed Tito" in spite of Foreign Office warning. Mr Eden sent a reply to the Prime Minister on September 15 pointing out that the danger had arisen because our policy towards Yugoslavia had been determined by considerations of short-term military expediency rather than by those of long-term political interest.

Eden is also on record as saying Churchill felt "somewhat disenchanted by his meeting with Tito".[12] Tito himself was well pleased. Djilas thought "the meeting with Churchill strengthened Tito's self-confidence and authority."[13]

Djilas admits that while they were attacking the Chetniks in Montenegro that August and were suffering heavy casualties, Tito persuaded Maclean to seek help in evacuating the wounded. This was when Churchill and his entourage were denying they were taking sides in the Yugoslav civil war. Over a thousand Partisan casualities were picked up and flown out to Italy in a single day. This relieved the pressure on the Partisans, who were able to make a breakthrough that same evening. According to Djilas "they stole up to the Chetniks' position and killed off three to four hundred of them."

With British help the Partisans had, in mid-July, established a new headquarters on the mainland to which some of the Allied missions moved, though not Tito himself. Tito now demanded the release of all British-trained Yugoslav air mechanics working for the Balkan Air Force. He wanted to establish workshops for his own air force, which he hoped to set up as soon as Yugoslavia was liberated. That this Partisan air force was merely a figment of the future, whereas the mechanics were needed immediately to win the war against the Germans, apparently did not cross Tito's mind. SOE head Colin Gubbins is on record as indicating that aiding the Italian resistance was "paying a far better and more immediate dividend ... than Tito's very half-hearted efforts in Yugoslavia". Gubbins felt "Tito was having us for a sucker."[14]

During August the prospect of an Allied landing on the Dalmatian coast reappeared. The intention was to link up with Tito's forces to capture Trieste, then to advance on Vienna through the Ljubljana

gap. Churchill wired Roosevelt on 28 August 1944 urging such a landing and saying, "Tito's people will be waiting for us in Istria."[15] The
Americans again refused, which perhaps was just as well. Tito had
ordered his men to be on the lookout for any such landing and to
oppose it forcibly. One of his generals, Stane Semic-Daki, recalled in
his memoirs, *The Best Have Fallen*, how he was instructed to ready his
troops to move towards the sea: "This would be necessary if Anglo-
American troops landed on the Yugoslav coast as the Supreme Commander Marshal Tito was opposed to the establishment of a second
front on Yugoslav territory." Tito's close colleague Edvard Kardelj, in
his memoirs *The Struggle for Recognition and Independence*, says they
seriously considered blowing up bridges to slow the Allied advance.

Earlier in the summer, while Tito was enjoying British hospitality
on Vis, the Partisans had again proposed to the Germans joint action
to oppose an Allied landing in Venezia Giulia. Field Marshal Alexander's later offer in February 1945 to send Allied troops to help the
Partisans hasten the German retreat was turned down out of hand by
Tito. It might have spared thousands of Partisan lives and perhaps
shortened the war. Such was the Partisan leadership's paranoia of an
Allied presence in Yugoslavia that Kardelj was to claim Tito's refusal
"saved our revolution"!

The Red Army reached the Yugoslav border on 6 September
1944 and entered Bulgaria three days later. The former Axis power
had changed sides following a coup and had already begun aiding the
Allies. This prompted the Germans to begin withdrawing in earnest
their 300,000 or so troops from Greece. The British hoped Tito
would harass their retreat through Yugoslavia. To that end supplies
were stepped up to him, but to Churchill's great annoyance they
were again used to kill Mihailovic's anti-communists instead of Germans. He telegraphed Tito on 16 September: "I have been increasingly concerned to see how large a proportion of our ammunition
and supplies is being used against your own countrymen rather than
against the Germans."[16] The main route of the German withdrawal
from Greece was of course through Serbia, where Tito still had little
presence. He determined now to seek Soviet help in ridding Serbia
of his political opponents. Djilas reveals how "once it came into our
own territory the Red Army became a part of our own realities, out-
smarting the Brtitish, outmanoeuvering the Americans, and outfox-
ing the Bulgarians."

Without telling his British hosts, Tito on 21 September smuggled
himself out of Vis by air to Moscow (via Bari and Cralova in

Romania, which had recently been captured by the Red Army) in an American-built plane flown by Russians. Churchill was furious. Ever after he described Tito as having "levanted" – the Oxford English Dictionary definition of "levanting" being to abscond or bolt, especially with betting or gaming losses unpaid! It was obviously a well-planned operation. The Soviet air representative at Allied head-quarters in Italy had, some time before, requested permission for Soviet pilots to practice night landings and take-offs on narrow airstrips. This had readily been granted. He had then arranged for this practice to be undertaken on Vis's tiny airfield. Apparently nobody on the British side thought this unusual or suspicious! For several nights in succession the British guards there saw a Soviet plane take off and land. On the last night the plane contained Tito and the head of the Russian mission, General Korneyev. They noticed that it did not land again!

On the day Tito levanted to Moscow, Heinrich Himmler, Hitler's SS Chief, addressed some of his officers at Jagerhohe in Germany. Tito, he said, "had the nerve actually to fool and humiliate the British and Americans in the most comical way." Henniker-Major, in his memoirs, describes how he was given the fruitless task of "chasing round Serbia hunting for Tito to try to get him to come back to Vis". He was

> always, even at the time, amazed that Winston seemed to think that after he had deigned to meet him, Tito should be his faithful sup-porter, even stooge. It seemed to me perfectly obvious that Tito saw himself as a free agent able to pursue his relations as he saw fit with the Allies, and especially with the Russians – his original protectors ... After all, Tito was never anything other than a dedicated communist.

Maclean had meanwhile been organising an operation named "Ratweek" – meant perhaps to suggest swimmers leaving sinking ships! On 1 September Partisans, armed with British weapons and enjoying Allied air-cover, were to invade Serbia, ostensibly to catch Germans retreating from Greece, as Churchill had constantly implored Tito to do. But Tito had his sights set on his political rival Mihailovic. It was Mihailovic's supporters who were the rats in Tito's book. He now insisted to Maclean that British liaison officers with the subordinate Partisan commands be withdrawn, leaving only those at headquarters. He did not want Maclean's men to hinder the final liquidation of his political opponents. He also prevented British attempts to locate themselves on the Adriatic coast near the ports of Trieste and Fiume to harass German shipping. He had his eyes on those ports. A British presence might prevent him from acquiring them. That such a presence might shorten the war and reduce the loss of Allied life clearly did not interest him. When British raiders did go ashore there they were promptly detained by the Partisans and released only after much diplomatic wrangling.

To open Ratweek the Balkan Air Force bombed Leskovac, a populous town far to the south of Belgrade, where it was claimed the Germans had concentrated armour and motor transport. Fifty American Flying Fortresses were used to flatten the town. In Maclean's words it "lay enveloped in a pall of smoke; several buildings seemed to be burning fiercely. Even the Partisans seemed subdued ... the civilian casualties had been heavy." Maclean had witnessed the bombing: "The whole of Leskovac seemed to rise bodily into the air in a tornado of dust and smoke and debris, and a great rending noise fell on our ears." Hundreds of Serbs were killed and the whole area traumatised. It was clear from Maclean's account – the phrase used was "it seemed rather like taking a sledgehammer to crack a walnut" – that the small German garrison had not merited such a large-scale raid.

Tito had evidently asked for Leskovac to be bombed. Vane Ivanovic says:

> The Partisans needed not only all the propaganda value they could get from the fact of Allied recognition and military aid, but also a spectacular and easily understood demonstration by violence that, with the support of *all* the Allies, they would stop at nothing in order to prevail in Serbia. This demonstration Maclean provided when they got the Americans to raze Leskovac. The destruction of this town in support of the Partisans' march northwards, and in the presence of the chief of the British mission, was taken in Serbia, as I have had it since the War from dozens of people who were in Serbia at the time, as a clear signal that there was now no alternative to a Communist-led Partisan take-over of the entire country.

Other Serbian towns received similar treatment. Inevitably there were casualties, too, among the Allied aircrews doing the Partisans' bidding.

Tito was anxious that the Red Army should accomplish for him what he had been unable to do himself, namely clear Serbia of Mihailovic and his forces. That Mihailovic, as a counter to Maclean's Ratweek, had issued his long-awaited call for an uprising to expel the Germans before the Russians arrived made Tito all the more anxious. It was claimed forty thousand had answered the call, though

Mihailovic had few weapons to offer them other than those gleaned from the State Guard in Belgrade. The paucity of arms did not stop his forces having initial successes, including the early capture of the German-garrisoned town of Lazarevac, less than thirty miles from Belgrade. This was promptly announced as a Partisan success by the BBC. Enigma decrypts were to reveal German reports of widespread sabotaging throughout Serbia that week, such as the severing of railway lines and attacks on road convoys. But the rug was almost immediately pulled from under Mihailovic. King Peter was persuaded by Maclean to call upon all Serbs to rally to Tito. In a BBC broadcast on 12 September he suggested that those who did not would risk "the stigma of treason".[17]

Tito now met Stalin for the first time. A subterfuge was agreed: a formal request by the Red Army to Tito for permission to enter Yugoslav territory bordering on Hungary to block the German retreat from Greece. As this area was Serbia, most people saw through it. The Russians entered Yugoslavia on 22 September from Romania. A token force of Partisans linked up with the Red Army on 4 October to liberate Belgrade, which was achieved on 20 October. Because no other Allies were on the scene in force, it meant the *de facto* recognition of Tito's takeover of Yugoslavia. A message was sent from the British King George VI to the Yugoslav King Peter congratulating him on the liberation of Belgrade "by the forces of our gallant Soviet ally, helped by the stout resistance of its citizens".[18] None was sent to Tito. A telegram from the British Foreign Office to Cairo on 21 October noted, "we do not propose that any message should be sent to Tito whose troops in any case have played little or no part in Belgrade's liberation".[19]

The scale of Partisan participation in the liberation of Belgrade remains controversial. Moscow's official line at the time was that "the Soviet command courteously complied with the wishes by Partisan leaders, and by Tito personally, that Yugoslav troops should be the first to enter the capital". It emerged later that the Red Army's operational commander, General A. Zhdanov, had brushed aside requests for Partisan participation in the battle for Belgrade with the remark, quoted in Stephen Clissold's *Djilas: The Progress of a Revolutionary*: "I am advancing according to my own plan, and you may use yours and advance if you can. The enemy is weak and I shall simply walk over him ... Come tomorrow and have tea with me in Belgrade!" Stalin was to remind Tito in May 1948:

The Soviet army came to the aid of the Yugoslav people, crushed the German invader, liberated Belgrade and in this way created the conditions which were necessary for the Communist Party of Yugoslavia to achieve power. Unfortunately the Soviet army did not and could not render such assistance to the French and Italian communist parties.[20]

Many of Mihailovic's men had joined the Red Army in fighting the Germans. But, once Belgrade was taken, they were handed over to the Partisans who straightaway shot them. Mihailovic complained about this to Allied HQ in Italy in a signal on 8 November. He also stated that the Partisans had fired on them while they were attacking Germans. No reply was received. Djilas admits in his *Wartime* memoirs that extensive killings took place at this time and says:

> To be sure, among the executed there were also those whom the worst, most unjust court would have spared. But wars, and especially revolutions and counter-revolutions, are waged according to dogmatic and ideological criteria – criteria which in the course of extermination become a passion and a practice, a custom and a virtue: a person is guilty not necessarily of having done something, but simply of having belonged to something.

Thus Tito won control of Serbia without defeating Mihailovic in any decisive military or political contest. The Soviets did it for him. It was only now that the Soviets began supplying the Partisans in earnest. Djilas says Stalin offered to equip twelve infantry divisions and to supply planes for two airforce divisions. It was while Tito was in Moscow that Stalin urged him to appease the British by reinstating the King: "You don't have to take him back forever. Just temporarily, and then at the right moment – a knife in the back"![21]

While in Romania, Tito had met Marko Mesic, a Croat who had been an officer in the Royal Yugoslav Army before the war. He had deserted during the German invasion and then joined the Ustashi, participating in their murderous activities against the Serbs of Croatia. Subsequently he volunteered to fight for the Germans against the Russians and was awarded the Iron Cross for his efforts. Captured at Stalingrad in February 1943, he enlisted in the Free Yugoslav Legion set up within the Red Army for Yugoslav prisoners-of-war prepared to fight against the Germans. Djilas says Mesic undertook a "rigorous physical and political training programme ... such a 're-education' of men was something we hadn't known until that time". Mesic worked his way up through the ranks to become the Legion's commander, though Djilas, who met him during his visit to Russia earlier that year, claims "his command was a pure formality".[22] The Legion, about three thousand strong, took part in the liberation of Belgrade and was eventually absorbed into the Partisan army. Tito decorated Mesic with one of the highest Partisan awards!

Jasper Rootham, a liaison officer with Mihailovic, recalled a BBC broadcast that had enthused over Mesic's "repentance": "It is hard to describe the rage, and I am afraid I must say contempt, roused in Serb listeners by this effort." He remembered, too, another BBC broadcast at that time warning the Ustashi to join the Partisans "before it is too late", which caused a sensation in Serbia:

> This phrase, coming as it did from London, shocked the Serbs very much because, although they had maintained for some time that Tito had been accepting Ustashi into his ranks, they had not before received any indication that the British approved of it, and this they could not understand.[23]

Officers from the Ustasha militia were given the same rank in the Partisan army as they had held previously.

Relations between the Red Army and the liberated Yugoslavs quickly deteriorated. Raping and looting by the Russian troops, and the boorishness of some of their officers, shocked puritanical party functionaries like Djilas. He contrasted this with the gentlemanly behaviour of the British personnel they had met. Stalin replied to his complaints in person in April 1945, in the presence of Tito, Djilas and most of the top Soviet leadership:

> Imagine a man who has fought from Stalingrad to Belgrade – over thousands of kilometres of his own devastated land, across the dead bodies of his comrades and dearest ones! How can such a man react normally? And what is so awful in his amusing himself with a woman, after such horrors.[24]

Stalin never forgave Djilas for his criticism. Soviet agents put it about that he was a Trotskyist – the ultimate Stalinist sin!

Tito had remained with his Soviet hosts until 27 October 1944. He arrived by boat in Belgrade from Romania a week after the Yugoslav capital's liberation and took up residence in Prince Paul's former home, the White Palace. Henceforth he acted as head of state, despite his pledge to Churchill to share power with the London Yugoslavs. Djilas says that, before choosing the White Palace, Tito toured all the royal dwellings in Belgrade and ordered their restoration. He insisted that the furniture, china and other contents be safeguarded: "In the eyes of the people, palaces are the seats and symbols of power." A member of Tito's politburo, Andrija Hebrang, complained to the Soviets that Tito was more interested in repairing palaces than in fighting Germans.

Tito created a ceremonial guard under his personal command and formalised his secret police, the now dreaded OZNA. Its initials stood in Serbo-Croat for Department for the Protection of the People. In Tito's own words, its purpose was "to strike terror into the bones of those who do not like our kind of Yugoslavia". According to the historian Jozo Tomasevich, towards the end of 1944 a crucial meeting was held in Belgrade of the top OZNA officials when it was decided to eliminate all the Partisans' domestic enemies. It is an event, he says, "Yugoslavs do not write about" although, "politically, it was one of the most important decisions of the entire war period, and it cost a great deal of blood". He maintains it was unlikely to have been taken without "consultation with the Party-Army leadership – that is, with Tito and the other top leaders".[25]

In March 1946 OZNA changed its name to UDBA – State Security Administration. It was given unrestricted powers to arrest, imprison and even execute, without public charge or trial, those it deemed the regime's political opponents. Stalin had arranged for Yugoslav intelligence officers to be trained by KGB agents and he provided Tito with a bodyguard composed of KGB men. This was a source of much criticism within Tito's circle, especially when they were later shown to have been spying on Moscow's behalf. Stalin also gave Tito a bulletproof Packard limousine similar to his own.

Djilas mentions in *Wartime* that, when party functionaries began reaching Belgrade in November 1944, there was an unseemly scramble for villas in the fashionable suburbs abandoned by their owners. When these had all been taken, there was an even more shameful expropriation of properties whose owners were thought less than enthusiastic about communism. "Social climbing, jealousy, and backbiting", he says, came to the fore. "Special shops with token prices were set up for high officials, their supplies commensurate with the rank of their privileged clientele ... Privilege begins as a necessity and then becomes established as a right."

Djilas complains that, through Soviet influence, these shops became hierarchical:

> On the highest level was the diplomatic store, supplying foreign diplomats, Central Committee members, and the highest federal officials; next came the one for generals and higher officers, then the

one for leaders of the republics, then an officers' store, and so on. Prices in these stores were nominal. There was instant abuse. One high official ordered forty quilts for his relatives ... even after the special stores were abolished, members of the Politburo and a lesser number of top officials continued to have privileged sources of supply. They were fed by Tito's farms and, through his staff, were provided with first-class merchandise at advantageous prices.[26]

Fitzroy Maclean, in *Eastern Approaches*, states:

Tito, with his natural liking for the good things in life, soon settled into his new surrounding as if he had lived in palaces all his life. His suits and uniforms were made by the best tailor in Belgrade; his shirts came from the most fashionable shirt-maker; he ate the best food and drank the best wine; the horses he rode were the finest in the country.

Maclean noted how, on his first visit to the White Palace, he found Tito's mistress Olga "busily engaged in having the royal cipher unpicked from the bed-linen".

Franklin Lindsay, by this time head of the American military mission in Belgrade,

marveled at how Tito, the peasant's son, Communist underground organiser and Partisan leader in the forest, had so quickly adapted to life as the ruler. Personal vanity was apparent in his new uniforms. They were perfectly tailored and generously adorned with gold braid and his marshal's insignia of rank ... His overcoat almost touched the ground. His visored cap carried much gold. Only the five-pointed red star was a reminder of his Communist career. He was a gracious host who entertained well, and his buffet tables were always loaded with delicacies of every variety, including Russian vodka and Caspian caviar. He adapted so easily that it seemed he might have been born a Hapsburg prince rather than the son of Croat peasants.[27]

In no time at all, Lindsay remarked,

the Yugoslavs were already hard at work building Tito into a larger-than-life world image. Honor guards, flags, uniforms, parades, speeches, books, and quotations by the great man were fulsomely deployed. One day I received a call from the general staff saying Tito would arrive back in Belgrade the next day. As head of the military mission I was told I was expected to be at the airport to greet him when he stepped off the plane. Together with the top party, government, and military leaders we all waited in line for our turn to shake his hand before he was driven off, surrounded by his bodyguards.

In a message to Maclean, who had been asked by Churchill to rebuke him for his levanting, Tito rubbed salt into the wound by declaring: "We are an independent state, and I, as Chairman of the National Committee and Supreme Commander, am not responsible to anyone outside the country for my actions." He told Maclean he had felt equally hurt Churchill had not informed *him* when he had gone off to meet Roosevelt in Quebec that same month, September 1944. It was a remark Churchill and his colleagues naturally thought offensive. Churchill's close friend, the South African Field-Marshal Smuts, wrote to him on 26 September: "In spite of all the help Tito has obtained only from us, he has not behaved loyally to us. I fear that our interests will suffer by his supremacy in Yugoslavia."[28]

On 9 October in Moscow, with the Red Army nearing Belgrade, Churchill reached his so-called "percentages agreement" with Stalin. He suggested they settle their affairs in the Balkans informally:

> Your armies are in Romania and Bulgaria. We have interests, missions and agents there. Don't let us get at cross-purposes in small ways. So far as Britain and Russia are concerned, how would it do for you to have 90 per cent predominance in Romania, for us to have 90 per cent of the say in Greece, and go 50-50 about Yugoslavia?

Apparently embarrassed at the brazenness of it, Stalin was reluctant to keep the paper on which Churchill had jotted the figures. He ticked it with a blue pencil and passed it back to him. Winston thought they should burn it. Stalin told him to keep it.

Churchill later referred to the paper in private as the "naughty document". It was not, of course, mentioned in the official record of the Moscow meetings. Ian Jacob of Churchill's staff told Sir Edward Bridges, Secretary to the Cabinet, on 26 October 1944 that any mention was "most inappropriate" as it would "give the impression to historians that these very important discussions were conducted in a most unfitting manner". Bridges dutifully ordered the deletion.[29] Churchill, however, detailed it all ten years later in his own memoirs, *Triumph and Tragedy*.

Regarding Yugoslavia, Julian Amery said to me:

> We weren't in a position to claim our 50 per cent because we had nobody there. In Greece we did. But in Greece in the end Stalin was good. I have a feeling that if we had got the troops into Yugoslavia we might have produced a coalition arrangement which would have spared the Yugoslav people forty years or more of a Communist dictatorship.

The Foreign Office worried that Tito's ambitions might not be limited to Yugoslavia. They were alarmed when Djilas claimed, at a rally in Belgrade soon after its liberation, that the Slav inhabitants of Greek Macedonia were being persecuted by the Greek authorities. He called for the incorporation of both Greek Macedonia and Bulgarian Macedonia into Yugoslavia's proposed new Macedonian Republic. Fitzroy Maclean was ordered to voice London's protest, as was the British Ambassador in Moscow, since it was thought the Soviets were probably behind the move.

Churchill's close colleague Sir John Slessor, later head of the Royal Air Force but then Deputy Allied Air Commander-in-Chief, Mediterranean, had been persuaded in February 1944 by Maclean (against his better judgement, so he said) to equip the Partisans with a couple of squadrons. He fretted over Soviet intentions in the Balkans and how our promotion of Tito was facilitating a Soviet hegemony there. He was especially disgusted at the Russians' refusal to help the British drop supplies to the inhabitants of Warsaw when they rose up against the Germans in August 1944, assuming the Red Army was about to take the Polish capital. The Russians delayed their attack until the Germans had ruthlessly put down the uprising. Stalin had refused to co-operate because, he claimed, "the outbreak in Warsaw is purely the work of adventurers and the Soviet government cannot lend its hand to it". By "adventurers" Stalin meant anti-communists and he relished the Germans ridding him of them.

The airdrops attempted by the British at such a long distance had led to the loss of more than two hundred aircrew and the destruction of thirty-one planes. Slessor agonised over this in his memoirs, *The Central Blue*, and pondered "how, after the fall of Warsaw, any responsible statesman could trust any Russian Communist further than he could kick him, passes the comprehension of ordinary men". Churchill had been exasperated, too, on that occasion, recalling perhaps his previous misgivings about the Bolsheviks.

By mid-November, with Tito safely in control of Serbia, the Red Army quit Yugoslavia for Hungary. The Partisans, now equipped by the Soviets, were left to complete the task of eliminating Tito's political opponents elsewhere in the country. Bulgarian troops, who had previously helped the Germans subdue the Serbs and had been notorious for their brutality, were absorbed into the Partisan "liberating" force. Bulgaria had changed sides in early September. The British and American military chiefs disapproved. They had not been consulted.

Within days the Germans consolidated along a front pivoting on the Srem. They wished to protect a possible retreat route to southern Germany, and to keep open their main lines of communication to the east towards Hungary and to the south towards Montenegro and Greece, where their troops were still withdrawing. The Srem was the wedge of territory bounded by the rivers Sava, Drava and Danube, sixty miles north-west of Belgrade. The front then stretched from the coast east of Fiume to Mostar and Sarajevo and thence northwards to the Danube at Vukovar, north-east of Belgrade. The Germans successfully defended it until mid-April 1945, with only a few minor setbacks. During that time they were able to transfer five divisions, over half of their force, to help delay the Red Army's conquest of Hungary.

Milovan Djilas, in his *Wartime* memoirs, painfully details the Partisan failures and inadequacies on this front, although they were numerically superior. Tito had called up all Yugoslav men aged sixteen and over for military service. The call-up changed the character of the Partisan army. Few of the 800,000 conscripts were communists. They were given scant training before being hurled into action. Their losses – more than 25,000 killed – were the heaviest of the war. In one action alone, the siege of Knin, secured by 3,000 Germans, the Partisans lost 8,000 men.

Nor did the communists during their campaigning let up on the purge of "internal enemies". Ljubo Sirc comments in his memoirs that, when men disappeared in this way, they were said to have "been been sent to the 13th Battalion, which in communist language meant killed by the authorities". The Partisans were also facing a rebellion in their rear from anti-communists in Kosovo, mostly Albanians who were not pro-Serb either. They had been as much against Mihailovic's forces as against Tito's and now resented being reincorporated into a Yugoslav state. Having left it late to resolve their predicament, they were that much more desperate. Their resistance was not finally extinguished until late 1945, and not before many thousands on both sides had perished.

Meanwhile Tito did not let up on Mihailovic who, after the debacle at Belgrade, had escaped with several thousand men to north-eastern Bosnia. There they spent the winter of 1944-45. On 13 November 1944 Mihailovic made an offer to General Wilson, Supreme Allied Commander in the Mediterranean, repeated on 29 November to his successor, General Alexander, to place his troops, claimed to be more than 50,000 strong, under Allied command to harass the German retreat from Greece through Yugoslavia. His offers were ignored, even though the German withdrawal went unmolested by the Partisans, who preferred hounding Mihailovic's forces. The Allied-trained and Allied-equipped Partisan airforce also bombed them relentlessly.

Beset by typhus and hunger, lacking medical and other essential supplies, Mihailovic's force was soon reduced to a mere ragtag and bobtail. He persuaded most of them to go northwards to seek sanctuary with the western allies. He and a few close companions returned to Serbia in the spring of 1945. He was to maintain his resistance there until his capture the following year after a country-wide manhunt for him. Tito was anxious Mihailovic should not escape Yugoslavia. Once outside he could well have become a focus of international opposition to the Partisans.

The Germans largely remained in control as they withdrew through Montenegro and Bosnia: 113,000 strong, they did not finally capitulate in Yugoslavia until 15 May 1945, a week after the war ended elsewhere in Europe. Djilas says the Partisans were spurred to break out at Srem in April 1945 only because of rumours that proponents of the Croatian Peasant Party were plotting to overthrow the Ustasha leader, Ante Pavelic, and declare an independent Croatia under the protection of the Western powers. By the time they entered Zagreb on 8 May, the Partisans had lost another 36,000 men. They had taken Ljubljana, Slovenia's capital, the day before. Djilas claimed at least 305,000 Partisans lost their lives during the war. The total for all Yugoslavs, including victims of the Ustasha massacres, the reprisals, the bombings, the death camps and the killings in the civil war, was about a million. The SOE's official historian William Mackenzie maintains it was, when you include the near-destruction of the country, "out of all proportion to the damage inflicted on the enemy". He considered these losses "a heavy burden of responsibility to bear". They were far greater than those of any other warring participant, save Russia and Poland.

The Partisans were reluctant to accept humanitarian aid, except from the Soviets, who were hardly in a position to offer much. The West extended help through the United Nations Relief and Rehabilitation Administration (UNRRA), set up to bring succour to peoples suffering from the war. The Partisans insisted that they, rather than UNRRA's own representatives, should distribute the food, clothing and medicines within their country. All the while they denounced

UNRRA in their propaganda as "the Trojan horse of American capitalism"! Faced with starvation, they eventually compromised, agreeing
to a Soviet colonel heading the UNRRA mission in Yugoslavia.
Meanwhile two grain ships waiting in Dubrovnik in late December
1944 had been rerouted elsewhere by impatient UNRRA officials.
Donald Hamilton-Hill, in his memoirs *SOE Assignment*, details how
he and his colleagues had sought Maclean's help in persuading the
Partisans to let British personnel unload the grain. Fitzroy had
been unwilling to intervene. James Klugmann worked for a time for
UNRRA in Yugoslavia, after having spent four months with
Maclean's mission to Tito.

Local Partisan commanders raised difficulties over the landing of
British troops on the Dalmatian coast. British ships were refused
docking facilities at Split and Zadar. Even Allied minesweepers were
denied access to Yugoslav waters to clear routes for supply vessels.
Partisan shore batteries were instructed to fire on any boat not given
permission from Belgrade to enter a harbour. The Partisans would
permit equipment to be unloaded, but not soldiers. Two British
colonels sent ahead to co-ordinate matters were detained while their
credentials were forwarded to Tito's headquarters.

According to Ljubo Sirc, in Split at this time with the Partisans,
"the Communists considered the British their "class enemies" and
behaved accordingly, forever suspecting them of foul play. Naturally
the British did not like this attitude, so there were continual clashes."
The Partisan officers, he maintained, "distinguished themselves
mostly by their boorishness and unpleasantness". His

> eagerness to help in the war had evaporated after a few weeks under
> the Communists' combination of pettiness and murderousness ...
> The hatred displayed towards the British, and, to a somewhat lesser
> degree towards the Americans, was hard to believe. In the middle of
> the harbour lay a British destroyer out-of-bounds to everybody.
> To the townspeople who must have remembered days of festivities
> before the war when the British Mediterranean fleet visited Yugoslav
> ports, it must have looked odd to see solitary British naval officers
> going for walks without anybody daring to smile at them, let alone
> address a word to them.

He recalled, when in Slovenia a few months later, being lectured
"on British-American treachery" by his Partisan colleagues even
though

> we were all in British battle-dress, ate food mostly supplied by the
> Allies and had arms dropped by them, yet the Communists incessantly

sneered at Allied help and never stopped talking about Soviet aid, of which I never saw or heard a trace in Slovenia. Allegedly, Soviet planes always came by night.

Sirc says that, when he once spoke admiringly of some British and American equipment, he was taken aside by a friendly officer and warned it was risky to speak well of the Allies. Evidently the Partisan leadership were embarrassed by their continuing reliance on Allied aid. It was suggested in their propaganda that the initials U.S. on the planes delivering the supplies stood for Unione Sovetica!

Franklin Lindsay, an OSS representative with the Partisans in Slovenia at this time, recalls in his memoirs how he and his colleagues' relations with the Partisan command "had undergone a marked change. We were no longer treated as close allies and friends." Previously they had been allowed to question the downed Allied airmen and escaped prisoners-of-war they met en route, as well as the occasional defecting German soldier. Now they were prevented from doing so. Lindsay observed:

> We were literally never out of sight of at least our individual Partisan couriers or bodyguards. We were told they were there to provide us with constant protection. Their other purpose, however, was to see to it that we had no contacts that had not been authorized by the commissars of the units we were with. The Partisans were, in fact, in a position to block any activity they deemed not in their own interests.

There were times when he and his British colleagues "were for all practical purposes prisoners of the Partisans. I radioed in mid-October: 'We have been virtually under house arrest for the last month'." Refused contact with the Partisan leadership and given no information, they felt it was pointless remaining. Meanwhile the Allies continued sending supplies to the Partisans in ever increasing quantities, although it had become clear they were not being used against Germans. In his final report to OSS headquarters, Lindsay remarked:

> The incidents of non-co-operation, bad faith, and obstructionism became so numerous that it is impossible to explain them as carelessness or ignorance on the part of individual staff officers.. We came to the conclusion that these events could only be explained by a basic Partisan policy that had become one of all obstruction short of an open break with the West and the stoppage of air and sea supplies.

Lindsay cites the instance of a New Zealand army surgeon who was performing numerous operations daily on the Partisan wounded.

Whenever he became friendly with any of the nurses and attendants they were promptly withdrawn. He discovered later that the Partisan leadership feared he might recruit them as spies! Matters came to a head when the allocation of the medical supplies he had come with was taken out of his hands. He decided he had had enough. Lindsay claims the Partisans were anxious to minimise their dependence on the West:

> The story was spread widely among the Partisans, for example, that these arms, medical supplies, and clothing from the West were not gifts, but would have to be paid for at full price at the end of the war. Of course it was not true. To the Western capitalist Allies the blood of the Partisans was not sufficient payment, they said.

Lindsay also noted the increasing inequality within the Partisan ranks:

> There is far greater differentiation between officers and men in clothing, food, equipment, shelter, and privileges than is found in the British or American armies ... Nearly all the officers had "Tito" jackets tailored from British and American greatcoats supplied in our airdrops, then took second greatcoats to wear over the jackets. Meanwhile, the troops shivered in ragged remnants of civilian clothes and German uniforms.

Donald Hamilton-Hill, in *SOE Assignment*, complains of the Partisans becoming "more difficult and arrogant as time went on. Their demands became more and more exacting, and they began to start little pinpricks of annoyance."

Churchill wrote on 23 November 1944 to his son Randolph who was with the Partisans in Croatia: "I have been much disappointed with Tito, who has not responded to the generous manner in which I have approached and dealt with him."[30] One of Maclean's subordinates, Lieutenant-Colonel Peter Moore, visiting the Partisans in Slovenia that autumn and winter, found them concerned solely with their political objectives. They had "lost interest in fighting the Germans" and were "conserving their forces for ... the occupation of Trieste and all North Eastern Italy up to the Tagliamento to permit a *fait accompli* at the peace conference ... [and] Klagenfurt and Villach [in Carinthia]." Although still dependent on Allied aid they were "most uncomfortable at being under an obligation to us ... and every petty humiliation to British and American personnel, and discreditable story is employed to combat this."[31] The Foreign Office minuted on their copy of Moore's report dated 14 February 1945 that the "intention [of the Partisans] is to conserve their strength for the capture, after the German collapse in the Balkans, of Ljubljana, Venezia Giulia and Carinthia."[32]

Earlier, on 27 April 1944, another SOE Lieutenant-Colonel, Peter Wilkinson, later British Ambassador in Vienna, had reported that the Partisans in Slovenia were "violently Nationalist and bent on recovering those Slovene territories formerly belonging to Austria and Italy, including the town of Trieste". He found them "predominantly Communist" and

> overwhelmingly pro-Russian. We are a bad second and the Americans nowhere at all ... They are hostile to the monarchy [and] are not particularly interested in the European war as a whole [such that] there is little hope of persuading them to make big disinterested sacrifices for the general Allied cause.

He said Maclean was "inclined to underrate the extremely pro-Russian and Communist character of the Partisan movement".[33]

With the Allies bogged down in northern Italy, Churchill was keen to bypass the German positions there and land by sea on the Istrian peninsula. He could then capture the ports of Trieste and Fiume and thus threaten the German rear. But Tito had his eyes on this part of Italy. He felt it should be given to Yugoslavia to compensate for the destruction and trauma wrought by the Italian occupiers. He wanted to get there before the British. He worried that the presence of Allied forces in Yugoslavia might influence, if not dictate, the shape of its post-war government. It might even force the return of the monarchy. During the last week of November 1944 he demanded that all British forces be withdrawn from the Dubrovnik area, where they had been harassing the Germans.

Life was already being made difficult for the British soldiers there, through night curfews and a ban on their using bars in the towns. Their identity papers were constantly being checked by Tito's police. They were not allowed to fraternise with the civilian population. News correspondents were also deterred from visiting Yugoslavia, unless they were known to be sympathetic to the Partisans.

All too late it was being realised that Tito put political considerations ahead of military needs. Evelyn Waugh was in Split at this time and refers in his diary to

> the deliberate rudeness of the local Partisans. They are ill at ease in Dalmatia, where the cultured townsmen dislike them heartily. The

Partisans react by a regime of suspicion, arrests by the secret police, and discourtesy to the [British Liaison Officers]. A British cruiser is moored in the harbour, the *Delhi*, and greatly resented.

Waugh went on to be Fitzroy Maclean's representative in Dubrovnik. His diary entries illustrate what he saw as the increasingly peremptory manner in which the Partisans were treating their British allies. He quotes a colleague, Brigadier George Davy, in charge of Land Forces Adriatic, as saying, "I do not believe the Partisans have any intention of taking a serious part in the war once their country is cleared. They want to get on with politics." The Partisans particularly resented Waugh's concern for the Croat Catholics, about whose harassment he continually complained. He eventually wrote a report on the subject that found its way to the Vatican. But by then he had been expelled from Yugoslavia. Maclean had not resisted.

When the Germans began withdrawing from Greece, the British determined to make it difficult for them in every way. They hoped the Partisans would do so too, but they had other priorities. Henniker-Major, Maclean's man in Serbia then, admits the Partisan efforts were "half-hearted". A unit of British troops, codenamed "Floydforce" after their commander Brigadier Henry Floyd, complete with artillery, had been put ashore at Dubrovnik in late October. They were to hinder the German withdrawal through the difficult mountainous terrain of Montenegro to the south. They had some success but were to maintain they would have had much more if Tito's officials had not hampered them all the way. In the end they chose to leave before being forced to do so. Consequently the forty thousand Germans of the 21st Mountain Corps withdrawing from Greece via Montenegro were able to join the main German concentration in central Yugoslavia, near Sarajevo, by mid-January – "with a vast loss of stores but otherwise virtually intact" according to SOE's official historian William Mackenzie.

So paranoid was Tito that apparently he was convinced Floydforce was part of a wicked British plot to link up with Mihailovic and cheat him of his political prize at the last minute! A British officer turned historian, Michael McConville, in his account of these times entitled *A Small War in the Balkans*, details

the obstructionism, the suspicion, the unexplained delays and militarily inexplicable changes of plan, the restrictive boorishness of official attitudes to off-duty British troops ... [so that] the feeling among Floydforce upon departure was of let-down, disillusionment and irritation.

Churchill was becoming increasingly irritated too. He telegraphed Tito on 3 December, warning him he was copying the message to Marshal Stalin:

> As you know we have made an arrangement with the Marshal and the Soviet Government to pursue as far as possible a joint policy towards Yugoslavia, and that our influence there should be held on equal balance. But you seem to be treating us in an increasingly invidious fashion. It may be you have fears that your ambitions about occupying Italian territories in the North of the Adriatic lead you to view with suspicion and dislike every military operation on your coast we make against the Germans. I have already assured you that all territorial questions will be reserved for the peace conference, when they will be judged irrespective of war time occupations, and certainly such issues ought not to hamper military operations now.[34]

Winston cabled Smuts in South Africa that same day. The Yugoslav "percentage" was not working. "Tito has turned very nasty and is of course thinking now only of grabbing Trieste, Istria, Fiume, etc., for a virtually Communist Yugoslavia".[35] Three days later he fretted to Roosevelt: most of the German forces in the Balkans were escaping home. On 19 December he told Eden: "I have come to the conclusion that in Tito we have nursed a viper. But up till recently he has been biting Huns. Now that he has started biting us, I feel much less sympathetic."[36]

British diplomats in November 1944 feared Tito might be aiming to annex Greek Macedonia. He was assembling an armed force just across the border in Yugoslavia. This force might also intervene on the side of the Greek communists, it was thought, especially as the local partisan commander had ordered the British liaison officer with him to leave. Tito claimed the force was largely composed of Greek refugees anxious to fight the Germans. No one believed him. Matters came to a head on 23 December when Tito's Partisans tried to prevent British airborne supplies from reaching the Royalist Greeks by refusing to pack them. This prompted Churchill to telegraph William Deakin in Bari the next day to threaten that if the Yugoslav troops did not co-operate "a complete shut-down will be established on all supplies to Yugoslavia".[37]

Churchill minuted Eden on 1 January 1945: the Tito-Subasic agreements were "hopelessly one-sided and [could] mean nothing but the dictatorship of Tito, that well-drilled Communist". Even so, he proposed advising the king to accept "as it preserves at least for a short while the principle of monarchy".[38] Under the agreements the executive powers of the Yugoslav government-in-exile were to be surrendered to Tito's National Committee. Tito would be prime minister and Subasic foreign minister. The royal prerogatives would be transferred to a regency of three until the future of the monarchy was decided by a popular vote. When pressed to recognise all this, King Peter demurred. On 11 January 1945 he denounced the agreements and refused to dismiss his Serb ministers as stipulated in them.

Churchill had apparently confided to Subasic on 8 January:

> Tito holds all power in the country. Tito has the arms and ammunition and he is everything in the country. The real power is in his hands and that of his men. They will carry out the agreement and everything that you signed as they see fit. That is the reality.[39]

Churchill's godson Lord Birkenhead reported from Belgrade on 10 January: "These people have been steadily engaged during the past few months in setting up the machinery of a totalitarian state. All instruments of public expression are under state control."[40]

Nevertheless Churchill telegraphed Stalin on 12 January that Britain would still "favour the idea" of recognising a Tito-Subasic government, "set up under the Regency as the Royal Yugoslavian Government". He would send an ambassador to Belgrade and receive a Yugoslav one in London: "I hope you will think this is a good way out of the difficulty until there is a free and fair expression of the people's will."[41] What Stalin made of the reference to "free and fair expression of the people's will" is not recorded! Churchill cabled Roosevelt two days later: "You know my views on these matters so well that I do not have to repeat that we should insist, so far as is possible, on full and fair elections deciding the future regime of the Yugoslav people or peoples."[42]

In the House of Commons on 18 January, Churchill, showing his frustration at the predicament in which he had placed himself, overrode King Peter's reluctance:

> It is a matter of days within which an agreement must be reached upon this matter and, if we are so unfortunate as not to obtain the consent of King Peter, the matter will have to go ahead, his assent being presumed. We have no special interest in the political regime which prevails in Yugoslavia. Few people in Britain, I imagine, are going to be more cheerful or more downcast because of the future constitution of Yugoslavia.

Peter had in fact dismissed Subasic and his government. He was soon to be persuaded to rescind this as neither Subasic nor the Foreign Office would recognise the order. Churchill threatened to deport the young king, his family and entourage to Belgrade, and allegedly had RAF planes standing by. Clearly he found it easier to bully Peter than to bully Tito. The king's mother thought he was not standing up enough to Churchill. She wanted him to abdicate in favour of his younger brother Tomislav. On the evening of 23 January Churchill told his private secretary John Colville, when going to bed: "Make no mistake, all the Balkans, except Greece, are going to be Bolshevised; and there is nothing I can do to prevent it. There is nothing I can do for poor Poland either."[43]

On 9 February Molotov pressed Eden at Yalta – the Big Three Summit meeting on Soviet soil – to put the Tito-Subasic agreements into effect "before the termination of the Crimea Conference". Eden had been seeking assurances from Tito that all the members of the pre-war Parliament "other than those who had compromised themselves" should be included in the Anti-Fascist Assembly of National Liberation and also that the legislation of the National Liberation Assembly should ultimately "be confirmed by the Constituent Assembly". After some initial reluctance, Stalin eventually accepted these two amendments, as Molotov called them – or assurances, as Eden insisted on describing them.

Eden had wanted a third assurance: that the Government formed under the Tito-Subasic agreements be considered temporary, pending the free expression of the will of the Yugoslav people. Stalin objected. It would appear humiliating to Tito and Subasic. Churchill later reminded Stalin that Tito had said "when elections took place in Yugoslavia he would not object to Russian, British and American observers being present to report impartially to the world that they had been carried out fairly". Apparently Stalin did not react to this. He knew full well they would *not* be "carried out fairly"!

Thus the agreed Report of the Yalta Conference, signed by Churchill, Roosevelt and Stalin on 11 February, included a recommendation to Tito and Subasic that their agreement "be put into effect immediately, and that a new Government should be formed on the basis of that agreement". Tito's so-called Anti-Fascist Council of National Liberation of Yugoslavia would be enlarged "to include members of the last Yugoslav Parliament (Skupshina) who have not compromised themselves by collaboration with the enemy, thus forming a body to be known as a temporary Parliament".[44] It was left to Tito to decide who had "compromised themselves". He took full advantage to weed out all likely opponents! Also, having agreed to "democratic procedures", it was again left to him to define what they should be. That he would put into practice a political system that was the very antithesis of what Churchill and his circle meant by democracy was perhaps only par for the communist course!

The king now submitted, persuaded by Eden and by the assurances Churchill had got from Stalin at Yalta. The Americans likewise acceded, though without enthusiasm. The Tito-Subasic provisional government was proclaimed on 7 March and took office with Tito as Prime Minister and Subasic as Foreign Minister. Under pressure from the British, Milan Grol, the leader of the pre-war Democratic Party, was named as vice premier, and Juraj Sutej, a party colleague of Subasic, was made a minister without portfolio. Four other members of the former royal government were given minor posts. The twelve major positions all went to Tito appointees. Similarly, a Regency Council of three men, all, as vouched by Djilas, "favourable to Tito", temporarily took over the function of the Crown.

The Big Three speedily recognised the new arrangement, as did most other important governments. Within days their ambassadors were making their way to Belgrade. But Subasic soon found himself isolated: he was merely a figurehead, if not a fig leaf. The other noncommunists in the government quickly discovered that, behind the façade of the People's Front (Tito's euphemism for his supporters), all power was in the hands of the communists. They were never consulted, nor allowed to create their own party organisations. They complained to Churchill. He had already minuted Eden on 11 March that, with Tito's assumption of the premiership, communist predominance seemed complete, and the "fifty-fifty-percentage" a thing of the past:

> My feeling is that henceforward our inclination should be to back Italy against Tito. Tito can be left to himself in his mountains to stew in Balkan juice, which is bitter ... I have lost my relish for Yugoslavia ... On the other hand, I hope we may still save Italy from the Bolshevik pestilence.[45]

Eden, who had never been a Tito fan, reminded Churchill a week later:

> The United States Government have never been enthusiastic about our pro-Partisan policy, and it has always been with great difficulty that we have dragged them along reluctantly behind us. Are we now

to have to explain to them that after all Tito has not turned out to be what we had hoped for?[46]

Britain had gone ahead on 12 March with appointing an ambassador to Belgrade, inevitably Ralph Stevenson. The British Embassy there reopened two days later. In his reply of 18 March Eden tried to soften the blow for Churchill: "Yugoslavia has not the same long-term strategic and political importance for us as Greece or for that matter as Italy". It "lies outside or rather on the edge of the area of our major interests". Because of the fifty-fifty agreement, it "should be a sort of neutral area between British and Russian zones of influence". In that way it would better protect "our position in Greece and to a lesser extent in Italy as well". Even so, Eden maintained, from the political point of view "we should not draw out and leave the whole business to Tito and Moscow". He did agree that "Tito has certainly behaved ungratefully and ungraciously towards us."[47]

The Americans were blunter. Their ambassador reported to Washington that Tito had established "a complete dictatorship" in Yugoslavia, which was "under almost complete Soviet control". There was "no freedom of speech or press". Tito was a "thorough Communist, and his economic and political philosophy is not ours". The ambassador's number two went further in likening conditions in Yugoslavia to a "ruthless totalitarian police regime". He was pessimistic about the prospects of truly free elections being held there. He expected them to be a mockery.[48]

On 28 April Churchill complained to Stalin:

> The way things have worked out in Yugoslavia certainly does not give me the feeling of a fifty-fifty interest and influence as between our two countries. Marshal Tito has become a complete dictator. He has proclaimed that his prime loyalties are to Soviet Russia. Although he allowed members of the Royal Yugoslav Government to enter his Government, they only number six as against 25 of his own nominees. We have the impression that they are not taken into consultation on matters of high policy, and that it is becoming a one-party regime.[49]

At Potsdam in July 1945 Churchill reminded Stalin it had been agreed at Yalta that the government in Yugoslavia be shared equally between Tito and Subasic. Tito was now in total control. Stalin stalled. Yugoslav representatives should be summoned to answer Churchill's complaints in person. He was against the country being "tried in its absence". But Harold Truman, President since the death of Roosevelt that April, would not countenance any delay in the proceedings. He had other bones to pick with Stalin, more basic to American interests. The matter was effectively dropped, especially as Churchill was voted out of office in Britain within the month. Besides, the Soviets had already installed puppet governments in their other eastern European satellites. According to Edward Stettinius, US Secretary of State at the time of the Yalta Conference, Stalin let the cat out of the bag at Potsdam by requesting

> the United States to recognise the various governments in eastern Europe before the elections provided in the Yalta agreement had been held. Stalin said: "A freely elected government in any of these countries would be anti-Soviet, and that we cannot allow".[50]

Although diplomats in London worried about Tito's sincerity, those on the spot bent over backwards to defend him. A report from the Belgrade embassy reaching London on 26 July maintained Tito was relatively moderate, open to reason and anxious to preserve some ties with the West. But, increasingly bypassed by more militant subordinates who might end by manipulating him altogether: "Tito, in our opinion, puts Yugoslavia first and his subordinates put communism first."[51] By contrast the Foreign Office's official historian was to record that London considered

> the Yugoslav Government was not a true fusion of the former Royal Cabinet and Marshal Tito's *de facto* administration. The state was run by Marshal Tito and his Partisans. Their regime was totalitarian, and not democratic in the western sense of the term. The administration, as in the Soviet Union, was carried out by a series of superimposed committees, nominated – in spite of the pretence of election – by the central authority. Political activity was limited to the National Liberation Front and the press was merely the expression of the Government. No adverse criticism was allowed, and a secret police, with unlimited powers of arrest and detention without trial, enforced uniformity. Marshal Tito had said that he would never agree to the return of the monarchy because it was incompatible with the new regime. Yugoslavia was thus in effect a Soviet satellite.

Djilas was later to admit Tito was "an even more absolute monarch than King Alexander had been".[52]

One by one the non-communist ministers were forced out or resigned – Grol left on 18 August, followed by Subasic and Sutej a few weeks later. Tito had made sure they had no influence or power. King Peter withdrew on 8 August his grant of authority to the regents on the grounds that "they have ignored their oath and their obligations to me". An "election" was held on 11 November for a Constituent Assembly to decide Yugoslavia's future government. The new British Prime Minister Clement Attlee, a socialist, called such communist elections "races with one horse". All parties were invited to participate, though only the People's Front (Tito's euphemism for the communists) were allowed access to the radio and official press. In theory others could establish their own newspapers. A few did. They were immediately subjected to printers' strikes, arson or just plain thuggery, and soon closed. Michael Petrovic, then an official at the American embassy but later Professor of Russian and Balkan history at the University of Wisconsin-Madison, witnessed

> a paperboy who was selling copies of Grol's newspaper *Demokratija* on a Belgrade street burned when his newspapers were doused with gasoline and set on fire by a Communist gang, a gang whose identity the otherwise vigilant authorities allegedly could not determine.[53]

Djilas and his agitprop cohorts saw to it that all non-communist participants were vilified as fascists or as having collaborated with the enemy during the war. Those deemed to have collaborated or to have adhered to "fascist" organisations were denied the vote. The few opposition meetings held were invariably broken up by Tito's secret police, already all-pervasive within the country. Non-communist journalists described conditions as a "reign of terror". Most opposition candidates boycotted the election, at which one voted by dropping a metal counter into one of two boxes marked People's Front or Opposition Candidates. The latter, dubbed the "widow's urn" by wags, was made of tin so that metal counters dropping into it were readily audible! As the voting boxes were in full gaze of everyone, it was not a secret ballot. The voter was not given a list of candidates but merely told the names of the boxes, beside each of which stood a member of the authorities. It took a brave person to vote against Tito. Party officials holding lists ticked off the names of those doing so. It is hardly surprising Tito's candidates obtained 96 per cent of the vote, or so it was claimed.

The Constituent Assembly promptly abolished the monarchy on 29 November and proclaimed a republic, thus undoing the agreement Tito had struck with Subasic the previous year. Ivan Ribar became president and Tito prime minister. Fortune for the Yugoslav Communists had come full circle: Dr Ribar had presided over the Constituent Assembly that had banned the Yugoslav Communist Party in 1920!

A member of Franklin Lindsay's staff in Belgrade at the time said of the election:

> Slogans such as "Ballots for Tito, Bullets for Grol", and the unmistakable impression that all who voted against the government would be considered traitors only helped to create an atmosphere of widespread fear. A hidden but very real fear of a bloody war of retribution, particularly between the Serbs and the Croats, inspired many to vote for the Popular Front.[54]

Stephen Clissold, then press attaché at the Belgrade Embassy, toured Serbia in late October and reported to the Foreign Office of "widespread dissatisfaction", with peasants complaining of the "oppressive measures of the authorities ... the Government takes everything from us and gives us nothing in return ... this is not what we fought for". They would be voting "since they order us to ... we must, or it will be the worse for us".[55] Earlier in the year, Captain J.C. Lambie, a liaison officer in Slovenia, recounted to London how few of the civilians he had met there "had any belief in Communism"; they "did not wish the Partisan policy to continue after the war". Some had said to him, "Before the Partisans came we were like slaves, but now we are worse than slaves." Lambie had also found

> the Partisan leaders were always deeply mistrustful of British intentions towards Yugoslavia, and lost no opportunity of impressing this attitude on Partisans and civilians alike. Britain and America were always classed together as the "western capitalist nations" who were working solely for the subjugation and control of the future Yugoslavia.[56]

Intimidation continued even after the voting. Anyone criticising the election result was deemed a collaborationist and hence could be shot on sight. Informers were everywhere. In the towns and cities party cells were established in each residential block. Everyone was required to attend regular meetings and take part in "spontaneous demonstrations" denouncing the "enemies of the people". "People's courts" were set up where the sentences were pre-determined. The property of collaborators and "enemies of the people" was confiscated. Neighbour was encouraged to incriminate neighbour, and could earn part of the spoils for doing so. As the Party controlled the judiciary as well as the security services and the army, it was easily able to impose a repressive, dogmatic regime.

The day after the war had ended, Lindsay had been summoned to Tito's Chief of Staff, General Arso Jovanovic, and told he must close the American military mission and leave immediately. Lindsay reminded him of the western Allies' bounteous aid and waited for some words of appreciation:

> His response was that it was the Partisans' right to receive this support and our duty as allies to provide it. In any case it was less than it should have been. Therefore no expression of appreciation was called for.

That same month the American embassy had reported to Washington:

> Visitors tell us they are often questioned after leaving the Embassy; two Embassy employees were arrested during the past week; we asked for an explanation which has not yet been given ... dozens of Yugoslavs have since been arrested after attending parties where American and British soldiers were present. Some were told quite frankly that their arrest was due to their association with British and Americans.[57]

Although the American Ambassador had urged his government not to do so, declaring that in Yugoslavia "democracy, freedom and civil liberty, as we understand these terms do not exist", the United States duly recognised Tito's government on 22 December 1945. They indicated that this "should not be interpreted as implying approval of the policies of the regime ... or its failure to implement the guarantees of personal freedom promised its people". Tito brushed aside such reservations. He had got his recognition, which was all that concerned him.

The Constituent Assembly agreed on 31 January 1946 a federal constitution similar to the Soviet one of ten years before. Six federated provinces were established: Bosnia-Herzegovina, Serbia, Slovenia, Croatia, Montenegro and Macedonia. But, as with the Soviets, the federalism was fictitious. Tito's rule was as centralised as King Alexander's had been in the 1920s and 1930s. He was determined to cut Serbia down to size. Macedonia, known previously as south Serbia, was split off and Montenegro's separate historical identity recognised. Serbia was reduced further when two so-called "autonomous regions", Kosovo and Vojvodina, were carved out of it. The latter was rich farming land north of the Danube that had been annexed by Serbia from the wreckage of the Habsburg Empire in 1918. It was populated now mostly by Serbs, with a scattering of Hungarians, Romanians and other minorities. Previously half a million Germans had lived there, most of whom had fled in the closing

months of the war. Those remaining had been expelled almost immediately afterwards. The Serbs cherished Kosovo, often referred to as
"old Serbia". It was the cradle of their great medieval empire, though
more than three quarters of its population was now Albanian. Tito
even considered, in 1945, shifting the capital out of Serbia from
Belgrade to Sarajevo.

He was determined to create a balance between Serbs and Croats.
Almost half the Serbs lived outside Serbia. Bosnia-Herzegovina was
an area of mixed nationalities, with Moslems in a slight majority.
Bosnian Moslems were now recognised as a separate nationality,
though Tito was convinced all ethnic differences would become
submerged. He believed that under Communism, with its slogan
"brotherhood and unity", conflicts of nationality would wither away.
Relief that the war was over, coupled with the ruthlessness of his
secret police, made this seem possible. But soon there was neither
brotherhood nor unity. Typically, when nationalism did rear its head,
it was blamed in Serbia on the Chetniks, in Croatia on the Ustashi,
and in Slovenia on the anti-communist White Guard. Using the
language of the civil war served to continue it. Serbs blamed Croats
for introducing Communism to Yugoslavia. Croats claimed Serbs
were benefiting more: they filled most of the top jobs, particularly in
the army. The old enmities were not disappearing. They were merely
biding their time to reappear, with a vengeance, at a later date.

There was a titular parliament called the Federal People's Assembly, and other symbolic bodies, but total power was held by the Party.
Its leader controlled the judiciary and the secret police, and was
commander-in-chief of the army. In theory all Yugoslavs had freedom of speech and of the press, as well as exemption from arbitrary
arrest and imprisonment. But these rights could be suspended in the
interests of state security, so in practice there was no free press, no
right to demonstrate against the government and hence no opposition to the communists. While there was no official censor, under
Yugoslavia's penal code it was a criminal offence to engage in "propaganda against the state". Any political comment could be defined as
propaganda; whether it was "against the state" was decided by the
judiciary, and hence the party officials who controlled it. Journalists,
writers and broadcasters were forever looking over their shoulders.

By the summer of 1946 Yugoslavia had become a fully-fledged
communist state – a one-party dictatorship with Tito as the overlord.
Henniker-Major had returned to the Foreign Service after the war
and been posted to Belgrade as Second Secretary in the embassy

there. He had had enough of it by the spring of 1946 and managed to get himself appointed assistant private secretary to the new British Foreign Secretary Ernest Bevin. In his memoirs he says:

> By then the shoddiness of communist rule, of plodding and inefficient bureaucracy, petty corruption, increasing unfriendliness, and the absence of any appearance of warmth generated by our presence and help in the war, had brought me close to exhaustion and dark disillusion. I felt then, and for several years afterwards, almost totally exhausted and drained by the experience.

Within the year the non-communist ministers who had left the government were put on trial for alleged treasonable contacts with Britain and the United States. All were given stiff sentences. Already Tito's regime had shown itself even more intransigent towards the Western powers than the Soviets. Not only over Trieste, as we will now see, but also at various conferences attended by the foreign ministers of the victorious Allies who were trying to conclude peace treaties with former enemies such as Italy, Romania, Bulgaria, Hungary and Finland. Yugoslavia had become Stalin's most devoted satellite, supporting his foreign policy on almost every issue, while pursuing in domestic affairs his hardline path of collectivisation, nationalisation, and the suppression of individual freedom.

The Americans soon became alarmed at Tito's role as an agent of Soviet imperialism. Concerned about communism spreading to Italy and Greece, they worried that Yugoslavia as a victorious ally had no limit on the size of its armed forces, which added to Moscow's military potential. Although those forces needed modernising, their officer corps made up in fanaticism what they lacked in military skill. Moreover the Soviets were handling the training of those forces as well as their refurbishment.

Djilas was to say, when interviewed in *Encounter* in December 1979:

> During the War and for a couple of years after, the Yugoslav Communists were more closely welded to the Soviet Communist Party than any I can think of... We were certainly an absolute dictatorship... In our ideology, political policies, and security arrangements there was not much to distinguish us from the Soviet Union.

CHAPTER TEN

Exasperation over Trieste

"This, it was agreed, was
a hell of a way to end a war"
GEOFFREY COX

HAVING GOT THE RED ARMY to rid Serbia of Mihailovic's men, Tito's next priority was to rush as quickly as possible north-westwards to reach the Istrian peninsula and the ports of Trieste and Fiume – the area known as Venezia Giulia – before the British and Americans, coming up the Italian peninsula. Most of Venezia Giulia had been Austrian since the fourteenth century. Trieste was the southern terminus of the railway from Vienna through the Ljubljana Gap in the eastern Alps. It had been given to Italy after the First World War as a reward for helping the Allies defeat the Habsburgs' Austro-Hungarian Empire. While the citizens of Trieste, Gorizia and Monfalcone were nearly all Italians, the country around was populated mostly by Slovenes and Croats. In 1941 Venezia Giulia had been offered to Prince Paul's government as an inducement to enter the war on the British side. The offer had not been taken up. The Partisans laid claim thereafter. Churchill let it be known, after Italy changed sides in late 1943, that he preferred leaving it Italian. The American position was that everything should be decided at the peace conferences after the war.

Churchill had told Tito in August 1944 that, pending a peace treaty, Venezia Giulia would be administered by Allied military government. Tito had argued that, as one of the victorious Allies, the Partisans should participate in that government. They deserved some spoils of victory. This should have sounded alarm bells among the Allied military chiefs, especially when American intelligence agents discovered Milovan Djilas and Edvard Kardelj had secretly met the Italian Communist leader Palmiro Togliatti in Rome that autumn. Djilas says Togliatti proposed joint Yugoslav-Italian sovereignty over Trieste. The Yugoslavs had been smuggling weapons to

235

the Italian communists for some time. Many of the Italian partisan groups operating near Trieste had put themselves under Tito's command. The British Foreign Secretary, Anthony Eden, had proposed at Yalta in February 1945 that the British, Americans and Soviets agree a demarcation line in Venezia Giulia and that the Allies and the Partisans should share its occupation. The Americans had opposed this, insisting Venezia Giulia be placed under Allied military government, pending a peace treaty.

Meanwhile Tito's communists had been organising secret resistance committees in all the towns and cities of Venezia Giulia and arming groups of guerrillas in the surrounding hills and forests. The intention was to take over the area once the Germans looked like leaving. Churchill had expressed concern to his military chiefs on 9 September 1944 regarding the capture of Trieste and Istria:

> We know that the partisans have actually fought for the outskirts of Fiume, and are increasingly powerful over the whole region. I have asked Tito to make every effort to move his forces northwards instead of using our weapons against his own countrymen.[1]

Churchill was to rue encouraging Tito to hurry northwards. Assisted from the air by the Allies, the Partisans launched their offensive along the Dalmatian coast towards Trieste, some 120 miles away, on 20 March 1945. They had asked from Alexander, the Supreme Allied Commander in the Mediterranean, and surprisingly been given, yet more weapons, ammunition and fuel, even tanks and artillery, as well as medical supplies and food. All of this was shipped in by sea. Alexander had argued ingenuously to London: "If I have to negotiate an agreement with Tito over Venezia Giulia it will be easier for me to get what I want from a grateful Tito who will be under some obligation to me for the help I have given him." He also hoped the Partisans would draw off into Yugoslavia some of the German troops facing the Allied forces in Italy. The opposite was to happen!

The Partisans took Bihac on 27 March and Senj, halfway to the Italian frontier at Fiume, on 8 April. Fiume was reached on 20 April. Here the Germans had strengthened the fortified line Mussolini had built in the 1930s. Manned with a full army corps, it was intended to cover the retreat into Austria of the German forces from Yugoslavia and Greece. As well as attacking it frontally, the Yugoslavs tried to bypass it: first, with difficulty, to the north through the heavily forested mountains, some five thousand feet high; and then, more successfully, to the south. Leapfrogging the coastal islands, they landed on the Istrian peninsula on 23 April, though only in light numbers, and pushed on towards Trieste. Under pressure from Belgrade, and suffering heavy casualties, the bigger force to the north outflanked the Germans on 28 April and reached the outskirts of Trieste on 1 May. The Yugoslavs entered the city next day just hours before the New Zealanders, who had raced from the river Po following the German surrender in northern Italy that had come into effect that same day.

The Allied offensive there had begun on 9 April and led to an early German collapse. Negotiations over the German surrender had been held up for four days while Moscow was consulted. For a time the Soviets opposed the surrender. It emerged later the delay on the Soviets' part had been purely to allow Tito time to reach Trieste. The New Zealanders had also been held up at Monfalcone, twenty miles to the west of Trieste, by a ploy of the local partisan commander. He offered to arrange a meeting with his superior to avoid any, as he put it, "unnecessary confrontations between the two forces". Needless to say the superior never showed up.

Meanwhile, since 30 April the communist committees had taken over the running of Trieste, including its radio station and newspapers. They had begun eliminating its Italian administrators. Even the Italian resistance groups who had been co-operating with the Yugoslav communists were given short shrift. The Yugoslav flag was flying from every public building. Armed, red-scarved Partisans with red stars on their caps patrolled the streets. Portraits of Tito were pasted on walls with pro-Partisan slogans painted alongside them. The New Zealanders, though, were able to grab the vital docks and obvious strongpoints such as the mediaeval castle and the law courts. They also collared the best hotel for their brigade headquarters. Pockets of Germans had been holding out against the Partisans, waiting to surrender to the New Zealanders. About seven thousand of them now did so, increasing the confusion. The anti-communist Italians, who had concealed themselves during the uprising, came out to greet the New Zealanders ecstatically, adding to the chaos.

Both sides demanded the other withdraw. When they did not, they dug in to await further orders. It was an uneasy peace, especially for the New Zealanders, as the Yugoslavs effectively controlled the city. They had imposed a curfew and even changed the clocks to conform to Belgrade time. All civilian vehicles had been requisitioned. Any movement within the region was banned except with their permission. They continued purging civilians opposed to their point of view, tightening their political grip on the whole region. Their internal security police and "people's courts" were already operating in the countryside. Belgrade had ordered that the Italians be "driven out without any discussion". Twenty thousand are thought to have suffered in this way. Decades later a gorge was discovered at Basso-vizza in the Istrian mountains filled with corpses that had been stripped, shot and mutilated. Other rock fissures nearby were found to contain human remains dating from this period.

Fear spread throughout Trieste and citizens looked to the New Zealanders for redress. Confrontation loomed. Tito's Chief of Staff, Arso Jovanovic, demanded that the New Zealanders withdraw, warning that the Yugoslavs would not be held responsible for anything that might happen if the request was not met. The Yugoslavs also called for the immediate withdrawal of all Allied liaison officers and military missions with the Partisans. The New Zealanders insisted they had been ordered to stay where they were. They would ensure no trouble broke out but "would meet force by force if necessary". To show the Allies meant business, the New Zealanders were reinforced with a battalion of the Scots Guards and an equivalent number of American infantry.

Both armies settled down to what one of the participants described as "a mutual siege", relieved only by the occasional football match or other sporting event arranged between them. Partisan and Allied sentries stood side by side "in irritated silence" at every bridge and strategic position.[2] Patrols of both armies moved continuously through the city, eyeing each other cautiously. Tanks cruised the streets and country roads, trying to avoid each other. This was brinkmanship before the term came to be used in the Cold War. Indeed, this was the first major confrontation of the Cold War. It was to last five weeks.

The major snag for the Allies was that the Partisans controlled the civil administration of Venezia Giulia, in particular its policing. This allowed the Partisans to merge the province bit by bit into Yugoslavia, which they set about without delay. The banks and the law courts, for instance, were replaced by Yugoslav ones. Any opposition to these moves was ruthlessly suppressed. Arrests and executions became commonplace. More than two thousand such murders occurred in a matter of days. Properties were seized and looting was condoned. The Italians looked to the Allied soldiers for help, but they were under strict orders not to intervene. The longer the process was allowed to continue, however, the more difficult it was going to be to prise the province back from the Partisans, said to number sixty thousand.

Sir Geoffrey Cox, then senior intelligence officer of the 2nd New Zealand Division, and later Editor of Independent Television News in London, recalls in his memoir, *The Race for Trieste*, what he found when he reached the city on the evening of 2 May:

> It was an outcome highly unpalatable to both the Yugoslavs and the Western Allies. An area to which both Yugoslavia and Italy had strong claims was now under the control not of one army under one command, but under two armies responsible to two very different sets of powers. Overnight Trieste changed from a meeting place of victors in a shared cause to an arena of potential conflict between powers who were still formally allies in arms. The rest of the embattled world still glowed with the wartime unity against the common foe. But in this corner of the Mediterranean that glow was fading rapidly. In the outside world the crowds who gathered to rejoice in the streets of London, Washington and Moscow felt only the relief and radiance of victory. The thought of new tensions and new conflicts, the knowledge of the harsh words which were already finding their way into the diplomatic telegrams were not in their minds. But for us the transition was immediate. In Trieste we were not only in a new area, but in a new era, the post-war era of the emerging Cold War.

Tito was summoned to Moscow on 5 April 1945 to sign a treaty of friendship, mutual aid and post-war collaboration with the Soviet Union. He wore an even more resplendent uniform than on his previous visit, and was accompanied by most of the top Partisan leadership. This visit annoyed the Allies intensely, particularly Churchill. Djilas observed:

> The Soviet government lost no time in underscoring its dominant role in Yugoslavia through the mutual aid treaty ... part of a pattern by which the Soviet government was establishing and reinforcing its influence.[3]

On 18 April Churchill wired Eden, who was in Washington:

> This is another proof of how vain it is to throw away our substance in a losing game with Soviet Russia in Titoland. The harmony of British, United States and Italian interests about the Adriatic should henceforward be one of our main themes.

He agreed with Eden's suggestion that "all supplies to Tito should be shut down on the best pretext that can be found".[4] John Colville, one of Churchill's private secretaries, confided to his diary on 19 April that the Prime Minister was

> annoyed with Tito who now looks almost exclusively to Russia, oblivious of past favours from us. He feels we should now back Italy (from whom Tito will claim Trieste, etc.) and thus aim at splitting the Italian Communist party.[5]

Churchill, determined more than ever to prevent Tito grabbing Trieste, was prepared for it to remain wholly in Italian hands. He saw that backing Italy, as the Americans privately favoured, would provide a counter to Tito's ambitions. When on 20 April Belgrade asked for British support for air training schools in Yugoslavia, Churchill refused point-blank, minuting Sir Orme Sargent at the Foreign Office:

> If the Russians are willing to aid the Yugoslav Air Force, why have we got to divert from our scanty store the valuable material in officers and men? The great changes which have taken place in the connections and centre of gravity of the Yugoslav Government since we talked about providing them with an Air Force must not fall unnoticed. They have thrown themselves wholeheartedly into the hands of Russia. In these circumstances, I should deprecate our making any serious sacrifices for the right to play a losing game.[6]

Later that day Churchill read another telegram from Belgrade reporting Tito's words: "we count primarily on the Soviet Union which has already begun to help us".[7] He straightaway minuted Orme Sargent that these

> kind remarks should encourage the fading away of British arms and, so far as possible, supplies of food… It is no use our running a race with Russia in bringing the utmost help to Marshal Tito. Let him continue to count primarily on the Soviet Union.[8]

On 25 April Churchill was writing to the Chiefs of Staff:

> In view of the unsatisfactory attitude recently shown by Marshal Tito and of his ingratitude for the substantial help which we have provided for his forces, I consider the time has now come to discontinue the assistance which we have hitherto afforded.[9]

On 28 April the Combined Anglo-American Chiefs of Staff issued formal orders for Venezia Giulia to be administered by Allied military government. Two days later they put forward a plan to take over the Istrian Peninsula, the port of Fiume and the hinterland of Trieste, to which they would seek Tito's agreement. Churchill telegraphed Truman, the new American President:

> It is surely a delusion to suppose the Yugoslav Government, with the Soviet Government behind them, would agree to our entering or taking control of Venezia Giulia including Fiume etc. They will undoubtedly try to overrun all this territory and will claim and occupy the ports of Trieste, Pola and Fiume, and once they get there I do not think they will go. No one is more keen than I to play absolutely fair with the Soviet on matters of surrender of the German armies, and as you see the messages we have both sent to Stalin have completely restored his confidence in this respect. On the other hand we have never undertaken to be limited in our advance to clear Italy, including these Adriatic Provinces, of the Germans by the approval either of the Yugoslavs or of the Russians, nor to report to them the military movements our Commanders think it right to make.[10]

That same day, 30 April, Alexander informed Tito that, as troops under his command were approaching Venezia Giulia, he wished to secure Trieste and the lines of communication to Austria:

> I presume that any of your forces which may be in the area affected by my operations will come under my command, as you suggested during our recent discussions in Belgrade, and that you will issue orders to that effect.

He also reminded Tito that Allied military government would exercise control of the civil administration in Venezia Giulia.

The discussions to which Alexander referred had taken place on 21 February 1945. He had, he said, been adamant about his need to control Trieste and Pola in particular. They were essential supply ports for his armies as they moved into central Europe. While he came away with the firm impression that, once Anglo-American troops joined up with the Partisans outside Yugoslavia's frontiers, they would come under his command, he was less sure what would happen if the Partisans got to Trieste before his forces did. When Harold Macmillan met Alexander following his Belgrade visit, he noted in his diary: "Alex much enjoyed his visits to Marshal Tito and Tolbukhin [a senior Red Army general]. He seems to have formed a very favourable opinion of Tito (rather too favourable, I thought)."

Tito replied promptly to Alexander's signal. The situation had changed appreciably since the Belgrade talks. While he was happy for the Allies to use the ports of Trieste and Pola, and the railway lines to Austria, he would not agree to his troops coming under Alexander's command – other than those which happened to be on the Italian side of the Isonzo River (where there were none).

Churchill telegraphed Alexander on 1 May:

> There is also of course going to be a frightful outcry between the Italians and the Yugoslavs for these territories. I am in favour of backing up the Italians because that will split their Communist forces and will also fit in with the very friendly interest the Americans have in Italy and which I should like also to share. I imagine the Italians care more about Trieste and Istria than about Communism, and it would be a good thing to have a settled Government in Italy which was united to the two western democracies. I doubt very much whether Tito will agree, if he got there, to you turning him out. He is claiming all sorts of territories.[11]

Alexander replied:

> Tito's regular forces are now fighting in Trieste and have already occupied most of Istria. I am quite certain that he will not withdraw his troops if ordered to do so unless the Russians tell him to. If I am ordered by the Combined Chiefs of Staff to occupy the whole of Venezia Giulia by force if necessary, we shall certainly be committed to a fight with the Yugoslav Army, who will have at least the moral backing of the Russians. Before we are committed I think it as well to consider the feelings of our own troops in this matter. They have a profound admiration for Tito's Partisan Army, and a great sympathy for them in their struggle for freedom. We must be very careful therefore before we ask them to turn away from the common enemy to fight an Ally.

When it became clear the Yugoslavs had reached Trieste first, and securing western control over the whole of Venezia Giulia was going to be difficult, the Foreign Office advised Churchill to "make the best compromise we can". They reminded him that

> the obvious, and indeed the only, bargaining counter we would have in such negotiations [to get Tito out of Trieste] would be the fact that the Americans are in occupation of a large part of the Russian zone of Germany.[12]

Churchill seemed to share this view, but he knew that to utilise that bargaining counter he needed President Truman's firm backing. He had the impression Truman was not anxious to pick a fight just yet over Trieste. Hence he cautioned restraint when he telegraphed

Alexander on 2 May: "Should unco-operative contact be made, no violence should occur except in self-defence … A quarrel with the Yugoslavs would be a matter for the Peace Table and not for the field."[13]

John Colville, one of Churchill's private secretaries, confided to his diary that evening:

> Tito has beaten us in the race for Trieste and Venezia Giulia and, backed as he is by Russia (which has also, unilaterally, established its own puppet government in Vienna) it is hard to see how he can ever be dislodged. Still by backing Italy against Tito's claim to possess Trieste we may split the Italian Communist party and thus at least save Italy from the Russian imperialist clutches. As it is, the Soviet looks like dominating Europe east of a line drawn from the North Cape to Trieste and soon the pressure will be turned on Turkey.

The Partisans that reached Trieste on 30 April, just hours before the New Zealanders, were few in number. The Allies, being in greater force, took the surrender of the German garrison. Being outnumbered did not prevent Tito's men from behaving with what one of the New Zealand intelligence officers described as "provocative truculence". Because the Partisans refused to withdraw immediately, Churchill threatened to stop all military supplies to Tito. He telegraphed Eden on 4 May:

> You have no doubt read the telegram showing Tito's breach of faith with Alexander, and that Freyberg's New Zealanders only just got into Trieste, Monfalcone and Gorizia ahead of the Tito-ite patrols. The awkward moment was avoided by the fact that we were in heavy strength and they were no more than patrols pegging out claims.[14]

Two days later Churchill was telegraphing Field Marshal Alexander:

> I am very glad you got into Trieste, Gorizia and Monfalcone in time to put your foot in the door. Tito, backed by Russia, will push hard, but I do not think that they will dare attack you in your present position … To avoid leading Tito or the Yugoslav commanders into any temptation, it would be wise to have a solid mass of troops in this area, with a great superiority of modern weapons and frequent demonstrations of the Air Force … I suppose you have cleared the approaches to Trieste so that you can soon have strong naval forces there. Strength is safety and peace.[15]

On 7 May he was again stressing his concern to Alexander that Tito might take over Istria: "Let me know what you are doing in massing forces against this Muscovite tentacle, of which Tito is the crook."[16]

Alexander decided to send his Chief of Staff, General William Morgan, to Belgrade to try to persuade Tito to accept a purely military demarcation. This would give the western Allies the main road and railway through Venezia Giulia needed to support advance units moving into Austria. Tito refused, unless he was granted the territories he claimed. He also demanded the immediate return of all liberated Yugoslav prisoners of war. The majority were reluctant to do so voluntarily. Captured during the German invasion in April 1941, they were mostly anti-communist.

Franklin Lindsay, who attended the negotiations with Morgan on behalf of the United States, described the scene:

> Tito sat in the center of a long table. Four senior Partisan generals, now in smartly tailored grey uniforms with the insignia of general on their collars and sleeves, were arrayed along Tito's side of the table. These new Yugoslav uniforms, rumoured to have been tailored in Moscow to Tito's specifications, bordered on the gaudy, with their generous use of gold braid. They were not what one would have expected from the leaders of a people's revolution, fresh from fighting in the forest.[17]

The British Ambassador in Belgrade, Ralph Stevenson, argued to London that the crux of the matter was whether Tito had Soviet backing "particularly in the event of a show-down with the United States". He doubted it and suggested calling his bluff. He said his American colleague agreed with him:

> If we let Tito get away with Trieste he would lay claim to Southern Austria, onto which his troops were now advancing, and would help the Communists in the Macedonian provinces of Greece to rebel against Athens. I do not think it too fanciful to say that the interests of future peace in South East Europe are now at stake.

Stevenson was clearly regretting his previous promotion of Tito's interests. Alexander's forces were anxious to push northwards into Austria as speedily as possible, to get there before the Soviets who were advancing from Vienna and the Hungarian border. The Germans had virtually ceased fighting in front of the British. The passes into Austria were clogged with retreating troops and refugees.

Signals flashed between London, Washington and Alexander's headquarters in Italy as the British and Americans pondered the possibility of armed conflict with Tito's Partisans. This was when the Germans had finally surrendered and the war in Europe was at an end. With an ear perhaps to events in Trieste, Churchill in his Victory broadcast noted:

On the continent of Europe we have yet to make sure that the simple and honourable purposes for which we have entered the war are not brushed aside or overlooked in the months following our success, and that the words "freedom, democracy and liberation" are not distorted from their true meaning as we have understood them.

Alexander wrote to Churchill on 9 May that, like Stevenson, "I am not too sure that Tito has the full backing of Moscow, and I think he will agree to my proposals in the end." Orme Sargent for the Foreign Office reminded Churchill (not that he needed reminding):

> If we use force to push Tito out this will constitute a direct challenge to the Russians ... If we want to force Tito from his present positions, it is essential that we should carry the Americans with us, not only politically, but militarily.[18]

Churchill knew he needed Washington's backing, but was reluctant to press Roosevelt's successor Harold Truman, whom he did not yet know. Truman seemed prepared to give political support but did not want military participation. Japan had still to be defeated and the Americans were anxious to withdraw forces from Europe as soon as possible for that task. They were hoping, too, for Russia's help against Japan. He did not want to risk a quarrel with Moscow at this juncture.

Meanwhile Alexander argued with his political bosses over the extra forces he would need should armed conflict become necessary. Macmillan confided to his diary on 9 May: "I feel that we must be very careful. Neither British nor American troops will care for a new campaign in order to save Trieste for the 'Eyeties' [Italians]." Alexander signalled the Combined Chiefs of Staff on 11 May: "Even if the Russians did not give [Tito] material support, but ... nevertheless he decided to resist us by force, I should require a total of eleven divisions." Alexander indicated this estimate assumed his forces

> would display the same fighting spirit and high endeavour in battle as hitherto. In view of the announcement of VE Day, and the long publicity given to Tito's operations in aid of the Allied cause, I am doubtful whether in fact this would be the case. In my view, both United States and British troops would be very reluctant to engage at this stage of the war in a fresh conflict against the Yugoslavs.

Alexander noted too that his total strength was eighteen divisions, of which only four were British. Of the other fourteen, few could be counted on to undertake any action against Tito's Partisans.[19]

The walls of Trieste were plastered next day with posters proclaiming the city an autonomous territory within the Republic of Yugoslavia – clearly meant to raise the political stakes. It was the day Truman chose to send Churchill what Churchill described to Alexander as a "most robust and encouraging telegram".[20]

Truman declared he had

> become increasingly concerned over the implication of Tito's actions in Venezia Giulia. You are no doubt receiving the same reports which indicate that he has no intention of abandoning the territory or of permitting a peaceful solution of this century old problem as part of a general pacific post-war settlement. I have come to the conclusion that we must decide now whether we should uphold the fundamental principles of territorial settlement by orderly process against force, intimidation or blackmail. It seems that Tito has an identical claim ready for South Austria, in Carinthia and Styria and may have similar designs on parts of Hungary and Greece if his methods in Venezia Giulia succeed. Although the stability of Italy and the future orientation of that country with respect to Russia may well be at stake the present issue, as I see it, is not a question of taking sides in a dispute between Italy and Yugoslavia or of becoming involved in internal Balkan politics. The problem is essentially one of deciding whether our two countries are going to permit our Allies to engage in uncontrolled land grabbing or tactics which are all too reminiscent of those of Hitler and Japan. Yugoslav occupation of Trieste, the key to that area and a vital outlet for large areas of Central Europe, would, as I know you will agree, have more far-reaching consequences than the immediate territory involved. In these circumstances I believe the minimumn we should insist upon is that Field Marshal Alexander should obtain complete and exclusive control of Trieste and Pola, the line of communication through Gorizia and Monfalcone, and an area sufficiently to the east of this line to permit proper administrative control. The line suggested by Alexander at Allied Force Headquarters in March [the "Morgan line"] extended to include Pola would, I believe, be adequate. Tito seems unsure of himself and might not put up more than a show of resistance, although we should be prepared to consider if necessary further steps to effect his withdrawal. I note that Alexander, who has lost patience with Tito's latest moves, is prepared to go ahead if we agree.

Truman concluded: "If we stand firm on this issue ... we can hope to avoid a host of other similar encroachments." Stalin was to be informed of the Anglo-American stance and Tito to be told immediately to toe the line.[21]

Few realized then what a watershed Truman's telegram was in committing the United States to resisting Soviet expansion. It was Washington's first reaction to the Cold War, the forerunner of decisions in 1946 to insist that Russia evacuate northern Persia. In 1947 this would take from Britain the financial burden of supporting the anti-communist government in Greece. It would lead to the even greater decision later that year which came to be called the Truman Doctrine: that the United States would resist Soviet expansion wherever it occurred. The doctrine was soon to be tested in the West's response to Stalin's blockade of Berlin in 1948, and to North Korea's invasion of South Korea in 1950. Moscow's perfidy over Poland had evidently disgusted Truman, as had Molotov's intransigence during negotiations leading to the establishment of the United Nations.

In his prompt reply to Truman's welcome telegram, which exceeded his wildest hopes, Churchill did not conceal his delight at its tough stance:

> I agree with every word you say, and will work with all my strength on the line you propose... If it is handled firmly before our strength is dispersed, Europe can be saved another bloodbath. Otherwise the whole fruits of our victory may be cast away and none of the purposes of World Organisation to prevent territorial aggression and future wars will be attained... [Your telegram] shows how gravely we both view the situation.[22]

He repeated his main point to Alexander: "This action if pursued with firmness may well prevent a renewal of the World War."[23] Truman telegraphed Churchill on 14 May that, if Tito should "attack our Allied Forces anywhere, I would expect Field Marshal Alexander to use as many troops of all nationalities in his Command as are necessary."[24]

With Truman's approval, Churchill telegraphed Stalin the following day:

> Yugoslav occupation and administration of the whole province [of Istria] would be in contradiction with the principle, which we seek to maintain, that the fate of the province must not be decided by conquest and by one-sided establishment of sovereignty by military occupation.[25]

Alexander's hint of his troops' possible unwillingness to fight Tito's men had alarmed Churchill. He cabled Alexander on 16 May:

> If the Western Allies cannot now resist land-grabbing and other encroachments by Tito, and have to put up with some weak compromise,

this may well breed a danger far greater than we now face at the head of the Adriatic. I am very anxious about the general attitude of the Russians, especially if they feel they have only war-wearied armies and trembling administrations in front of them.[26]

Alexander's reply the next day was reassuring:

Yugoslav behaviour both in Austria and Venezia Giulia is making a very unfavourable impression on Allied troops, both United States and British. Our men are obliged to look on without power to intervene whilst actions which offend their traditional sense of justice are permitted. Further, our men feel that by taking no action they are condoning such behaviour. As a result feeling against Yugoslavs is now strong and is getting stronger daily.[27]

Those witnessing Yugoslav violence against the Italians were becoming disgruntled at the orders not to intervene. They were only too ready to make a show of force. The Partisans they met in Trieste did not match the romantic image they had held of "brave and worthy allies". Besides, they were anxious to go home, or at least to move on. As Geoffrey Cox put it, "this, it was agreed, was a hell of a way to end a war".

But Tito on 18 May still refused to withdraw. Responding to Truman's recommendation of a show of force, Eisenhower, then Supreme Allied Commander in Europe, offered to send five American armoured divisions to the Brenner Pass north of Trieste. Units of the Mediterranean Fleet were ordered to the Adriatic. Several air squadrons were put on standby to move at a moment's notice to airfields in Italy close to Trieste. Embassy staffs in Belgrade began openly to evacuate their offices and homes. British and American officials there were alerted to be ready to leave swiftly.

On 19 May Alexander issued his troops an Order of the Day written by Harold Macmillan, warning them of

Marshal Tito's apparent intention to establish his claims to Venezia Giulia and territory around Villach and Klagenfurt by force of arms and by military occupation. Action of this kind would be all too reminiscent of Hitler, Mussolini and Japan. It is to prevent such actions that we have been fighting this war.[28]

Churchill and Truman cabled Stalin the following day criticising Tito's behaviour and insisting they would not compromise on the principles of an orderly, just settlement.

The pressure worked. That same day Tito withdrew his troops from Austria. He also offered to relinquish control of Venezia Giulia up to the Morgan Line provided that he could participate in the Allied military government of the region and the Allies work through the Yugoslav civil administration already established there. Alexander rejected these conditions but indicated he was prepared to negotiate. He kept up the pressure by occupying, on 22 May, key crossroads along the Morgan Line and moving his troops forward into several strategic positions. He even visited Trieste with some of his commanders. The Yugoslavs also reinforced their garrisons, but it was obvious who was the stronger. More importantly it was becoming clear Stalin would not intervene on Tito's behalf. Negotiations began in Belgrade, but dragged on. This was partly because the Allies were not totally agreed on what should be done about the port of Pola on the southern extremity of the Istrian peninsula. Washington and London thought it should remain in Allied hands. Alexander considered it militarily untenable.

Churchill showed his annoyance with Alexander over Pola in a telegram of 29 May:

> We do not seem to be looking at the situation from the same angle. I regard it as of first importance not to back down before Tito's encroachments or to give the impression to the Balkans or to Russia that we are unable in the last resort to use force. I am sure that if we begin giving way at this juncture there is no limit to which we shall not be pushed.[29]

He got his own way and by 2 June was telling Truman that Alexander was ready to

> eject the enemy from their positions... The fact that the Russians have so far remained quiescent is important. If we once let it be thought that there is no point beyond which we cannot be pushed about, there will be no future for Europe except another war more terrible than anything that the world has yet seen. But by showing a firm front in circumstances and a locality which are favourable to us, we may reach a satisfactory and solid foundation for peace and justice.[30]

The firm stance worked. On 11 June Tito agreed to withdraw from Pola.

An accord was reached on 9 June whereby, pending a final settlement at a peace conference, Venezia Giulia would be divided into two along the Morgan Line. The major towns of Trieste, Gorizia, Monfalcone and Pola, together with the countryside up to and including the lines of communication to Austria, would come under direct Allied military administration. The rest of the province would remain under Yugoslav control. The Yugoslavs were to return all residents they had arrested and deported except "those possessing Yugoslav nationality in 1939". They were to make restitution of all property confiscated or removed. They were also to withdraw to the Morgan Line by 12 June – which they did, though not before they had, according to the official New Zealand War History, "stripped machinery and accessories from garages, and emptied some barracks, hotels and houses of their contents; the amount of loot seemed to be limited only by the paucity of transport."

In the subsequent Italian Peace Treaty of 1947, Tito received part of the Allied zone, including Pola, but not Gorizia or Monfalcone. These went to Italy, along with the larger part of western Venezia Giulia. Trieste and the area to the south of it was designated a "Free Territory", to be governed by a representative of the United Nations Security Council. Bickering over this appointment led to the Territory being divided into two zones. Zone A included the city and the surrounding area and was governed jointly by the British and American military. Zone B, the larger south and east region, was administered by the Yugoslavs. As the Soviets and the western Allies were still unable to agree on a governor for the whole Territory, in October 1954 the Anglo-American zone was handed back to the Italians while the Yugoslav zone was incorporated into Slovenia. There were some last-minute border adjustments in favour of the Italians. To obtain these, the Yugoslavs were sweetened by grants from the United States and Britain said to total twenty million dollars and two million pounds respectively!

The Trieste crisis had not excited much interest in Britain that summer of 1945. People there were still euphoric about the ending of the war in Europe. And a general election was in the offing, as Churchill's great wartime coalition had been dissolved. Evelyn Waugh, calling himself "A British soldier lately in Yugoslavia", wrote a bitter letter to *The Times* published on 23 May:

> If when the truth is published, it is revealed that the regime of Marshal Tito has all the characteristics of Nazism – a secret political police, unscrupulous propaganda bureaux, judicial murder of political opponents, the regimentation of children into fanatical, hero-worshipping gangs, the arrests and disappearance of civilians for no other reason than that they spoke English ... if these things are true, the nation will see where its duty lies towards people threatened with an extension of this regime.

"Another British Officer from Yugoslavia", who Waugh identified as Fitzroy Maclean, replied three days later, dismissing Waugh's strictures as a "disturbing example of the way prejudice is formed, when half-knowledge is disguised as expert knowledge".

Stalin's not intervening on his behalf must have come as a great shock to Tito. Until then he had been behaving as though he was hand in glove with the Soviet leader. Stalin had certainly appeared to be encouraging Tito wholeheartedly. When Tito had visited Moscow in April 1945 to sign the treaty of friendship with the Soviets, Stalin had granted him the rare privilege of a triumphal tour of the Soviet Union. He had been welcomed everywhere as a war hero. Then, in May 1946, at the funeral of the Soviet President, Mikhail Kalinin, Tito walked with Stalin to the Lenin Mausoleum. He joined him in taking the salute at the military parade that followed the funeral cortège. Diplomats recorded that this showed him to be *persona gratissima* with Stalin.

No doubt to Stalin control of Trieste was a mere detail in his increasingly intricate pattern of relationships with Britain and America. As a Mediterranean port it had strategic value, but he had his eyes on other ports. Critically, the Americans had not yet withdrawn from all the areas they occupied in the proposed Soviet zone in Germany. To risk those vital territories so that Tito could secure a relatively tiny part of Italy did not make much sense to Stalin. He was keen, too, to join in the Anglo-American war against Japan so as to gain frontier changes crucial to his security in the Far East. Also, his spies in the United States kept him in the picture that spring and summer of 1945 regarding the progress of the Anglo-American project to make an atom bomb. He knew its final testing was near. He could not have been confident of success in a military confrontation with the Americans, especially if they were to possess a working atom bomb.

Tito's attempt to capture Trieste was clearly the final straw for Churchill, though he had begun to show his disenchantment with the Partisan leader much earlier. At Potsdam on 18 July Churchill complained to Stalin that their fifty-fifty agreement regarding Yugoslavia had become "99-1 against Britain". Stalin disagreed, but remarked that Tito "had done several things he ought not to have done".[31] Because Tito had not honoured the Yalta agreement, Churchill hoped to persuade Stalin and Truman to issue a joint rebuff. Stalin was reluctant to do this without letting Tito make his case in person. Truman was anxious to move on to discuss what his delegation considered more urgent matters. Churchill had to content himself for the moment with merely putting his dissatisfaction with Tito on record. His opportunity to press the point further disappeared within days when he fell from power in Britain after the general election. As the wags in SOE sadly put it, the man who had ordered Europe to be set ablaze was himself now extinguished.

It was reported in both the 13 December 1945 edition of the Belgian magazine *Europe-Amerique* and the 29 December 1945 issue of the British political weekly *Time and Tide* that, at a recent private dinner party in Brussels, Churchill was heard to declare: "During the war I thought I could trust Tito. He had promised me to observe the agreement he had concluded with Subasic, but now I am well aware that I committed one of the biggest mistakes in the war." When asked to comment, Churchill's former secretary John Colville minuted the Foreign Office on 15 January 1946:

> This certainly represents Mr Churchill's views and I don't suppose he would mind it being known, but I doubt if he will say so publicly except under provocation. He certainly won't accept any arguments to the contrary.[32]

Peter Woodard, in *The Sunday Telegraph* on 5 August 1990, recalled hearing Anthony Eden addressing a meeting of the Coningsby Club late in life and being asked, "What is most on your conscience now, towards the end of your political career?" He replied, apparently without hesitation: "Our betrayal of Mihailovic."

CHAPTER ELEVEN

Post-war Butchery

"This is not a state;
it is a slaughterhouse"
MILAN GROL

IT WAS NOT JUST Trieste to which Tito laid claim. He had his eyes also on Carinthia, the southern province of Austria, bordering Yugoslavia. To that end he had begun a propaganda campaign as early as September 1944. The Americans and the British had sent agents into southern Austria a few months previously in the hope of stirring up anti-German feeling, to facilitate an Allied takeover from within, but without success. The rumours of an embryonic Austrian resistance movement turned out to be wide of the mark. The Soviet infiltration at that time of twenty-seven Austrian former prisoners-of-war met similar failure, though one of them stayed on to become boss of Austria's Communist Party.

It was in Carinthia in May 1945 that the remnants of many of the German armies converged. They preferred to surrender to the Western Allies rather than to the Russians, believing the former would treat them better. Carinthia was also where the anti-communist Croats, Slovenes and Serbs fled, including Mihailovic's men who eluded the clutches of the Partisans en route. A considerable number of Partisans had entered Carinthia too, reaching Klagenfurt, the capital, about the same time as the British did, on 8 May 1945. Although Carinthia was within the designated British zone of occupation in Austria, to which the Soviets had agreed, the Partisans issued a proclamation in effect annexing it to Yugoslavia. The Austrians, they said, were persecuting the Slovenian minority there, who had asked Tito for protection. They began holding pro-Tito rallies and distributing propaganda leaflets. But, as they were looting, raping and otherwise intimidating the local population, and beating up the Austrian police, they were not exactly winning friends or influencing neutrals. Harold Macmillan described it to London as a "minor reign of terror". Because of this lawlessness and truculence, the British troops took an instant dislike to them. One witness thought them "a murderous Balkan rabble, hanging on the wings like jackals and killing and looting indiscriminately".

Macmillan went to see for himself and noted in his diary on 13 May:

> With the same idea as in Venezia Giulia – that possession is nine-tenths of the law – [the Yugoslavs] have raced us into Austria. They actually reached Klagenfurt a few hours after us, so we could secure the best buildings and put sentries in them. We have, however, not enough men to occupy and guard every place. The Yugoslavs are bringing in considerable numbers – partly regulars and partly irregular forces – and repeating the Venezia Giulia tactics. We put up [Allied Military Government] notices. They pull ours down and put up their own. They requisition and loot and arrest so-called Nazis and Fascists. We have to look on, more or less helplessly, since our present plan is *not* to promote an incident.

He reported to London on 18 May:

> Situation in Austria most unsatisfactory and has deteriorated. The Yugoslavs are endeavouring to set up their own Government and have posted proclamations. They are looting shops and houses and are maltreating the local inhabitants.[1]

The British 8th Army's Fifth Corps was responsible for occupying Carinthia. Its War Diary mentioned a meeting held in Klagenfurt on 16 May at which a Provisional National Liberation Committee was elected unanimously, and commented: "Meeting obviously packed since unanimous audience all brought in by Yugoslav military transport"![2]

Unlike at Trieste, the Allies made no attempt at a show of force in Carinthia. They bought off Tito's territorial ambitions by handing over to him willingly – some thought too willingly – political opponents of his who had surrendered to the British troops. The clear understanding was that they would be protected from the Partisans known to seek their extinction. No doubt there were practical reasons why the British wished to be rid of them: feeding and housing them was difficult. But questions of humanity seem to have been forgotten in the rush to strike a deal to get the Partisans out of Carinthia as quickly as possible, before the crisis there grew into another Trieste.

This rush left even some senior Yugoslavs bewildered. Milovan Djilas, a member of Tito's politburo in 1945, said in *Encounter* magazine in December 1979:

We didn't at all understand why the British insisted on returning these people. We believed, in the ideological context prevailing at the time, that the British would have a good deal of sympathy with these refugees, seeing that they had fled Communism. We thought the British would show "class solidarity" with them, and some of us even feared that they would enlist them for future use against Communist governments, especially our own. Yet, to our great surprise, they did none of these things but delivered them into our hands.

Tito sanctioned the deal, although he wanted the Partisans to remain in Carinthia. With Soviet help he hoped to secure it for the new Yugoslavia. He is said to have sat up through the night of 18 May awaiting instructions from Moscow to stay put in Carinthia. When they did not come, he was pressed by his colleagues to accept the tempting British deal. This was swiftly struck on 19 and 20 May between senior officers on the staff of Alexander's subordinate commander in the area, Lieutenant-General Charles Keightley, and equivalents of the Partisan Third and Fourth armies. The withdrawal of the Partisans from Carinthia and the handover of their victims were to be completed before the end of the month. The prisoners were said to total about 35,000 though some believe the true number was nearer twice that. Even so, there were still some Partisan troops in Carinthia as late as 3 July, although they were offered British transport to speed them on their way.

The 35,000 figure did not of course include the 200,000 or so anti-communist refugees, mainly Croats, who had tried to cross from Yugoslavia into Carinthia and had been stopped by British troops stationed along the border. Forced to remain within Yugoslavia, they were easy pickings for the Partisans. Harold Macmillan's official biographer, the distinguished historian Sir Alistair Horne, comments: "whatever the figure, the repatriations reflect badly on the British".[3] Macmillan, as the political adviser to the British generals, came in for much of the blame, particularly from Nikolai Tolstoy. Alexander was to describe the return of the Yugoslavs to Tito as a "military necessity", but he had not been able to "deal with the anti-Tito Yugoslavs as he would have liked".[4]

The order from General Keightley's headquarters was that the so-called "non-Tito Yugoslav nationals" be disarmed immediately, but they would "*not* [original italics] be told of their destination".[5] Most of the victims – they included priests as well as women and children – were deceived by the British into believing they were being transferred to Italy. The War Diary of the 1st Guards Brigade specifically states: "Croats not told of their destination, believing they are going to Italy ... some escape from Tito by swimming the Drava [river]". The handover was described in the War Diary for 18 May as

> this most unpleasant task ... the Croats have been given no warning of their fate, and are being allowed to believe that their destination is not Yugoslavia but Italy, until the actual moment of their handover... British troops have the utmost distaste in carrying out their orders.[6]

It was only when the trains were firmly locked with them inside that the victims began to have doubts. Those doubts were soon confirmed as the trains, instead of proceeding westwards towards Italy, turned south to enter the long Rosenbach tunnel through the Karavanke Mountains, the other side of which was Yugoslavia. Onlookers recall the deafening hammering on the inside of the coaches as what lay in store dawned on the occupants. Many broke windows and threw themselves out to certain deaths; others committed suicide en route. Partisan troops had even been allowed to hide in the guards vans of many of the trains.

The British soldiers often had to resort to force to persuade the victims to enter the trains (One private who protested when ordered to use force was arrested). They had been led to believe, however, that only those convicted of war crimes after a fair trial would be punished. The rest would be allowed to lead normal lives. Their order stated: "The Yugoslavs have guaranteed full rights of surrendered personnel and agreed to trial of nominated war criminals by Allied court."[7] The soldiers had read only laudatory articles about Tito and his Partisans in the British Army press and had heard stories extolling them on the BBC. They could not have been expected to believe that Tito and his men were capable of barbarity on a par with the Nazis. Some handed over at the frontier by British officers were machine-gunned down within earshot of those officers. Other soldiers recalled victims pleading to be shot rather than handed over to the Partisans.

Nigel Nicolson, the publisher and Conservative MP, then intelligence officer to the 1st Guards Brigade, was involved in the handovers. Because he described the task as "most unsavoury" in one of his Situation Reports, he was reprimanded and taken off the job. In his final intelligence report of 13 June 1945 he said of the non-Tito Yugoslav nationals:

> The only point on which they were unanimous was in their fear that we should return them to Tito, and this was unfortunately exactly

what we intended to do. They were not told of our intentions till they saw for themselves the Tito guards boarding their train.[8]

He was to say that it was "the most horrible experience of my life".[9]

Tony Crosland, a future Labour Cabinet Minister, then a captain in intelligence in the Royal Welch Fusiliers, confided to his diary on 18 May:

> The problem of the anti-Tito Croats and Slovenes is almost causing a civil war within the British Army. We have on our hands at the moment some 50,000 of them. When we accepted their surrender, they certainly assumed that they would not be returned by us to Yugoslavia. It was then decided as a matter of higher policy that they were to be handed back to Tito. The armed lot south of the Drava were dealt with thus: our troops all withdrew north of the river, and behind them took out the centre section of the bridge; after we had gone, firing broke out, a number of Croats swam back across the river, and more tried to repair the broken bridge: so we put up wire and other obstacles to stop them getting back to safety. The unarmed lot were shepherded into trains and told they were going to Italy: they crowded on in the best of spirits, and were driven off under a British guard to the entrance of a tunnel at the frontier: there the guard left them, and the train drove off into the tunnel. Among officers here, there is great revolt and resentment against the deception and dishonesty involved.

Crosland described it in a letter to his Oxford friend Philip Williams as "the most nauseating and cold-blooded act of war I have ever taken part in".[10]

The War Diary of the 3rd Battalion of the Welsh Guards for 19 May 1945 reads:

> Lovely day. Evacuation of Croats began. Order of most sinister duplicity received i.e. to send Croats to their foes i.e. Tits [Tito forces] to Yugoslavia under the impression that they were to go to Italy. Tit guards on train hidden in guards van.[11]

The official British stance was that they were repatriating only those Yugoslavs willing to go!

Most were massacred within hours of their arrival on Yugoslav soil, in remote forests close to the Slovenian border. The victims were first looted of their private property. Gold teeth were brutally smashed from jaws and rings severed from fingers in the greedy haste. Victims were then beaten or attacked with axes, pitchforks and jagged knives fastened to poles before being pushed, still alive, into limestone pits. Dynamite was hurled in and soil bulldozed over them. Incredibly, some survived to tell the tale. Eventually larch trees and shrubs were planted over the graves to complete the concealment, in the same way as the Soviets had hidden the pits filled with Polish army officers butchered in the forests of Katyn in 1940. Tito's murderers, it seems, looked to Moscow for guidance in their systematic savagery. Extermination squads were rewarded with cameras and watches, or given holidays at Dalmatian coastal resorts. Tito's ministers decorated their bosses with medals. Many, though, were to suffer nervous breakdowns and even epileptic fits later in life, which came to be known as "Partisan sickness". Only after Slovenia's secession from Yugoslavia in the early 1990s were official attempts made to locate and unearth the gruesome pits and give the victims a more fitting burial.

Djilas gives chapter and verse in *Wartime* on the murderous treatment meted out to his fellow countrymen who were "repatriated". Nikolai Tolstoy does likewise in even more distasteful and devastating detail in *The Minister and the Massacres* published in 1986. "A story, long buried, of British treachery and Communist savagery", one reviewer described it. Tolstoy quotes Kosta Nadj, commander of the Partisan Third Army responsible for the fate of many of the surrendered prisoners. He boasted in January 1985, in the Belgrade weekly *Reporter*, that his army had "liquidated" 150,000 of them. Many of the Croats were forced to march endlessly around the country while people en route were urged to attack them with whatever weapons were to hand. The marches ended only when all the victims had perished. It was a way of implicating the populace in the eradication of the regime's enemies, as well as deterring would-be opponents.

Djilas admits that the anti-communists who fell into their hands were executed in "senseless acts of wrathful retribution". The Partisans "killed far too many people ... an atmosphere of revenge prevailed ... these killings were sheer frenzy". He pleads in mitigation that "massacres are the fruit of bitterness and of the calculations of leaders". He mentions complaints from the Slovenian Central Committee "because underground rivers were casting up bodies. They also said that piles of corpses were heaving up as they rotted in shallow mass graves, so that the very earth seemed to breathe."

In his December 1979 *Encounter* interview Djilas maintained:

> The great majority of the people the British forced back from Austria were simple peasants. They had no murders on their hands ... Their only crime was fear of Communism and the reputation of the

Communists. Their sole motivation for leaving the country was panic. If the British had handed over to us "Quisling" leaders such as Nedic, and police-agents who had collaborated with the Nazis in torturing and killing people, or had done it on their own, there could be no question of the morality of the British action. But this is not what they did. They forced back the lot – and this was profoundly wrong… It was astonishing that the British, with their fine sense of justice and the administration of law, should have been so thoroughly remiss in examining the sort of justice that was likely to be meted out to the repatriates.

He thought the British had "a pretty shrewd idea of what we'd be doing with them. We had a British Military Mission attached to us."

The atrocities and the horrors within Yugoslavia during the months immediately following the war were not confined to those sorry souls handed over by the British from Carinthia. Cyrus Sulzberger of *The New York Times* estimated there were fifty thousand anti-communist guerrillas active inside Yugoslavia in 1945. Djilas admits the figure was probably accurate, although he ridiculed it at the time. Tito's secret police methodically hunted them down. They were summarily shot when caught. Arbitrary arrests, torture and forced labour became the order of the day. The powers of the secret police were unrestricted. People were executed simply for not supporting the Partisans sufficiently during the war. Milan Grol, one of the non-communist ministers in Tito's first government, wrote to his friends in London in late 1945: "This is not a state; it is a slaughter-house."

Djilas acknowledged that they fabricated charges of collaboration with the enemy against those whom they feared or simply disliked, or whose property they coveted. At this time, he said, "the absolute power that victory had brought Tito was transforming his person-ality into a cult alongside the cult of Stalin." Djilas maintained he had been against such cults because "they signified undeniably and surely the transformation of a revolutionary movement into a power-grasping bureaucratic one". Tellingly, just as Stalin's birthplace was a shrine in the Soviet Union, Tito saw to it that his own became a focus of pilgrimage. Djilas found "the new state more and more resembled an absolutist police state".

Tito believed that for his revolution to succeed the Serbian national movement had to be crushed. He sought to make Mihailovic's loyalists traitors and devils. He introduced a brutal,

Stalinist-style regime which sanctioned mass killings and reprisals. The judiciary were required to administer "class justice", denying anti-communists the protection of the law. Any presumed anti-communist that fell into their hands was promptly executed. Tito had declared on 19 June 1945:

> The People's Defence is an organ of security which has sprung from the people. If it strikes fear into the bones of some of those gentry abroad, that is not our fault. But certainly, I think it an advantage if OZNA strikes fear into those who do not like the new Yugoslavia.

Rankovic, who headed the secret police, admitted later how much Tito feared opposition. In the reign of terror after the war people were punished for collaborating with the enemy who had in fact spent the war in concentration camps.

The British Consul in Ljubljana, Frank Waddams, who had been a liaison officer with the Partisans, reported in 1946:

> The most unpleasant feature of life in Yugoslavia today is the existence of the all-powerful OZNA, the political police. This body is responsible for the murder of thousands of Yugoslavs, for the maltreatment in concentration camps of thousands more and for the permanent terror in which the vast bulk of the population lives. It possesses its agents in every block of flats, in every street, in every village and in every barrack room. These agents report on the conduct of the inhabitants of their flat, street, village or barrack to the OZNA section of their local council or military unit. On the results of these reports is built up the *karakteristka* or conduct-sheet of every citizen, which assesses each man's reliability (or lack of reliability) from the Communist point of view. OZNA has complete control over the life, liberty and property of all citizens and if it chooses to arrest, to imprison without trial, to deport or "to liquidate" anybody, no one may protest or ask the reason why. That is why the populace is in such a state of terror.[12]

Stephen Clissold, a member of Fitzroy Maclean's mission with Tito during the war and press attaché at the Belgrade embassy immediately afterwards, observed:

> The tentacles of OZNA already reached out to every citizen in Yugoslavia. It examined his war-time record and his class loyalties, recorded the way he voted at elections, checked up his attendances at meetings and demonstrations, investigated any contacts he might have with foreigners, read his correspondence, set his very children to spy on his political "reliability".[13]

Frank Waddams was to compare the Yugoslav concentration camps to Dachau and Buchenwald. He was convinced that in Slovenia alone nearly thirty thousand were imprisoned out of a population of 1,200,000. The general belief, he reported, was that the Allies had contributed little to the successful outcome of the war. It owed everything to the Soviets and their supporters.

In Slovenia, according to Ljubo Sirc in *Between Hitler and Tito*,

> people had been taken away by the hundred from their homes all over the region, never to be seen again. Among them were petty collaborators, but also people whose only fault was that some Communist disliked them. I knew that some 300 people in my home town were taken by truck to a forest nearby and shot one by one. We were told about it by old truck drivers who used to work for our factory and one of our relations was among the victims.

Sirc adds: "all the personal belongings of the condemned were taken away and distributed among the communist hierarchy. The best villas in Ljubljana went to communist leaders."

Sirc, who had been a Partisan officer, claimed "in the end it no longer mattered what you had done during the War". He had thought his record with the resistance would protect him: "on the contrary that was sometimes considered as an aggravating circumstance because you were alleged to have betrayed the partisan cause". People were being shot for no obvious reason. Others were imprisoned simply because a party member disapproved of them. He "once calculated on the basis of the figures we had in Slovenia that there must have been at least 200,000 such people in prison at any one time". Meaning more than a million Yugoslavs were imprisoned between 1945 and 1950 – one in ten of the adult population. Alexander Petrovica claimed to me that within the secret police there circulated "a 'list with black spots', about 8,000 of them, people who were marked for elimination for not offering sufficient support to the Partisans during the war".

The purpose of the reign of terror, described as "The Bloody Two Years" or "The Red Spring", was to deter any thought of resistance to those in power. The liquidations went on until "at a meeting of the Central Committee Tito cried out in disgust, 'enough of all these death sentences and all this killing! The death sentence no longer has any effect! No one fears death anymore!'" Even so, according to Djilas, "the hatreds and divisions continued to bring destruction and death, both inside and outside the country".

Recent estimates of the total killings at that time vary between 250,000 and 300,000. The Oxford historian Mark Almond, in *Europe's Backyard War*, says:

> Just as his contemporary Franco was able to live out a long life quietly because of the terror that his name still inspired even in senile decay, so too Tito was able to live off the capital of fear which he stored up during the savage reprisals against his opponents after 1944. For as long as he lived, everyone in Yugoslavia feared, though few dared to say, that the old man might turn nasty again.

The Serb historian Milan St Protic, later a visiting professor at the University of California, told me when I met him in Belgrade:

> Tito was absolutely sure he had to crush the Serbia national movement in order for his revolution to be successful. That was why the terror over the Chetniks at the end of the war and in the first years after the war was so tremendous. He had to behead the anti-communist Serbian resistance that still existed, armed, in certain parts of Serbia. Some of them survived until 1949 and were still fighting the Communists. The movement had to be crushed and moreover it had to be shown as a traitor movement. It had to be blamed. Tito had to develop a blasphemy over the Chetnik movement, making them anti-angels, devils of the Serbian people.

Tito's key devil, Mihailovic, was captured on 13 March 1946 after a ten-month countrywide search involving most of the Yugoslav army. He was found exhausted and half-blind, hiding in a foxhole on the Bosnia-Serbia border, living off snails and herbs. His supporters outside Yugoslavia had tried to persuade him to seek safety abroad, but he had been adamant about staying put to the bitter end. David Martin, in *Ally Betrayed*, published in 1946, quotes a letter Mihailovic wrote to a supporter in Switzerland on 2 February that year:

> Under no conceivable circumstances will I leave my country and my people. "You cannot carry your country with you on the soles of your shoes", said Danton when he was urged to leave France. I can do no more than repeat those very words today. For I am not Josip Broz Tito, who has nothing in common with this land and these people, so that I should run away at the first sign of danger and seek refuge on some isolated island.

He was brought to trial on 10 June 1946 with all the cynical panoply a Stalin clone like Tito could muster. A special courtroom was created in a former barracks on the outskirts of Belgrade, to which the world's media were invited. No expense was spared to get them there. To help blacken his name, Mihailovic was tried alongside twenty-three obvious collaborators with the Germans, including some of quisling Nedic's top officials. Nedic had fled to Austria in 1945, where he had been captured by the British and turned over to the Partisans. The Partisans claimed he committed suicide in February 1946 by throwing himself out of a third-floor window of the building in Belgrade where he was being held for questioning. Mixing real traitors with alleged ones had been a common practice at the Moscow show trials of the 1930s, which Tito had witnessed. It did not augur well for Mihailovic when his prosecutor Milos Minic, later Tito's Foreign Minister, declared at the outset that the purpose of the judiciary was not to resolve disputes but to liquidate the class enemy!

The atmosphere at the trial was extremely hostile towards Mihailovic and his co-defendants. The hand-picked audience in the courtroom punctuated every remark they made with hisses, jeers and shouts of "hang them!" Incredibly, Britain and the United States were accused of having supported the defendants in their alleged collaboration with the Germans, thereby seeking to prevent the liberation of Yugoslavia! The proceedings were broadcast throughout Yugoslavia. Mihailovic had wanted to shave off his beard but was prevented from doing so. No doubt Tito thought a bearded Mihailovic projected a more menacing image.

Churchill, obviously embarrassed, tried to persuade Attlee to intervene, but the British Prime Minister had problems closer to home. When Lord Halifax lobbied Ernest Bevin on the matter, the Labour Foreign Secretary replied on 29 March: "Action by us on his behalf would not be well received by our Party."[14] However, the Foreign Office did pass on to Belgrade a deposition on Mihailovic's behalf compiled by Colonel Bailey and six others who had served as liaison officers with his forces during the war. Bill Hudson offered to appear as a witness for the defence but was told that if he set foot in the country he would be arrested and charged with war crimes for co-operating with Mihailovic!

Others tried to intervene too. Two hundred of the American airmen who had been succoured by Mihailovic's forces in 1944 signed statements on his behalf and offered to appear as witnesses at his trial. At their request the State Department persisted with Tito, but was told that because the guilt of Mihailovic is already decided, there is no purpose in these Americans coming over to testify ... the crimes of the traitor Draza Mihailovic against the people of Yugoslavia are far too big and horrible that it could be or should be allowed to be discussed whether he is guilty or not.[15]

Belgrade maintained Mihailovic had rescued the airmen solely to secure American political and financial support.

The trial lasted barely a fortnight. Within forty-eight hours of the sentence being passed, and without any suggestion of an appeal, Mihailovic was executed by firing squad on 17 July 1946. "I never wanted the old Yugoslavia back, but I had a difficult legacy," he said in his final speech.

> I was confronted with the aims and tendencies of my own Government. I had against me a competitive organisation – the Yugoslav Communist Party, which seeks its own ends without compromise. I found myself in a whirl of events and intrigues ... Fate was merciless to me when it threw me into this maelstrom. I wanted much. I started much, but the whirlwind of history carried me and my work away.

Djilas revealed that Mihailovic had been promised his life would be spared if he co-operated with the prosecution – which he had. Djilas also hints Mihailovic may have been drugged throughout the proceedings. One of his lawyers was punished for over-zealously defending him. Charged on a technicality, he was sentenced to forced labour which he did not survive. Mihailovic's execution represented the climax of the bloodletting. A mystic, a fatalist, a stubborn and brave, rather muddled, much misunderstood man, he had not realised the war was altering everything. The whirlwind of history indeed swept him away. A lone and tragic figure, he has, however, flowered into a Serbian folk hero.

Roosevelt had never been a Tito fan. His successor, Harold Truman, was not one either. He protested to Belgrade at the way Mihailovic's trial had been conducted. The United States Congress set up a committee to consider the trial. They concluded it had been a sham and that Mihailovic was innocent of treason. On 29 March 1948 Truman awarded him posthumously the Legion of Merit in the Degree of Commander-in-Chief in recognition of his help in rescuing and evacuating American airmen from Yugoslavia and for his contribution to the Allied victory. To appease his diplomats, this was not disclosed until twenty years later! Truman also refused to hand over to Belgrade the gold the Royalist Yugoslav government had deposited in Washington in 1941.

Having rid himself of the Chetnik devil, Tito sought to fill the vacuum by littering the country with massive monuments to the alleged achievements of the Partisans. That most were mythical did not trouble his propagandists or his supporters in the West. He had learned from Stalin that history is as history is written, and so the national archives were taken into the Party's custody. In this way the written and the spoken word came under his control. In true Marxist-Leninist fashion, he set about rewriting history to suit himself. In this he was helped by his British fans, who wrote their own heroic versions of his life. In Michael Lees's phrase, "Titomania became literarily profitable."[16] Through constant repetition over the years, the Partisan myths and legends came to be accepted as fact. And after June 1948 Yugoslav history was rewritten a second time to show that Tito had always pursued an independent, liberal-minded, anti-Stalinist line. Many in the West were to swallow that too!

William Deakin's former pupil, Mark Wheeler, who had at one time been commissioned to write the official history of SOE in Yugoslavia (it has yet to be written) is on record as saying: "if history is the propaganda of the victors, then it is natural that the story of Tito and the Partisans has been more widely propagated than that of the loser Mihailovic."[17] Others have put it more bluntly: "The victors make their own history while the vanquished must endure in silence." This has certainly been true in Britain. Tito benefited from the fact that many of the liaison officers with him were outstanding men in their own right, and some had close relationships with Churchill. The portrait they painted of the Partisan war was profoundly romantic. So prolific was their writing it was almost a mini-industry. Many of these memoirs – "Partisan Pictures" as Basil Davidson called them – came out just as decision-makers in the West were beginning to question Tito's worth, especially in view of his intransigence over Trieste.

Undoubtedly it griped with some of those liaison officers who had served with Mihailovic that they were not sought out by publishers to tell their stories. In the words of Michael Lees, "they disappeared into the woodwork, fighting other wars and making their living". It hurt that their opposite numbers with the Partisans made names for themselves and "quite a business out of their Partisan experiences". Lees mentions particularly "Fitzroy Maclean's beautifully written though rather fanciful *Eastern Approaches*", which came out in 1949, followed in 1957 by a somewhat sycophantic biography of Tito, *Disputed Barricade*.

> These two books became accepted as gospel, and the theories and contentions in them have been widely quoted. Even before *Eastern Approaches* came out, Basil Davidson, who claimed in his later book, *Special Operations Europe*, to have started it all in the M04 [SOE] Cairo office, rushed out *Partisan Picture* already in 1946... His books, with their convincing enthusiasm, like those of Fitzroy Maclean, made a great case for the *received wisdom*... These Partisan participant books together with purportedly "historical" works by Seton-Watson and others ... created a pro-Partisan climate in general public as well as scholarly circles, which was of course reinforced dramatically when, in due course, the lead figure and historical guru, Deakin, published *The Embattled Mountain*. Deakin, a prewar don, a researcher for the great man Churchill, hero of Mount Durmitor, and a postwar academic of distinction, quietly moved into a key position when he became chairman of the British Committee for the History of the Second World War – thus very much one of the Great and the Good. This position has enabled him, inevitably, to give extra weight and leverage to the Titoite side. No one among the British participants has put forth the other point of view in detail.

Lees went further:

> *Received wisdom* was, of course, being built up and reinforced in Belgrade by the Tito government's public relations people ... the material from Belgrade has been drawn on heavily by academics studying, writing, and taking part in symposiums on the subject and has, in this manner, achieved gospel status. The "note on sources" in Deakin's *The Embattled Mountain* shows the extent to which he relied on Partisan sources. All of that Belgrade material – until the revisionists came along – had one underlying political purpose, namely to smear Mihailovic and the Loyalist Cetniks and thus ensure that no ideas foreign to Tito's image, Tito's legend, and Tito's despotic rule could blossom.[18]

Michael Lees told me that many of the liaison officers who had been with Mihailovic were ostracised at SOE's own social venue, the Special Forces Club, when it was established in Knightsbridge after the war. The Club became, in his terms, a fortress of the "received wisdom" – though he agreed with me "perceived history" was perhaps a better description. It was the liaison officers who had been with Tito who shaped the writing of history on Allied involvement in Yugoslavia during the Second World War. Not just because of their personal relationship with Churchill and the fact that they wrote bestselling books, but because the official position came to coincide with their version of history.

Deakin helped Churchill write his wartime memoirs. The six-volume *The Second World War* became a bestseller too, and for a loyal generation the accepted version of that war. Significantly, Robert Blake and Roger Louis, in the introduction to their 1993 compilation *Churchill*, quote him as saying to Deakin during the writing of *The Second World* War: "This is not history, this is my case."[19] Years before, in the 1930s, Churchill had alarmed another Oxford historian, Maurice Ashley, while helping with the biography of his ancestor the first Duke of Marlborough: "Give me the facts, Ashley, and I will twist them the way I want to suit my argument."[20]

Vane Ivanovic was at school with Deakin and, despite their differing viewpoints, maintained a close friendship with him for the rest of his life. He observes:

> there has been no symposium or discussion in Great Britain or elsewhere in Europe on the role of SOE in the last War in which Deakin has not taken a prominent part. In each of these, the version of events in Yugoslavia that has been aired is that of the victorious pro-Partisan faction inside SOE. On the British side, I have not come across any views or interpretations of the other side within SOE.[21]

Indeed, Deakin was to remain for another generation Britain's most widely recognised expert on wartime Yugoslavia.

Nora Beloff, in *Tito's Flawed Legacy*, recalls attending the Anglo-Yugoslav colloquia held by the British section of the International Committee for the History of the Second World War organised by the Imperial War Museum in London, and chaired, certainly in 1984, by William Deakin. She says the Yugoslav view was exclusively represented by the officially authorised historians who,

> like their British opposite numbers, have come to believe their own legend: perceiving Tito and the other Partisan commanders as fellow-fighters in the Allied war effort rather than as a politically motivated minority, using the Second World War as an occasion for acquiring a Communist monopoly of power in the new Yugoslavia.[22]

Milan Deroc, in *British Special Operations Explored*, relates Bill Hudson's experience at a conference in Oxford in 1962 chaired by Deakin. No one seemed interested in hearing his views, despite his being a major participant in British wartime involvement in Yugoslavia, pre-dating Deakin:

> The general impression gained from following Hudson's repeated attempts to intervene in the discussion at the conference is that he met with obstruction from some historians with committed views. Eventually he was dismissed by snubbing him as if he were a little boy. *Inter alia*, he was being referred to as "... our dear Hudson ..."

Deroc remarks it was "no wonder that, since this experience, Colonel Hudson has become reticent about volunteering any further statements and giving interviews". At that same conference, although Hudson was in their midst, some of the historians present were complaining of "the problem of sources" on the Mihailovic side!

Just as the BBC played a prominent role in promoting Tito and his Communists during the war, so after 1945 it helped sustain the Partisan myths. When I joined BBC Television in 1958, documentaries were being produced peddling a pro-Tito line. My department – I was a member of the production team of the daily programme *Tonight*, which I eventually edited – was located at Lime Grove in west London. Fitzroy Maclean – by this time Sir Fitzroy – was a frequent visitor and was on friendly terms with many of the senior executives. His view of wartime events in Yugoslavia was the accepted one within the BBC then. I recall an hour-long programme entitled *The Life and Times of Marshal Tito*, fulsomely narrated and presented by Maclean, that included a particularly reverential interview with Tito.

Nor had the situation changed by 1991, when I was commissioned to produce two documentaries for BBC2 to mark the centenary of Tito's birth. I argued for a revisionist approach and, mistakenly as it turned out, believed I had convinced the powers that be. Certainly no conditions were imposed on me. I completed the films precisely as indicated in my original proposal and handed them in, edited, dubbed, and ready for transmission. The first of them was crudely and savagely re-edited behind my back to fit in with the "perceived history".They softened my criticisms of Sir Fitzroy Maclean and Sir William Deakin, and especially of Maclean's controversial, and by then largely discredited, 1943 "Blockbuster" Report. Mentions of Ustasha atrocities were removed and references to skulduggery in high places excised or watered down, as were references to Tito's anti-British attitudes during the war. Even hints of Churchill's ill health in December 1943 were removed. Deakin's relationship with Churchill was downplayed; Maclean's extravagant claims of elite German divisions allegedly tied down by the Partisans went unchallenged. It was the, by now customary, shameless covering-up. Two hundred changes, it was boasted, needed to be made to the first programme alone. For a while BBC production personnel were forbidden to speak to me or contact me in any fashion. I was even denied access to BBC premises when my pass card was electronically cancelled!

That this wanton and petty censorship was extremely costly and produced anachronistic howlers as well as wilful errors did not bother the BBC hierarchy, who would not budge from their established viewpoint. One BBC executive concerned bragged to me how Maclean had been one of his "boyhood heroes"! Even when the blatant inaccuracies were pointed out in detail, in time for them to have been corrected before transmission, I was ignored. Maclean was said to have spent "a few months in Yugoslavia" before writing his report: in fact he was there barely a few weeks. Archive film was wrongly attributed: sequences of Tito in May 1944 were passed off as September 1943; images of Churchill in December 1943 were said to have dated from January. Truth became a victim of political safety.

The BBC had apparently feared legal action by Maclean – evidence of his continuing sway with that pillar of the British Establishment even then. When I mentioned this to a former wartime colleague of his, who had also participated in the programmes, he assured me Fitzroy was not a litigious individual, preferring more subtle means of getting his own way. Besides, he said somewhat enigmatically, Fitzroy was too shrewd a chap to put himself at risk of lawyers finding skeletons in *his* cupboard!

I told the BBC Maclean was disinclined to issue writs, whereas some of the other participants might be less reluctant. Again I was not listened to. I did, though, cause a sufficient stir for the second of the two films, dealing with the post-war Tito story, eventually to be transmitted largely untouched. As expected, many of the participants were horrified when they found out what changes had been made to the first film – the BBC not having had the courtesy to inform them of the mutilation of some individual contributions. Michael Lees, who had been censored the most, immediately posted a complaint from his Dorset home. Alas, on his way back from the mailbox, he suffered a heart attack and died. His widow persisted with his complaint. It found its way to the Broadcasting Complaints Commission, which upheld it in part, as it did a similar complaint from another participant who had been excised entirely.

*

Relations between Yugoslavia and the United States deteriorated further during August 1946. Yugoslav fighters forced an American plane flying between Vienna and Udine in Italy to land on Yugoslav territory. A Turkish passenger was wounded and the eight Americans on board detained. A few days later they shot down a second plane, killing its five-man crew. *The New York Daily News* called for an atom bomb to be dropped on the Yugoslav capital! The US ambassador accused Tito of "first degree murder" and moved his family from Belgrade to Switzerland. Embassy officials in Belgrade had long been complaining of intolerable working conditions, amounting almost to a siege. They claimed they were unable to function properly as few Yugoslavs would risk communicating with them. Many had already ended up in prison for doing so.

One senior American diplomat described the regime's attitude towards the US as "cold unyielding hatred". Another labelled Tito Moscow's "most faithful and conscientious collaborator ... spearhead of dynamic expansionist Communism".[23] Ljubo Sirc, who immediately after the war worked for the official Yugoslav news agency, Tanjug, in Ljubljana, remarks in his memoirs how at this time Yugoslav journalists were invariably subservient to the Soviets and "deliberately rude" towards the West.

Djilas says Molotov congratulated them on the plane incidents but cautioned against any repetition. Nevertheless two months later the Yugoslav mining of Albanian waters off Corfu led to the loss of two British warships and forty-four British lives. This was at a time when the Yugoslavs had renewed their truculence over Trieste. The Americans sent ships, extra soldiers and planes to the area. Tito was given an ultimatum. At Stalin's insistence he apologised, released the crew of the first plane and paid $150,000 in compensation to the families of the dead crew of the second. This did not stop UNRRA aid being suspended, largely because American dockers refused to handle shipments to Yugoslavia. Tito came to depend more and more on the Soviets.

Yugoslavia had been devastated economically by the war. A tenth of its population had been killed and most of its productive facilities destroyed. Its industrial potential had been reduced to a third of its pre-war value. One in four of its people had been rendered homeless. More than half of its livestock had been lost. Mass starvation was avoided only by aid from UNRRA, 94 per cent of whose funds and supplies came from the USA, Great Britain and Canada, each of which contributed one per cent of its national income. The USA was easily the largest single contributor. In three years supplies worth more than two billion dollars were shipped to Europe: two-thirds went to countries in Eastern and Central Europe, including the Soviet Ukraine, Byelorussia and Poland. Yugoslavia received almost half a billion dollars' worth in the eighteen months following the end of the war – a fifth of UNRRA's total budget and the largest amount given to any European country. This was at a time when bread was rationed in Britain, which had not happened even during the war.

It rankled with many in the West, particularly during the Trieste crisis, that UNRRA supplies were being used by Tito to feed and equip his 750,000-strong army. His troops were uniformed from new textile mills provided from UNRRA funds. They relied on UNRRA trucks and jeeps for transport. Tito and his party officials drove around in UNRRA cars. It embarrassed American diplomats, as one of them, Eric Pridonoff, points out in his memoirs, *Tito's Yugoslavia*, to be invited to receptions at Tito's White Palace where the tables literally groaned with the choicest delicacies and wines. Elsewhere ordinary Yugoslavs went hungry.

Most UNRRA officials were American, British or Canadian, which Tito's communists resented. But there was no alternative. The Soviets were in no position to help. The aid was decisive in averting disaster for Yugoslavia, as even Tito's official biographer Vladimir Dedijer, in *Tito Speaks*, admits: "There is no doubt that the aid UNRRA extended to Yugoslavia during those days played an enormous role in alleviating hardship. It was sent urgently, when most required." It was accepted grudgingly, with the fiction in the Yugoslav media that most of it was coming from the Soviets. It was even put about that the aid emanated from a town beyond the Urals called Unrra! As the internal distribution of UNRRA supplies was effectively in the hands of Tito's lieutenants, they were used to enhance the Partisans' political position. Opponents or waverers got nothing. Although the supplies were provided free, some were sold openly on the "black market", the Party pocketing the proceeds. It is astonishing the Western powers put up with such contemptuous behaviour.

Despite the economic difficulties, Tito and his lieutenants were determined to introduce such doctrinaire measures as the destruction of the property-owning classes. The urban bourgeoisie were in a state of shock after the war and the revolution, and hence more malleable, but the peasants were a different kettle of fish. Yugoslavia was still essentially a land of smallholdings. In lieu of collectivisation, the peasants were set production quotas. They were forced to sell only to the state, usually at rock-bottom prices. Most chose instead to cultivate the bare minimum for their own needs. This led to shortages for the rest of the population, especially those living in the cities and major towns. Rationing was introduced, which quickly led to a black market in essential foods. Corruption became rampant. All commercial and industrial enterprises were nationalised. Most of them had been taken over by the Germans during the war, or at least controlled by them. Many were now confiscated on the dubious grounds that the previous owners, by "allowing" their factories or other facilities to continue in production, had collaborated with the enemy.

In June 1947 UNRRA was ended. The United States then launched the Marshall Plan to aid countries like Yugoslavia still suffering economically from the war. It was also intended to prevent nations such as Italy and France from going communist and to act as a counter-balance to Moscow's rising power through its eastern European bloc. The Soviets realised this and denounced the Plan as an imperialist plot. Their satellites were discouraged from participating. Belgrade obeyed Moscow's bidding and declined the American largesse. Thus Yugoslavia and the other eastern European communist nations became even more dependent on the Soviet Union, which tightened its political grip on them. At this time Yugoslavia got all of its coal and coke and almost all of its specialised machinery, steel tubes, locomotives and rolling stock from the Soviet bloc, as well as 80 per cent of its pig iron and fertiliser, and 60 per cent of its petroleum products.

Yugoslavia now pursued the Soviet industrial route. Tito aped Stalin in launching a Five-Year Plan in the spring of 1947, with the usual communist emphasis on heavy industry and disregard for consumer goods. As with the Soviets in the 1920s and 1930s, personal consumption was severely restricted. The aim was to free Yugoslavia from dependence on agriculture and turn its peasantry into an urban proletariat. The national income would hopefully double within five years, but at the cost of the nation becoming highly centralised and dependent on detailed planning. It turned out to be an extravagant misuse of Yugoslavia's puny resources. The country was soon in difficulties. Djilas had boasted at the time of Yugoslavia catching up with England, in terms of *per capita* production of goods, within ten years. He was to admit they were the victims of their own ideology as industrialisation was considered "the very premise of the classless society to come".[24] He was to admit, too, to their "doctrinaire, Stalinist, mythological obsession with heavy industry".[25]

The Soviets would have preferred the Yugoslavs to remain agrarian and to rely for their industrial needs on the USSR in exchange for their raw materials. Nevertheless they offered to build them oil refineries, steel plants, copper and aluminium rolling mills and the like, though at high cost. Stalin, like Hitler, had his eyes on Yugoslavia's mineral deposits, which he longed to exploit exclusively for his own needs. General Soldatov, one of the Soviet military instructors attached to the Yugoslav army, told a group of his students in 1947: "Yugoslavia is a small country which can exist only with the support of the Soviet Union. We Russians and no one else liberated Yugoslavia, and we are entitled to request you to do what we require and what we tell you to."[26] Soon many Yugoslavs were complaining of "economic enslavement".

Tito was determined to control religious practices and beliefs, if necessary to abolish them. The churches were, by their nature, antagonistic to communism. Knowing how immense their influence had been in pre-war Yugoslavia, he resolved to break their political power. Religious teaching ended in state schools. Church schools were taken over. Obligatory civil weddings were introduced. Church lands were nationalised, church property confiscated. Religious associations, including orphanages, were closed down. Religious newspapers were curbed. Many priests were imprisoned, others physically abused or denounced; some were accused of spying for Western powers and tried for treason. Lengthy sentences were imposed and prison conditions made unduly harsh. The intention was to frighten the clergy and deter them from resisting the regime.

The Orthodox and Muslim religious leaders mostly allowed themselves to be coerced. The Roman Catholic Church was more intransigent. Tito feared it might become a focus for opponents of his regime. Many former Ustashi had re-entered Yugoslavia from Austria and Italy and were urging supporters to join them in the wooded mountains of northern and western Croatia. Tito had wanted the Church to repudiate its obedience to Rome. In return he was prepared to grant certain privileges and to tolerate its existence. But in the Archbishop of Zagreb, Aloysius Stepinac, head of the Catholic Church in Yugoslavia, Tito met his stubborn match.

The Catholic Church in Croatia did not have a good war record. Many priests had collaborated with the Ustashi in murdering Serbs.

Some were arrested and executed immediately after the war, Pavelic and most of his lieutenants escaped Tito's clutches. The Vatican facilitated their flight to Italy in the closing days of the war. To Tito's annoyance they continued to enjoy Rome's protection. Western intelligence services turned a blind eye: they were not anxious to do Tito a favour. The show trial that would have followed Pavelic's extradition to Belgrade would most likely have been an anti-Western propaganda exercise. Pavelic ended up in Peron's Argentina. Other senior Ustasha figures found their way to Australia, Canada and the United States. Some thirty thousand Ustashi are thought to have escaped Tito's justice in this way.

Tito was prepared to end his persecution of the Catholic Church if it submitted to his will, Stepinac, backed by Rome, was not prepared to do so. He stepped up his denunciations of Tito's anti-clerical campaign. Matters came to a head when Stepinac was arrested on 18 September 1946, just two months after Mihailovic's execution. He was charged with collaborating with the Germans, being complicit in Ustasha crimes, associating with Mihailovic and conspiring with foreign powers to intervene in Yugoslav affairs. He was tried alongside the notorious Ustasha police chief Colonel Erih Lisak and sentenced on 11 October 1946 to sixteen years' imprisonment at hard labour, with an additional five years' loss of civil rights. Lisak was sentenced to death. The Vatican promptly excommunicated everyone concerned with the trial. The United States Congress passed a resolution condemning it. Many senators urged the US to break off diplomatic relations with Yugoslavia. Other western governments protested too, including the United Kingdom. Tito was reviled throughout North America and most of Europe. Newspaper cartoonists compared his corpulent, bemedalled, uniformed figure to that of Herman Goering!

In response, Tito intensified his harassment of the remaining Catholic bishops and clergy. He claimed they were conspiring with organisations abroad to subvert Yugoslavia's independence. Two bishops were called up for military service and assigned to cavalry regiments as grooms! Others were harried while touring their dioceses by officially organised jeering claques who on occasion pelted them with stones and rotten vegetables. Some priests were killed in such disturbances. Several hundred lingered in prison. Children were expelled from school for going to church.

In 1950 Tito offered to release Stepinac if he would resign his archbishopric and leave the country. Stepinac refused. A year later he was released conditionally on the grounds of failing health but remained under house arrest. In 1952 he was made a cardinal, to the fury of Tito, who promptly broke off diplomatic relations with the Vatican. They were not restored until 1970. Stepinac died on 10 February 1960 and was buried in Zagreb cathedral – to the surprise of most Yugoslavs, who had not expected Tito to allow it. Tito had softened his stance after Stalin's death in 1953. The Croatian Church still refused to apologise for, let alone acknowledge, the Ustasha crimes committed against Serbs during the war. This rankled with Orthodox Christians.

Determined to stamp out any hint of opposition, Tito saw to it that all remaining non-communist politicians were arrested in 1947 and tried on trumped-up charges. They included those who had been in the Tito-Subasic administration two years before. The favourite indictment was spying for British or American intelligence services. Sentences were stiff; some even received the death penalty. Djilas was later to admit: "we needed to silence them". Told by Rankovic, his police chief, that finding a charge might be difficult for one opposition politician – Dragoljub Jovanovic, the leader of the Serb Peasant Party – Tito responded: "Then make him guilty of something!"[27]

One of those charged was Ljubo Sirc, a former Partisan. Arrested on 24 May 1947, he was accused of being a British spy, having allegedly befriended the British consul in Ljubljana and helped one of the consul's secretaries to complete complicated official forms. He was also indicted of having aided the formation of an opposition party. Sirc was convinced the secret police were paranoid then about contacts with foreigners, especially the British. One of his co-defendants was charged with having translated George Orwell's *Animal Farm* into Serbo-Croat!

Sirc details in his memoirs how during his interrogations he was not allowed to sleep but could only sit in his cell on a backless chair with the lights constantly on. After a month of this he was so exhausted he became confused. Everything he said was turned into the confession of a terrible crime. Step by step he lost all sense of reality. His family, too, were harassed. After the mockery of a Stalinist-style trial he was sentenced to death, along with other members of his alleged spy ring. One was immediately hanged to encourage the others to co-operate with the secret police.

Sirc's sentence was later reduced to twenty years' forced labour. He was offered release – and the release of his father too – if he would become a police informer. He refused. His father had had nothing to do with his son's activities but was nevertheless arrested and sent to prison, where he eventually died. Sirc was made to translate for the secret police the lengthy transcripts of trials of Soviet agents in the West. He was released after more than seven years, most of it spent in solitary confinement.

Fitzroy Maclean was in Yugoslavia during the period of the show trials, enjoying a hunting holiday with Tito. He found him "remarkably affable, considering the existing tensions between our two countries". Like William Deakin and many other British officers who had been with the Partisans during the war, Maclean bent over backwards to excuse Tito. On this occasion he reported formally to the Foreign Office:

> Living as he now does, in magnificent palaces and castles, he is no longer as closely in touch with the people of the country and their everyday affairs as when he shared their dangers and hardships as a Partisan. He has been obliged, too, to delegate authority to some who are unworthy of it. Thus he is not, I think, aware of a good deal that goes on in his own country and in the world at large and suffers also from the lack of someone who will tell him unpleasant truths.[28]

At the United Nations General Assembly in 1947, the Yugoslav delegates outdid the Soviets in ranting against the Western democracies, the United States in particular. Edvard Kardelj, Tito's Foreign Minister at this time, reveals in his memoirs how, during the peace treaty conferences, he breakfasted almost every day with his Soviet opposite number, Molotov, to co-ordinate their strategy – or rather to be told what he was expected to do.

Tito had already fallen foul of the western Allies by backing the communist insurgents in the Greek civil war. He sent them arms, trained their fighters, gave them refuge within Yugoslavia when pressed by Greek government forces, and saw to it their wounded received medical treatment. He also furnished them with a propaganda radio station, Radio Free Greece, located on Yugoslav soil though purporting to come from inside Greece. He even sent two divisions of Yugoslav troops, together with an air regiment, into Albania, ostensibly to protect that country when it looked as if the Greek government might pursue communist guerrillas who had retreated there.

He fell further foul by backing revolutionary movements in British Malaya, Dutch Indonesia and French Indo-China. He also supported the Chinese Communists in their war against Chiang Kai-Shek and sided with the Soviet Union in its dispute with Britain over Iran. He was so openly enthusiastic in his championing of Stalin in his disputes with the West that political commentators there dubbed Yugoslavia "Soviet Satellite Number One". Yugoslav schoolchildren were taught to chant "Hail Stalin, Stalin hail! In every way your views prevail!"

Stalin urged caution over Greece. He did not wish to pick a quarrel with the United States, at least not until he had his own atom bomb. But Tito had his sights on a Balkan federation embracing Bulgaria, Albania and a communist Greece, with him at its head. To that end he had started negotiations with the Bulgarian Communist Party during the autumn of 1944. Although not wholly averse to the idea, the Bulgarians worried that the Yugoslavs might swallow them up. Tito confided to his colleagues that he intended expanding Yugoslavia's Macedonian province at the expense of Bulgaria and Greece. The western Allies opposed a Balkan federation.

The Albanian leader Enver Hoxha did not welcome Tito's troops in his country. He complained to Stalin, fearing it might lead to Albania's subjugation by Yugoslavia. Though facing hunger themselves, the Yugoslavs shipped food to the Albanians; they loaned them experts of all kinds, when they were seeking technical help from the Soviets. Tito was keen to take over Albania. It would solve the problem of Kosovo and its substantial Albanian majority. He thought he had Stalin's blessing. Djilas, in *Conversations with Stalin*, says the Soviet leader told him in January 1948: "We agree to Yugoslavia swallowing Albania ... the sooner the better." As if to emphasise the point, he "gathered together the fingers of his right hand and, bringing them to his mouth, he made as if to swallow them".

Regarding Greece, Tito did not know Stalin had agreed with Churchill in October 1944 that it should be strictly a British sphere of influence. Stalin did of course not mind the Yugoslavs, Bulgars and Albanians being his surrogates in promoting communism there. A crisis was reached in March 1947 when the British decided they could no longer bear the cost of backing the anti-communists in the Greek civil war. The problem was passed to the Americans, who stepped up aid to the anti-communists. This annoyed Stalin. Prepared to countenance British influence in the area, he did not want it replaced by a more powerful American presence.

The American initiative led to the promulgation that same month of what became known as the Truman Doctrine. The United States

pledged "to support free peoples who are resisting attempted subjugation by armed minorities or by outside pressure". Greece was
specifically mentioned. Stalin blamed the upset on Tito, who was slow
to get the message that the Soviets were unwilling to take on the
United States over the issue. In December 1947 the Yugoslav-
operated Radio Free Greece announced the formation of a provisional Greek Democratic Government. Stalin had had enough. Two
months later he told Djilas and Kardelj in Moscow:

> The uprising in Greece will have to fold up ... they have no prospect
> of success at all. Do you think ... the United States, the most power-
> ful state in the world, will permit you to break their line of commun-
> ication in the Mediterranean? Nonsense. And we have no navy. The
> uprising in Greece must be stopped, and as quickly as possible.[29]

CHAPTER TWELVE

Breaking with Stalin

"Tito may be a scoundrel,
but he's our scoundrel"

ERNEST BEVIN

DURING HIS JUNE 1946 visit to Moscow, Tito suggested reviving the old Communist International, dissolved in 1943 when it was thought provocative to the western Allies. But Stalin preferred a new organisation to co-ordinate the views of the world's communist parties, as well as to exert his control over their destinies and those of the Soviet satellites. In October 1947 the Communist Information Bureau was formed and quickly dubbed Cominform. Its head-quarters was in Belgrade – a favour to Tito and perhaps a way of diverting his attention from Greece.

Djilas and Kardelj were named as the Yugoslav delegates to the Bureau. Evidently Stalin encouraged them to play a prominent role in its affairs. Membership was confined to the communist parties of the Soviet Union and its eastern European satellites, plus those of France and Italy, the strongest then in Western Europe. Djilas describes their enthusiasm over the Cominform: they "were bursting with childlike pride and joy". He wrote in the Party newspaper *Borba*: "The peoples of Yugoslavia can be proud that their capital has become the place where Communist parties will carry out future consultation and reach agreements on the struggle against the insti-gators of new wars and their henchmen." To him "the very founding of the Cominform – still more, its establishment in Belgrade – implied harmony with the Soviet Union".[1] The West saw it simply as Moscow's response to such American initiatives as the Marshall Plan and the Truman Doctrine, both aimed at containing communism. Tito spoke much at this time of communism resuming its advance through the creation of popular fronts. He hinted at militancy, par-ticularly strikes, to bring this about within Western countries. Soon he was acting as if the Cominform was his baby.

By now the glorification of Tito in Yugoslavia almost equalled that of Stalin in the Soviet Union. Ageless photographs of him, usually in his marshal's uniform, were everywhere. There was a city named Titograd or something similar in almost every region of the country – eight eventually including Titov Drvar and Titovo Uzice, both associated with him during the war. Podgorica, Montenegro's new capital, became Titograd. There was also a Tito Street in every town and most villages. His name was painted on walls, fashioned out on hilly slopes and even carved from giant rocks on mountainsides. Every day tiny tots in schools stood with clenched fists touching the red stars on their hats, responding "Onward!" as their teachers roared out "For the Fatherland with Tito!" When he spoke in public, his audience were expected not just to applaud but to chant, "Tito is ours; we are Tito's." He even adopted the regal tradition of acting as godfather to every ninth son and of bestowing freshly printed banknotes as he went around the countryside. Because the newspapers were censored, no criticism of him was ever circulated. He would not have been aware of any unfavourable comment, surrounded as he was by sycophants.

As with Stalin, the security ringing Tito was intense. Everywhere he went he was accompanied by hundreds of bodyguards; soldiers lined the streets and marksmen occupied the rooftops. His bulletproof car was driven at great speed, usually in convoy. Bystanders rarely saw him, or he them. The American diplomat Eric Pridonoff describes, in *Tito's Yugoslavia*, preparations for Tito's first visit to the embassy in Belgrade. It was

> searched from top to bottom. The surrounding areas and streets were subjected to minute scrutiny. The streets were cleared of all civilians by the troops and the roofs, balconies and windows of all buildings near the Embassy were smothered with soldiers; some of them were even stationed inside the entrance of the Embassy itself.

Relations between Stalin and Tito had cooled over Greece. But it was the proposed Balkan federation, incorporating Yugoslavia, Bulgaria and Albania, which Tito saw himself as topping, that brought matters to a head. Stalin saw a threat to his own standing in the communist bloc. Mooted in November 1944, the idea had been revived in August 1947 when Gheorghi Dimitrov, previously head of the Comintern but now leading the Bulgarian communist party, visited Tito while on holiday in Slovenia. Tito hinted it could eventually embrace Romania, Hungary, Czechoslovakia, Poland and even

Greece. As a preliminary, they agreed to a federal union of their two countries. This was announced three months later when Tito visited Sofia to sign a treaty of alliance. Neither had discussed it with Stalin or informed him in advance. They were both summoned to Moscow in early February 1948.

Tito feigned illness and sent Djilas, Kardelj and Vladimir Bakaric, the top Croatian communist, which displeased Stalin. Djilas was already in Moscow. He had been summoned a month earlier by Stalin to discuss Yugoslavia's relations with Albania, most likely as a result of Enver Hoxha's complaint. Djilas had then been kept waiting; Stalin, it seemed, wished to discuss other matters with him. He was accompanied by a military delegation as the Yugoslavs were seeking to re-equip their army with Soviet help.

Dimitrov was prepared to accept a reprimand over the Balkan federation. The Yugoslavs were not, though. Kardelj was persuaded to sign a document to the effect that Yugoslavia would not take any foreign policy initiative in future without first consulting Moscow. Tito was displeased and would not confirm Kardelj's signature when asked by Stalin to do so. Nevertheless, in reporting to Tito, Djilas maintained his faith in Stalin and his confidence in the outcome of the discussions – "idolatry dies hard", he said.[2] The Yugoslavs declared their enthusiasm for the communist *coup d'état* in Czechoslovakia that same month and backed Soviet protests over the West's decisions concerning Germany.

The Bucharest correspondent of the French newspaper *Le Figaro* had already reported, on 12 February, seeing portraits of Tito being removed from public buildings in Romania. A Yugoslav trade delegation to Moscow negotiating the renewal of their agreement with the Soviet Union, due to lapse that April, were suddenly told to leave before the end of February. On 18 March Stalin announced the withdrawal from Yugoslavia of Soviet military experts and instructors training the Yugoslav army. The next day the Soviet *chargé d'affaires* in Belgrade informed Tito that civilian advisers, too, would leave because they were "surrounded by an absence of comradeship and treated with hostility".

Tito sought an explanation from Moscow. On 27 March he received an angry letter from Stalin accusing him of spying on Soviet officials in Yugoslavia, pursuing non-communist economic policies and covertly criticising the Soviet Communist Party. Stalin also described Djilas, Rankovic, Boris Kidric, Svetozar Vukmanovic-Tempo and Vladimir Velebit as "dubious Marxists". Velebit was even accused of being "an English spy" – although the Soviets had asked him in May 1944 to spy for them in London! Apparently Velebit had refused, during the recent trade negotiations, to accept what he considered to be onerous conditions.

To appease Stalin, Tito suspended Velebit from his duties while the allegations of espionage were investigated. (He would later become ambassador to Italy and then to Britain.) At the same time Tito reiterated Yugoslavia's loyalty to the Soviet Union and invited Moscow to send a delegation to Belgrade to discuss matters. Stalin was not to be mollified. On 4 May he announced that the Cominform would meet in Bucharest the following month to consider the dispute.

Tito had by then exacerbated the situation by expelling from the Yugoslav Communist Party the two most pro-Stalinist members of his administration, Andrija Hebrang, once minister of industry though recently demoted to Chairman of the Federal Planning Commission, and Sreten Zujovic, a former Partisan general, now finance minister and a member of the politburo, and a close chum of the Soviet Ambassador to Yugoslavia. Both were accused of leaking to Moscow Tito's discussions with colleagues on the issue in question. It transpired they had been Soviet agents for some time. Within weeks they were arrested. The following year Hebrang was said to have committed suicide in prison. Few believed this and presumed he had been murdered on Tito's orders, particularly when it was revealed he had been Stalin's choice to replace Tito. Zujovic was never tried. After spending two years in prison, he recanted publicly and was allowed to rejoin the Party. He died of natural causes in 1976.

Tito declined to send a delegation to the Bucharest meeting, just a statement to the effect that the Yugoslav Communist Party remained "true to its policy of solidarity and of the closest cooperation" with the Soviet and other communist parties. On 28 June 1948 a dumbfounded world heard that Yugoslavia had been expelled from the Cominform for "pursuing an unfriendly policy towards the Soviet Union". The Cominform headquarters was switched from Belgrade to Bucharest. Tito, Kardelj, Djilas and Rankovic were singled out for rebuke. The Cominform called upon "healthy elements" within the Yugoslav Communist Party to replace its leadership with one friendlier to the Soviet Union.[3] Molotov went further, describing the Yugoslav leadership as "this hired gang of criminals";[4] Malenkov dubbed them "American agents carrying out espionage assignments against the USSR".[5] The Yugoslav Ambassador to Moscow was expelled in October 1949 for allegedly engaging in "subversive activities in the Soviet Union".[6] Even James Klugmann, the Stalinist pro-Partisan mole within wartime SOE Cairo and later a leading member of the British Communist Party, published, in 1951, *From Trotsky to Tito* in which he denounced his Yugoslav hero's "treachery" that had been "long and carefully concealed"!

Stalin's breach with Tito happened when the West was diverted by the Soviet blockade of Berlin, begun in late March 1948. This was Moscow's reaction to its failure, at the Four-Power conference in December 1947, to get its own way over the administration of Germany, of Berlin in particular. The edginess between East and West was heightened by the Communist coup in Czechoslovakia in late February 1948. The CIA's director had warned President Truman that war was likely. The five major West European nations quickly concluded a pact of self-defence, the Brussels Treaty, forerunner of NATO. Meeting in London on 1 June, the Western Allies announced their intention to establish a separate West German State. The Berlin airlift began on 26 June, just two days before the announcement of the Stalin-Tito rift.

While privately welcoming the rupture between Tito and Stalin, the British Foreign Secretary, Ernest Bevin, was cautious in public. His biographer Alan Bullock recalled:

> The Yugoslavs had been the most aggressive of the East European Governments in attacking British policy – over Trieste, Austria, Greece, Albania, the Balkan and Italian peace treaties. [Bevin] had sat through too many anti-Western tirades by Djilas and others at the Paris Peace Conference and in the United Nations to be easily convinced that this was a real breach.

Indeed Bevin had advised his colleagues, "it would be wrong to read too much into the Yugoslav-Russian exchanges. It was a family quarrel and did not mean that the Communist empire in Eastern Europe was crumbling."[7] He initially thought the split a "put up job". Others in the Foreign Office believed "it might have been a trick to deceive the West". Most American diplomats thought so too. They expected at best it was merely temporary. The official line on Yugoslavia was still that it was one of Moscow's "satellite police states" assisting the Soviets in their "drive toward world conquest".

Washington continued to abhor Tito. That April, President Truman had declared to a group of magazine editors: "I am told that Tito murdered more than 400,000 of the opposition in Yugoslavia before he got himself firmly established there as a dictator."[8] Because the breach occurred during the blockade of Berlin, it was to be welcomed. Thus Tito was thought worthy of "discreet and unostentatious support". Attempts by Stalin to crush Tito should be thwarted "without provoking him in the process".[9]

Tito and his colleagues in 1948 did not consider themselves dissidents, launching a rival brand of communism or socialism. They felt they were the purest of Marxist-Leninists, the staunchest of Stalinists. It was the Soviets who were straying from the party line. There was no ideological clash with the Kremlin. In his December 1979 *Encounter* interview, Djilas maintained:

> We were, up to the time of our break with Moscow, far from being opposed to the Soviet Union, least of all for nationalistic reasons. If anything, we supported the Soviet Union with unbounded loyalty and enthusiasm. Nothing the Russians did was too absurd for us to rationalise and defend.

Anxious to display their credentials, Tito and his lieutenants immediately set about tightening discipline within their party and vigorously pursuing traditional communist policies. Stung by Stalin's accusation that they were slow to nationalise industry and collectivise the land, they now pushed ahead with what Djilas describes as "dogmatic zeal". They forced the selling of grain and other crops. They took into state ownership such service industries as insurance companies, retail shops, hotels, cafes and restaurants, as well as many small businesses – 3,100 enterprises were nationalised in a single month in 1948.

The chaos that quickly ensued exacerbated the steadily worsening economic situation. Food became desperately short in the towns. Many peasants refused to give up their land and were imprisoned. At least fifty were killed resisting the forced takeovers. Livestock and crops were eaten rather than yielded to the authorities. Protest rallies were even held at cemeteries under the slogan "Arise, ye dead, change your places with the living."[10] Djilas claims he and his colleagues were soon "outrivaling in perfidy Moscow's own methods of double-dealing and retaliation".[11] Agricultural production dropped to below pre-war levels. Three poor harvests in a row, and a severe drought in 1950, did not help. The suffering of the peasants was appalling. Industrial output slumped. Run on Soviet lines, Yugoslav factories were woefully inefficient. With food shortages, rampant inflation and increasing foreign debts, the country soon found itself near to economic collapse. Tito was forced in early 1953 to reverse collectivisation. By the end of 1954 only 3 per cent of arable land remained in collective farms.

Thereafter, as Yugoslavia became dependent on the West, particularly for food and defence, its brand of communism (socialism, it was now called) was bound to change. It was a matter of expediency, not deliberate choice. For ordinary Yugoslavs it meant a higher standard of living than in other communist states, including the Soviet Union. After March 1953 peasants could sell their produce directly at reasonable prices. Small businesses, including shops and restaurants, were no longer discouraged.

Tito's fans in the West portrayed the break with Stalin as having been instigated by him. But it is clear it had been unexpected and unwanted by Tito and his politburo. According to Djilas's biographer Stephen Clissold, "the bottom had been knocked out of their Marxist world". It seems the gall-bladder problems from which Tito was to suffer for the rest of his life were brought on by his anxieties over expulsion from the Cominform. Djilas says that for Tito it

> came as a bitter psychological and intellectual blow ... with those close to him Tito did not conceal what he was going through. In those months he was fretful, easily agitated, and broke out suddenly into expressions of intimacy and warmth towards his closest and most trusted comrades – an intimacy and warmth he had lost toward the end of the war and in the early postwar years.[12]

There were no ideological differences between Tito and Stalin. Yugoslavia's communist system was based on the Stalinist template. As Djilas maintains, Yugoslavia in 1948 was "the most hard-line" of all Communist countries.[13] It was simply that, in Stalin's eyes, Tito had become a bit too big for his boots. It was a raw struggle for political power.

There was wounded vanity on Stalin's part. Khrushchev was to tell the Soviet Party congress in 1956 that Stalin believed he had only to wag his little finger "and there will be no more Tito. He will fall."[14] Stalin was, in today's parlance, a control freak. Tito's standing threatened that control, whatever his protestations of loyalty. He may have accepted Stalin's pre-eminence, but he undoubtedly considered himself Stalin's successor. As Stalin got older, his paranoia about conspiracies against him became more marked. Tito was a threat to his personal authority.

Taken aback by the vehemence of the Soviet stance, Tito and his colleagues fought back. Their power within Yugoslavia was at stake. The Soviets were accusing them of heresy, of Trotskyism, of revisionism, of Menshevikism – all the errors in the communist lexicon. To support their "innocence", the correspondence with Moscow was published. A congress of the Yugoslav Communist Party was called for 21 July 1948 – the first since 1928! Ironically, Stalin had berated Tito for not having arranged one immediately after the war.

Held in Belgrade and attended by more than two thousand delegates, the congress lasted nine days. All stops were pulled out to present a united Party behind its leadership. In this they were helped by the inept anti-Tito propaganda pushed out by the Cominform. Moscow spread rumours that Belgrade was in a state of siege, which was clearly untrue. Djilas says, though, that at the congress site "the surrounding woods, as well as the clearings around the White Palace and the Old Palace, were packed with antiaircraft batteries and machine guns 'just in case'".[15] Tito clearly thought the Soviets might be tempted to interfere. Yugoslavs in the Soviet bloc were being harassed, which was adding to the tension. Stalin had downgraded Tito's Kremlin codename from *Orel* ("Eagle") to *Stervyatnik* ("Carrion Crow")![16]

Overt criticism of the Soviet Union – especially of Stalin – was avoided at the congress. Instead there were ritual resolutions applauding Stalin and the USSR. Tito devoted most of his opening speech to explainng how faithful the Party had always been. The Partisan movement had been created in 1941 to help the Soviets in their hour of need. He concluded with a ringing, "Long Live Stalin!" Foreign Minister Kardelj reaffirmed Yugoslavia's place in the "camp of anti-imperialist forces headed by the Soviet Union". He continued peddling the Soviet line in United Nations debates that autumn. When NATO was created the following year, Belgrade followed Moscow's lead in labelling it a "serious threat to peace and international co-operation" and "a plan for the forcible establishment of Anglo-American world domination". Djilas, however, found the July 1948 congress "somewhat strained".[17]

The hall – used previously for the show trial of Draza Mihailovic – was filled with the usual portaits of Stalin, Lenin, Marx and Engels, though they were noticeably smaller than those of Tito! Soon, however, all photographs of Stalin, Lenin, Marx and Engels disappeared from Yugoslavia's walls as Tito's increased in number and size. When Stalin celebrated his seventieth birthday in 1949, the Soviet satellites vied with each other to send suitable gifts. Yugoslavia did not send a present. According to Vladimir Dedijer, the suggestion of the Belgrade wags was to send Stalin a trainload of his redundant portraits!

Such criticism as there was at the congress was focused on the Cominform and on those within the Party who had not immediately and wholeheartedly supported Tito. This was a prelude to the brutal purging of such "traitors", the pro-Stalinists, whom Tito and his lieutenants chose to describe Cominformists. The Soviets had embedded within the Yugoslav Party substantial numbers loyal to their point of view, a point of view hitherto the conventional wisdom. Now anyone showing any hint of such "loyalty", or even faintly criticising Tito, was disposed of mercilessly. It was an opportunity to weed out anyone considered a dissident.

"Offences" included listening to Radio Prague or Radio Moscow, or even admiring Russian music. Under an emergency law people could be interned for up to three years without trial. More than fifty thousand are thought to have been imprisoned. Sentences ranged from two to sixteen years. Among those jailed were nearly two thousand former secret policemen and almost seven thousand army officers. They included several generals, as well as many senior air force personnel who had been trained in the USSR.

Because of the numbers, the existing prisons could not cope. New ones were needed. A labour camp, complete with stone quarries, on the desolate Adriatic island of Goli Otok, south of Riyeka, became, according to Vladimir Dedijer, "a perfect miniature reproduction of a Stalinist Siberia". Djilas claims it was Tito's idea alone: he did not consult any colleague apart from Rankovic. At least fifteen thousand are thought to have experienced, between July 1949 and December 1952, Goli Otok's torrid summers and freezing, windswept winters, as well as its other perverse and brutish delights. A colleague who visited the island told Djilas that Rankovic's secret police "had devised and applied corrective methods that were possibly the most diabolical in history". He detailed the torture. Prisoners often "had their heads plunged into pails of human excrement [and] were forced to wear placards that read 'Traitor'".[18]

There was a procedure known as the *stroj* or line. New captives, unloaded from the ships,

> were forced to run a gauntlet of crazed prisoners who were obliged to demonstrate their reform by beating them. Depending on the account one reads, the *stroj* was as short as five hundred metres or as

long as fifteen hundred. By the end, the victims were dazed and stag-gering: "I no longer know what they did with me. I only know I was wrenched, bloodied, my skin pounded to a pulp, and that I ran the gauntlet of 4,000 prisoners barefoot and naked – because we had to take off our shoes and clothes – over the rocks for a kilometre and a half... Many fell unconscious along the way, but I saw with my own eyes that those who fell were picked up and beaten. Many wanted to kill themselves and leaped headlong upon the rocks".[19]

According to Djilas:

> If gouged eyes were a rarity, broken teeth and ribs were not ... the inmates had no visitation rights. They received neither letters nor packages – at least not in the early period. Until word leaked out unofficially, their families had no idea where they were; letters were addressed to a number, as to soldiers in wartime.

The "re-education" of the prisoners

> was made the responsibility of certain inmates – the "reconstructed" ones – who in effect collaborated with Security. The latter involved itself as little as possible, leaving the re-education to "self-managing units" made up of reconstructed inmates, who went to inhuman extremes to ingratiate themselves and win their own release. They were inventive in driving their fellow victims similarly to "recon-struct" themselves ... there is no limit to the hatred and meanness of the new convert toward yesterday's coreligionists.

Sentences were limited to two years, but there was no bar on their renewal. Djilas claims that "inmates who languished there for ten years were not uncommon."[20]

Those condemned to work in the stone quarries had to carry rocks uphill and down again. The pointlessness of their labour was part of the torture. There were hundreds of deaths on the island, including suicides. The authorities did everything possible to deny its existence. Release required public repentance, usually in the press or in the presence of Party members. A condition of discharge was not to mention the camp or their experiences to anyone, even their own families. Otherwise they would be returned to the island. The deterrent worked. To Djilas, "Goli Otok was the darkest and most shameful fact in the history of Yugoslav Communism."[21]

Nor were the top prisoners, even former generals, spared these procedures. Tito's wartime chief of staff, General Arso Jovanovic, was shot dead trying to cross into Romania one night in mid-August 1948. Two other high-ranking officers with him were captured and imprisoned. He had recently returned from Moscow where he might well have been encouraged to mount a coup against Tito. Another general succeeded in escaping the country. That these events happened after the Party congress suggests the officers in question might have concluded a putsch was no longer possible in view of the strong popular support for Tito. Many other senior officers were arrested and tried. Several diplomats absconded to the Soviet bloc.

More than two thousand hard line communists fled Yugoslavia. Some Yugoslavs overseas defected, including Tito's ambassador to Romania, his press attaché in Washington, the *chargé d'affaires* in Budapest, the military attaché in Stockholm and an official in Oslo. Several hundred students and technocrats on courses in communist countries opted not to return home, in many cases under pressure from the authorities there. Much was made publicly of their actions. Publicity was given, too, to the formation of international brigades of volunteers in Hungary, Romania and Bulgaria, prepared, apparently, to overthrow the regime in Yugoslavia. Six thousand East Germans were said to have signed up for one of these brigades. The wartime Radio Free Yugoslavia was re-established, this time in Bucharest, airing anti-Tito propaganda daily!

There were clashes at Yugoslav universities between pro-Soviet and pro-Tito groups, which led to at least one death. Other disturbances resulted in casualties the authorities, anxious to downplay the extent of the opposition, concealed. According to Yugoslav official statistics, between 1949 and 1951 504 infiltrators from neighbouring countries bent on subversion or sabotage were captured. Allegedly more than a hundred Yugoslavs were killed by them. There were reports, too, of military properties having been damaged. In October 1952 an opposition political party was formed with Soviet support by a group of defectors with the extravagant title League of Yugoslav Patriots for the Liberation of the Peoples of Yugoslavia from the Yoke of the Tito-Rankovic Clique and Imperialist Slavery! It did not long survive Stalin's death. Yugoslav *émigrés* in the Soviet Union continued, though, to have their own newspaper, financed by the Kremlin, throughout the Khrushchev period.

Stalin took the opportunity to encourage purges of dissidents in the Cominform countries. It was too good a chance to get rid of people he did not like! Many were imprisoned or even executed on the grounds of having been friends of Tito, or of having been hospitable to Tito's colleagues. Any whisper of favouring Tito was dealt with harshly, as was any hint of criticism of his expulsion by Stalin. He also turned the economic screw on Tito by delaying deliveries of equipment vital for the Yugoslav Five-Year Plan, which was soon in a shambles. The other Cominform countries followed suit. The few supplies that arrived were invariably defective, or so the Yugoslavs claimed: machinery did not work or had essential parts missing. Romania for a while even severed all rail and postal communications with Yugoslavia. Yugoslav shipping was prevented from reaching the Black Sea by way of the Danube.

In January 1949 the Cominform established a Council for Mutual Economic Assistance (dubbed Comecon), from which the Yugoslavs were excluded. It was to organise an economic boycott of Yugoslavia. Trade between the Cominform countries and Yugoslavia was in any case dwindling. By the end of 1949 it had virtually ceased. The ambitious industrialisation schemes of the Five-Year Plan were put on hold. Rumours of a Soviet invasion prompted an increase in military expenditure. Roads near the eastern borders were mined and bunkers prepared there. Food was stockpiled. The state archives were evacuated from Belgrade.

Under the guise of extended military exercises, the Soviet Union and its satellites deployed troops close to Yugoslavia's borders. There were numerous "incidents", some extremely provocative. More than forty Yugoslav frontier guards were said to have been killed. Soviet planes flew daily across Yugoslav territory from bases in her Communist-controlled neighbours. Moscow sent a diplomatic note on 18 August 1949 protesting against the alleged maltreatment of Soviet citizens. It concluded with a threat: the Soviet Government "will not reconcile itself to such a state of affairs … it will be compelled to resort to other, more effective means". This was taken by Tito as a declaration of war.[22] Earlier that month, addressing army commanders in Skopje, he had declared Yugoslavia would resist any invasion. Tension rose when the Soviets exploded an atom bomb in September 1949. Tito put his troops on full alert.

The USA and Britain declared jointly that an attack on Yugoslavia would have serious consequences. When Kardelj spoke at the United Nations in New York later that autumn, the British Foreign Secretary, Ernest Bevin, ostentatiously shook his hand in full view of the Soviet delegation and for the benefit of the press cameras. The Americans successfully lobbied, against vitriolic opposition from the Soviets, for Yugoslavia to fill a vacant seat with a two-year term on the UN Security Council. Djilas was present and vouched: "the Soviet delegation did everything to block our election, from public accusations about charter violations and our breaking a "gentleman's agreement", to surreptitious blackmail and threats."[23]

The "gentleman's agreement" was the unofficial arrangement whereby seats on the Security Council, other than those of the five permanent members, would include two from eastern Europe and two from Commonwealth states. Bevin worried that the lobbying was unduly provocative to the Soviets, who were backing Czechoslovakia for the eastern vacancy. He was anxious Moscow should not veto his Commonwealth candidates and was persuaded to support the United States only at the last minute. It was Britain's vote that swung it Tito's way.

The Yugoslavs abstained on the initial vote in the Security Council on 25 June 1950, following North Korea's invasion of South Korea, which demanded its immediate withdrawal. They voted against the more crucial resolution two days later endorsing American military intervention, however, and subsequently disapproved of American troops entering North Korean territory. When, on 1 August, the Soviets moved to oust Nationalist China from the United Nations, the Yugoslavs voted with them. This did not stop President Truman sending a note to Congress on 29 November supporting a Yugoslav Emergency Relief Act: "the continued independence of Yugoslavia is of great importance to the security of the United States ... keeping Soviet power out of one of Europe's most strategic areas ... is clearly in our national interest". The Yugoslavs received $38,000,000 to alleviate the effects of a drought that year. Some of this money was used to feed the Yugoslav military, against the wishes of the Americans. Even so, Congress granted a further $20,000,000 for famine relief two years later, when there was another drought. The Yugoslavs received $650,000,000 in food aid from the United States during the 1950s.

In November 1951 Yugoslavia complained to the United Nations about Soviet intimidation. Moscow ridiculed the charges as "nothing but a tissue of lies and calumnies" but the UN General Assembly voted 47 to 5 in Yugoslavia's favour. To Stalin's fury, they recommended their differences be settled "in accordance with the spirit of the United Nations."[24] The Hungarian defector General Bela Kiraly, then a commander in the Hungarian army, claimed that, but for the Korean War, a Soviet invasion of Yugoslavia supported by Hungarian and Romanian troops would have taken place in 1950. The Russians were deterred by the fear that the Americans would intervene in Yugoslavia as they had in Korea.

Khrushchev was later to assert that he was "absolutely sure that if the Soviet Union had a common border with Yugoslavia, Stalin would have intervened militarily."[25] Milovan Djilas was convinced the Americans would never have allowed the Russians to invade Yugoslavia, and that Tito believed this too. In his biography of Tito, he quotes him as saying: "The Americans are not fools. They won't let the Russians reach the Adriatic." The US military seriously considered using the atom bomb against targets in the Soviet satellites, though not in the Soviet Union itself. The US State Department and President Truman never favoured this.

Franklin Lindsay, head of the American military mission in Belgrade during the final months of the war, was now asked to renew his contacts with the Tito leadership. He was told the Yugoslavs

> desperately needed arms to strengthen their defense against the possibility of an attack by Hungarian, Romanian, and Soviet forces. Yet Tito believed that the open acceptance of arms from the United States could provide just the pretext Stalin needed for actual invasion. We agreed upon an initial secret shipment ... five shiploads of arms in innocently marked boxes were loaded out of Philadelphia aboard ships bound for Yugoslav Adriatic ports. With this in hand Tito felt sufficiently secure to receive openly additional support from the West. Over the next ten years the United States openly provided more than one billion dollars of military and economic aid to Yugoslavia. Britain provided similar support.[26]

In the following decade that billion quadrupled!

Later exchanges were even more open. Tito's military chief, General Koca Popovic, visited the Pentagon in the summer of 1951 and his American opposite number went to Belgrade that autumn; the US Assistant Secretary of Defence met with Tito the following summer. The American military was keen to include Yugoslav forces in NATO's defence of Western Europe and was to claim Belgrade had agreed to it. The US State Department was maybe more realistic in its retrospective assessment that "the Yugoslavs probably fooled us a great deal" on this.[27]

Djilas says a Soviet plot was discovered to assassinate the whole of the Yugoslav politburo while they were playing billiards at Tito's residence. The head of Tito's bodyguard turned out to be a Soviet agent! The Soviets made other attempts to assassinate Tito, right up until Stalin's death in 1953. Stephen Dorril, in *MI6: Fifty Years of Special Operations*, maintains:

One attempt envisaged an agent spraying a dose of lethal bacteria on the leader, another killing him with a specialised silent weapon during a trip to London. MI6 forewarned Tito at least twice of Soviet attempts on his life. The plans were dropped when Stalin died.

The would-be assassins included the man who had made the first, almost successful attempt on Trotsky's life in Mexico City in May 1940. In the early 1950s he had become Costa Rica's non-resident envoy to Yugoslavia! Christopher Andrew, in *The Mitrokhin Archive*, reveals that the report on this last attempt on Tito's life reached Stalin just hours before his fatal stroke during the morning of 2 March 1953. It may well have been the last official document he read. Simon Sebag Montefiore, in his massive biography *Stalin: The Court of the Red Tsar*, claims that among the five letters found by Khrushchev under a sheet of newspaper in Stalin's desk after he died was one from Tito dated 1950: "Stop sending assassins to murder me ... If this doesn't stop, I will send a man to Moscow and there'll be no need to send any more."

Yugoslavia's communist neighbours now took the opportunity to press their territorial claims. Albania stirred up trouble in Kosovo, where Albanians were an overwhelming majority. Albania was also the first of the communist-run countries to renounce its treaties with Yugoslavia. With Moscow's blessing, Bulgaria renewed its interest in Macedonia. Hungary and Romania incited their minorities in Yugoslavia, and made life difficult for Yugoslavs within their own borders. The Soviets encouraged separatist movements in Croatia and Montenegro. The Greek communists were persuaded to break off relations with Tito's regime. This was to their detriment: the Yugoslavs closed their borders to them in July 1949, stopped aid and expelled those who had sought sanctuary there. This effectively ended the civil war in Greece; the non-communist Greek government was the victor. Moscow denounced Yugoslavia's "act of perfidy ... they stabbed the national liberation army of Greece in the back at the most difficult moment in its struggle against the monarchofascist army and its Anglo-American patrons".[28] Ambassadors were exchanged between Greece and Yugoslavia in December 1950. Within months rail and air links were reopened and trade resumed between the two neighbours.

The various treaties of friendship and mutual assistance into which Yugoslavia had solemnly entered with its communist neighbours were all abrogated, as was the Soviet-Yugoslav pact signed in April 1945, meant to last twenty years. The Soviets withdrew their support for Yugoslavia's territorial claims in Carinthia and Venezia Giulia. At last peace treaties with Italy and Austria became possible.

Moscow's attempted economic strangulation was to prove a blessing in disguise for Tito. It forced him to replace his over-ambitious Five Year Plan with more realistic targets, and to seek alternative sources for his imports and fresh outlets for his exports. These were in the West. He was able to take advantage of the wider opportunities of trade, aid and technology. Tito did not have to turn to the West for help. It turned to him. His expulsion from the Cominform had been greeted enthusiastically in many Western capitals. Although Yugoslavia's continuing belligerency towards Italy over Trieste was causing alarm, anyone prepared to break the solid strength of the Soviet bloc was clearly welcome. The US *chargé d'affaires* in Belgrade reported to Washington: "No event could be more momentous for the attainment of our foreign policy objectives than the permanent alienation from the Soviet Union of this key regime." The US Secretary of State, George Marshall, agreed: "by this act the aura of mystical omnipotence and infallibility that surrounded the Kremlin has been broken".

Washington was watching events with great interest. They made a "gesture" before Tito's Party Congress, releasing the $30,000,000 worth of gold deposited at Fort Knox by the royalist Yugoslav government-in-exile. In return the Yugoslavs compensated Americans whose businesses had been nationalised by Tito. The Americans and the British also responded favourably to a request for several thousand tons of crude oil. Washington now went further and granted loans to buy raw materials and industrial equipment. Over the next decade these were to amount to more than $2 billion. Tito did not display much gratitude in public. Nor was he prepared to change his ways: "The West will have to take us as we are."[29] Despite requests from Washington not to, he recognised Ho Chi Minh and his Vietminh movement in northern Vietnam, who were engaged in a bitter guerrilla struggle with France.

The decision had been taken in western capitals to "keep Yugoslavia afloat" (British Foreign Secretary Ernest Bevin's phrase) rather than have it become more subservient to Moscow than before. The venerable American Senator William Fulbright thought it "an act of enlightened self-interest". Trade agreements were concluded with other western countries. The World Bank and the International Monetary Fund chipped in too, with loans on which the Yugoslavs would be forever dependent. The Yugoslav press and radio ceased to attack western statesmen. A British Labour Party delegation visited Yugoslavia in 1950. The following year a Yugoslav one went to London, seeking financial and military aid. They were well received by British Prime Minister Clement Attlee and Opposition leader Winston Churchill. That same year the UN Secretary General, Trygve Lie, visited Yugoslavia.

US military aid was used to re-equip, within the decade, eight of Yugoslavia's twenty-seven infantry divisions. It allowed the Yugoslavs to discard much of the out-of-date military hardware the Soviets had foisted on them. The Americans even dangled membership of NATO before Tito, though the French and British were not so keen. Nor were they favourably disposed to offering military aid should the Soviets invade. Tito realised that joining NATO might be the last straw for Stalin; and Stalin now had the atom bomb. He never seriously countenanced it, but is said to have told the Americans that, if the Soviets attacked Greece, West Germany or Italy, he would offer his forces to NATO.

Tito's fans in the West resurfaced invigorated. Many claimed they had always believed he would seek independence from the Soviet bloc at the first opportunity: "Look, we said that if we supported Tito in the war we could woo him away from communism. We have been vindicated." Fitzroy Maclean, back to being a Conservative MP, and William Deakin, now Warden of St Antony's College, Oxford, unashamedly lobbied on his behalf. Maclean went so far as to suggest he spotted Tito's independent-mindedness before Tito recognised it himself! According to the Oxford historian Mark Almond,

> when Tito turned westward again at the height of the Cold War, there were many willing pens waiting to rekindle his myth and perhaps bask once more in his reflected glory. 1948 marked the rebirth of the Tito myth which proved so dominant in establishment circles at Westminster and the universities for decades to come.[30]

Fortunately for Tito – though not for the Yugoslav people – the West imposed no conditions on the aid thrust at him. Yugoslavia did not have to become a democracy, nor its judges independent and impartial. Its secret police did not have to be disbanded. Free elections were not demanded. Nationalised banks and industries did not have to be privatised. The collectivised economy did not have to be replaced by a competitive one. Tito could remain a dictator. Yugoslavia was underpinned ideologically by the East but sustained economically by the West.

Tito was to benefit most from the Cold War because it enabled him to play off one side against the other. He was courted by both sides, fêted by both sides. He used the Americans to safeguard himself from the Soviets: he and his colleagues must have laughed themselves sick over how credulous the West was! Djilas, however, remained sceptical:

> Communists are not able to cast off one dogma or mythology without adopting another: the revolution which had been accomplished in covert fashion quickly acquired, after 1948, a dogmatic mythology of its own.

Nora Beloff quotes Tito's close confidant Svetozar Vukmanovic-Tempo as saying:

> We did not shrink from publishing fictitious data in official documents so as to obtain more aid and thus enable our own resources to be diverted for financing industrialisation. In this operation we had considerable success.

Clearly the aid was given not for economic but for political reasons. The British were perhaps a shade shrewder and more pragmatic than the Americans. Foreign Secretary Ernest Bevin remarked to Dean Acheson: "Tito may be a scoundrel, but he's our scoundrel."[31]

CHAPTER THIRTEEN
Life after Stalin

"that traitor Djilas"

TITO

IN MAY 1952 Tito married Jovanka Budisavljevic. She had nursed him after his operation for gallstones earlier that year. She was his fourth wife. Thirty-two years younger than him, she was a Serb born in Croatia. Not very well educated, she is thought to have been a captain in the secret police; for some time she was described as Tito's personal secretary. Tito's entourage never liked her. She tended to interfere in their routines. Nor did Tito's two sons, though perhaps that was natural. Although she always travelled with him, she was not well known outside his circle, and was never popular. She and Tito had no children, though Djilas says she desperately wanted them. At Tito's suggestion, Vladimir Velebit, Yugoslavia's ambassador to Rome, invited Jovanka to stay at the embassy so that he, and more especially his wife Vera, could instruct her in the etiquette and diplomatic niceties of being a president's wife! The first westerner to be told of the marriage, and to meet the new wife, was Anthony Eden, who visited Belgrade in September 1952. Once again British Foreign Secretary after Churchill's victory in the polls the year before, Eden had himself recently remarried.

One of the purposes of Eden's trip was to invite Tito on a state visit to Britain the following spring. Tito readily accepted although he had been warned he might be heckled by Roman Catholics objecting to his imprisonment of Cardinal Stepinac. He might have been less enthusiastic had he known the Soviets planned to assassinate him in London. But just eleven days before he arrived on 16 March 1953, Stalin died and the assassination attempt was called off. Even so, security was tight throughout the visit: anti-Tito demonstrators were kept at a distance. The microphones of cinema newsreels were able, though, for the record, to catch their shouts of protest, and the explosion of a magnesium flare just forty yards from him. It was his first venture outside the Soviet bloc as leader of his country.

As the point of the visit for the British government was to show to the world, and especially Stalin's successors, how closely identified with the West Tito had become, they clearly did not want him harmed. He had come by sea and was met at Westminster Pier in the heart of London by Churchill, Eden and the Duke of Edinburgh. The red carpet was run out for him. He dined with Churchill at 10 Downing Street and lunched with the Queen at Buckingham Palace. The possibility of Yugoslavia joining NATO was one of the topics Churchill and Eden discussed with him. Tito managed to convince his hosts that membership was not appropriate at that time. He was awaiting developments in Moscow following Stalin's death.

At the Sixth Party Congress in November 1952 the Yugoslav party's name had been changed to League of Communists, meant to symbolise its difference from the Soviets. The Politburo became the Executive Committee. Its membership was still Pijade, Kardelj, Rankovic and Djilas. Rankovic ran the secret police and was responsible for state security. Pijade and Kardelj were entrusted with guiding the party line. Djilas was in charge of education and propaganda. He also edited the biggest official daily newspaper *Borba*. Tito had given him free rein to attack the Soviet Union and expose the horrors of Stalin's purges. But he also criticised the corruption of the communist state, in particular the acquisitive lifestyle of party bureaucrats. In his eyes they were a bunch of self-serving toadies. That a movement claiming to speak for the underprivileged should become just another bunch of exploiters, rankled with him. His colleagues resented such censures, knowing they applied to them. They complained to Tito, who for the moment was prepared to let Djilas have his head.

Djilas says "Stalin's death was greeted with relief and even rejoicing by the Yugoslav leadership." But

> Tito began to stress the need for dispensing with American aid as soon as possible… We all agreed on putting an end to the aid and thereby our dependence on the West. But the way he harped on it hinted at the coming reversal in domestic policy, when the process of democratisation would be halted.

By June 1953 Tito was complaining to Djilas that too much "was being written and spoken against the bureaucracy and bureaucratism".[1] Tito clearly had in mind the articles Djilas had been publishing in *Borba*. For instance, he had written:

The bureaucracy contains the worst characteristics of all previous classes. It is ravenous and insatiable like the bourgeoisie, but without its spirit of enterprise and thrift. It is heedless of the value of human labour like the feudal lords and the slave owners of antiquity, but it lacks their spiritual culture.[2]

Also: "In its role in the process of production, the bureaucracy in the USSR does not differ significantly from previous ruling classes." And:

Because it has achieved a lordship over all forms of social life that has never been achieved by any other class, we can conclude that it is prepared to perpetrate crime on a scale never attained by any class in history.[3]

Such comments were dynamite in a closed society. Djilas maintained he was describing only the Soviet bureaucracy, but Tito knew his comments applied to Yugoslavia too.

Djilas says that after Stalin's death Tito began to regard criticism of the Soviets as counter-productive. The new men in Moscow were seeking a *détente* with Yugoslavia. Nikita Khrushchev had effectively taken over from Stalin, though for a while he shared power with Marshal Bulganin. They began wooing Tito back into the Soviet bloc and within three months of Stalin's death diplomatic relations were restored. According to Djilas, Tito showed his independence of the West by acting forcibly that summer over Trieste. He moved troops up to the Italian border, while a mob attacked the United States Information Service offices in Belgrade. He also halted further moves towards democratisation within Yugoslavia.

Djilas claims that the Soviets indicated he was an obstacle to their normalising relations. He quotes Khrushchev as saying to Tito: "You [eliminate] Djilas, we Beria." Beria was head of the Soviet secret police who had organised the assassination attempts on Tito. Yugoslavia's Ambassador to Moscow, Veljko Micunovic, relates in *Moscow Diary* that, during the 1956 Hungarian Uprising Khrushchev congratulated him: "How well you solved the question of Djilas." When he took up his appointment an elaborate network of bugging devices was discovered within the embassy complex!

In June 1953 Tito called a meeting of the Central Committee on the island of Brioni where he was holidaying. He wanted to agree a new policy towards Moscow and halt further liberalisation of the economy. As well as disapproving of the changes, Djilas objected to the choice of venue. He was to write later:

> There was an uneasiness in the atmosphere and the arrangements:
> there we were, former guerrilla fighters and defenders of the oppres-
> sed, in the lap of luxury, but also in a sort of fortress, with a superflu-
> ous escort of guards everywhere.[4]

His colleagues did not share his concerns. Thereafter, like Tito, they
began distancing themselves from him.

Matters came to a head over a further series of articles Djilas
wrote for *Borba* that autumn. He not only continued his criticism of
the party bureaucracy but made such comments as: "The greatest
crimes of horror in history, from the fires of the inquisition to
Hitler's concentration camps and Stalin's labour camps, occurred
ultimately through the absence of free thought."[5]

He called for a multi-party system in which voters could elect candidates they really wanted, not "people imposed from above". What
was needed was "more democracy, more free discussion, more free
elections to social, state and economic organs, more strict adherence
to the law". Only in this way could be countered "those outmoded
and reactionary forces which cling to the notion that they represent
the whole of social reality, that they are the only legal representatives
of society". The various forms of "favouritism and privilege" were
listed by which those without proper qualifications were granted
jobs, pensions, special medical treatment, superior accommodation
and other perks, all as a result of the "protection" they enjoyed in
high places. "Waste, profligacy and arbitrariness are everywhere rampant. Billions are thus dissipated – and all that in a poor, underdevel-
oped country." These were devastating comments for a communist
leader to utter in such a claustrophobic community as Yugoslavia still
was in 1953!

Midway through the publication of the articles the usual one-
party election to the National Assembly was held on 22 November.
Djilas received 98.8 per cent of the votes cast in his constituency, a
bigger percentage even than Tito. Also he was unanimously elected
President of the Assembly.

Allegedly pressed by his colleagues, who saw their own futures
threatened, Tito called a special meeting of the Party's Central Committee in Belgrade on 16 January 1954. They were to be given the
opportunity to air their grievances against Djilas and for him to
answer them. (Meanwhile *Borba* announced on 10 January the sus-
pension of Djilas's articles and its rejection of his views.) The proceedings were broadcast live and foreign pressmen allowed to attend.
Djilas was accused by Tito of "advocating democracy at any price"

and by Kardelj of "revisionism", the ultimate communist sin. Mosa Pijade reminded him that he owned "a villa and two cars and so forth ... far more than those whom he has described as a repulsive caste". The others piled in. Only Djilas's former wife Mitra Mitrovic and his friend Vladimir Dedijer spoke on his behalf.

Ljubo Sirc and his fellow prisoners listened to the proceedings avidly. Sirc recalled later:

> It was sad to hear Djilas's former friends and comrades attacking him, one after another, for having taken the slogans about equality and legality seriously. Djilas at first appeared to resist, then caved in. Many were shocked by his behaviour, but they probably did not realise what it meant to stand alone, confronted by a body of former friends criticising you in the name of ideas you had ardently believed in yourself not so long ago.

Djilas found the ordeal "much more frightening and painful than anything I had sensed or could foresee".[6]

That night Djilas decided to recant his criticisms, and did so the next day. He and his second wife Stefanija had evidently considered joint suicide. He abjectly admitted to ideological errors and promised to pursue in future only the dictates of the Party. He even voted against himself – to the end the disciplined, die-hard communist! But his colleagues were unwilling to forgive him readily and stripped him of his governmental and Party positions. They hinted they were prepared to expel him from the party if he did not mend his ways. Six weeks later he turned in his party membership card, saying he no longer considered himself a communist.

Many of Djilas's friends in the West wrote to Tito pleading his case, and some also that of Dedijer who was being threatened with punishment too. They were assured no action would be taken against them, but Djilas and Dedijer needed to re-apply for their state pensions and these were discontinued six months later when they spoke to foreign journalists. Thereafter they had to live off the fees and royalties from articles and books they managed to publish outside Yugoslavia. Djilas's pension was reinstated only in 1967. Members of their families suffered too. Some lost their jobs; others were harassed. Visitors to Djilas were intimidated. His flat was bugged and his movements monitored. Even the street named after him was re-labelled! After Djilas's fall, Tito re-introduced that Stalinist mainstay, "voluntary" mass physical labour for youth. Djilas had largely been responsible for ending it in Yugoslavia. Tito blamed its earlier abolition on "that traitor Djilas".[7] Four years later, in 1958, Tito was to speak publicly of "the revisionist and anarchic ravings of that lunatic [Djilas] ...traitor and renegade, who spat at the finest achievements of the revolution".

The political commentator Richard West, who spent much time in Yugoslavia during the 1950s and 1960s, writes:

> The young communists, such as the students I knew in Belgrade and Sarajevo, were thunderstruck by the fall of their hero, but their response was disillusion rather than rage. To them, Djilas had been the incarnation of pride in the revolution and hope of building social-ism. After the Djilas affair, they started to lose their ideals. From that time on, I cannot remember meeting a Communist true believer. Most of my friends in the 1950s and 1960s were Party members, but only so as to hold their jobs as doctors, lawyers, journalists, teachers or policemen. In private, none was a Marxist or even left wing.[8]

More than 72,000 had been expelled from the Party in 1953. A fur-ther 30,000 had resigned. During the next two years nearly 300,000 were ousted. The most heavily purged were the peasants. Worryingly for Tito, the Party ceased to interest the young.

The Soviets relaxed their economic pressure and sought to renew trade agreements with Yugoslavia, as did the Soviet satellites. Border crossings were reopened and hostile propaganda ended. Khrushchev was helped by the general lowering of political and military tension between East and West after Stalin's death. Tito realised Russia's courtship could strengthen his bargaining power with the West. The Soviets thought the West might be weakened if Yugoslavia could be enticed back into their camp. The stage was set for Tito to play East and West off against each other.

Most, including Djilas himself, were convinced he had been sacri-ficed as a sop to the Soviets. They had openly welcomed his sacking. Even so, Tito continued to cultivate his contacts in the West. In April 1954 he visited Turkey and in July Greece. That August he signed a pact of mutual defence with Greece and Turkey, both NATO members, which in effect brought him under the NATO defence umbrella. The following year the Greek king and queen paid a state visit to Yugoslavia, while he visited Ethiopia, India and Burma. In India he struck up a close friendship with Pandit Nehru. This led in 1956 to the founding of the "non-aligned movement" with Colonel Nasser, whom Tito met on his way home. Nasser had just ousted the Egyptian king, Farouk, and was pursuing a strong anti-colonialist, anti-British line.

Although Nasser had suppressed the communist party in Egypt, Tito felt a strong affinity with him that boded ill for the West. It was Tito who persuaded Khrushchev to fund Nasser's High Dam when the United States pulled out. The Americans had hoped to bring Nasser to heel. The reverse happened. With Soviet money and military aid, Nasser was able to cock a snook at the West – to the delight of the Arab world, whose leader he aspired to become. Tito had earlier recommended that Moscow supply Nasser with arms, vouching in May 1955 for his socialist credentials. In *Khrushchev Remembers*, the Soviet leader observes how Tito assured him "Nasser was a young man without much political experience", but "if we gave Nasser the benefit of the doubt, we might later be able to exert a beneficial influence on him, both for the sake of the Communist movement and for the sake of the Egyptian people." Khrushchev had "thought at the time that Tito had put this idea [funding the Aswan Dam] in the Egyptians' heads": whenever they met, Tito "always defended Nasser vigorously and praised him to the skies".

Tito had clearly hoped Djilas would go quietly. Instead he continued to speak out, especially to western newsmen. On 25 December 1954 *The New York Times* ran an interview in which he urged the introduction of a multi-party system in Yugoslavia. This was heresy as far as Tito and his hardline colleagues were concerned. The following month Djilas and Dedijer, who had stood loyally by him, were charged with engaging in hostile activities against the state by talking to western journalists. Both were found guilty. Djilas was sentenced to eighteen months in prison and Dedijer to six months, though the sentences were suspended. One of Dedijer's sons committed suicide after being taunted at school about his father's dissent. Another was killed while mountaineering. Dedijer himself was in and out of hospital for a time before seeking an academic career overseas.

Meanwhile the reconciliation with the Soviet Union went on apace. Khrushchev invited himself to Belgrade in May 1955, with some of the other Soviet leaders, but not Molotov. He was said to be heavily engaged in establishing the Warsaw Pact, the Soviet riposte to NATO. It was later revealed he refused to go to Belgrade because he felt it was humiliating for the Russians: the Yugoslavs should have come to Moscow.

At the airport Khrushchev apologised for Stalin's expulsion of Tito in June 1948, blaming it on Lavrenty Beria, the former head of the KGB, who had been executed shortly after Stalin's death. The apology was well received, though Tito and his colleagues did not believe Beria bore any blame. Khrushchev confided later that the Yugoslavs initially "irritated" him with their "sarcastic remarks" and scornful smiles.[9] He was "somewhat disappointed by the cool reception at the airport", and when they toured the country their "reception in cities and towns was restrained". He claimed the lack of enthusiasm had been orchestrated. No doubt it had![10]

Nevertheless, Tito was as eager as Khrushchev to make up differences. Their signatures to the so-called Belgrade Declaration following the 1955 visit were a start. The Soviets recognised Yugoslavia's right to seek its own road to socialism and agreed to show "respect for the sovereignty, independence, integrity, and equality of states in their relations with each other". As a sop to the Soviets, Tito agreed to Communist China's joining the United Nations. Khrushchev denounced Stalin in a sensational speech to the Twentieth Congress of the Soviet Communist Party in February 1956. He revealed the terrible extent of the Purges and reviled Stalin's "cult of the personality". Khrushchev referred also to Stalin's "shameful role" in the dispute with Yugoslavia and how he had magnified his differences with Tito "in a monstrous manner".[11] Within days Tito received a copy of the speech. The Yugoslavs and Soviets had been exchanging military delegations since the previous summer.

The Cominform was dissolved in April 1956. Stalin's closest supporters amongst Soviet bloc leaders were weeded out. Those who had backed Tito were rehabilitated, in some cases posthumously. In May 1956 Molotov, associated closely with Yugoslavia's expulsion from the Cominform, having co-signed Stalin's derogatory letters to Tito, was sacked as foreign minister. All photographs of Stalin disappeared from official buildings in the Soviet Union. Stalingrad was renamed Volgograd. Tito obtained $85,000,000 in compensation from Hungary for breaches of contracts made before June 1948.

Tito paid a three-week state visit to Moscow in June 1956. The Russians bent over backwards to please him, with banquets and paeans of praise. The Yugoslav ambassador commented in his diary how "all the Soviet leaders seemed to be competing among themselves to see who could condemn Stalin's policy against Yugoslavia in the sharpest terms".[12] Visits to Leningrad, Kiev and the Crimea were laid on too. Tito declared:

> I feel at home in the Soviet Union because we are part of the same family: the family of Socialism ... in time of war as in time of peace. Yugoslavia marches shoulder-to-shoulder with the Soviet people towards the same goal – the victory of socialism.[13]

Whereas the Belgrade Declaration had regularised relations between the two states, the Moscow Declaration of 20 June 1956 restored ties between the Soviet and Yugoslav communist parties on the basis of "complete voluntariness and equality". Increased trade between the two countries was promised and large loans proffered by the Soviets. Before returning home, Tito visited Romania. He was rapturously received and addressed a large public meeting in Bucharest. Apparently some of Khrushchev's colleagues were disconcerted at the warm reception Tito got from ordinary Russians.

Many in the West were narked, particularly when his friend Nasser nationalised the Anglo-French-owned Suez Canal in July 1956 and Tito supported him. That summer Khrushchev had problems of his own. Anti-Russian riots in Poland led to Wladislav Gomulka taking over there. Gomulka had been imprisoned in 1949 as an alleged Tito sympathiser but released in 1955 after Stalin's death. Marshal Rokossovsky, the Polish-born Red Army officer in charge of the Polish army, was forced to resign. This did not stop Khrushchev visiting Tito in September and Tito returning the courtesy in the Crimea later the same month. Both meetings were linked with events in Poland.

There was even worse trouble in Hungary: anti-Soviet demonstrators toppled statues of Stalin and demolished other symbols of the Communist Party. The hardline Stalinist leadership at last gave way to a more moderate one. It was still not liberal enough for the protesters. They got their way and the Soviets panicked, sending in tanks. It was the same day that Britain and France invaded Egypt following Nasser's nationalisation of the Suez Canal. British and French paratroopers dropping over Port Said got much more publicity than Soviet tanks battering Hungarian patriots in Budapest. The Americans seemed far more annoyed about the former. By the time the United States had forced the British and French to desist, the Russians had eradicated all opposition in Hungary.

Tito supported the Egyptians but not the Hungarians. Yugoslavia's reconciliation with the Soviet Union was more important to him than helping Hungarian dissidents. He realised that any threat to his hold on power was more likely to come from the East than the West. This is why he was also to endorse in 1968 the Soviet line over Czechoslovakia. Besides, the scenes of communist leaders hanging from lampposts in Budapest were a little too close for comfort. At the height of the Hungarian crisis, when Imre Nagy, the liberal Hungarian leader, announced Hungary's withdrawal from the Warsaw Pact, Khrushchev and Georgi Malenkov flew at night in atrocious weather to meet Tito at his palace on the island of Brioni. They landed in a storm, the plane having for a time lost contact with ground control.

Khrushchev explains: "Tito was on the island because he was ill and his physicians had prescribed saltwater baths for him."[14] They got Tito's backing for the Red Army's intervention. Like Khrushchev, Tito feared a full-blooded counter-revolution in Hungary that could end communism in Eastern Europe and eventually in the Soviet Union. He had worried that Djilas's criticisms might lead to a counter-revolution in Yugoslavia that would sweep him from power. He gave his blessing to the eradication of Nagy, whom some Hungarians likened to Tito.

Khrushchev was to recall how "pleasantly surprised" he and Malenkov were that Tito

> said we were absolutely right and that we should send our soldiers into action as quickly as possible ... We had been ready for resistance, but instead we received his whole-hearted support. I would even say he went further than we did in urging a speedy and decisive resolution of the problem.[15]

In his later memoirs Khrushchev quotes Tito as saying: "You must do it. But do it yourself. Don't involve any other socialist countries."[16] Evidently Tito had kissed Khrushchev on arrival in the Russian manner, which previously he had shunned. He did not approve of men kissing men. According to Khrushchev, "We said farewell like old friends and kissed each other on both cheeks. He wished us a good journey and success in what we had to do."[17]

The Soviet leaders returned to Moscow and ordered the tanks into Budapest. It took just twenty-four hours to put down the rebellion. Nagy and forty-one of his colleagues were given sanctuary in the Yugoslav embassy on 4 November. Russian tanks surrounded it, firing into the building and killing a Yugoslav diplomat. The surrender of the refugees was demanded. On 22 November they were handed over to the new Hungarian government, put in power by the Russians. The Yugoslavs were assured, so they said, that no charges would be brought against the Hungarians, but the Russians were to deny that any assurances had been given or asked for. The Hungarians were promptly kidnapped and imprisoned in Romania. In June 1958 Nagy and three of his colleagues were executed.

*

Russia's brutal suppression of the Hungarian uprising led to mass resignations from communist parties round the world. In a speech on 11 November 1956 to party activists in Pula, Tito was unrepentant: "if it meant saving socialism in Hungary then ... the Soviet intervention was necessary".[18] He hinted to counter-revolutionaries in Yugoslavia that they could expect similar treatment: "We must not permit various individuals, various elements to blabber just anything. People from underneath, the masses, must silence them and prevent them from sowing dissension." This implicit threat led to a further rift between Tito and Djilas.

Eight days after Tito's Pula speech the American weekly *New Leader* carried an article by Djilas. Describing the Hungarian uprising as "a new chapter ... in the history of humanity", he criticised the Yugoslav government for being unable "to depart from its narrow ideological and bureaucratic class interests" and for betraying "those principles of equality and non-interference in internal affairs on which all its successes in the struggle with Moscow had been based".[19] He also gave a statement to *Agence France Presse* attacking Yugoslavia's abstention in the United Nations Security Council vote condemning the Soviet intervention in Hungary. The Yugoslavs had earlier opposed a resolution in the UN General Assembly condemning it.

Djilas was arrested and charged with violating the conditions of his suspended prison sentence. It was claimed he had promised no further "hostile propaganda" against Yugoslavia. He was tried in secret on 27 November 1956 and sentenced to three years' imprisonment, which was not suspended. The prison chosen for his incarceration was the same one in which the royalist government had detained him in the 1930s! More than half the time he was in solitary confinement. Thereafter he was allowed monthly visits from his family, but these were sometimes cut short, with no reason given. When they met, he was not allowed to embrace his wife and son.

In August 1957 Djilas's book *The New Class* was published in London and New York. It was a critique of communist ruling cliques who had appropriated privileges and wealth stripped from the bourgeoisie. He lambasted party bureaucracies which were richly rewarded so that they had a vested interest in preserving the regime: "at the core of the party are the all-powerful exploiters and masters". Djilas argued that, instead of creating a classless society, communists had added a new class, top state officials and party *apparatchiks* who held all economic and legal power. They owned all the property of the state and took to themselves its benefits and rewards.

This new class was

> more highly organized and more highly class-conscious than any class in recorded history ... no other class in history has been as cohesive and single-minded in defending itself and in controlling that which it holds – collective and monopolistic ownership and totalitarian authority.

To him

> the so-called "dictatorship of the proletariat" ... inevitably evolves into the dictatorship of the leaders ... extravagance and love of power are inevitable, and so is corruption ... a special type of corruption caused by the fact that the government is in the hands of a single political group and is the source of all privileges.

He warned that "the stifling of every divergent thought, the exclusive monopoly over thinking for the purpose of defending their personal interests, will nail the Communists to a cross of shame in history."

Djilas was critical of the Soviet bloc set-up: "the Communist East European countries did not become satellites of the U.S.S.R. because they benefited from it, but because they were too weak to prevent it." The Soviet leadership abhorred the book, possession of which was said to bring an automatic jail sentence of at least three years, and sometimes exile to Siberia. The Ukrainian dissident Danylo Shumuk received a fifteen-year sentence in 1972 for circulating it. Already in prison, Djilas was charged with attempting "to compromise socialism as an idea and the international workers' movement". Tried again in secret, he was sentenced to a further six years' imprisonment.

Tito was growing ever closer to the Soviet Union. It was thought no coincidence that, just a few weeks before Djilas's extended sentence was passed, Tito had again met Khrushchev, this time in Romania, to iron out recent differences. No doubt Djilas was one of those differences. Khrushchev says Tito had wanted the meeting kept secret, suggesting it take place on a boat on the Danube near the Romanian border. But news leaked out and the venue was switched to Bucharest. To the great annoyance of the West, Tito chose now to recognise the hardline East German regime of the obdurate old Stalinist Walter Ulbricht. West Germany severed diplomatic relations with Yugoslavia.

Top Yugoslav and Soviet generals, including the wartime commander Marshal Zhukov, held military discussions in Moscow and

Belgrade during 1957. Tito's colleagues Kardelj and Rankovic spent their annual holidays in southern Russia, meeting their Soviet opposite numbers as well as Khrushchev himself. Clearly the Soviets were keen to improve relations with the Yugoslavs.

The Yugoslavs made even greater efforts to improve relations with the Soviets. On the occasion of the fortieth anniversary of the Russian Revolution they signed Khrushchev's "peace manifesto", blaming the United States for the cold war. In 1958 Tito went out of his way to justify the creation of the Warsaw Pact three years earlier, declaring it "a natural defensive reaction" to NATO and West German rearmament.

Tito attended the annual meeting of the General Assembly of the United Nations in September 1960, his first visit to the United States. It followed the abortive May 1960 summit in Paris at which Khrushchev had walked out because of the U-2 spying flight over the Soviet Union. It too was stormy, with Khrushchev banging his shoes on the desk in front of him to interrupt the speeches he disliked. Fidel Castro of Cuba also attended. His overthrow in January 1959 of the pro-American dictator Battista had alarmed the USA since it brought a Communist regime within ninety miles of its shores.

Nevertheless the West, in particular the United States, continued its massive economic aid, without which Yugoslavia would long since have foundered. Tito had the good fortune to have George Kennan as the American ambassador to Belgrade between 1961 and 1963. He was perhaps the USA's leading expert on communism, and its most distinguished post-war diplomat. Kennan became Tito's most enthusiastic apologist at a time when a strong and noisy anti-Tito lobby was emerging in the United States, promoted by the half a million Serbs and Croats who had fled there after the war. Kennan thought Tito worth backing as long as Yugoslavia remained outside the Warsaw Pact: the Yugoslav army provided "a highly useful barrier between the southern European NATO forces and the forces of the Soviet bloc". But Kennan was realistic enough to recognise that the Soviet-dominated communist movement remained for Tito, "through all vicissitudes, his proper family; and it was *its* opinion of him, not ours, that really counted".[20]

Tito's friendship with the Egyptian dictator, Abdel Nasser, and the Indian Premier, Pandit Nehru, blossomed into the Non-Aligned Movement. Nehru is said to have coined the name. It was an informal association of mainly African and Asian nations belonging to neither NATO nor the Warsaw Pact: largely so-called Third World or developing countries. Many were former British, French, Dutch, Belgian or American colonies. By associating with developing countries, Tito could play down his dependence on the western world. John Lewis Gaddis, in *We Now Know: Rethinking Cold War History*, entertains the interesting theory that, unlike Mao Tse-Tung and Ho Chi Minh, who were ideologues and bandwagoners, Tito, Nasser and Nehru

> were balancers: the ideologies they proclaimed only occasionally dictated their actions; non-alignment allowed them to tilt this way or that, thereby playing both sides in the Cold War off against one another.

Although the three of them founded the movement, Tito was recognised as its leader. He hosted in Belgrade its first get-together in September 1961. Delegates from twenty-five countries attended. By its next conference in 1964, in Cairo, the number had grown to forty-seven, all African or Asian except for Cuba and Yugoslavia. The movement lent credibility to these minor countries. Many of them were authoritarian, one-party dictatorships like Yugoslavia, ruled by some of the most vicious tyrants of the post-war world: Idi Amin in Uganda, Sukarno in Indonesia, Bokassa in the Central African Republic. Tito depicted them as "the conscience of mankind"! Yasser Arafat of the Palestine Liberation Organisation (PLO) used to attend Non-Aligned conferences in battledress, flourishing a gun – a fitting symbol of a movement financed by a series of lucrative arms deals between particularly nasty people. Tito became a role model for these new dictators.

Most had gained power by promising their followers living standards as high as those of their former colonial masters. When the expectations were not met, Tito provided the anti-capitalist rhetoric to blame it all on multi-national corporations and the like. Tito's ideologue, Edvard Kardelj, considered the movement's *raison d'être* was to rupture the capitalist world. Others saw its purpose as encouraging poor countries to gang up against rich ones. Either way it allowed Tito to make speeches condemning the division of the world into antagonistic blocs. It put him on the world stage: the third world stage, the feeblest one, but the most populous and the noisiest. Tito relished the attention it brought him, particularly at the United Nations. It provided a further opportunity to play off East against West.

His leadership of the movement gave Tito an influence out of all proportion to the size and wealth of his country. A thousand or so journalists and broadcasters were regularly attracted to the movement's conferences. For a small, relatively backward nation like Yugoslavia, Tito was able to carve out an enhanced international presence. But this hardly helped solve Yugoslavia's problems: it is not easy to see what material benefits his countrymen gained. Some claimed it opened markets for Yugoslav exports such as engineering goods, ships and armaments. Certainly considerable amounts of Yugoslav-made weapons were sold to Non-Aligned countries and dissident groups like the Algerian rebels, the FLN who fought the French between 1954 and 1962. Tito gave the FLN leaders an international platform. Belgrade became a base for their propagandising. Badly wounded FLN soldiers were treated in Yugoslav hospitals and Tito provided doctors to train FLN medics and therapists. After independence, the FLN leader Ben Bella became a strong supporter of the Non-Aligned Movement, as did his successor Houari Boumedienne. The 1973 conference was held in Algiers.

Some Yugoslavs complained of the expense of maintaining legations and embassies in so many mini-states of Africa and Asia. By 1968 Yugoslavia had 65 embassies and 99 diplomatic and consular missions worldwide, an enormous burden. Some sixty foreign ambassadors were permanently accredited in Belgrade, half of them from Africa and Asia.

The movement gave Tito the opportunity to travel, which he clearly enjoyed. During the early 1960s he used his ocean-going yacht, accompanied by bustling naval and air escorts. A considerable retinue was carried on board, or met him at various destinations en route. He had a chance to wear his ever more resplendent uniforms and scarcely less flashy civilian attire. There were opportunities to bestow, and have bestowed, ever more dazzling decorations. Tito loved the elaborate protocol of it all. He is said to have made fifty-six foreign tours and to have visited every continent except Australia (he feared to set foot there because of its violent dissident Croat community). The Soviets revelled in Tito's growing influence in Asia and Africa, areas of acute interest to them. They showered him with honours when he visited Moscow in 1967, the fiftieth anniversary of the Revolution. Many Yugoslavs grumbled at his frequent absences and envied his luxurious travel, but some were delighted with the attention their previously neglected country was receiving.

Tito was perhaps the first of those flamboyant heads of state who became much better known than their countries, who indeed came to identify their countries. He was certainly the Non-Aligned Movement's most visible and active spokesman (unsurprisingly, it did not survive his death). It helped his reconciliation with the Soviets. They had welcomed the strongly anti-western tone adopted at the initial 1961 Belgrade Conference, and were relieved at its non-reaction to their resumption of nuclear testing and the erection of the Berlin Wall. Despite its title, it was from the outset not a neutral body. It was a thinly disguised anti-western, pro-Soviet lobby group. As such, it was a bane of the United States, particularly at the United Nations. The Security Council's five vetoing powers being spread between the Cold War protagonists, it was rendered virtually inactive. Hence attention was focused on the General Assembly. Because of the increased membership, largely due to decolonisation, it had a built-in anti-western majority after 1960. The Assembly became an anti-western talking shop dominated by spokesmen of the Non-Aligned Movement. Their antics were to discredit the movement in the eyes of many in the world.

That the movement annoyed the United States much more than the Soviet Union pleased Moscow and won Tito brownie points there. The communiqué at the end of the first non-aligned conference held in New Delhi in 1982 (after Tito's death) was attended by delegates from 104 countries and carried 23 separate denunciations of the United States, but none of the Soviet Union. Yet the Soviets had recently invaded Afghanistan, a member of the Non-Aligned Movement!

Tito was also close to the Campaign for Nuclear Disarmament and other "world peace movements". Belgrade became a venue for many a conference on "peaceful coexistence", "general and complete disarmament" or "banning all nuclear weapons". When some at those gatherings protested against the resumption of Soviet nuclear tests in 1961, in breach of the moratorium on such testing agreed at Geneva in 1958, Tito successfully silenced them, no doubt to Moscow's relief.

Tito was persuaded to release Djilas in January 1961, halfway through his sentence. Djilas allegedly promised to refrain from any further hostile writing and not to permit a reprint of *The New Class*. His release improved Tito's image in the West. But it was not long before Djilas was in trouble again. He wrote a book critical of Stalin based on his experiences of him during his visits to Moscow in 1944,

1945 and 1948. As no Yugoslav publisher would touch *Conversations with Stalin*, he sought an outlet in the United States. The book was published there in May 1962, having been serialised in some American newspapers beforehand. Djilas did not simply criticise Stalin, he denounced him as "the greatest criminal in history – and, let us hope, for all time to come ... history does not know a despot as brutal and as cynical as Stalin." He "was one of those rare and terrible dogmatists capable of destroying nine-tenths of the human race to 'make happy' the remaining tenth." He attacked Stalin's successors as being equally responsible for Stalinism. One of them, Andrei Gromyko, now Khrushchev's Foreign Minister, was about to visit Tito.

To placate the Soviets, Djilas was re-arrested on 7 April 1962 and charged with betraying state secrets. He was tried on 14 May and sentenced to five years' imprisonment to run in addition to the three years or so remaining from his previous sentences. There was an immediate outcry in the West. *The New York Times* denounced the trial as a blatant relapse into Stalinism. Tito ignored the clamour: he was more concerned about relations with Moscow. Tanks bought from the Soviets, the first since 1948, figured in Yugoslavia's May Day parade that year. The Soviet head of state visited him in September. Three months later, Tito was rewarded with a state visit to Moscow, where he was granted the rare privilege of addressing the Supreme Soviet. He maintained that their two countries had identical aims in foreign and domestic policies and fulsomely praised Khrushchev for his handling of the Cuban Missile Crisis that autumn. Khrushchev had saved the world from nuclear disaster! Khrushchev visited Yugoslavia the following summer.

When Tito went to the United States in October 1963, such were the hostile demonstrations against him that he and his entourage needed to be lodged outside Washington, in Colonial Williamsburg. They were helicoptered in to meet President Kennedy. Their reception in New York was worse, largely because the police were more tolerant of the demonstrators. Some entered the hotel where the Yugoslavs were staying. He next embarked on a series of meetings with eastern European communist leaders, including the hardliners Novotny of Czechoslovakia and Ulbricht of East Germany and culminating in a visit to Leningrad in June 1964 to meet Khrushchev. Having fallen out with the Peking leadership, Khrushchev was seeking support against the Chinese.

This anti-Mao crusade was not to his Kremlin colleagues' liking, nor had they admired as much as Tito Khrushchev's handling of the

Cuban Missile Crisis. He was replaced that autumn by Leonid Brezhnev. Abroad at the time and clearly surprised, Tito hastily returned to assure Brezhnev of his wish to "continue constructively to promote close co-operation with the Soviet Union and with other socialist countries". He visited Brezhnev in June 1965. The communiqué at the end of their talks "noted with satisfaction that contacts between [their two countries had] become broader and stronger in recent years".[21] Tito had declared publicly that "if difficult times were to come", Yugoslavia would stand firmly with the Soviet people. A meeting a year later of Yugoslav and Soviet foreign ministers "reaffirmed the closeness or identity of the two countries' views on the chief problems of the present international situation".[22] On the Vietnam conflict and other world issues, Tito merely repeated Russian criticisms of the West. When seventeen non-aligned countries promoted without success a solution to the Vietnam War on neutralist lines, he encouraged them to blame their failure on the United States. He was rewarded by Brezhnev's visit to Belgrade in September 1966.

Djilas was not alone in being harassed for what he wrote. Mihajlo Mihajlov, a Russian Tsarist refugee who occasionally lectured in philosophy, wrote an article in a Belgrade literary magazine in January 1965 criticising Lenin. He accused him in particular of being responsible for the system of forced labour camps in the Soviet Union. Moscow protested. He was arrested and charged with disseminating hostile propaganda and contempt for a foreign state. Without waiting for the court's verdict, Tito branded him a "reactionary". His university sacked him. His sentence of nine months' imprisonment was suspended but the magazine was banned. In July 1966 Mihajlov announced the publication of a new intellectual magazine intended to appeal to Slovene Catholics, Croat nationalists and Serb liberals, and to lead to the establishment of a new political party. He was re-arrested, convicted of "inciting nationalism" and sentenced to a year's imprisonment that was not suspended. Later, for writing in *The New York Times* and in the American magazine *The New Leader*, he was charged with disseminating "hostile propaganda" and sentenced to a further seven years, less time already served.

Earlier, in 1958, two elderly former politicians and two equally long-toothed academics had been charged in Belgrade with plotting to overthrow the regime. They were given prison sentences ranging from four to eight years. Apparently they met from time to time to exchange opinions on the government. One of them had written a book critical of Tito which he had attempted, without success, to get published in the West. Another group of academics was convicted in Ljubljana in 1964 for criticising the regime in a magazine called *Perspektiva*. Later, some law lecturers at Belgrade University were sacked for encouraging students to criticise the regime, while during the 1969 elections a Serbian Orthodox priest standing for a rural constituency caused a minor sensation by predicting the imminent end of communist rule. He was prevented from further campaigning and sentenced to twenty days' imprisonment before polling day. In April 1970 a Youth League journal in Zagreb was banned for reproducing a film poster with a caption said to be insulting to Tito. When private editions of books and pamphlets began appearing, the authorities sought to deter them by intimidating the printers. In June 1970 Tito reminded an audience of academics that Marxism assigned to learning the role of changing the world rather than explaining it!

The Belgrade students' union paper *Student* was frequently banned during the 1968 troubles. Thereafter its reputation as an opposition voice grew and its circulation widened. The authorities tried to curb its influence by pressuring the university administrators to sack its editors. When that did not work, they arrested one of its prime movers on a trumped-up charge, and had him sent to prison in October 1970. This prompted student demonstrations in Belgrade and elsewhere in the country. In 1978 the editor of a mimeographed literary journal entitled *The Clock*, boasting no more than five hundred copies, to which Djilas had contributed, was imprisoned for a month.

CHAPTER FOURTEEN

Economic Mayhem

"for those who believe in worker-control,
we have shown how *not* to do it"

WITHOUT AID FROM the West after 1948, particularly low-interest loans from the World Bank and International Monetary Fund (IMF), Yugoslavia would have been bankrupt within months. Instead, in a relatively short time Yugoslavs were enjoying a far higher standard of living than anyone else in the communist bloc. Industrial production increased and more and more people moved from the villages into towns. This had a disadvantage: the country ceased to be self-sufficient in food production and became a major importer of it. The Soviet-style command economy had been denounced as "state capitalism", considered by many (including Djilas) to be worse than the private kind. It became bureaucratised and corrupted, and was in no way responsible to the people. However in June 1950 Yugoslavia chose the route of so-called "socialist self-management".

"The factories to the workers" became the new slogan. They were to be run not centrally by bureaucrats, but locally by the workers themselves. Central planning was dismantled and market incentives introduced. "Market socialism" it was termed. Nationalised industries were gradually transferred to the control of workers' councils elected annually by employees. These councils chose the management. Some enterprises were allowed to operate in the market, and occasionally to engage in foreign trade. But it was never a totally free market, even for goods and services; and there was a considerable delay in establishing a market for labour and capital. It was claimed to be a halfway point between communism and capitalism.

Djilas and Kardelj were its principal proponents. It was they who initially convinced Tito. For Djilas, "the concept of self-management was born from the struggle against Stalinist tyranny and from visions of a true democratic socialism".[1] Later he would claim: "we believed

that at last we had discovered the definitive road leading to the with-
ering away of the state and therefore to a classless society".[2] Tito was
to remain sceptical of such an anti-Stalinist approach to the economy and was to maintain it had been forced on them by circumstances. But in the confusion after 1948, especially the disintegration
of the Five-Year Plan, he saw the propaganda value of appearing to
hand over management of the means of production to the workers –
though not, of course, its control or ownership. It enabled him to
sound more communist than the Soviets and more democratic than
the West.

In time self-management came to embrace almost every institution in the land, including health, welfare, education and cultural
activities, though never the military. It was enshrined in a new
Constitutional Law in January 1953. This also introduced the office
of President of the Republic. He was also head of the state, the government and the army. Inevitably Tito was "elected". The individual
republics lost the rights of secession and sovereignty granted in the
1946 Constitution. Sovereignty now rested with the people. A new
federal Chamber of Producers was established to represent workers'
councils, though it was all merely symbolic. Khrushchev, intrigued by
"self-management", thought

> all their talk about participation in ownership seemed like so much
> window dressing. No matter what they said, it still looked to me as
> though the government prescribed their output plan and tightly con-
> trolled how it was put into effect.

He claimed that, when visiting Yugoslavia, he expressed these
doubts: the "Yugoslav comrades ... seemed to be half in agreement
with me".[3]

The origin of "self-management", for Djilas, lay in syndicalism,
though Kardelj maintained it sprang from the wartime experiences
of the Partisans. It was to go through many phases. To some it
appeared a form of direct democracy. In practice it was merely
decentralised, undemocratic, patronage politics under a different
name. All appointments remained in the gift of Party officials. The
workers did not own their enterprises; these remained the property
of the state. The selection and supervision of the workers' councils
was operated through local "people's committees" that also raised
taxes and organised welfare services. The trade unions played a
prominent role in drawing up lists of candidates for election to the
committees, as did the Party bureaucrats.

Usually these committees insisted on near-equal wages, a dis-incentive to skilled workers or for workers to achieve skills. They tended to choose Party activists for managers. Many had barely primary education, let alone any business training. This was frustrating for those better educated but not close to the Party. The literacy level in the country then was only about 75 per cent. More importantly, these committees invariably ignored the compelling logic of matching supply to demand. They competed with each other to produce more and more goods and services not needed in an under-developed country like Yugoslavia while not producing enough of those goods and services that were sorely needed – which inevitably led to inflation.

Although certainly better than a Stalinist command economy, self-management had serious defects, which soon became apparent. The Belgrade wags were quick to dub it self-*mis*management! It created obstacles to the movement of capital, skilled labour, management and technology. Consequently the less developed regions continued to lag behind. It helped widen the wealth divide between the richer northern republics of Slovenia and Croatia, and the poorer southern ones of Serbia, Montenegro, Macedonia, and Bosnia-Herzegovina. From 1945 to 1965 the difference in income levels between Slovenia, the most developed region, and Kosovo, the least developed, doubled. The average *per capita* income in Slovenia in 1965 was six times that in Kosovo. Croatia's income per head was almost twice that of Montenegro or Macedonia.

According to Nora Beloff, self-management produced

> high inflation, black markets in currency and commodities, smuggling, speculation, almost ubiquitous corruption and massive moonlighting in working hours. "The world owed Yugoslavia a debt", said a thoughtful young Yugoslav, representing his country abroad, "for those who believe in worker-control, we have shown how *not* to do it".[4]

Because food prices were kept artificially low, peasants streamed out of the countryside into the cities, reducing the food supply and increasing urban unemployment. Belatedly, Kardelj decontrolled some prices, phased out a few food, energy, housing and transport subsidies, and devalued the currency. It did not alleviate the problem. The cost of living rose by 30 per cent between 1959 and 1962. Thereafter annual rates of inflation of 10 per cent became commonplace. Some prices were re-controlled and a wage freeze was introduced.

The liberalising of foreign trade was reversed. Unemployment still rose and unrest grew. In 1958 there occurred communist Yugoslavia's first serious strike, a three-day stoppage at the Trbovlje coal mines in Slovenia over pay. It was settled in the strikers' favour. The strikes increased. By the 1970s there were a thousand a year. Some became violent, requiring police and even army intervention. Absenteeism was high. Experts claimed it was reducing Yugoslavia's productivity by nearly 2 per cent.

Occasionally the stoppages led to street demonstrations and the destruction of social property. Tito blamed them on "excessive liberalisation". Others were bewildered as to why employees should in effect be striking against themselves. It showed the shallowness of "self-management". Tito censured the workers' councils for their lack of "socialist morality" in overpaying their employees, which he claimed had brought about the inflation! He would have preferred a return to central planning. But by 1965 the country was well on the road to becoming a market economy, albeit a rocky road.

Because workers could not buy and sell the assets of their enterprises, the system was open to conflicts of interest. This hampered efficiency. All business decisions were effectively taken by the government, whether in the guise of the Party or the people's committees. It led to what managerial pundits dub "organisational rigidity". Managers were party appointees and, unlike their employees, were hired for a fixed term, usually four years. They looked to pleasing the party bosses rather than their customers. Much of their time was spent attending party meetings, where they negotiated allocations of foreign exchange and sought permission to raise prices or to import necessary supplies. They were reluctant to take risks or to change anything. Most had come up through the party ranks, and were of low calibre and unequal to managerial tasks.

The introduction of self-management was a convenient way of weakening the power of Belgrade and opening the door to federalism. Authority was at first devolved mainly to the communes. With the resurgence of nationalism in the 1960s, federalism was established as part of the "Economic Reform". This led to yet more duplication of investment projects. Every republic and province wanted its own bank, iron-ore plant, steel mill or oil refinery. They all competed with each other for what was a relatively small internal market. Slovenia was allowed its own airline, which competed with Yugoslavia's national one. There was more trade with the outside world than between the republics and provinces. It was difficult to transfer bank accounts when moving between the republics. Bizarrely, "Serbian capital" could not be transferred to Croatia, and vice versa. The quality of products varied, and was usually poorer the further south you got. Sometimes 40 per cent of the output of the car factory at Kragujevac in Serbia did not pass muster. Tito complained in 1962 that the country's warehouses were full of poor quality goods that were unsaleable.

Examples of wasteful investment abounded. A steel mill at Niksic in Montenegro in 1953 had to wait eight years for a rail connection to the nearest port and more than ten years for a paved highway to anywhere. The raw materials for a refrigerator factory built at Cetinje in the interior of Montenegro had to come in by sea and be transported on unpaved roads over mountainous terrain that for much of the year was impassable. The finished products had to be trucked to the coast for shipment to a northern port on the Adriatic with a rail link to the rest of Yugoslavia. Apart from being costly, the quality of the refrigerators was poor, as were those from another factory in southern Macedonia. The construction of the two factories was clearly politically motivated. There was already a refrigerator factory in Slovenia, located on a railway line, whose products were of better quality. It could easily have been expanded to meet the whole country's needs.

A giant iron-ore processing plant at Kavadarci in southern Macedonia was founded in the 1960s despite the local ore being inferior. Financed with the help of foreign loans, its total overseas debt soon rose to $437,000,000. Supposed to provide an annual income of $160,000,000, it only ever made losses and was eventually scrapped after some of its directors were convicted of fraud. An aluminium smelting plant, begun building at Obrovac in Croatia in 1961 to utilise local bauxite and electricity, was still not completed by 1974, when electricity prices soared because of the oil crisis, meaning it would never be profitable. The local bauxite proved inadequate, so supplies had to be imported. It was closed in 1983. Another aluminium smelting plant at Zvornik in Bosnia-Herzegovina, boasted as the largest in Europe, never made a profit either.

Other loss-makers included the massive artificial fertiliser plant, INA-Petrokemija, and the Trepca lead and zinc plant in Kosovo, then the largest in Europe. Again the local ores proved sub-standard and supplies had to be imported. It never made a profit. A hydro-electric scheme at Mratinje in Montenegro went three times over budget. An aluminium smelting plant located nearby to take advantage of the hoped-for cheap electricity was almost immediately undermined by the collapse in world aluminium prices from 1972.

Many of these vast projects were begun on the whim of local party bosses, to inflate their egos or because others were initiating similar ventures. They were dubbed "political factories": they were not built for economic reasons. Business crime and corruption increased sharply during the late 1960s and early 1970s.

In April 1963 the Constitution was further amended. Tito's presidency was now in effect for life. Yugoslavia was designated a "Socialist" instead of a "People's" Federal Republic. Government was decentralised and job rotation introduced for all elective posts. The holding of state and party offices simultaneously was disallowed. But this rotation merely confused matters and led to greater inefficiency. It was ironical, if not comical, how the Yugoslav communists were so punctilious in punctuating every administrative change with a new constitution or an amendment to an existing one, when, as in all communist states, constitutional procedures did not count for much. It was party affairs that really mattered. Tito after all was a dictator. As long as he commanded the loyalty of his army he could do what he damn well liked! Many saw this constitution-writing as, at best, a game for party nerds; at worst it was a smokescreen to distract attention from the constant bickering within the party bureaucracy.

In 1963 Yugoslavs were allowed to travel freely to the West, unlike the rest of communist Europe, and non-Yugoslavs were permitted to enter the country. A massive migration of workers followed, to Belgium, Sweden, West Germany and Austria, in search of jobs. By the end of the decade one Yugoslav adult in six worked outside the country. The number grew to more than a million and they came to be known as Yugoslavia's "Seventh Republic". By the mid-1970s a period of employment abroad became almost a standard part of the Yugoslav way of life. Their remittances home, averaging $2 billion a year, were a substantial source of hard currency and soon became vital to Yugoslavia's balance of payments. Not all of their earnings were remitted, though. According to Zagreb University's Research Centre for Migrations, some $7 billion was held by Yugoslav workers in West German banks alone at the end of 1977.

Critical to the country's balance of payments was the revenue from the tourists now welcomed to the coastal resorts of Dalmatia and skiing centres in Slovenia – nearly 4 million a year by 1967, already providing more than $130,000,000 in hard currency. In time that revenue became crucial to the Yugoslav economy. Many were to argue that the tourist industry was the economy's saviour. But because 90 per cent of the spending was in Croatia and Slovenia it exacerbated the nationalities problem. The disparity in incomes between Croats and Slovenes and the rest of Yugoslavia increased over the years. The citizens of Zagreb and Ljubljana came to look down on the Kosovan and Bosnian peasants hanging around their railway stations, hoping for work. Needing to rely on remittances from their emigrant workers and the spending of western tourists to solve the country's hard currency problems was a political embarrassment to the leaders of the Yugoslav Communist Party. They tried to laugh it off with the slogan "Through tourism to socialism". Few were taken in by this. It became clear Yugoslavia was popular with western tourists simply because it was so cheap.

Many had hoped economic reform, in particular decentralisation, would reduce nationalism. It did not. For one thing the individual republics had to deposit a percentage of their foreign currency earnings in the state central bank in Belgrade. This was greatly resented in Zagreb and Ljubljana, whose citizens objected to subsidising their less entrepreneurial and, in their opinion, less hard-working Serbian, Bosnian, Montenegrin and Macedonian fellow countrymen. The different economic experiences of Slovenia and Croatia, who benefited from economic liberalisation and the introduction of tourism, and Serbia, Bosnia, Montenegro and Macedonia who did not, led to a resurgence in nationalist discord. Croats claimed they were providing 40 per cent of Yugoslavia's hard currency earnings. Slovenia, with 8.3 per cent of Yugoslavia's population, accounted for 16.5 per cent of the country's Gross National Product and more than 20 per cent of its foreign trade.

The visitors brought new ideas, and returning workers new expectations not always welcome to the regime. The Soviets had long resisted opening their borders, fearing tourism would introduce western influences, such as a demand for consumer products. To this the Yugoslav authorities now had to respond. The workers abroad experienced a freedom of political life unknown at home. Small-scale private employment was now permitted and even contacts with trading partners overseas. Foreign investors, too, were welcomed and allowed to export their profits.

Tito, however, grew ever more sceptical of self-management after Djilas's fall from grace. He blocked Kardelj's attempt in the early

1960s to liberalise trade further and introduce a free market economy. He preferred old-style Stalinist centralism. Kardelj was sidelined and Tito came to rely for advice on the remaining member of his previous kitchen cabinet, the hardline Aleksandar Rankovic. Head of the secret police, he was now also organisational secretary of the Party. In 1963 Rankovic became Vice-President, a post specially created for him. This was thought to signify his choice as Tito's heir-apparent. But three years later he was accused of corruption and of bugging the phones of many top leaders, including Tito. He was expelled from the Party and removed from his official positions, though not prosecuted. Thereafter he took a back seat, remaining loyally silent. He never undermined Tito, whom he outlived by three years.

Not everyone was convinced of Rankovic's guilt. Some suspected that Tito was paranoid about being ousted: Rankovic had become powerful within the Party bureaucracy. Others thought Tito was anxious to show the West that he had not stopped liberalising Yugoslavia. Rankovic was associated with the old-guard communists and had visited Moscow four months earlier. Brezhnev is said to have tried to intercede on his behalf during a visit to Yugoslavia in September 1966.

Tito feigned surprise at the extent of personal surveillance in the country and promised to reduce it. He set about purging the secret police and the state security services, which he now ran himself, almost as personal fiefs. The mechanism of surveillance had remained intact throughout the period of alleged "liberalisation". For a while Yugoslav newspapers were full of stories of kickbacks paid to police officials, organised cross-border smuggling, prison inmates building villas for state security bosses and stolen property being misappropriated.

Kardelj, who knew his phone was being tapped but presumed it was at the behest of Tito (or so he said to Tito after the event), now came back into favour. Djilas also benefited from Rankovic's downfall. He was released from prison on 31 December 1966, though he remained under police surveillance for the rest of his life. A condition of his release was that he would not take part in politics for at least five years. He abided by this but continued to write, though his books remained banned in Yugoslavia until long after Tito's death.

Surprisingly no action was taken against him when his *Wartime* memoirs were published in 1977 in New York and London. They divulged the controversial March 1943 negotiations between the

Partisans and the Germans. A truce had been agreed with the Germans while the Partisans fought Mihailovic's forces. Djilas also revealed that the parleying was intended to lead to the Partisans co-operating with the Germans in resisting an Allied landing in the Balkans. Tito continued to claim the negotiators had exceeded their instructions.

Many Yugoslavs wondered why Tito had not rid himself of Djilas, as he had of Andrija Hebrang, for instance. Apparently he told his cronies he preferred Djilas to suffer "political death". Ironically, while both are now physically dead, it is Tito who is politically dead too, whereas Djilas is in many ways still politically alive. Djilas will go down as having helped nail the coffin of international communism. He certainly punctured Tito's reputation and that of the Partisans.

Under Tito the economy, during the 1970s, reverted to state control. It was described, however, as "federalised socialist self-management" because it was organised not centrally but by the eight constituent republics and semi-autonomous political units. Competition yielded to compromise, which led to further duplication of industrial capacity and yet more inefficiency. Inflation and unemployment increased as each administrative unit strove after self-sufficiency.

The Yugoslav economy was too feeble to withstand the pressures when the world economy went into recession following the 1973 oil crisis. It declined as oil prices more than doubled: 40 per cent of its energy requirements were imported and a sizeable proportion was oil. Party bureaucrats took fright when they saw control of the economy slipping from their hands. Their counter was the 1976 Law on Associated Labour. Government intervention was increased and the power of the managers weakened by fragmenting their enterprises. They could no longer appoint or dismiss their staff and were unable to reward good work. The increase in regulation led to yet more inefficiency. Price controls were eventually re-introduced as the inflation rate climbed. By 1980 the annual rate was 30 per cent.

CHAPTER FIFTEEN

The Ethnic Powder Keg

"The claim that Yugoslav socialism
was resolving ethnic rivalries
was exposed as an illusion"
CHRISTOPHER ANDREW

ISRAEL ATTACKED EGYPT in June 1967. The Arab armies were routed in a pre-emptive strike in what is known as the Six-Day War. Tito urged Brezhnev to help his friend Nasser and offered Soviet planes refuelling facilities in Yugoslavia. Some aid reached Egypt in this way. Mohamed Heikal, Nasser's closest adviser, says Tito told Brezhnev: "As far as Egypt is concerned, I am no longer non-aligned."[1] Tito had met Nasser a dozen or so times in the run-up to the war, which Nasser had been planning for months. He had boasted to his Arab neighbours that this was their chance "to deal Israel a mortal blow of annihilation". The United Nations peace-keepers manning the border between Egypt and Israel had been expelled in mid-May. When Tito realised Nasser had been out-smarted, he flew secretly to Moscow to discuss with Brezhnev and other Soviet bloc leaders what should be done. Nothing came of this, apart from their breaking off diplomatic relations with Israel. But Tito was firmly back in the Soviet camp. He and the Warsaw Pact countries issued a joint communiqué blaming the Israeli victory on "a conspiracy of certain imperialist powers, the United States in the first place, against the Arab countries". He was rewarded with a state visit to Moscow that November and again had the honour of address-ing the Supreme Soviet.

Tito was drawn into the Czechoslovakia crisis known as "Prague Spring", the following year. Alexander Dubcek, who had taken over from the Stalinist hardliner Anton Novotny, sought to liberalise the country – to give communism, as he put it, "a human face". He intended a radical democratisation of political life that would include a free press, guarantees of personal liberty, honest electoral

processes, equal rights for all national groups, and the rehabilitation
of political victims. The Party would have a guiding rather than a
controlling role. Industrial decision-making would be decentralised,
and the country opened to world markets. Initially Dubcek received
much support in Yugoslavia, particularly among the young. *Borba*,
Belgrade's largest newspaper, gave a full and approving account of his
reform programme. But when, in March 1968, writers in Czechoslovakia began openly to criticise the Soviet Union and the communist system, Brezhnev reacted sharply. Tito was summoned to Moscow
to give advice. Apparently he urged caution.

By May the excitement had spread to Belgrade. Students demon-
strated against rising prices, bad housing and poor job prospects.
They called for greater political freedom. University buildings were
decorated with banners demanding "A Better and Freer University",
"Dismiss the Incompetent Politicians" and "Down with the Princes
of Socialism". Lecture halls were blocked and campuses occupied.
There were clashes with the police, leading to almost two hundred
injuries, including gunshot wounds. Tito was alarmed but managed to
end the sit-ins by promising to improve student grants and living
conditions. He warned them to guard against infiltration by "alien
elements". This did not stop the disquiet spreading to other Yugoslav
universities. It was the serious turn events in Czechoslovakia had
taken that had prompted Tito's intervention.

The leaders of the Warsaw Pact countries, apart from Nicolai
Ceausescu of Romania, issued Dubcek with an ultimatum. They
could not "consent to hostile forces compelling your country to leave
the Socialist path and threatening to tear Czechoslovakia away from
the Socialist commonwealth. This is no longer your concern alone."
He must defeat the "forces of counter-revolution".

Ceausescu had befriended Tito. They had met several times.
Although Romania's communism was more Stalinist than Yugoslavia's, Ceausescu took an independent line on foreign policy, which
intrigued Tito. The two countries co-operated in building military
planes, such as the YU-ROM fighter, for sale to Third World countries. General Ion Pacepa, one of Ceausescu's top aides until his
defection to the West in 1978, says they relied heavily for such production "on the illegal or semi-legal import of Western equipment
forbidden to Communist countries". Tito apparently boasted to
Ceausescu in Pacepa's presence:

> Both of us enjoy privileged positions because of our public attitude
> towards Moscow. It is at least ten times easier for both of us to get

our hands on Western military secrets than it is for the Soviets... We wouldn't be able to get anything from the West by riding on Moscow's coat-tails, and without Western money and technology there wouldn't be any Communist society in our countries... They call it "Tito's Triangle". I set up three basic guidelines: friendly smile toward the West, maximum take from it, and no contamination from capitalism.[2]

Pacepa revealed that by 1976 Tito had established training centres for Yassar Arafat's PLO within Yugoslavia and was aiding dissident groups in Italy, including the notorious Red Brigades:

Secret military and financial support for the Red Brigades was a significant part of the Yugoslav intelligence operations for undermining the political stability of Italy, Yugoslavia's NATO neighbour... Yugoslav involvement in the Red Brigades started in the mid-1960s.

The symbol of the Red Brigades, a five-pointed red star, was identical to the one in the Yugoslav flag, complemented by a machine gun![3]

A meeting between Dubcek and Brezhnev on 29 July 1968 at the Czechoslovak-Soviet border seemed to reduce the tension. Tito visited Prague on 9 August to urge caution. He had already been to Moscow to see Brezhnev. But eleven days later the Warsaw Pact countries, apart from Romania, invaded Czechoslovakia. Dubcek and his colleagues were imprisoned. Tito protested to the Soviets, though not as vehemently as Ceausescu did. He warned his fellow Yugoslavs their turn might be next. It did the trick, uniting the country round him and removing popular support for the rioting students. No one outside Yugoslavia seriously believed the Soviets had designs on Tito!

In November 1968 there were further student protests in Pristina, the chief city of Kosovo. These were mainly of a nationalist nature. They called for teaching to be in Albanian instead of Serbo-Croat, which was granted. Conceded, too, was permission to fly the black-eagled red flag of Albania. The Kosovans were given more autonomy within Serbia and promised increased investment. Unemployment and illiteracy were high among Kosovans, most of the best jobs were held by the Serb minority. Tito was anxious to keep the lid on Kosovan nationalism. A separate university was promised, as well as more official posts for Kosovans. Previously Pristina College had been merely a branch of the University of Belgrade. It did not stop further mass demonstrations and calls for union with Albania, which Belgrade tried to hush up.

In May that year the popular Serb writer Dobrica Cosic, a member of the Party's Central Committee, had caused a stir by criticising the anti-Serbian mood in Kosovo, about which he claimed the Belgrade authorities were doing nothing. He also denounced Tito's decision to make the Moslems a separate nation and to grant provincial autonomy to the Vojvodina. He was expelled from the Committee and resigned his Party membership, but he was not silenced. His rallying of support for his views increased the tension. After Tito's death, Cosic was briefly federal President.

Moscow's policy of reserving the right to intervene militarily to preserve a communist regime became known as "the Brezhnev doctrine":

> When internal and external forces that are hostile to socialism try to turn the development of some socialist country towards the restoration of a capitalist regime ... it becomes not only a problem of the people of the country concerned, but a common problem and concern of all socialist countries.

Tito never repudiated this, though it ran counter to his professed thesis of "separate roads to socialism". A few years later he told a visiting group of Czech officers:

> Formally we are not members of the Warsaw Pact, but if the cause of socialism, of Communism, of the working class, should be endangered, we know where we stand ... we hold our aims in common with the Soviet Union.[4]

Although relations between Tito and Brezhnev cooled a little after the crushing of Dubcek, they knew they needed each other. For Brezhnev Tito's friendship was a useful prop in the Cold War. Tito realised the dangers of moving too close to the West. This did not stop him, however, hosting visits to Belgrade from, in September 1970, United States President Richard Nixon and, in October 1972, Queen Elizabeth II and the Duke of Edinburgh. In October 1970 he visited West Germany, France, Belgium, Holland and Luxembourg to drum up trade. The European Economic Community already took 39 per cent of Yugoslav exports and provided 49 per cent of her imports. Brezhnev visited Belgrade in September 1971. Tito went to Moscow in June 1972 to receive the Order of Lenin. The Soviets offered to lend the Yugoslavs a billion dollars. Tito could pick and choose his creditors. He was successfully playing the East-West poker game!

During the Yom Kippur War of 1973 between the Egyptians and Israelis Tito once more persuaded Moscow to take the Arab side. He flew at short notice to meet Brezhnev and press his case. Again he provided refuelling facilities for the Soviet airlift of aid. More than a thousand Soviet planes used them during the two weeks of the war. It was revealed later that Tito had urged Anwar Sadat, Nasser's successor, to bomb Tel Aviv when the Egyptian forces were in danger of being annihilated – to the alarm of the Americans listening in to his conversation! Tito was also to provide refuelling facilities when the Soviets airlifted aid to the Angolan communists in 1976 and to the Ethiopians and South Yemenis later in that decade. He also provided docking and repair facilities for the Soviet Mediterranean fleet at ports along the Dalmatian coast. The Soviet Navy even installed its own floating dry dock in the Bay of Kotor.

The US Secretary of State, Henry Kissinger, complained of Tito's bias in dealings with the two super-powers when he visited Belgrade in 1974. According to Dusko Doder, *Washington Post* correspondent in Belgrade between 1973 and 1976, Tito replied: "You know, they are near and you are far, far away."[5] Tito attended the Soviet-sponsored gathering of European communist parties in East Berlin in June 1976. Later that year, Brezhnev visited Belgrade and declared their two parties were now equal partners.

Nationalism re-surfaced in Croatia during the early 1970s. The people there had become richer compared to those in Serbia and felt their economic success merited increased political power. They protested against the hold the Belgrade banks had on the tourist economy of Dalmatia. They complained, too, about the official version of the Serbo-Croat language, which they claimed was dominated by Serbian forms of words. A federal project for a single Serbo-Croat dictionary was then slowly coming to fruition. They called for the recognition of Croato-Serb as well as Serbo-Croat and the ending of discrimination in official correspondence and documentation. They wanted the exclusive use of Croato-Serb in Croatian schools, universities, government and business circles. At times the dispute became passionate. Advertising signs in the Cyrillic alphabet were torn down in Zagreb. It spelled the end of the single dictionary, which was quietly dropped.

The Slovenes and Macedonians also pressed for greater recognition of their languages at the federal level. A separate Macedonian Academy of the Arts was instituted as a counter-balance to the well-established academies in Belgrade, Zagreb and Ljubljana. An autonomous Macedonian Orthodox Church had already been allowed. Now, with government approval, a Macedonian archbishop-ric was established. This annoyed the Serbian Orthodox hierarchy, who saw it as a further weakening by Tito of Serbian cultural influence.

The Slovenes had in 1969 precipitated a crisis that almost toppled the federal government, whose prime minister then happened to be a Slovene. Tito had negotiated a World Bank loan to construct Yugoslavia's first network of motorways but had omitted from the agreed projects a pet Ljubljana scheme linking it with the Austrian and Italian borders. So vehement were their protests that Belgrade had to back down and yield to the Slovenes at the expense of a favoured Serbian motorway.

Hitherto Tito had been able to keep the lid on the ethnic squabbles only through the ruthlessness of Rankovic's secret police, backed up by a nation-wide network of paid informers. But Rankovic was no more and there were too many western influences at work for the problem to be restrained as easily as before. Student demons-trators in Zagreb in November 1971 carried banners declaring "Stop the Plunder of Croatia" and "A Separate Seat for Croatia at the United Nations". Complaints were voiced of foreigners backed by Belgrade "buying up the Croatian economy". A strike was called in support of Croatia retaining its earnings in foreign currency, espe-cially its profits from tourism. Croatian flags – the now familiar red and white chequerboard without the obligatory Yugoslav red star – were being waved in public.

When the local party leaders seemed reluctant to crack down, Tito intervened. He sacked many of them and arrested several hundred nationalist activists, some of whom were given long prison sentences. Further demonstrations were banned. In a show of force, army helicopters hovered over the meeting-place in Zagreb and the city was awash with police in riot helmets.

More than a thousand party officials were purged in Croatia. A year later it was Serbia and Slovenia's turn. Dissidents there were accused of "anarcho-liberalism" and pro-Western sympathies. Hun-dreds were purged with the help of the army, the duty of which, Tito said, was to "protect the achievements of the revolution within the country itself".[6] By this time the army was absorbing two thirds of the federal budget! Christopher Andrew in *The Mitrokhin Archive* maintains "the claim that Yugoslav socialism was resolving ethnic rivalries was exposed as an illusion".

*

Tito sought to buy time by amending the constitution in 1971. The six republics and the two provinces were granted sovereignty in all rights of government not assigned specifically to federal institutions. Three years later he introduced a completely new constitution designed to ease the evolution of the Yugoslav state into a loose federation under a collective leadership which would take over when he died. The Yugoslav presidency was to rotate annually among the constituent republics. Meanwhile he would be advised by a federal presidential council comprising three representatives from each republic and two from each of the autonomous regions of Kosovo and Vojvodina.

Each constituent republic and each autonomous region was to have its own central bank and separate police, educational and judicial systems. The two regions would elect deputies to the Serbian parliament, as well as to their own assemblies. Each republic would have a veto on all proposed legislation, but as all matters, apart from national defence and foreign policy, were to be devolved to the republics, this was not expected to be a problem. Each republic would have the right to secede from the confederation. To increase the representation of interest groups, the federal assembly was to include delegates from workers' councils, peasants and farmers, the professions and the army as well as from the party and state bodies. Tito wanted to reduce Serbia's power in relation to the other constituent republics. Originally with a population of ten million, twice that of Croatia, over the years it had been pared down to, in Tito's eyes, a more manageable six million.

The new constitution, the fourth in less than thirty years, was not adopted until February 1974. It ran to almost a hundred thousand words and was claimed to be the longest in the world! Compared to it, the eight-thousand-word American Constitution seemed unduly meagre! Its preamble was perhaps intended as an epitaph for Tito:

> In view of the historic role of Josip Broz Tito in the National Liberation War and the Socialist Revolution, in the creation and development of the Socialist Federal Republic of Yugoslavia, the development of Yugoslav socialist self-management society, the achievement of the brotherhood and unity of the nations and nationalities of Yugoslavia, the consolidation of the independence of the country and of its position in international relations and in the struggle for peace in the world, and in line with the expressed will of the working people and citizens, nations and nationalities, the Socialist Federal Republic of Yugoslavia Assembly may, on the proposal of

the Assemblies of the Republics and the Assemblies of the Autonomous provinces, elect Josip Broz Tito President of the Republic for
an unlimited term of office.[7]

In practice he had always been boss of both state and party. Now at
last he was legally so!

The purpose of the new constitution had also been "to kill nationalism by kindness". To some extent it was successful, though not
before there had been further demonstrations in Croatia, Serbia and
Slovenia. These were again brutally put down by the police, with
the army's help. The economic difficulties the country was facing
sharpened the unrest. The cost of living had steadily risen. Perennial
deficits in the balance of payments necessitated successive currency
devaluations. New notes now needed to be introduced, one new
dinar replacing a hundred old ones. Inflation soared and unemployment leapt. Graft and corruption became widespread. Living standards dipped. Dangerous disparities of wealth emerged, breeding yet
more resentment among urban workers and peasant farmers.

In the early 1970s Tito took back direct control of the mass
media. To keep order he was prepared more and more now to use the
army. Because it had brought him to power, he always saw it as the
mainstay of his regime. He never relinquished being its commander-
in-chief. He bought its loyalty by liberally bestowing on senior
officers promotions, medals and perquisites, such as the best accommodation in Belgrade and access to luxury holiday villas along the
Dalmatian coast. Significantly, they were not allowed to travel privately overseas. He involved them increasingly in Party affairs; 95 per
cent of officers were Party members. Under the new constitution
they were allocated seats in the federal and provincial assemblies.
Their voting power at the federal level was on a par with the
republics, such that they were dubbed "the ninth republic"! In many
ways they had become a praetorian guard. From 1969 schoolchildren
regularly received military training, including weapons instruction.

The early 1970s saw a revival in Ustasha militancy outside Yugoslavia.
In April 1971 Croatian terrorists murdered Tito's ambassador in
Sweden. The following year Ustasha agents planted a bomb on a
Yugoslav airlines plane that exploded over Czechoslovakia with the
loss of all on board – except for a Montenegrin air hostess who
survived a fall of 33,330 feet without a parachute and merited an entry
in the *Guinness Book of Records*. In 1972 the Ustasha hijacked a plane

flying from Chicago to Paris and used it to drop leaflets over London. Earlier, in 1968, bombs had been exploded in Yugoslav diplomatic and consular missions in Paris, New York and Klagenfurt, causing injuries and damage. There were also bomb attacks on Yugoslav agencies in Australia. The most violent of the Ustasha organisations, the Croatian Revolutionary Brotherhood, had moved its headquarters there that year from West Germany. In 1969 an attempt on the life of the head of the Yugoslav military mission in West Berlin had been followed by a series of unexplained murders of Yugoslav expatriates in West Germany, France, Sweden and Spain – almost certainly the work of the Yugoslav security forces. West German police reopened enquiries into some of them in 2011.

There were also Ustasha bomb incidents inside Yugoslavia that the authorities tried to hush up, including one at the main Belgrade railway station; and even, in 1975, an attempt on Tito's life in Zagreb. This provoked a wave of arrests in Yugoslavia, verging at times on the farcical. A harmless British tourist found spotting aeroplanes was held in custody for several weeks. Other "offences" included singing anti-Tito songs, reciting verses critical of the regime, and membership of *émigré* organisations. The British secret service claimed links between the Irish Republican Army and Croatian nationalists, which Belgrade did not deny. Belgrade newspapers were among the few in Europe then to support unequivocally the British stance in Northern Ireland.

Although Tito resisted real political freedom to the bitter end, he did relax censorship. Local translations of George Orwell's *1984* and *Animal Farm* were published. People were allowed to travel and to think, though not to question the system. Repression could still be swift and brutal.

In 1977, a few months before the issue of human rights was to be discussed at the Belgrade Conference on European Peace and Security (the so-called Helsinki Accords), Djilas embarrassed Tito by asserting there were at least six hundred political prisoners in Yugoslavia. Substantially more than in any other European country, save the Soviet Union, it was more too than there had been under Yugoslavia's pre-war royal dictatorship. Amnesty International put the number nearer a thousand.

CHAPTER SIXTEEN

Tito's Cult of Personality

"the first Communist king"

MOHAMED HEIKAL

TITO HAD ENCOURAGED a cult of universal adulation of himself, beginning during the war. Perhaps its most absurd manifestation was the annual *Titova Stafeta* that took place on his official birthday, 25 May. This was a massive relay race covering the whole country in which tens of thousands of young Yugoslavs participated, culminating in the presentation to him of a decorated baton in Belgrade's main sports stadium. It had been heavily promoted after June 1948. By 1952 the number taking part exceeded a million and a half. The length of the course extended to more than eighty thousand miles. Thereafter the course's length steadily declined to a more manageable eight thousand or so miles and the number of participants to about a hundred thousand. In 1957, to mark his having reached the conventional retirement age of 65, the race was somewhat bizarrely renamed The Festival of Youth! Significantly, 25 May was the principal ceremonial occasion, not 1 May, International Workers' Day, as elsewhere in the communist world.

His image appeared, of course, on the country's postage stamps and coins, which delighted him. Confectioners sold cakes in the shape of his head. Paintings and photographs of him in ever more resplendent uniforms were everywhere. Schools, factories and even cities were named after him. The paths he had trod during the war, and the places where he had been holed-up, all became shrines. Schoolchildren learned his life story and achievements by rote. Commentators did not talk of Yugoslavia, but of "Tito's Yugoslavia". Some even spoke of "Tito's epoch". Television news bulletins invariably led with coverage of his latest activity, no matter how trivial: a visit to a new factory, his receiving a message of goodwill from some political group. When he spoke in public, his audience were expected not just to applaud but to chant, "Tito is ours, and we are Tito's."

He loved being given presents and was said to receive an average of eight a day. Those he did not use went on display at the Museum of 25 May, close to his Belgrade residence. On occasion he was given wild animals, which were housed in a private zoo in the grounds of his summer villa at Brioni. Because of his reign of terror in the first years of his power, there was always the fear he might return to such methods. This helped to deter any kind of political opposition. People were always in awe of him and that was a part of his charisma. He had a capacity to alarm at the same time as charm.

He had always had a love of showy clothes, of uniforms in particular. When he appointed himself Marshal in 1943 he could not wait to have a splendid outfit to match his new title. The Soviets kindly provided one. Thereafter he had umpteen such outfits bedecked with gold braid and decorations to suit every occasion. He enjoyed wearing them on his official travels, as cinema newsreels recorded. They became ever more elaborate. Sartorial splendour became increasingly important to him, though discerning visitors likened his style to doormen at Las Vegas hotels. When not in uniform, he favoured bright white suits: he tried to look like a film star even into his seventies. His wardrobe included hundreds of silk shirts and tailored suits, and, it was said, 538 ties. His jewellery, too, he enjoyed flaunting. "His belt buckle was made out of pure gold and was so heavy", Djilas pointed out, "that it kept slipping down. He wrote with a heavy gold pen."[1] Apparently he ate off gold plates even in private.

Collecting medals was another of his passions. Exchanging them with visiting dignitaries became a required routine. Most of those he gave marked national anniversaries associated with him. Although he denied having been recommended for a medal while serving in the Austro-Hungarian Army on the Russian Front during the First World War, Djilas says he eagerly accepted it during a visit to Vienna after the Second World War!

Djilas maintains that from the outset Tito expected to be treated differently from his colleagues, certainly as regards accommodation and food. After the war his concern for special treatment showed signs of paranoia, even when it came to seating-plans at casual meetings. He developed his own procedure: "his chair was impressive and always placed at the centre of the room. He changed his clothes as often as four times a day, according to the occasion and the impressions he wished to create."[2] He relished luxury and came to expect it.

He revelled in the pageantry and splendour of political power: the ritual gun salutes, the resplendent retinues, the lavish banquets and glittering receptions, the fleets of limousines, the military bands and the parades with saluting escorts. Djilas writes: "Pomp was indispensable to him. It satisfied his strong *nouveau riche* instincts; it also compensated for his ideological deficiency, his inadequate education."[3] Again Djilas:

> Luxury was the hallmark of his palaces, his vehicles, his hunting grounds and yachts. More than merely an attachment to luxury, these manifested power. To Tito, flamboyance was inseparable from political leadership, from state administration.[4]

He loved showing off his worldly possessions. The proletariat having won the class war, he as its rightful representative wanted to be seen to be enjoying the same trappings of power as hereditary kings and barons. Djilas points out that Tito's

> personal expenses were inseparable from those of the state. Building costs and the expenses of refurbishment were charged to a special state account, and Tito simply ordered the Ministry of Finance to make the payments.[5]

He lived initially in the White Palace belonging to Prince Paul in the semi-rural suburb of Dedinje, favoured by Belgrade's diplomats and the pre-war rich. After he had a modern villa built for him nearby, the White Palace was retained for his official duties. The Croatian provincial government erected an enormous palace for him in Zagreb in 1964. Not to be outdone, in 1976 the authorities in Montenegro built a similarly large luxury villa at Igalo, where he went every summer to watch his army on manoeuvres. The Bosnians built another near Sarajevo. The house in Kumrovec where he had been born became a place of pilgrimage and was turned into a national museum. The new road leading to it was always kept in top condition and the hotel built to lodge VIPs had a suite reserved for him, until the whole thing was converted into a private residence for him. The royal military stud farm became a racing stable; the horses were always referred to as the "Marshal's horses". He took over hunting lodges, beach houses and the like around the country. By 1947 he could choose from twenty-five residences; seven more were added before his death.

Tito also had at his disposal a specially equipped Boeing 727 airliner, two sea-going yachts and two river boats, plus a well-appointed personal train and, of course, numerous cars, including a Rolls-

Royce. Monumentally vain, he enjoyed being called "the Marshal". His unique uniform became his symbol as more and more he established a quasi-regal routine. Djilas says: "he took great pains to collect and appropriate all that had belonged to the former court."[6] Just after the war, Tito's office and entourage were often referred to as "the Court"; later they were more usually called "the Marshal's headquarters". Nasser's closest adviser Mohamed Heikal described Tito as "the first Communist king". Tito's flaunting of his wealth irritated Nasser.

In the winter he spent much time in the sixteenth-century castle of Brdo in Slovenia, where Prince Paul had often lived before March 1941. But his favourite residence was his villa, or complex of villas as it eventually became, on the island of Brioni off the Istrian coast. Because of its healthy climate, Brioni had been popular with the Romans, and later with the Venetians, as a summer retreat.

Much of the construction work on Tito's residences, especially on Brioni, was carried out by prisoners. Djilas quotes Svetozar Vukmanovic-Tempo as saying that Tito boasted to him: "all that is great in history was built by slaves."[7] Fedor Burlatsky, a Kremlin speech-writer, tells of a visit to Brioni with Yuri Andropov, Brezhnev's successor:

> Marshal Tito's residence in Brioni was a relatively small three-storey rectangular white building with a flat roof reminiscent of Greek architecture. On a small terrace paved with marble stood a statue of a naked woman in an erotic pose. During the talks between our delegation and the Yugoslavs, Tito at one point came out onto the terrace where we were standing. Approaching the figure, he affectionately patted her in a delicate place and the statue slowly and invitingly began to turn. "Pretty, isn't she?" he asked us. And then he told us how he had had his eye on Brioni as a future residence even when fighting with the partisans nearby.[8]

Tito's many residences were adorned with works of art "borrowed" from Yugoslav museums and galleries or "obtained" by his friend Ante Topic-Mimara, a controversial character. Tito commissioned him after 1945 to seek out and have returned those Yugoslav works of art the Nazis had purloined. Topic-Mimara garnered a remarkably wide and varied art collection of his own which, on his death in 1987, was bequeathed to the city of Zagreb.

Although not artistic or intellectual, or remotely interested in cultural matters, Tito enjoyed the company of writers, artists and intellectuals. No doubt their presence flattered him and inflated his prestige even in his own eyes. He played poker and was a keen photographer. An avid movie-watcher, he had his own private cinema. He particularly enjoyed viewing films about himself! He is said to have personally backed the making of the three-hour epic of the Partisan war, *The Battle of the Neretva*, starring Yul Brynner, Kurt Jurgens and Orson Welles, for which he supplied the Yugoslav Army free of charge!

Although none of them, Tito included, had been hunters before the war, massive hunting parties with lavish feasts became part of the routine for top Party officials. Other Balkan communist potentates were occasionally invited, along with Belgrade's diplomatic corps. As Djilas put it, "we went hunting less to relax than to exhibit our power and our prestige."[9] The hunting preserves with their bears, wild boars and stags were declared federal property and became, in Djilas's phrase, "the postwar prerogative of high functionaries". Only rabbits were left for ordinary people to hunt.[10] When Tito went hunting locally, no one else was allowed to carry live ammunition!

Tito enjoyed his food and had a predilection for smoked meats, sausages and thick soups. He was perennially overweight and suffered heart attacks. But he was not a heavy drinker. He rarely sipped the popular plum brandy, *sljivovica*, preferring whisky, sometimes mixed with Coca-Cola. Nevertheless, he had problems with his liver. And he smoked too much – more than a hundred a day, in a silver-studded wooden pipe-shaped cigarette-holder as favoured by Yugoslav men of his generation. His lungs were affected. Eventually his sight deteriorated. He also suffered from sciatica and needed the help of a stick to walk. He cut down on rich food and smoked only cigars, which made him even more bad-tempered. To conceal his ageing he resorted to colouring his hair or wearing a toupée. He maintained his tan through regular use of a sun lamp.

Corruption was rife among those close to Tito. The opportunities were perhaps too tempting. Partisans with a "good" war record had always enjoyed immense patronage in Tito's Yugoslavia, which led inevitably to abuse. They had watched Tito spearhead the rush to greed. Djilas records that Tito's chauffeur "was caught selling tyres and spare parts from Tito's well-stocked garage, and, unable to face the scandal and imprisonment, he killed himself."[11] Djilas reminds himself:

We Communists at the top moved from villa to villa; we moved often and easily; we ordered objects from state storage, furnishings and paintings the value of which we rarely assessed ... [it] assumed the proportions of a comfortable disease ... luxury hotels and villas were transformed into restricted recreational centres.[12]

Franklin Lindsay remarks how quickly Tito

succumbed to the sybaritic life of a secure and unchallenged potentate. Several luxurious villas and hunting lodges throughout the country were his. His huge yacht would have been the envy of the most self-indulgent capitalist multimillionaires. Meanwhile the country and the economy drifted.[13]

According to Djilas,

Tito's impulse to identify himself with history was kindled by his vanity, which ranged from pettiness to megalomania. He jealously guarded every trinket in his possession, and at the same time encouraged and supervised the construction of monuments and museums dedicated to himself.[14]

Like the Russians, the Yugoslavs sublimated their political frustrations in their humour. Tito tried in 1974 to ban ethnic and political jokes, happily without success, although severe penalties were prescribed. Some went to prison for telling jokes about him. A favourite Belgrade joke was: "What is the difference between Yugoslavia and the USA?" Answer: "In the USA you work for forty years and then become President for four; in Yugoslavia you fight for four years and then become President for forty". Another, quoted by Dusko Doder in *The Yugoslavs*, concerned the banking system:

A man received five thousand dollars willed to him by an aunt who died in the United States. He went to the bank, deposited the money and asked the teller, somewhat apprehensively, whether the funds were safe. "What if the bank collapses?" he inquired. The teller said that was unlikely, but all deposits are insured with the National Bank. "What if the National Bank goes under?" the man inquired. "Look," said the teller, "the bank's integrity is guaranteed by the federal government." "But what happens if the government collapses?" the man inquired. The teller looked around, lowered his voice and said, "Wouldn't it be cheap to get rid of the Communists for only five thousand dollars?"

CHAPTER SEVENTEEN

No Tito Two

IN HIS OLD AGE, having outlived most of his wartime comrades (Kardelj died in February 1979), Tito came to rely on his secret police, not just for intelligence but for day-to-day control. Once again the country's administration was in the hands of a close clique of his cronies. He spent less and less time in Belgrade and saw fewer and fewer people. He was mostly at his hunting lodge or his villa at Brioni, surrounded by flatterers and office-seekers. Rumours were rife of strokes and other terminal ailments. He certainly had a heart attack in the spring of 1973. While attending the fifth non-aligned conference in Colombo in the summer of 1976 he suffered further cardiac complications.

Tito never concerned himself with grooming or suggesting a successor. He had sons, but made no attempt to create a dynasty. He relished the "After Tito, what?" speculation in newspaper columns around the world (it was firmly discouraged within Yugoslavia itself). Djilas observes:

> Communist leaders are more absolute than the most absolute rulers of all time, but they leave no heirs. Not because they cannot find any, nor even because they cannot think of themselves as expendable, but because they simply do not want to be replaced. Megalomaniacs, they are convinced of their irreplaceability, convinced that they will endlessly endure in an endless, indestructible Party, convinced of their eternal presence in the life of the nation.[1]

In 1978, however, Tito did put in place a collective leadership, intended perhaps to avoid an unseemly struggle for succession in his lifetime or, more likely, immediately after his death. Others saw it as intended to show that a *single* individual could not replace him. The Belgrade wags tagged the collective leadership "Tito and the Eight Dwarfs". Djilas says Tito "made certain" he had no political heir:

> He valued himself and his work to such a degree that towards the end of his life he ordered a constitutional change to introduce collective

leadership, which insured that no one who came after him would command such power as he held, no one could ever use it to blacken his memory. In making his role impossible to duplicate, Tito sought to project himself into history.[2]

A campaign to secure for him, on his eighty-fifth birthday, the Nobel Peace Prize came to naught. He had to make do with being named at home a People's Hero for the third time.

Tito was not a family man. He maintained little contact with his blood relations. His son Aleksandar-Misa, known as Misha, born in 1941 from his marriage to Herta Haas, came to live with him for a while shortly after the war. But there was little love lost between Tito and his elder son Zarko. Zarko, who died in 1995, did at least provide Tito with three grandchildren, Josip, Zlatica and Edi. Josip, the eldest, clearly named after his grandfather, was working as a cook in a restaurant in the Zemun area of Belgrade in September 2002, according to the London newspaper *The Independent*. He was then fifty-five. Zlatica and Edi were then both living in Yugoslavia too. Later, in December 2010, it was reported that Josip, now a pensioner aged sixty-three, had founded in Belgrade a new political party, evidently communist in purpose, intended "to restore the dignity of the people". Misha's children live abroad. Tito's brother Martin, with whom he had lodged in Vienna before the First World War, visited him once in 1946. His youngest sister Teresa was present at his birthday lunch in 1977. The Belgrade daily newspaper *Politika* said she was living in an old people's home in Zagreb in March 1990.

Apparently the KGB had approached Tito's first wife, Pelagija, shortly after Yugoslavia's expulsion from the Cominform in June 1948, asking her to return to Yugoslavia on their behalf and contact Tito. She refused, and was rearrested and imprisoned. After Stalin's death she was released and continued to live in the Soviet Union. Evidently she harboured a desire to visit Yugoslavia, though she knew Tito had no interest in seeing her again. Their son Zarko offered to arrange her visit but fell ill. Before he recovered she died, in 1967, at the age of sixty-three. Lucia Bauer survived Stalin's purges and when released from prison shunned politics, living quietly in the Soviet Union. According to Jasper Ridley, a biographer of Tito, she was still alive in 1990. Herta Haas died in March 2010.

Women had been important to Tito. Of all his wives and mistresses, he is said to have been closest to his wartime companion Zdenka, whom most of his entourage could not easily tolerate. When she died of tuberculosis on 1 May 1946, at the age of twenty-seven, Tito was apparently devastated. He arranged for her to be buried in the garden of the White Palace in Belgrade.

After Zdenka's death, Tito had courted the Yugoslav-born opera singer Zinca Kunc Milanov, who had made her name at the Metropolitan Opera in New York. Although flattered by his attention, she showed little enthusiasm for prolonging it and married a Partisan general who had fought in the Spanish Civil War.

Soon after his eighty-fifth birthday in May 1977, Tito and his wife Jovanka separated. He is said to have grown annoyed about her lavish spending and incessant quarrelling with his staff; she about the minders who surrounded him in his old age. Thereafter he was totally in their hands: they decided who he should and should not see. He became increasingly isolated.

Tito was taken ill on New Year's Eve 1979, with circulatory difficulties in his right leg. Three days later he entered a clinic in Ljubljana. The treatment there was not successful and his leg was amputated on 20 January 1980. Zarko and Misha visited him in the clinic, as did Jovanka who told her friends she had found him cheerful. Within weeks he developed kidney problems, followed by pneumonia and heart trouble. Finally his liver failed. He died at 3.05pm on 4 May 1980, a few days before his eighty-eighth birthday. It was not until 6pm that evening that the country was told.

Tito's body was brought from Ljubljana in his private train for burial in the grounds of his Belgrade residence. His tomb said simply: "Tito 1892-1980". He had been impressed by Roosevelt's white marble tomb at his home in upper New York State, which bore only his name and dates. But whereas Roosevelt, in his will, had eschewed all military pomp, Tito had prescribed daily ceremonials at his graveside similar to those at Lenin's mausoleum in Moscow's Red Square.

Immediately after his death, four further towns in Yugoslavia were named after him and yet more statues erected. His face was still to be seen everywhere. In 1982 he received the ultimate Soviet accolade: a square in Moscow was named after him. Near Krassyn Street, Josip Broz Tito Square is located where old Moscow gives way to the newer suburbs. The plaque mentions his being "an eminent combatant for the Communist and Workers' movement". Every year for a decade, at 3.05pm precisely on 4 May, wailing sirens throughout Yugoslavia demanded the observance of a minute's silence in his memory. Wreaths were laid on his tomb and at other locations associated with him. In those ten years fourteen million people are said to have filed past his grave.

Party bureaucrats continued to cash in on his name. Slogans such as "And after Tito, Tito!" or "What will there be now? There will be Tito" merely showed how ideologically bankrupt they were. They still referred to "Tito's Yugoslavia". Laws were enacted protecting his name. His collective works were published and scores of books about him were written around the world. But suddenly respect for him crumbled as the country's economy collapsed during the oil crisis of the 1980s. The follies of self-management and of the collective leadership were laid bare.

Criticism of him, hitherto taboo, now it came in a torrent. In a short while he fell from hero to villain. He was blamed for everything. The Serbs maintained he had discriminated against them; the Croats that he had curtailed their national re-awakening to appease the Serbs. The rotating presidency became unworkable as the country came apart at the seams. Nationalism, never far below the surface, reared its head. Paralysis seized the system as the Party machine began to buckle under the weight of its enormous bureaucracy.

By the early 1980s Yugoslavia's foreign debt had soared to more than $20 billion. Tito's economic policy of muddling through on the back of western loans was coming home to roost. Because of government restrictions on the repatriation of funds, Yugoslav workers abroad were now reluctant to remit their earnings home. In any case these remittances had been declining since the mid-1970s as the recession in Western Europe began to bite. Most of the Yugoslav *gastarbeiters* had returned, adding to Yugoslavia's unemployment problem. At one time their remittances had financed half of Yugoslavia's trade deficit. The balance of payments predicament led to imports being reduced, which stifled the economy still further. Yugoslav exports had been dwindling since the mid-1970s, largely because of Western Europe's trade barriers. The *dinar* was twice devalued, with little effect, and then allowed to float. Its value declined 90 per cent between 1979 and 1985. It fell a further 75 per cent during 1986 and was devalued twice within two months in 1987.

Meanwhile, inflation spiralled. In 1979 the annual rate had been 21 per cent. By 1981 it reached 42 per cent and by 1989 a staggering 2,714 per cent! This led to a collapse of confidence in the currency. The number of dinars to the dollar slipped from twenty in 1979 to more than a thousand in 1988.

Production dipped and unemployment soared. Wages fell in real terms by almost a third between 1979 and 1985. Food subsidies were abandoned in 1982 and the prices of petrol, heating fuel, food and transportation increased by a third the following year. By 1987 workers were beginning to rebel, as were students. Nearly 40 per cent of people under twenty-five were unemployed. Strikes became more and more frequent: there were over fifteen hundred in 1987 alone. A miners' strike in Croatia lasted thirty-three days. The following year throngs of workers descended on Belgrade from Croatia, Bosnia and elsewhere in Serbia. It was the first time there had been such protests in the lifetime of communist Yugoslavia. That October the federal parliament was weakened when the Croat and Slovene delegations withdrew, refusing to continue to contribute to the federal budget. The Slovenes were already secretly printing their own currency. Soon Slovenia dropped "socialist" from its official title. Before the decade was out, the Party journal *Kommunist* folded. *Borba* discarded "Proletarians of the World Unite" from its masthead: everyone was for uniting but no one was for being proletarian any more!

Shortages of food and other necessities led to further unrest. More than a quarter of the population fell below the poverty level. City dwellers felt the austerity most, particularly the burgeoning artisan and professional classes. Import restrictions meant scientists and other academics were denied access to foreign periodicals, which they found demoralising. Corruption grew. In 1987 several top Party officials were convicted and imprisoned because of a near-$900,000,000 financial scandal involving a string of factory farms called Agrokomerc based in Bosnia and employing twelve thousand people. The money had been issued in the form of unsecured promissory notes to at least fifty-seven banks countrywide. There were similar embarrassments involving an aluminium plant at Zvornik. The National Bank in Belgrade was found to have been secretly printing money to lend to the local Serbian government to prop up loss-making enterprises. It was revealed, too, that senior officers of the Yugoslav army had been embroiled in arms deals with shady third-world dictatorships.

Then the whole communist edifice in Eastern Europe and in the Soviet Union abruptly crumpled. The West no longer needed Yugoslavia. The Cold War was over. No more could Belgrade expect special treatment from Washington, London or Paris.

As well as an economic crisis, Tito bequeathed social unrest. Serbians, Bosnians, Montenegrins and Macedonians were becoming worse off faster than Croats and Slovenes. The latter two grumbled that the calamities were not their fault, but Belgrade's, and the Serbians' in particular. They felt they could run their economies much better on their own. The republics of Montenegro and Macedonia verged on bankruptcy. The nation's health suffered. Infant mortality rose and diseases thought eradicated re-emerged. With the drop in foreign earnings, there were critical shortages of imported drugs. Education standards slumped too. Schools and universities were short of funds.

Tito left an explosive situation in Kosovo. It was regarded by Serbs as their historic heartland and referred to fondly as "Old Serbia". Thanks to his policies, the Albanian proportion of the Kosovan population had grown to 85 per cent. The shrinking Serbian minority felt threatened and became restless. When the Albanian majority flexed its muscles in April 1981, the Serbian authorities reacted violently. At least nine were killed and hundreds wounded. This led to both sides taking up ever more extreme positions. The Kosovan Serbs now looked for deliverance to Belgrade. Ambitious politicians there were jockeying for position in the post-Tito period. Many were eager to take up their cause and turn it into a nationalistic crusade. The possibility of losing holy Kosovo to the Moslem infidel was to prove too much for the ultra-Serbs.

Tito had not left a proper will. His failure to distinguish between what was his personal property and what was the state's made it extremely difficult for his recognised heirs, his wife Jovanka and his two sons, Zarko and Misha. A commission was established to decide what was theirs and what belonged to the state. It took them almost four years to do so, and even then the heirs contested the decision. It was not until 1990 that a settlement of sorts was reached with the sons. But not with Jovanka. Although given a handsome pension, she had to surrender her passport and allow herself to be confined to a mansion next door to Tito's former Belgrade residence. Zarko and Misha are said to have inherited very little, Jovanka nothing at all. *The Independent* carried a report on 21 January 2006 that Jovanka, then aged eighty-one, was living in Belgrade in a dilapidated state-owned house with a leaking roof and no central heating. Later that year, however, it was reported that the Serbian government had granted her a pension of about £740 a month, her Yugoslav pension having long since lapsed. Some of Tito's residences were sold off, with his yachts and cars. His island retreat on Brioni was turned into a national park. His private train, with its oak-panelled interiors, velvet carpets and leather chairs, became a tourist attraction.

As the demystification of Tito proceeded, much gossip emerged, particularly about his private life. It was claimed he had had thirteen mistresses, with whom he had spawned seventeen illegitimate children. Questions were asked about the provenance of his art collection. By the tenth anniversary of his death, Serbia's daily newspaper *Politika* could proclaim: "The myth of Tito is today to all intents and purposes totally dead." He had become the scapegoat for all Yugoslavia's ills. While his debunking was most extensive in Croatia, it was most intense within Serbia. His portraits quickly disappeared from public places. His statues were removed and the Tito-streets and Tito-towns renamed. Banknotes bearing his image were called in. The guard of honour was withdrawn from his grave. The museums of his memorabilia and Partisan myths were closed or redesigned to tell a different story. The publication of his collected works was halted: barely half of the intended sixty or so volumes had appeared. By May 1986 his official birthday was ignored in much of the popular press. Two years later the annual *Titova Stafeta* birthday relay was discontinued.

The street in Belgrade once called King Milan Street, and, after 1945, Marshal Tito Avenue, now became Avenue of the Rulers of Serbia. Marshal Tito Boulevard reverted to its nineteenth-century name of Terazije (The Scissors). Marx-Engels Square is now Pasic Square after the Serbian statesman of the early twentieth century. A monument has been erected to Mihailovic, and Serbian patriots now speak with hatred of "the Croat Broz". The former King Peter's son and heir lives quietly in the White Palace in Belgrade. Elsewhere, in Zagreb, Marshal Tito Street is now Andrija Hebrang Street; The Square of the Victims of Fascism is The Square of Distinguished Croats. But Tito's birthplace in Kumrovec has been preserved and is open to visitors more readily than his tomb in Belgrade. In December 2004 a bomb blew off the head of a statue to him in the village.

During the 1990s many pits and caverns were discovered in Slovenia and Croatia filled with the remains of the victims of Tito's post-war purges. Former Partisans who had remained silent during his lifetime began telling their tales of butchery and mass slaughter.

For a while there was a mini industry in members of his coterie publishing their memoirs. His former food-taster, Colonel Branko Tribovic, revealed the extraordinary lengths taken to keep potential poisoners away from Tito's kitchens. His food was analysed in a private biochemical laboratory run by Tribovic to decide whether it was fit to be eaten; it was also tested for traces of explosives. Then epidemiologists, bacteriologists, toxicologists and radiologists examined it in turn. The ingredients of every meal he ate were recorded He usually took his own food on his travels, especially to Third World countries. When staying in foreign hotels, he would choose from the restaurant's menu, but Tribovic would cook the food for him in the hotel kitchen. If such procedures were not possible, Tito would simply pretend to eat, pushing the food around his plate. When possible, he preferred to have the simple Slav dishes Tribovic prepared for him, wherever he was in the world.

Undoubtedly Tito was a con man, a great fraud, a brilliant rogue. But he was also an ebullient figure, a sort of cross between Hermann Goering and Robert Maxwell. He saw communism as merely a tool for his own ambition. It is significant that his crowning achievement was to devise a constitution for Yugoslavia that proved unworkable after his death. It was doomed to fail and thus to show that only he could preserve Yugoslavia's peculiar ethnic patchwork. He would be remembered as the sole person who had held the country together and had kept the nationalities from getting at each other's throats. He knew how unstable a conglomerate Yugoslavia was.

But nobody knew him. Certainly no one in his closest entourage could ever be sure they would be forever in his favour. In time many who had helped him to power and in power lost that favour. He was the complete egomaniac. He was, of course, also an ambitious megalomaniac. Like most tyrants, he identified his own fate with the fate of his country. This allowed him to act in a way which was often ruthless and dishonest. He had a super-regal lifestyle, yet, as his heirs found out, very little of what he had was his own personal property. He controlled much but owned little. He was not interested in passing wealth on to his family. He hardly had a family as such. Nor was he interested in founding a dynasty. The name Tito was his alone. His wives and sons had no right to it. They were just plain Broz. There was going to be no Tito Two!

He was primarily interested in building his place in History. Already he has been compared to Cromwell, because his power stemmed from the loyalty of his army to him personally and because his regime dissolved in anarchy after his death. Others have pointed out that in his private life he resembled more Charles II.

It transpired there had never been such persons as Yugoslavs, only ever Serbs, Croats, Slovenes and others. Tito used to say he was the only Yugoslav. Perhaps he was right. Within a decade or so of his death Yugoslavia was no more. It has been replaced by an independent Slovenia, an independent Croatia, an independent Macedonia and Bosnia, and eventually an independent Serbia, Montenegro and Kosovo – though only after terrible bloodshed and unbelievable barbarism. As many had predicted, because Tito had fastened the lid so firmly on Yugoslavia, the upheaval after lifting it was all the worse when it came. He never allowed the peoples of Yugoslavia to decide freely on their sovereignty and international political status. He did little to prevent the historical prejudices from accumulating. There are many in the lands of the former Yugoslavia who wish there had never been a Tito. He certainly has much to answer for.

Notes

Unless stated to the contrary, references are to files at the National Archives in Kew:

CHAPTER ONE

1 Milovan Djilas, *Wartime*, p.103.
2 FO 371/44271, R8182.
3 Milovan Djilas, *Fall of the New Class*, p.187.
4 PREM 3 513/8.
5 Milovan Djilas, *Tito: The Story from Inside*, pp.26-8.
6 Stephen Clissold, *Yugoslavia and the Soviet Union 1939-1973: A Documentary Survey*, p.115.
7 Milovan Djilas, *Memoir of a Revolutionary*, p.333.
8 Ivan Avakumovic, *History of the Communist Party in Yugoslavia*, p.175.
9 Clissold, *op. cit.,* p.120.
10 Avakumovic, *op. cit.*, p.176.
11 Djilas, *Memoir of a Revolutionary*, p.332.
12 Avakumovic, *op. cit.,* pp.176-7.
13 *Ibid.,* pp.175-6.
14 Phyllis Auty & Richard Clogg (eds) *British Policy Towards Wartime Resistance in Yugoslavia and Greece*, p.286.

CHAPTER TWO

1 Robert Rhodes James (ed.), *Chips: The Diaries of Sir Henry Channon*, pp.136, 168, 238.
2 FO 371/20436.
3 John Colville, *The Fringes of Power: Downing Street Diaries 1939-1955*, p.360.
4 J.B. Hoptner, *Yugoslavia in Crisis 1934-1941*, p.236.
5 FO 371/30089.
6 David Dilks (ed.), *The Diaries of Sir Alexander Cadogan OM 1938-1945*, p.366.
7 Julian Amery, *Approach March*, p.227.
8 Dilks, *op. cit.,* p.366.
9 PREM 3 309/3.
10 Stephen Clissold, *Yugoslavia and the Soviet Union 1939-1973: A Documentary Survey*, p.125.
11 Milovan Djilas, *Memoir of a Revolutionary*, p.373.
12 *Documents on German Foreign Policy 1918-1945: Series D (1937-1945)*, Vol. XII: *The War Years February 1-June 22, 1941*, p.373.
13 *Ibid.*, p.403.
14 FO 371/30269.
15 Djilas, *Memoir of a Revolutionary*, pp.388-9.
16 Hoptner, *op. cit.*, p.288.
17 Clissold, *op. cit.,* p.129.
18 Milovan Djilas, *Wartime*, p.144.
19 FO 371/30215.

20 Milan Deroc, *British Special Operations Explored*, p.162.
21 Djilas, *Wartime*, p.8.
22 William Mackenzie, *The Secret History of SOE: The Special Operations Executive 1940-1945*, p.340.
23 Phyllis Auty & Richard Clogg (eds), *British Policy Towards Wartime Resistance in Yugoslavia and Greece*, p.284.
24 Amery, *op. cit.*, pp.245-6.
25 CAB 101/126.
26 Sir Llewellyn Woodward, *British Foreign Policy in the Second World War*, Vol. 3, p.280.
27 Simon Trew, *Britain, Mihailovic and the Chetniks, 1941-42*, p.77.
28 Ljubo Sirc, *Between Hitler and Tito*, pp.23, 26, 31.
29 FO 371/30220.
30 CAB 121/676.
31 FO 371/30220.
32 CAB 121/676.

CHAPTER THREE

1 Tito, *The Yugoslav People's Fight*, pp.13-14.
2 FO 371/30220.
3 Vladimir Dedijer, *War Diaries*, Vol. 3, p.188.
4 FO 371/30221.
5 Milovan Djilas, *Tito*, p.12.
6 *Documents on German Foreign Policy 1918-1945: Series D (1937-1945)*, Vol. XIII: *The War Years June 23-December 11, 1941*, p.946.
7 Milovan Djilas, *Wartime*, p.184.
8 Stephen Clissold, *Yugoslavia and the Soviet Union 1939-1973: A Documentary Survey*, p.146.
9 Djilas, *Wartime*, p.69.

CHAPTER FOUR

1 Vane Ivanovic, *LX: Memoirs of a Yugoslav*, p.272.
2 FO 371/30220.
3 Mark Wheeler, *Britain and the War for Yugoslavia, 1940-1943*, p.154.
4 *The Diaries of Sir Robert Bruce Lockhart*, Vol. 2: 1939-1965, p.127.
5 WO 208/2014.
6 FO 37133469.
7 Jozo Tomasevich, *War and Revolution in Yugoslavia 1941-1945: The Chetniks*, p.213.
8 William Deakin, *The Brutal Friendship*, pp.96-7.
9 *Ibid.*, pp.183-94.
10 *Ibid.*, pp.353-5.
11 PREM 3 510/5; FO371/33474.
12 CAB 101/126, COS 3407.

CHAPTER FIVE

1 Richard M. Leighton, "Overlord Revisited", *American Historical Review*, lxviii (1963).
2 Martin Gilbert, *Finest Hour: Winston S. Churchill 1939-1941*, pp.716, 852.
3 Martin Gilbert, *Road to Victory: Winston S. Churchill 1941-1945*, p.317.
4 FO 371/37579.

5   William Mackenzie, *The Secret History of SOE: The Special Operations Executive 1940-1945.* p.132.
6   Anthony Powell, *To Keep the Ball Rolling*, Vol. III: *Faces in My Time*, p.177.
7   WO 202/131.
8   FO 898/157.
9   CAB 121/676.
10 FO 371/37581.
11 *Trials of War Criminals before the Nuremberg Military Tribunals*, Vol. XI, Washington, US Government Printing Office, 1950, p.1016.
12 *Hitler e Mussolini, Lettere e Documenti*, Milan, 1946, p.133.
13 F.H. Hinsley, *British Intelligence in the Second World War*, Vol. 3, Pt 1, p.147.
14 FO 898/157.
15 WO 106/5689A.
16 FO 898/157.
17 FO 898/157.
18 FO 371/37584.
19 Winston S. Churchill, *The Second World War*, Vol. IV: *The Hinge of Fate*, pp.839-40.
20 Milovan Djilas, *Fall of the New Class*, p.38.
21 Wilhelm Hoettl, *The Secret Front*, p.164.
22 Milovan Djilas, *Wartime*, p.242.
23 Miso Lekovic, *Martovski Pregovori 1943*, p.27.
24 Djilas, *Wartime*, pp.242-4.
25 *Ibid.*, p.244.
26 *Ibid.*, p.240.
27 Hoettl, *op. cit.,* p.167.
28 David Martin, *The Web of Disinformation*, p.92.
29 WO 202/359.
30 WO 208/2026.
31 FO 898/157.
32 FO 898/157.
33 FO 371/37602.
34 INF 1/926.
35 INF 1/926.
36 FO 371/37602.
37 Franklin Lindsay, *Beacons in the Night: With the OSS and Tito's Partisans in Wartime Yugoslavia*, p.49.
38 CAB 121/676.
39 CAB 121/676.
40 Winston S. Churchill, *The Second World War*, Vol. V: *Closing The Ring*, p.410.
41 PREM 3 228/5.
42 FO 371/37610.
43 Fitzroy Maclean, *Eastern Approaches*, p.281.
44 Basil Davidson, *Special Operations Europe*, p.135.
45 Michael Lees, *The Rape of Serbia*, p.67.
46 Phyllis Auty & Richard Clogg (eds), *British Policy Towards Wartime Resistance in Yugoslavia and Greece*, p.225.
47 WO 208/3102.
48 Maclean, *op. cit.,* p.281.
49 Churchill papers 20/129.
50 PREM 3 136/5.
51 PREM 3 136/5.
52 Churchill papers 20/152.
53 Jozo Tomasevich, *War and Revolution in Yugoslavia 1941-1945: The Chetniks*, p.195.

CHAPTER SIX

1 Phyllis Auty & Richard Clogg (eds), *British Policy Towards Wartime Resistance in Yugoslavia and Greece*, p.239.
2 FO 371/37603.
3 FO 371/37603.
4 FO 371/37603.
5 FO 371/37615.
6 FO 371/37615.
7 Auty & Clogg, *op. cit.,* p.39.
8 Kirk Ford, *OSS and the Yugoslav Resistance 1943-1945*, p.54.
9 FO 371/37615.
10 FO 371/37612.
11 FO 371/37612.
12 David Martin, *The Web of Disinformation*, p.374.
13 WO 202/155.
14 Michael Lees, *The Rape of Serbia*, p.141.
15 *Times Literary Supplement*, May 19, 1972.
16 Milovan Djilas, *Wartime*, p.367.
17 Sir Llewellyn Woodward, *British Foreign Policy in the Second World War*, Vol. 3, p.278.
18 WO 202/140.
19 Franklin Lindsay, *Beacons in the Night: With the OSS and Tito's Partisans in Wartime Yugoslavia*, p.273.
20 F.H. Hinsley, *British Intelligence in the Second World War*, Vol. 3, Pt 1, p.151.
21 WO 202/140.
22 WO 202/131, WO 202/139, WO 202/140, WO 202/143 & WO 202/145.
23 FO 371/37590.
24 FO 371/37612.
25 WO 202/140.
26 FO 371/37616.
27 FO 898/159.
28 WO 202/140.
29 FO 371/37613.
30 FO 371/37591.
31 *The Diaries of Sir Robert Bruce Lockhart*, Vol. 2: 1939-1965, p.305.
32 *Ibid.,* p.728.
33 FO 371/44287.
34 FO 371/44287.
35 FO 371/44287.
36 FO 371/44289.
37 Auty & Clogg, *op. cit.,* p.23.

CHAPTER SEVEN

1 John Harvey (ed.), *The War Diaries of Oliver Harvey*, p.320.
2 FO 371/37618.
3 FO 371/37618.
4 FO 371/37617.
5 FO 371/37617.
6 PREM 3 136/10.
7 PREM 3 136/5.
8 Fitzroy Maclean, *Eastern Approaches*. pp.401-2.
9 PREM 3 510/10.

10 FO 371/44276.
11 FO 371/37618.
12 FO 371/37167.
13 FO 371/37618.
14 WO 202/139.
15 FO 371/37618.
16 WO 202/144.
17 WO 202/145.
18 WO 202/136.
19 WO 202/136.
20 WO 201/1599.
21 FO 371/37620.
22 FO 371/37620.
23 PREM 3 511/1.
24 WO 201/1599.
25 Maclean, *op. cit.,* pp.402-3.
26 Churchill papers 20/130.
27 David Dilks (ed.), *The Diaries of Sir Alexander Cadogan, OM 1938-1945*, p.583.
28 Martin Gilbert, *Road to Victory: Winston S. Churchill 1941-1945*, pp.601-2.
29 Field Marshal Lord Alanbrooke, *War Diaries 1939-1945*, Alex Danchev (ed.), p.493.
30 Gilbert, *op. cit.,* p.602.
31 Harold Macmillan, *War Diaries, Politics and War in the Mediterranean, January 1943-May 1945*, p.327.
32 PREM 3 511/2.
33 CAB 101/126.
34 WO 202/144.
35 PREM 3 511/2.
36 CAB 101/126.
37 PREM 3 511/2.
38 PREM 3 511/2.
39 PREM 3 511/2.
40 CAB 79/69.
41 FO 371/44245.
42 PREM 3 511/1.
43 FO 371/37615.
44 PREM 3 511/9.
45 Churchill Papers 1/381.
46 Elisabeth Barker, *British Policy in South-East Europe in the Second World War*, p.10.

CHAPTER EIGHT

1 Vane Ivanovic, *LX: Memoirs of a Yugoslav*, p.225.
2 Franklin Lindsay, *Beacons in the Night: With the OSS and Tito's Partisans in Wartime Yugoslavia*, pp.26-7.
3 Kirk Ford, *OSS and the Yugoslav Resistance 1943-1945*, p.139.
4 *Ibid.*, p.68.
5 PREM 3 511/8.
6 PREM 3 511/8.
7 PREM 3 511/8.
8 PREM 3 512/1.
9 Francis L. Loewenheim, Harold D. Langley & Manfred Jonas (eds), *Roosevelt and Churchill: Their Secret Wartime Correspondence*, p.482.
10 Loewenheim, *op. cit.,* p.483.

11 Ford, *op. cit.,* p.124.
12 Ljubo Sirc, *Between Hitler and Tito*, p.68.
13 PREM 3 510/2.
14 Richard Crossman, "The Ethics of Terrorism", *The New Statesman and Nation*, December 15, 1956.
15 PREM 3 511/6.
16 *The Diaries of Sir Robert Bruce Lockhart*, Vol. 2: 1939-1965, p.354.
17 Michael Davie (ed.), *The Diaries of Evelyn Waugh*, p.579.
18 FO 898/159.
19 Ford, *op. cit.,* pp.66-7.
20 Milovan Djilas, *Wartime*, p.373.
21 *Ibid.*, p.373.
22 Milovan Djilas, *Fall of the New Class*, p.13.
23 *Ibid.*, p.38.
24 Milovan Djilas, *Conversations with Stalin*, p.70.
25 Sir Llewellyn Woodward, *British Foreign Policy in the Second World War*, Vol. 3, pp.325-6.
26 Jozo Tomasevich, *War and Revolution in Yugoslavia 1941-1945: The Chetniks*, p.412.
27 Peter Wilkinson & Joan Bright Astley, *Gubbins and SOE*, p.199.
28 Ivanovic, *op. cit.,* p.225.
29 FO 371/44273.
30 FO 371/44273.
31 Winston S. Churchill, *The Second World War*, Vol. V: *Closing the Ring*, pp.422-3.
32 FO 371/43646.
33 Djilas, *Wartime*, p.400.
34 Ford, *op. cit.,* p.106.

CHAPTER NINE

1 PREM 3 512/7.
2 PREM 3 512/7.
3 PREM 3 511/2.
4 FO 371/44258.
5 CAB 101/126.
6 Piers Dixon, *Double Diploma*, p.99.
7 PREM 3 512/3.
8 Francis L. Loewenheim, Harold D. Langley & Manfred Jonas (eds), *Roosevelt and Churchill: Their Secret Wartime Correspondence*, p.561.
9 *To War With Whitaker: The Wartime Diaries of the Countess of Ranfurly 1939-45*, pp.262-3.
10 Kirk Ford, *OSS and the Yugoslav Resistance 1943-1945*, p.80.
11 CAB 120/729.
12 Anthony Eden, *The Eden Memoirs: The Reckoning*, p.470.
13 Milovan Djilas, *Wartime*, p.401.
14 Peter Wilkinson & Joan Bright Astley, *Gubbins and SOE*, pp.199-200.
15 PREM 3 472.
16 FO 371/44293.
17 FO 371/44306.
18 FO 371/44306.
19 FO 371/44306.
20 *The Soviet-Yugoslav Dispute*, Royal Institute of International Affairs, 1948, p.51.
21 Djilas, *Wartime*, p.407.
22 Milovan Djilas, *Conversations with Stalin*, p.40.

23 INF 1/926.
24 Djilas, *Conversations with Stalin*, p.102.
25 Jozo Tomasevich, *War and Revolution in Yugoslavia 1941-1945: The Chetniks*, p.438.
26 Milovan Djilas, *Rise and Fall*, pp.18-19.
27 Franklin Lindsay, *Beacons in the Night: With the OSS and Tito's Partisans in Wartime Yugoslavia*, p.249.
28 Winston S. Churchill, *The Second World War*, Vol. 6: *Triumph and Tragedy*, p.184.
29 CAB 120/158.
30 Churchill papers 20/142.
31 FO 371/48811.
32 FO 371/48811.
33 FO 371/44255.
34 PREM 3 512/10.
35 Churchill papers 20/176.
36 CAB 120/729.
37 Churchill papers 20/184.
38 PREM 3 513/2.
39 Ivo Banac, *With Stalin Against Tito*, p.16.
40 PREM 3 513/2.
41 PREM 3 513/2.
42 John Harvey (ed.), *The War Diaries of Oliver Harvey*, p.374.
43 John Colville, *The Fringes of Power: Downing Street Diaries 1939-1955*, p.555.
44 PREM 3 51/10.
45 PREM 3 513/6.
46 PREM 3 513/9.
47 FO 371/48823.
48 Lorraine Lees, *Keeping Tito Afloat*, pp.5-6.
49 PREM 3 356/6.
50 Edward Stettinius, *Roosevelt and the Russians*, p.273.
51 FO 371/48823.
52 Milovan Djilas, *Tito: The Story from Inside*, p.31.
53 Thomas T. Hammond (ed.), *Witnesses to the Origins of the Cold War*, p.51.
54 Lindsay, *op. cit.*, p.284.
55 FO 371/48874.
56 FO 371/48823.
57 Hammond, *op. cit.*, pp.54-5.

CHAPTER TEN

 1 Churchill papers 20/153.
 2 Geoffrey Cox, *The Race for Trieste*, pp.208-9.
 3 Milovan Djilas, *Wartime*, p.433.
 4 PREM 3 495/5.
 5 John Colville, *The Fringes of Power: Downing Street Diaries 1939-1955*, p.591.
 6 CAB 120/729.
 7 PREM 3 513/7.
 8 PREM 3 513/6.
 9 CAB 120/729.
10 PREM 3 473.
11 PREM 3 495/6.
12 PREM 3 495/6.
13 PREM 3 495/6.
14 Churchill papers 20/217.

15 WO 106/4059.
16 WO 106/4059.
17 Franklin Lindsay, *Beacons in the Night: With the OSS and Tito's Partisans in Wartime Yugoslavia*, pp.304-5.
18 PREM 3 495/6.
19 FO 1020/42.
20 WO 106/4059.
21 PREM 3 473.
22 PREM 3 495/7.
23 WO 106/4059.
24 PREM 3 473.
25 WO 106/4059.
26 PREM 3 495/9.
27 FO 371/48817.
28 PREM 3 495/10.
29 PREM 3 495/8.
30 PREM 3 473.
31 PREM 3 430/6.
32 FO 371/59517.

CHAPTER ELEVEN

1 FO 371/48817.
2 WO 170/4421.
3 Alistair Horne, *Macmillan 1894-1956*, Vol. 1 of *Official Biography*, p.273.
4 Anthony Cowgill, Lord Brimelow & Christopher Booker, *The Repatriations from Austria in 1945: The Report of an Inquiry*, p.152.
5 WO 170/4241.
6 WO 170/4404.
7 WO 170/4241.
8 WO 170/4404.
9 *The Economist*, 2 October, 2004, p.99.
10 Susan Crosland, *Tony Crosland*, pp.38-9.
11 WO 170/4982.
12 *Yugoslav Information Sheet*, Bromley, Kent, 1946 (quoted in Norah Beloff, *Tito's Flawed Legacy*, p.133).
13 Stephen Clissold, *Whirlwind*, p.237.
14 CAB 120/729.
15 Kirk Ford, *OSS and the Yugoslav Resistance 1943-1945*, p.177.
16 Michael Lees, *The Rape of Serbia*, p.10.
17 Mark Wheeler, *Britain and the War for Yugoslavia, 1940-1943*, p.74.
18 Lees, *op. cit.*, p.308.
19 Robert Blake & Roger Louis (eds), *Churchill*, p.4.
20 Norman Rose, *Churchill: An Unruly Life*, p.45.
21 Vane Ivanovic, *LX: Memoirs of a Yugoslav*, p.260.
22 Nora Beloff, *Tito's Flawed Legacy: Yugoslavia and the West 1939-84*, p.264.
23 Lorraine Lees, *Keeping Tito Afloat*, pp.33, 38.
24 Milovan Djilas, *Fall of the New Class*, p.66.
25 Milovan Djilas, *Rise and Fall*, p.22.
26 Vladimir Dedijer, *Tito Speaks*, p.270.
27 Djilas, *Rise and Fall*, p.45.
28 FO 371/67440.
29 Milovan Djilas, *Conversations with Stalin*, p.164.

CHAPTER TWELVE

1 Milovan Djilas, *Rise and Fall*, pp.139-40.
2 *Ibid.*, p.163.
3 Stephen Clissold, *Yugoslavia and the Soviet Union 1939-1973: A Documentary Survey*, pp.202-7.
4 *Ibid.*, p.239.
5 *Ibid.*, p.245.
6 *Ibid.*, p.223.
7 Alan Bullock, *Ernest Bevin, Foreign Secretary 1945-1951*, p.599.
8 Lorraine Lees, *Keeping Tito Afloat*, pp.46-7.
9 Dean Acheson, *Present at the Creation*, p.332.
10 Ivo Banac, *With Stalin Against Tito*, p.135.
11 Milovan Djilas, *Fall of the New Class*, p.20.
12 Milovan Djilas, *Tito: The Story from Inside*, p.31.
13 Djilas, *Fall of the New Class*, p.315.
14 Clissold, *op. cit.*, p.259.
15 Djilas, *Rise and Fall*, p.211.
16 Christopher Andrew & Vasili Mitrokhin, *The Mitrokhin Archive*, p.464.
17 Djilas, *Rise and Fall*, p.208.
18 Djilas, *Tito: The Story from Inside*, pp 81-7.
19 Banac, *op. cit.*, pp.248-9.
20 Djilas, *Rise and Fall*, p.241.
21 *Ibid.*, p.245.
22 Clissold, *op. cit.*, p.220.
23 Djilas, *Fall of the New Class*, p.114.
24 Clissold, *op. cit.*, pp.61, 243.
25 *Khrushchev Remembers: The Last Testament*, p.181.
26 Franklin Lindsay, *Beacons in the Night: With the OSS and Tito's Partisans in Wartime Yugoslavia*, p.337.
27 Lorraine Lees, *Keeping Tito Afloat*, p.110.
28 Clissold, *op. cit.*, p.237.
29 *Chicago Tribune*, March 16, 1951.
30 Mark Almond, *Europe's Backyard War*, p.154.
31 Dean Acheson, *Present at the Creation*, p.327.

CHAPTER THIRTEEN

1 Milovan Djilas, *Fall of the New Class*, pp.142-3.
2 Milovan Djilas, *Parts of a Lifetime*, p.173.
3 *Ibid.*, pp.174-5.
4 Milovan Djilas *The Unperfect Society*, p.21.
5 Djilas, *Parts of a Lifetime*, p.201.
6 Djilas, *The Unperfect Society*, p.173.
7 Milovan Djilas, *Rise and Fall*, p.321.
8 Richard West, *Tito and the Rise and Fall of Yugoslavia*, p.261.
9 *Khrushchev Remembers*, p.343.
10 *Ibid.*, pp.379-80.
11 *Ibid.*, pp.599-600.
12 Veljko Micunovic, *Moscow Diary*, p.66.
13 Fitzroy Maclean, *Disputed Barricade*, p.449.
14 *Khrushchev Remembers*, p.435.
15 *Ibid.*, p.421.

16 *Khrushchev Remembers: The Glasnost Tapes*, p.127.
17 *Ibid.*, p.422.
18 Stephen Clissold, *Yugoslavia and the Soviet Union 1939-1973: A Documentary Survey*, p.267.
19 Djilas, *Parts of a Lifetime*, pp.362-4.
20 George Kennan, *Memoirs 1950-1963*, pp.279-81.
21 Clissold, *op. cit.*, p.293.
22 *Ibid.*, p.293.

CHAPTER FOURTEEN

  1 Milovan Djilas, *Tito: The Story from Inside*, p.74.
  2 Milovan Djilas, *Fall of the New Class*, pp.116-17.
  3 *Khrushchev Remembers*, p.385.
  4 Nora Beloff, *Tito's Flawed Legacy: Yugoslavia and the West 1939-84*, p.218.

CHAPTER FIFTEEN

  1 Stephen Clissold, *Yugoslavia and the Soviet Union 1939-1973: A Documentary Survey*, p.110.
  2 Ion Mihai Pacepa, *Red Horizons*, pp.345-9.
  3 *Ibid.*, p.354.
  4 Stevan K. Pavlowitch, *The Improbable Survivor: Yugoslavia and its Problems 1918-1988*, p.120.
  5 Dusko Doder, *The Yugoslavs*, pp.134-5.
  6 *Ibid.*, p.147.
  7 Stevan K. Pavlowitch, *Tito*, p.79.

CHAPTER SIXTEEN

  1 Milovan Djilas, *Tito: The Story from Inside*, p.110.
  2 *Ibid.*, p.110.
  3 *Ibid.*, p.96.
  4 Milovan Djilas, *Fall of the New Class*, p.251.
  5 Djilas, *Tito: The Story from Inside*, p.99.
  6 Djilas, *Fall of the New Class*, p.251.
  7 Djilas, *Tito: The Story from Inside*, p.102.
  8 Fedor Burlatsky, *Krushchev and the First Russian Spring*, p.118.
  9 Djilas, *Tito: The Story from Inside*, p.105.
 10 Milovan Djilas, *Wartime*, p.328.
 11 Djilas, *Tito: The Story from Inside*, p.101.
 12 *Ibid.*, p.100.
 13 Franklin Lindsay, *Beacons in the Night: With the OSS and Tito's Partisans in Wartime Yugoslavia*, p.348.
 14 Djilas, *Tito: The Story from Inside*, pp.122-3.

CHAPTER SEVENTEEN

  1 Milovan Djilas, *Fall of the New Class*, p.209.
  2 Milovan Djilas, *Tito: The Story from Inside*, p.169.

Bibliography

Acheson, Dean, *Present at the Creation*, Hamish Hamilton, 1970.

Alanbrooke, Field Marshal Lord, *War Diaries 1939-1945*, Weidenfeld & Nicolson, 2001.

Alexander, Stella, *Church and State in Yugoslavia Since 1945*, CUP, 1979.

Allcock, John, *Explaining Yugoslavia*, Hurst, 2000.

Almond, Mark, *Europe's Backyard War: The War in the Balkans*, Heinemann, 1994.

Amery, Julian, *Approach March*, Hutchinson, 1973.

Andrew, Christopher & Mitrokhin,Vasili, *The Mitrokhin Archive*, Penguin, 2000.

Andrew, Christopher & Gordievsky, Oleg, *KGB: The Inside Story of its Foreign Operations from Lenin to Gorbachev*, Hodder & Stoughton, 1990.

Auty, Phyllis & Clogg, Richard (eds), *British Policy Towards Wartime Resistance in Yugoslavia and Greece*, Macmillan, 1975.

Avakumovic, Ivan, *History of the Communist Party in Yugoslavia*, Aberdeen University Press, 1964.

Balfour, Neil & Mackay, Sally, *Paul of Yugoslavia*, Hamish Hamilton, 1980.

Banac, Ivo, *With Stalin Against Tito*, Cornell University Press, 1988.

Barker, Elisabeth, *British Policy in South-East Europe in the Second World War*, Macmillan, 1976.

Barker, Thomas M., *Social Revolutionaries and Secret Agents: The Carinthian Slovene Partisans and Britain's Special Operations Executive*, Columbia University Press, NY, 1990.

Beloff, Nora, *Tito's Flawed Legacy: Yugoslavia and the West 1939-84*, Victor Gollancz, 1985.

Bennett, Ralph, *Ultra and Mediterranean Strategy*, William Morrow, 1989.

Blake, Robert & Louis, Roger (eds), *Churchill*, OUP, 1993.

Bond, Brian & Roy, Ian (eds), *War and Society*, Croom Helm, London, 1975.

Briggs, Asa, *The War of Words, History of Broadcasting in the United Kingdom*, Vol. 3, OUP, 1995.

Brown, Anthony Cave, *The Last Hero: Wild Bill Donovan*, Times Books, 1982.

Bullock, Alan, *Ernest Bevin, Foreign Secretary 1945-1951*, Heinemann, 1983.

Burlatsky, Fedor, *Krushchev and the First Russian Spring*, Weidenfeld & Nicolson, 1991.

Carter, Miranda, *Anthony Blunt: His Lives*, Macmillan, 2001.

Churchill, Winston S., *The Second World War*, Vol. 4: *The Hinge of Fate*, Cassell, 1951.

— Vol. 5: *Closing The Ring*, Cassell, 1952.

— Vol. 6: *Triumph and Tragedy*, Cassell, 1954.

Clissold, Stephen, *Whirlwind: An Account of Marshal Tito's Rise to Power*, Cresset, 1949.

— *Djilas: The Progress of a Revolutionary*, Temple Smith, 1983.

— (ed.), *Yugoslavia and the Soviet Union 1939-1973: A Documentary Survey*, OUP, 1975.

Colville, John, *The Fringes of Power: Downing Street Diaries 1939-1955*, Hodder & Stoughton, 1985.

Cookridge, E.H., *Inside SOE*, Arthur Barker, 1966.

Cooper, Artemis, *Cairo in Wartime 1939-1945*, Hamish Hamilton, 1989.

Cowgill, Anthony, Lord Brimelow & Booker, Christopher, *The Repatriations from Austria in 1945: The Report of an Inquiry and the Documentary Evidence*, Sinclair-Stevenson, 1990.

Cox, Geoffrey, *The Race for Trieste*, William Kimber, 1977.

Crampton, R.J., *Eastern Europe in the Twentieth Century – and After*, Routledge, 1997.

Crosland, Susan, *Tony Crosland*, Jonathan Cape, 1982.

Davidson, Basil, *Special Operations Europe*, Gollancz, 1980.

Davie, Michael (ed.), *The Diaries of Evelyn Waugh*, Weidenfeld & Nicolson, 1976.

Deakin, F.W., *The Brutal Friendship*, Weidenfeld & Nicolson, 1962.

— *The Embattled Mountain*, OUP, 1971.

Dedijer, Vladimir, *Tito Speaks*, Weidenfeld & Nicolson, 1953.

— *The War Diaries of Vladimir Dedijer*, University of Michigan Press, 1990.

Deroc, Milan, *British Special Operations Explored*, Columbia University Press, New York, 1988.

Dilks, David (ed.), *The Diaries of Sir Alexander Cadogan OM 1939-1945*, Cassell, 1971.

Dixon, Piers, *Double Diploma*, Hutchinson, 1968.

Djilas, Milovan, *The New Class*, Thames & Hudson, 1957.

— *Conversations with Stalin*, Rupert Hart Davis, 1962.

— *The Unperfect Society*, Methuen, 1969.

— *Memoir of a Revolutionary*, Harcourt Brace Jovanovich, 1973.

— *Parts of a Lifetime*, Harcourt Brace Jovanovich, 1975.

— *Wartime*, Secker & Warburg, 1977.

— *Tito: The Story from Inside*, Harcourt Brace Jovanovich, 1980.

— *Rise and Fall*, Macmillan, 1985.

— *Fall of the New Class*, Knopf, New York, 1998.

— *Documents on German Foreign Policy 1918-1945: Series D (1937-1945)*, Vol. XII: *The War Years, February 1-June 22, 1941*; Vol. XIII: *The War Years June 23-December 11, 1941*, HMSO, 1962; 1964.

Doder, Dusko, *The Yugoslavs*, Allen & Unwin, 1979.

Dorril, Stephen, *MI6: Fifty Years of Special Operations*, Fourth Estate, 2000.

Draskovich, Slobodan M., *Tito, Moscow's Trojan Horse*, Henry Regnery, Chicago, 1957.

Eade, Charles (comp.), *The Unrelenting Struggle: War Speeches by the Right Hon. Winston S. Churchill, CH, MP*, Cassell, 1951/2.

Eden, Anthony, *The Eden Memoirs: The Reckoning*, Cassell, 1965.

Foot, M.R.D., *Resistance*, Eyre Methuen, 1976.

— *SOE 1940-46*, Pimlico, 1999.

Ford, Kirk, *OSS and the Yugoslav Resistance, 1943-1945*, Texas A&M University Press, 1992.

Gaddis, John Lewis, *We Now Know: Rethinking Cold War History*, OUP, 1997.

Garnett, David, *The Secret History of PWE*, St Ermin's Press, 2002.

Gilbert, Martin, *Finest Hour: Winston S. Churchill 1939-1941*, Heinemann, 1983.

— *Road to Victory: Winston S. Churchill 1941-1945*, Heinemann, 1986.

— *Never Despair: Winston S. Churchill 1945-1965*, Heinemann, 1988.

Glen, Alexander, *Footholds Against a Whirlwind*, Hutchinson, 1975.

Glenny, Misha, *The Fall of Yugoslavia: The Third Balkan War*, Penguin, 1992.

Hamilton-Hill, Donald, *SOE Assignment*, William Kimber, 1973.

Hammond, Thomas Taylor (ed.), *Witnesses to the Origins of the Cold War*, University of Washington Press, 1982.

Harvey, John, *The War Diaries of Oliver Harvey 1941-1945*, Collins, 1978.

Healey, Denis, *The Time of My Life*, Michael Joseph, 1989.

Henniker, John, *Painful Extractions,* Thornham Books, 2002.

Hinsley, F.H., *British Intelligence in the Second World War*, Vol. 3, Pt 1, HMSO, 1984; Pt 2, HMSO, 1988.

Hoare, Marko Attila, *The History of Bosnia*, SAQI, 2007.

Hoettl, Wilhelm, *The Secret Front*, Weidenfeld & Nicolson, 1954.

Hoptner, J.B., *Yugoslavia in Crisis 1934-1941*, Columbia University Press, 1962.

Horne, Alistair, *Macmillan 1894-1956*, Vol. 1, *Official Biography*, Macmillan, 1988.

Howard, Michael, *The Mediterranean Strategy in the Second World War*, Weidenfeld & Nicolson, 1968.

— *Grand Strategy*, Vol. IV: *August 1942-September 1943*, HMSO, 1972.

— *British Intelligence in the Second World War*, Vol. 5, HMSO, 1990.

Ivanovic, Vane, *LX: Memoirs of a Yugoslav*, Weidenfeld & Nicolson, 1977.

James, Robert Rhodes (ed.), *Chips: The Diaries of Sir Henry Channon*, Weidenfeld & Nicolson, 1967.

Judt, Tony (ed.), *Resistance and Revolution in Mediterranean Europe 1939-1948*, Routledge, 1989.

Kardelj, Edvard, *Reminiscences – The Struggle for Recognition and Independence: The New Yugoslavia, 1944-1957*, Blond & Briggs, 1982.

Keegan, John, *The Second World War*, Hutchinson, 1989.

Kemp, Peter, *The Thorns of Memory,* Sinclair-Stevenson, 1990.

Kennan, George F., *Memoirs 1950-1963*, Hutchinson, 1973.

Khrushchev Remembers (ed. & trans. Strobe Talbott), Andre Deutsch, 1971.

Khrushchev Remembers: The Last Testament, Andre Deutsch, 1974.

Khrushchev Remembers: The Glasnost Tapes, Little, Brown, 1990.

Korbel, Josef, *Tito's Communism*, University of Denver Press, 1951.

Kyle, Keith, *Suez*, Weidenfeld & Nicolson, 1991.

Lamb, Richard, *Churchill as War Leader – Right or Wrong?*, Bloomsbury, 1991.

Lampe, John R., *Yugoslavia as History: Twice There was a Country*, Cambridge University Press, 2000.

Langhorne, Richard (ed.), *Diplomacy and Intelligence During the Second World War*, Cambridge University Press, 1985.

Lees, Lorraine, *Keeping Tito Afloat*, Pennsylvania State University Press, 1997.

Lees, Michael, *Secret Operations Executed,* William Kimber, 1986.

— *The Rape of Serbia,* Harcourt Brace Jovanovich, New York, 1990.

Lekovic, Miso, *Martovski Pregovori 1943*, Narodna Knjiga, Belgrade, 1985.

Lindsay, Franklin, *Beacons in the Night: With the OSS and Tito's Partisans in Wartime Yugoslavia*, Stanford University Press, 1993.

Loewenheim, Francis L., Langley, Harold D. & Jonas, Manfred (eds), *Roosevelt and Churchill: Their Secret Wartime Correspondence*, Barrie & Jenkins, 1975.

Lydall, Harold, *Yugoslavia in Crisis*, OUP, 1989.

Mackenzie, William, *The Secret History of SOE: The Special Operations Executive 1940-1945*, St Ermin's Press, 2000.

Maclean, Fitzroy, *Eastern Approaches*, Jonathan Cape, 1949.

— *Disputed Barricade*, Jonathan Cape, 1957.

Macmillan, Harold, *War Diaries, Politics and War in the Mediterranean, January 1943-May 1945*, Macmillan, 1984.

McConville, Michael, *A Small War in the Balkans,* Macmillan, 1986.

McLynn, Frank, *Fitzroy Maclean*, John Murray, 1992.

Marks, Leo, *Between Silk and Cyanide: The Story of SOE's Code War*, Harper-Collins, 1998.

Martin, David, *Ally Betrayed: The Uncensored Story of Tito and Mihailovic*, Prentice-Hall, New York, 1946.

— *The Web of Disinformation*, Harcourt Brace Jovanovich, New York, 1990.

Micunovic, Veljko, *Moscow Diary*, Doubleday, 1980.

Mihaljov, Mihaljo, *Russian Themes*, Macdonald, 1968.

Miller, Joan, *One Girl's War*, Brandon, 1986.

Montefiore, Simon Sebag, *Stalin: The Court of the Red Tsar*, Weidenfeld & Nicolson, 2003.

Muggeridge, Malcolm, *Chronicles of Wasted Time*, Vol. 2: *The Infernal Grove*, Collins, 1973.

Pacepa, Ion Mihai, *Red Horizons*, Heinemann, 1988.

Pavlowitch, Stevan K., *Yugoslavia*, Praeger, 1971.

— *Unconventional Perceptions of Yugoslavia 1940-1945*, Columbia University Press, 1985.

— *The Improbable Survivor: Yugoslavia and its Problems 1918-1988*, Hurst, 1988.

— *Tito*, Hurst, 1992.

— *Serbia: The History Behind the Name*, Hurst, 2002.

— *Hitler's New Disorder*, Columbia/Hurst, 2008.

Peter II, King of Yugoslavia, *A King's Heritage*, Cassell, 1955.

Pincher, Chapman, *Too Secret Too Long*, Sidgwick & Jackson, 1984.

Powell, Anthony, *To Keep the Ball Rolling*, Vol. III: *Faces in My Time*, Heinemann, 1980.

Pridonoff, Eric L. *Tito's Yugoslavia*, Public Affairs Press, Washington DC, 1955.

Ranfurly, Countess of, *To War With Whitaker: The Wartime Diaries of the Countess of Ranfurly 1939-45*, Heinemann, 1994.

Rendel, Sir George, *The Sword and the Olive*, Murray, 1957.

Ridley, Jasper, *Tito*, Constable, 1994.

Robertson, K.G. (ed.), *War, Resistance and Intelligence*, Leo Cooper, 1999.

Rootham, Jasper, *Miss Fire*, Chatto & Windus, 1946.

Rose, Norman, *Churchill: An Unruly Life*, Simon & Schuster, 1994.

Rusinow, Dennison, *The Yugoslav Experiment 1948-1974*, Hurst, 1977.

Seton-Watson, Hugh, *The East European Revolution*, Methuen, 1950.

Sirc, Ljubo, *Between Hitler and Tito*, Andre Deutsch, 1989.

— *The Yugoslav Economy under Self-Management*, Macmillan, 1979.

Slessor, Sir John, *The Central Blue*, Cassell, 1956.

Smith, Michael & Erskine, Ralph (eds), *Action This Day*, Bantam Press, 2001.

Stafford, David, *Britain and European Resistance 1940-1945*, Macmillan, 1980.

— *Camp X: SOE and the American Connection*, Viking, 1987.

— *Churchill and Secret Service*, John Murray, 1997.

Stenton, Michael, *Radio London and Resistance in Occupied Europe*, OUP, 2000.

Stettinius, Edward, *Roosevelt and the Russians: The Yalta Conference*, Jonathan Cape, 1950.

Sweet-Escott, Bickham, *Baker Street Irregular*, Methuen, 1965.

Thayer, Charles, *Hands Across the Caviar*, Michael Joseph, 1953.

— *The Soviet-Yugoslav Dispute*, Royal Institute of International Affairs, 1948.

— *The Trial of Dragoljub-Draza Mihailovic*, Union of Yugoslav Journalists, Belgrade, 1946.

Thomas, Hugh, *The Spanish Civil War*, Hamish Hamilton, 1977.

Tolstoy, Nikolai, *The Minister and the Massacres*, Century Hutchinson, 1986.

Tomasevich, Jozo, *War and Revolution in Yugoslavia 1941-1945: The Chetniks*, Stanford University Press, 1975.

— *War and Revolution in Yugoslavia 1941-1945: Occupation and Collaboration*, Stanford, 2001.

Trew, Simon, *Britain, Mihailovic and the Chetniks, 1941-42*, Macmillan, 1998.

Warlimont, Walter, *Inside Hitler's Headquarters 1939-45*, Weidenfeld & Nicolson, 1964.

West, Nigel, *Secret War: The Story of SOE*, Hodder & Stoughton, 1992.

West, Rebecca, *Black Lamb and Grey Falcon*, Macmillan, 1967.

West, Richard, *Tito and the Rise and Fall of Yugoslavia*, Sinclair-Stevenson, 1994.

Wheeler, Mark, *Britain and the War for Yugoslavia, 1940-1943*, Columbia University Press, 1980.

Wilkinson, Peter & Astley, Joan Bright, *Gubbins and SOE*, Leo Cooper, 1993.

Williams, Heather, *Parachutes, Patriots and Partisans*, Hurst, 2003.

Wilson, Henry Maitland, *Eight Years Overseas 1939-1947*, Hutchinson, 1950.

Woodward, Sir Llewellyn, *British Foreign Policy in the Second World War*, Vol. 3, HMSO, 1971.

Woodward, Susan, *Balkan Tragedy*, Brookings Institution, 1995.
Young, Kenneth (ed.), *The Diaries of Sir Robert Bruce Lockhart*, Vol. 2: 1939-
    1965, Macmillan, 1980.

Acknowledgements

THE AUTHOR IS GRATEFUL to the National Archives, London for permission to quote extensively from original documents. He is grateful, too, to the Churchill Archives Centre in Cambridge for being allowed to quote from the Churchill Papers held there. Two personal telegrams are reproduced by permission of Curtis Brown Ltd, London on behalf of the Estate of Sir Winston Churchill (Copyright © Winston S. Churchill). He is obliged also to The Random House Group Ltd for being allowed to quote at length from *Wartime* by Milovan Djilas, published by Secker and Warburg, and to Orion Publishing to quote from *Tito: The Story from Inside* by Milovan Djilas. Extracts by Fitzroy Maclean from *Eastern Approaches* (© The Estate of Fitzroy Maclean, 1949) are reproduced by permission of PFD (www.pfd.co.uk) on behalf of Fitzroy Maclean. Extracts by William Mackenzie from *The Secret History of SOE* published by St Ermin's Press are similarly reproduced by permission of PFD on behalf of William Mackenzie. Extracts from Ljubo Sirc's *Between Hitler and Tito* published by Andre Deutsch in 1989 are used by permission of the Carlton Publishing Group. Excerpts from *The Rape of Serbia: The British Role in Tito's Grab for Power 1943-1944*, copyright 1990 by Michael Lees, are reprinted by permission of Harcourt, Inc. Excerpts from *Beacons in the Night: With the OSS and Tito's Partisans in Wartime Yugoslavia* by Franklin Lindsay are used with the permission of Stanford University Press (www.sup.org) (copyright 1963 by the Board of Trustees of the Leland Stanford Jr. University, all rights reserved).

Copyright of the cover illustration is held by the Imperial War Museum, as is the photograph of Draza Mihailovic. Copyright of the wartime photograph of Tito and of the 1953 photograph of Tito and Winston Churchill is held by TopFoto. That of post-war Tito is held by Getty Images.

The author would like to acknowledge the help of Jean Desebrock and Anthony Werner with the MS.

Index